Matter of I
An Interdi:
Study of Relics and
Relic Veneration
in the Medieval Period

Edited by James
Robinson and
Lloyd de Beer
with Anna Harnden

CW00944396

The British
Museum

Publishers
The British Museum
Great Russell Street
London WC1B 3DG

Series editor
Sarah Faulks

Matter of Faith:
An Interdisciplinary Study of Relics and Relic Veneration
in the Medieval Period
Edited by James Robinson and Lloyd de Beer
with Anna Harnden

ISBN 978 086159 195 4
ISSN 1747 3640

© The Trustees of the British Museum 2014
Third printing 2020

Front cover: reliquary of St Eustace, *c.* 1210, Basel,
Switzerland, silver gilt over wood, rock crystal, chalcedony,
amethyst, cornelian, pearl and glass, wooden core with
gesso, 35 x 16.6 x 18.4cm. British Museum, London
(1850,1127.1)

Printed and bound in the UK by 4edge Ltd, Hockley

Papers used by The British Museum are recyclable products
made from wood grown in well-managed forests and other
controlled sources. The manufacturing processes conform to
the environmental regulations of the country of origin.

All British Museum images illustrated in this book are
© The Trustees of the British Museum.

Further information about the Museum and its collection
can be found at britishmuseum.org.

Contents

Preface

James Robinson

Matter of Faith was the working title for the exhibition *Treasures of Heaven: Saints, Relics and Devotion in Medieval Europe*. The exhibition was held at three venues: Cleveland Museum of Art, the Walters Art Museum, Baltimore, and the British Museum between October 2010 and October 2011. The final exhibition title was devised as a means of expressing more clearly the precious nature of the exhibits and for its allusion to the intercessionary power attributed to saints who are believed to serve as mediators between earth and heaven. However, *Matter of Faith* was considered too good a second choice to relinquish entirely and the decision was made to retain it for the title of the exhibition's academic conference and for this publication. Its value lies in its succinctness and ambiguity. The 'matter' it describes is at once the question of faith that underlies the belief system and the physical substances that empower it. The substances are not, however, solely the fragments of bone, stone, wood and textiles that for the most part comprise the sacred matter used in relic veneration, but also the precious commodities of gold, silver, crystal and gemstones that were used to make the reliquaries that enshrined the relics.

In his review for *The Sunday Times* of the British Museum's leg of the exhibition, Waldemar Januszczak lamented what he perceived as a lack of 'scholarly doubt' in its curation. He summed up his exasperation in the following passage:

> I certainly don't expect the British Museum…to mock any of the mad contents of its spectacularly ornate survey of Christian relic art. But a scholarly nay or two was probably in order.[1]

Januszczak's reading of the exhibition, his objection to the quiet dignity afforded to the subject matter and perhaps even his choice of vocabulary were heavily influenced by a much earlier commentator on the issue of relic veneration. This of course is the frequently cited and oft misquoted John Calvin (1509–64) whose *Treatise on Relics* published in 1543 has provided subsequent scholars with ample evidence of medieval superstition, malpractice and deceit. It is Calvin's rhetoric that Januszczak mirrors when he addresses a section of the exhibition that focused on reliquaries designed to contain purported relics of the True Cross:

> As for the precious fragments of the true cross that remain, not just in this show but far beyond it, used together they could provide enough timber to build a barn.[2]

Calvin, with characteristic humour, went further than Januszczak:

> Now let us consider how many relics of the true cross there are in the world. An account of those merely with which I am acquainted would fill a whole volume, for there is not a church, from a cathedral to the most miserable abbey or parish church, that does not contain a piece. Large splinters of it are preserved in various places, as for instance in the Holy Chapel at Paris, whilst at Rome they show a crucifix of considerable size made entirely, they say, from this wood. In short, if we were to collect all these pieces of the true cross exhibited in various parts, they would form a whole ship's cargo. The Gospel testifies that the cross could be borne by one single individual; how glaring, then, is the audacity now to pretend to display more relics of wood than three hundred men could carry![3]

Januszczak continues in the spirit of Calvin when he rails against 'the world of the medieval relic' as a 'world of fraud, greed, madness, delusion, cannibalism, gullibility and pretence'. He summarizes his opinion of the exhibition's content with a remark that reveals a historically entrenched attitude, 'all of which feels irreducibly popish and superstitious'.[4]

Certain other aspects of the review, however, imply a greater awareness of scholarly content at odds with Januszczak's initial, instinctive response to the exhibition. This is particularly true of his enjoyment of the Late Antique/early Christian narrative and his appreciation of the very material role that reliquary design played in elevating the senses beyond the mundane piece of bone, tooth or hair that might form the relic. When he makes the following comment, it appears that the metaphoric penny has finally dropped, albeit with a clunk:

> We are here to admire the packaging, not the contents. What is immediately obvious is that art played a critical role in the rise and conquest of Christianity. Art could make the incredible credible, the ugly beautiful. That was power indeed.[5]

His persistent reluctance to view this art as anything more than an elaborate stratagem to confound the witless masses does not pay due regard to the classical and biblical texts that supported complex medieval theories on the question of matter and the nature of God. The exhibition's primary intent was not to debunk myths or reveal fraudulent practices long ago exposed by Calvin and others, but to examine the relationship between sacred matter and precious materials as evidenced by relic veneration in the Middle Ages. In this context it was felt neither sympathetic nor instructive to recycle jokes that are almost 500 years old. It is undeniable that the exhibition featured reliquaries that were made to contain truly preposterous relics – perhaps the most outlandish was a silver-gilt figural reliquary of the Virgin and Child that was made to contain a supposed fragment of the infant Christ's umbilical cord. The reliquary was lent by the Musée de Cluny and is, incidentally, one of the finest surviving, documented examples of Parisian goldsmiths' work from the period around 1400.[6] The relic itself was destroyed by the bishop of Châlons in the early 18th century. The high artistic merit of the piece may have been obscured for visitors to the exhibition if the interpretation of the object had concentrated on the trade in fake relics and the gullibility of a duped congregation. In order to expand public understanding of the significance of relic veneration for a medieval audience, the reliquary was used instead to serve as a poetic discourse on the mysteries of the incarnation. This, after all, was the real value of such a sensational relic that speaks so viscerally of the relationship between mother and child.

The same might be said of the relic of the milk of the Virgin Mary. This was represented in the exhibition as one of the eight relics contained within the opulent gable-end reliquary of St Oda from the British Museum's collection,[7] discussed in a paper by Glenn Gates, Susan La Niece and Terry Drayman-Weisser in this publication.[8] Calvin, not surprisingly, demonstrated little empathy with the relic and irreverently compared the Virgin Mary with a dairy cow for her prodigious yield of milk: 'had the Virgin been a wet-nurse her whole life, or a dairy, she could not have produced more than is shown as hers in various parts'. Vibeke Olson tackles the Virgin's lactation issue with rather more sensitivity in her beautifully illustrated essay that explores the relic's salvific, medicinal and Eucharistic significance for medieval devotees.[9]

As Januszczak inferred, the grisly nature of many relics meant that the 'packaging' was indeed essential for the vital process of communication and contemplation. Martina Bagnoli's essay for this volume, 'Dressing the relics', explains that few relics were intended to be seen in the medieval period.[10] The gruesome exposure of whole cadavers or body parts, such as the eye of Edward Oldcorne at Stonyhurst College in Lancashire, was securely part of the climate of counter-Reformation where relics responded to a new brutal age of martyrdom in a very graphic way. This extreme language of relic veneration, illustrated in Andrea de Meo Arbore's paper,[11] was used not just to inspire piety, but probably to generate feelings of outrage and anger. It was, however, emphatically not the medieval experience which relied most usually instead on the power of beauty and the eloquence of precious materials.

Treasures of Heaven demonstrated with conviction that relics constituted more than 'Absurd things … put on show to manipulate Catholic audiences in unscrupulous ways'.[12] The belief in the power of the saints and their relics impacted on every aspect of medieval daily life from the cultivation of the land to the care of the sick to civil defence and international diplomacy. The amassing of Louis IX's veritable arsenal of relics at Sainte Chapelle, for instance, must be viewed within the system of belief that permitted it if it is to be fully appreciated. In many ways, Januszczak's largely unfavourable reading of *Treasures of Heaven* is not a surprise. Reviews even with a more sympathetic understanding of the exhibition's ambitions resorted to staple expressions drawn from stock post-Reformation, post-Enlightenment images that invoked the macabre and occasionally suggested a level of cultural superiority on the part of the writer. For instance, on 11 June 2011 the *Daily Telegraph Review* used the title 'Deathly Hallows: the British Museum digs deep into the grim, grisly, gorgeous world of religious relics' to announce a feature by Martin Gayford under the headline 'Bodysnatching, bones and the power of the undead'. Meanwhile, the article written by Eamon Duffy on the exhibition for the *Guardian* was presented under the headline 'The lovely bones', and so the list continues. The deeply embedded negative attitude towards relic veneration that the media response to the exhibition revealed was considered a potential challenge to the positive reception of *Treasures of Heaven* from the outset. Henk van Os remarked in the publication that accompanied his groundbreaking exhibition, *The Way to Heaven*, held in the Netherlands between 2000–1, that the study of reliquary art had been inhibited historically by exactly this sort of opinion:

> Humanists, reformers and revolutionaries hated reliquaries. For them the veneration of such objects represented the ultimate proof of the degenerate nature of the Christian Church or the utter stupidity of the Christian faith.[13]

Van Os's work in some ways heralded a new scholarly approach that placed greater insistence on investigating the significance of relics and reliquaries beyond the obvious, well-trodden, simplistic arguments of ecclesiastical abuse and repression. He cites authorities such as Peter Dinzelbacher and Arnold Angenendt as figures who have enlarged our understanding by engaging with a belief system that may at times seem impenetrable.[14] Many others, of course, have contributed to this process, including Derek Krueger and Alexander Nagel whose essays for the *Treasures of Heaven* exhibition catalogue expand the chronology of relic veneration respectively back into the ancient past and forward to the modern age.[15] This longer history places the ritualistic behaviour of veneration neatly within a universal human impulse to cherish physical objects that are somehow felt to be imbued with the character or personality of the individual who once owned or touched them. It becomes, therefore, no longer an alien, dark practice, unfathomable to the rational mind, but rather something to which we are all likely to subscribe at some point in our lives, even unwittingly. Steven Hooper expands on these ideas in his cross-cultural theory of relics, placed appropriately as the closing chapter of this fine collection of essays.[16]

The scholarly legacy of *Treasures of Heaven* was captured by its catalogue which is now a standard publication for teachers and students of medieval material culture. The exhibition also generated a digital research resource hosted by Columbia University.[17] The papers published in this volume represent yet another aspect of the exhibition's legacy. In October 2011 over a three-day period, a multitude of experts from a variety of disciplines – art history, history, archaeology, conservation and science, congregated at the British Museum to share their knowledge of and fascination with the study of relics, reliquaries, pilgrimage and the cult of saints. The international, interdisciplinary nature of the gathering has produced a volume of unique value for students and researchers in this field. The conference served partly as a vehicle for ideas that could not be adequately developed in the exhibition space and as a platform for papers that were inspired by the exhibition. The essays are arranged in three sections to convey a sense of place ('Pilgrimage and cult centres'), material culture ('Relics, reliquaries and their materials') and conflict ('Debate, doubt and later developments') emphasizing without any scholarly doubt the richness of the world of the medieval relic.

Acknowledgements

The interdisciplinary nature of the essays contained in *Matter of Faith* required a host of different peer reviewers who are all thanked for the contribution of their expertise and the timely submission of their comments. Thanks are also due to Jonathan Williams and Roger Bland at the British Museum for their support of the project. Careful readers of the endnotes will observe frequent mention of Anna Harnden who was project curator of *Treasures of Heaven* at the British Museum and handled all the organizational aspects of the conference with grace, charm and humour. Anna's successor as co-editor, Lloyd de Beer, has navigated the publication through its various stages with calm, clarity and confidence. Finally, however, the publication has benefitted from the rigour and determination of Sarah Faulks who has truly demonstrated the patience of a saint!

The exhibition and conference were made possible by the support of John Studzinski CBE; Judith and William Bollinger, Singapore; Betsy and Jack Ryan; Howard and Roberta Ahmanson; and the Hintze Family Charitable Foundation. In addition, John H. Rassweiler, Sir Paul and Lady Ruddock and Polly Devlin OBE kindly contributed to the conference and publication. All are thanked warmly for their generosity and encouragement.

Notes

1. http://www.waldemar.tv/2011/07/the-hand-of-god/ (*The Sunday Times*, 3 July 2011).
2. Ibid.
3. http://www.gutenberg.org/files/32136/32136-pdf.pdf p.173.
4. http://www.waldemar.tv/2011/07/the-hand-of-god/.
5. Ibid.
6. Bagnoli *et al.* 2010, cat. 124, 207.
7. Ibid., cat. 82, 176.
8. See Chapter 15, 116–25.
9. See Chapter 19, 151–7.
10. See Chapter 13, 100–9.
11. See Chapter 24, 183–9.
12. http://www.waldemar.tv/2011/07/the-hand-of-god/.
13. Van Os 2000, 12.
14. Ibid., 16.
15. Bagnoli *et al.* 2010, 5–17 and 211–22.
16. See Chapter 25, 190–9.
17. www.learn.columbia.edu/treasuresofheaven.

Bibliography

Bagnoli, M., Klein, H.A., Mann, C.G. and Robinson, J. (eds) 2010. *Treasures of Heaven: Saints, Relics and Devotion in Medieval Europe*, Baltimore and London.

Van Os, H. 2000. *The Way to Heaven: Relic Veneration in the Middle Ages*, Amsterdam.

Chapter 1
To Be a Pilgrim
Tactile Piety, Virtual Pilgrimage and the Experience of Place in Christian Pilgrimage

Dee Dyas

In Act One of Shakespeare's *Romeo and Juliet*, Romeo delivers one of the most unusual 'chat-up' lines in history. Deeply affected by his first glimpse of Juliet, he moves quickly to establish intimacy:

ROMEO   If I profane with my unworthiest hand
This holy shrine, the gentle fine is this:
My lips, two blushing pilgrims, ready stand
To smooth that rough touch with a tender kiss.

JULIET   Good pilgrim, you do wrong your hand too much,
Which mannerly devotion shows in this;
For saints have hands that pilgrims' hands do touch,
And palm to palm is holy palmers' kiss.

ROMEO   Have not saints lips, and holy palmers too?

JULIET   Ay, pilgrim, lips that they must use in prayer.

ROMEO   O, then, dear saint, let lips do what hands do.
They pray, grant thou, lest faith turn to despair.

Romeo and Juliet, I.V

And he plants a hearty kiss, demonstrating that he is clearly not one to hold back in his wooing. However, what this exchange also shows is that tactile piety (and Romeo is demonstrating a very tactile kind of piety) is clearly still deeply embedded in public consciousness. It seems that 50 years after the dissolution of the monasteries in England and the dismantling of saints' cults by reformers, knowledge of the concept of physical intimacy with saints can be assumed and used in this playful fashion. Everyone knows that pilgrims touch, and even kiss, saints.

There is a deeper question underlying this apparently still widespread cultural assumption so deftly employed by Shakespeare. How did Christianity, which in its earliest days moved away very deliberately from attaching importance to place and things, become so deeply pervaded by an emphasis on physical experience. And even more intriguingly, why did this happen and prove so resilient in the face of opposition? The literally dazzling objects on display in the *Treasures of Heaven* exhibition showed clearly why even non-believers might long to touch such superbly crafted objects, but the importance of touch in Christian devotional practice is not limited to the obviously beautiful or physically appealing. Indeed some of the saints' relics touched and kissed, both in the Middle Ages and still today, are not physically appealing at all. However, human remains that many societies (including pagan Rome) have regarded as actively polluting sacred space,[1] are not only treated with honour, but publicly displayed and enthusiastically embraced.

The closely related elements of place, proximity, sight and touch, which feature so strongly in attitudes to relics and reliquaries of the saints, are also intrinsic to the spread of pilgrimage and to the power associated with 'primary' holy places and the secondary network of sites which developed through belief in 'transferable holiness'.[2] The term 'tactile piety', as used by Robert Wilken in his book *The Land Called Holy*,[3] combines the meanings of the medieval word for piety ('pitie'), which the *Middle English Dictionary* defines as 'godliness, reverent and devout obedience to God', and 'devocioun', which offers the added dimension of awe and adoration.[4] This is not just piety in terms of obedience and holy living, but a quality of sensory experience which reveals an extraordinary degree of physicality at the heart of much Christian spirituality.

As will be seen in the following discussion, Christianity inherited a range of emphases from the Old Testament and New Testament. The Early Church chose to follow the New Testament teaching that God was available to all people, everywhere, through the Holy Spirit. However in the 4th century, there was a significant sea change as the cult of saints and pilgrimage to holy places really took hold in Christian thought and practice. Since that time onwards, Christian piety has struggled to reconcile belief in the omnipresence (and hence 'omni-availability') of an invisible, intangible God, and a strong human desire to experience visible, tangible evidence of God's presence and power within a particular location. The development of Christian holy places has from its earliest manifestations raised central theological questions: 'If some places are especially sacred, offering particular access to God, then are other places therefore less holy? Is God really more easily encountered in Jerusalem or Rome than in other locations? And if God is Spirit, invisible, intangible, what is the role or even the validity of tactile experience in such encounters?' In this essay I wish, therefore, to examine the essential paradox at the heart of tactile piety as it has emerged within Christianity, and to trace some of the reasons for its power and persistence through the centuries.

The paradox of tactile piety in Christianity

The biblical inheritance
Christianity has a long and complex history in terms of the interaction between faith, sight, place and touch. The biblical inheritance alone is surprisingly multifaceted. The Hebrew Bible provides two key approaches to the association between place and experience of God.[5] While Abraham, Jacob and Moses encounter God in particular places,[6] the primary focus for Moses in leading the Exodus and Abraham in seeking the land of Canaan is on journeying into the unknown *with* God. All places are locations where God can be known, for God travels with his people. Once the Promised Land is reached, however, a system of fixed-place pilgrimage evolves. A series of concentric circles emerges: the Land as a whole, Jerusalem, the Temple, the Holy of Holies, with the innermost circle linked to the most intense sense of God's presence. This model emphasizes journeying to a particular location to encounter God in a specific way.

There are also ambiguities regarding contact with God. The Book of Exodus makes it clear that sinful human beings may not look upon the face of God, let alone touch him or they will die (19:12; 33:20). Yet many of the images used in the Hebrew Bible to portray God are in fact profoundly tactile: he is the Shepherd who carries the lambs in his bosom (Isaiah 40:11); the bird sheltering its young under its feathers (Psalm 91:4); and the lover embracing the beloved in the Song of Songs (as in 2:6, for example).

In the New Testament much of this imagined contact is fulfilled as God becomes incarnate and physically present in the person of Jesus, a human being who is not only God made visible, but someone who touches and can be touched.[7] Here we have another paradox. The sense of Jerusalem and the Temple as the places where God is to be encountered fall away, for God is now to be found not in a place but in a person. Yet the physicality of place is replaced by the physicality of human touch. Physical contact with Jesus brings healing and cleansing and the crowds 'all wanted to touch him' (Luke 6:19). After the Resurrection, two encounters focus specifically on touch. Thomas is invited to overcome his doubts by touching Christ's wounds but told 'Blessed are they who have not seen yet believe' (John 20:29). Mary Magdalene is told 'Do *not* touch me for I have not yet ascended to the Father' (John 20:17).

Following the Ascension and Pentecost, God is only to be encountered through the Holy Spirit. Images of fatherhood (Matthew 6:9–13; Ephesians 3:14–15) and of the loving spouse remain (Ephesians 5:22–3), but God is intangible, invisible. He cannot be touched but he speaks, both directly and through messengers such as Peter and Paul. He also heals and there is an intriguing incident in the Acts of the Apostles when pieces of cloth (including handkerchiefs) that have been touched by Paul become channels of healing (Acts 19:6). It is clear from the Gospel of Luke and the Acts of the Apostles that God is viewed in these texts as omnipresent, able to work both inside and beyond the land formerly considered his special territory. The focus on 'place' in Jewish tradition is discarded by the Church. Christians are 'pilgrims and strangers' in the world (1 Peter 1:11); however they journey not to a holy place on earth, but to the heavenly Jerusalem.

Early Church attitudes
These New Testament emphases are also clear in the writings of the early Fathers. Writers from Clement of Rome at the end of the 1st century[8] to Augustine of Hippo[9] in the 4th century define pilgrimage as the daily journey of the people of God towards heaven. Clement of Alexandria (c. 160–215) quotes the poet Solon: 'The divine … is not capable of being approached with our eyes, or grasped with our hands' (*Stromata*, XII).[10] Similarly, Origen (c. 185–c. 254), writing in AD 248, declares 'We do not ask … "How shall we go to God?" as though we thought that God existed in some place… Celsus misrepresents us, when he says that we expect to see God with our bodily eyes … and to touch Him … with our hands.'[11] The motif of life as pilgrimage remained an overarching concept in Christian thought through succeeding centuries, and reformers and mystics repeatedly strove to root Christian experience in the spiritual rather than the physical. However, by the mid-4th century a revolution in Christian practice was well underway. A wave of tactile piety, attaching itself to both places and things, was sweeping across Christendom.[12]

Factors which facilitated change
How did a religion so 'inhospitable to the idea of holy places' become one that by the end of the 4th century was developing an ever-widening sacred geography?[13] Scholars generally agree that the chief external catalyst was Emperor Constantine's conversion to Christianity and his desire to create a Holy Land, and that the substantial internal shift in conviction was facilitated by the emergence of the cult of the martyrs. However, other factors also contributed to this complex series of events.

Plate 1 Ex voto offerings at Corinth

Plate 2 Ex voto offerings at the shrine of St William, York Minster. York Minster, St William Window N7 22b

The conversion of Constantine and the actions of Helena

Constantine's conversion and the activities of his mother Helena in Palestine were profoundly influential, not only in 'identifying' biblical sites and erecting churches upon them, but also in shaping the thinking of Eusebius (*c.* 260–339) and Cyril (*c.* 315–86).[14] Eusebius, as bishop of Caesarea (a city which had in recent years outranked Jerusalem), was initially reluctant. Cyril, as bishop of Jerusalem, understandably had less trouble weaving the concept of a Holy City and Holy Land into his theology and liturgical practice. However the new sacred topography opened the door to practices outlined below which sat uneasily with the teaching of the apostles.

The influence of pagan religion

Constantine was from a pagan background where it was customary for Roman emperors to erect sacred buildings, and his pursuit of this goal through Helena, in the context of his adopted faith, changed the face of Palestine. However, this is not the only pagan element which influenced Christian pilgrimage.[15] Christianity, as it spread across the Empire, had already encountered many polytheistic cults with a strongly developed sense of place. Geographical features such as mountains, caves or springs were believed to possess inherent sacredness.[16] Shrines attracted pilgrims seeking healing, guidance or the fulfilment of vows. Ex-voto offerings, revelations in dreams and the recording of miracles were key elements.[17] The gods were known through their images which were honoured on festival days and it was believed that they were not only symbols of their presence, but channels of their power.[18] Clearly these practices were also central to the cults of saints and sacred sites that sprang up in Christianity and continued into the era of medieval pilgrimage. There are very few differences between the pagan votive offerings which can still be seen at Corinth and objects displayed at the shrine of St William of York in the Middle Ages (**Pls 1–2**).[19] The absorption of aspects of pagan practice into Christianity did not go unnoticed and, ironically, the results were criticized by both sides. Christian devotion to the relics and tombs of saints shocked pagans, such as Julian the Apostate, by breaching the

customary distance maintained between the living and the dead.[20] On the other hand, Vigilantius, a cleric from Gaul, criticized what he saw as pagan practice absorbed wholesale into Christian saints' cults by complaining: 'Under the cloak of religion we see what is *all but a heathen ceremony* [author's italics] introduced into the churches'.[21] He was roundly rebutted by Jerome, but he had a point.

Visiting holy people

Tactile piety had been foreshadowed from the 3rd century onwards by the practice of visiting living holy figures, such as the 'Desert Fathers'.[22] Some came as disciples; others sought healing from people who patently lived close to God. The saints concerned did not seem to welcome the growing emphasis on proximity and touch. Many retreated further and further into the desert and it was apparently the intense desire of pilgrims to touch him and 'gain some blessing' which impelled Symeon the Elder (390–459) to become a stylite: 'He thought at first that this excess of honour was out of place, but then he found it annoying and tedious and therefore thought of standing on a column.'[23] Reverence for holy people was to a large extent the theological 'Trojan Horse' which breached Christian defences. Christian theology did not (at least in theory) accept the concept of inherent sacredness that identified pagan pilgrimage sites. However, Christians were prepared to honour people. Places particularly associated with the Trinity, or with the saints, could therefore qualify. This development fed the need for a historically based religion to remain rooted in its past (the events of the Bible and the age of the martyrs) and to demonstrate that the power of God was still real and active in the present.

Promotion and imitation

Cyril of Jerusalem, although more nuanced in his approach than Constantine,[24] nevertheless promoted the uniqueness of Jerusalem with vigour. In his *Catechetical Lectures* he proclaimed: 'Others only hear; we see and touch.'[25] He devised liturgical forms that employed the senses in acts of devotion, including kissing the cross. The links established in

Plate 3 Reliquary pendant for the Holy Thorn, c. 1340, French (Paris), gold, enamel (basse-taille), amethyst, glass and vellum, 4 x 2.65 x 2.5cm. British Museum, London (1902,0210.1)

the 4th-century narrative of the Spanish nun Egeria between holy places, the biblical text, appropriate prayers and the presence of 'holy' monks, together with her participation in the developing rituals in Jerusalem, shows how Christianity was weaving these elements into experiences which not only affected pilgrims at the time, but made them transmitters of beliefs and practices to others, stimulating both imitation and expectation.[26] Cyril put his city and diocese at the centre of the Christian world, demonstrating the power of pilgrimage to assert and reinforce political, ecclesiastical, theological and liturgical control.

Conflicts and controversy

But how did this heady mix fit with earlier Christian teaching? Significant voices raised concerns. Gregory of Nyssa (most of the time)[27] and Jerome (some of the time)[28] insisted that pilgrimage was not necessary, although Jerome was capable of arguing the case both ways.[29] The fact was that they and others faced an inescapable theological conundrum. If some places were especially holy, then, logically, other places must be less holy. Yet could it really be claimed that an omnipresent God was somehow more accessible in Jerusalem or Bethlehem than elsewhere? Jerome and Gregory, wearing their theological hats, both said that this was not the case. On the other hand, Gregory shed tears on visiting Jerusalem[30] and Jerome was no stranger to intensely tactile devotional experiences. He writes (like Egeria) of being in 'the very spot' where biblical events took place (*Letter* 66. 3, 9), of venerating the martyrs' tombs, applying their 'holy ashes' to his eyes and touching them with his lips (*Letter* 66.8). Urging a friend, Marcella, to visit Palestine, he says they will 'weep in the sepulchre of the Lord', and 'touch with their lips the wood of the cross' (*Letter* 46.13). He writes approvingly of the pilgrimage of another friend, Paula, undertaken around AD 386, describing how she 'fell down and worshipped before the Cross *as if she could see* [author's italics] the Lord hanging on it'. In the Tomb of the Resurrection 'she kissed the stone which the angel removed

from the sepulchre door … Her tears and lamentations there are known to all Jerusalem' (*Letter* 108). Interestingly, the intensity of Paula's emotion and her imaginative engagement with the sites visited, clearly commended by Jerome, is not unlike that expressed by another female pilgrim from a later era, Margery Kempe (*c.* 1373–after 1439). Kempe's responses, however, did not win similar approval from those around her as her companions tended to find her loud cries and tears irritating rather than praiseworthy.

When theology is ambushed by experience, experience tends to be the victor. However the growth of holy places and shrines created a paradox at the heart of Christianity which in time helped to provoke the Protestant Reformation in Europe in the 16th century and remains unresolved today.

In the 4th century, and during the following millennium, the adherents of tactile piety were dominant. For all the factors already cited, I want to suggest that the main reason was actually very simple. As we shall see, tactile piety fulfils something that is so instinctive and deeply rooted in human nature that it can overcome all manner of intellectual or social barriers.

The power of tactile piety

Once 'tactile piety' had taken hold, the Church found it very hard to regulate or suppress. It lay at the core of medieval pilgrimage to saints' shrines and to all the great destinations including Jerusalem, Rome and Santiago de Compostela. What makes visual and tactile expressions of piety so hard to resist?

The role of the senses in human development and experience

I suggest that the core reason for the appeal of tactile piety is not so much theological as physiological. Human beings, even from before birth, respond to touch and touch is the earliest mechanism through which we explore and experience the world around us. Even tiny infants possess a grasp reflex. They not only take and release objects, they also hold them in order to learn from them and bring them to their mouths.[31] The lips, tongue and fingers are the most sensitive parts of the body and have the greatest cortical representation.[32] Lips, as Romeo would attest, remain very important in human experience, whether kissing real or imagined saints. As infants develop, other senses come into play but touch, particularly in combination with sight, remains extremely powerful in communication and learning as well as in creating, reinforcing and perpetuating experience through memory. Educational experts tell us that we remember roughly 20% of what we hear, 30% of what we see, 50% of what we hear and see together, 70% of what we say (if we thin–k as we say it) and 90% of what we do.[33] This offers an interesting insight into the power inherent in combining ritual and place with the fullest possible use of the senses. Significantly, receiving the Eucharist usually involves sight, smell, hearing, taste and touch. Taking and holding things in our hands has a particular effect on us. To what extent was the power of the reliquary pendant for the Holy Thorn enhanced by the fact that it could nestle in the palm of one's hand (**Pl. 3**)?[34]

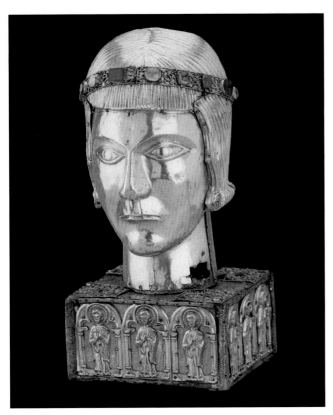

Plate 4 Reliquary head of St Eustace, *c.* 1210, Upper Rhenish (possibly Basel), silver gilt over wood, rock crystal, chalcedony, amethyst, cornelian, pearl, and glass, wooden core with gesso. British Museum, London (1850,1127.1)

Plate 5 Terracotta ampulla showing the Egyptian St Menas (died *c.* 309) between two camels, *c.* 480–650, Byzantine/Abu Mina (Egypt), h. 15.1cm. British Museum, London (1875,1012.16)

Particular spiritual benefits mediated through the senses

Providing evidence

Places and objects have frequently been seen as supplying proof of Christian teaching. Offering reasons to visit the Holy Land, William Wey quoted Pope Leo I: 'Why should the mind toil when the sight instructs?'[35] Seeing Bethlehem or Calvary made doctrine concrete, tangible. This was the real thing. And the very splendour of the architecture and the craftsmanship and materials used in shrines and reliquaries affirmed the eternal power which lay behind them. Simon Fitzsimons describes seeing the body of Thomas Becket in 1322 'in a case made of most pure gold and adorned with innumerable precious stones, with shining pearls like unto the gates of the [heavenly] Jerusalem, and sparkling' (*Western Pilgrims*, 3).[36] Pilgrims entering the cathedral at Compostela were greeted by the benevolent figure of St James, touched his foot and passed through the astonishing Portico of Glory. At the far end of the cathedral, bathed in flickering candlelight, with gold gleaming and incense rising, pilgrims embraced the statue of the saint (even today the shifting mass of pilgrims can make it look as if the statue itself is alive). Elsewhere tombs appeared to exude healing oil or sweet smells. It must have been hard *not* to believe in that context.

Offering a connection to the divine

In the early 5th century Paulinus of Nola wrote: 'No other sentiment draws men to Jerusalem but the desire to see and touch the places where Christ was physically present.'[37]

William Wey also noted: 'This is the stone on which Christ fell when he was carrying his cross and we kissed it.'[38] Pilgrims touch what Christ touched and the touch of Christ and the saints triggers a chain of contagious holiness, as the Veronica[39] and the Mandylion[40] demonstrate. A text found among the writings of Basil the Great asserts that: 'Those who touch the bones of the martyrs participate in their sanctity'.[41] Medieval pilgrims to Santiago de Compostela were exhorted to 'revere the sacred place' in which 'the most sacred limbs of the apostle *which touched God when present in the flesh* [author's italics], are stored'.[42] Here we do not have the 'six degrees of separation' which are said to link all human beings, but two degrees of connection. Pilgrims can touch the man who himself touched Christ. Felix Fabri records that he and his companions 'crawled to the socket-hole of the cross, kissed the place with exceeding great devotion' and placed their 'face, eyes and mouth over the hole, from whence …there breathes forth an exceeding sweet scent'. This won them a plenary (full) indulgence.[43] Shrines and relics provide a bridge to an invisible God and 'speaking reliquaries' (which visually describe their contents), such as those of St Baudime or St Eustace (**Pl. 4**), make this point particularly strongly. Constance Classen observes that tactile language is also used in medieval religious texts 'to convey the immediacy of God's love'[44] citing Bernard of Clairvaux who imagines Christ urging, 'touch me with the hand of faith, the finger of desire, the embrace of love'.

Providing a process of exchange

Pilgrims of all classes[45] frequently take away objects, stones, earth, badges and flasks and these *eulogia* or takeaway 'blessings' are believed to carry transferable holiness (**Pl. 5**).[46] Pilgrims also often leave something of themselves behind. Ex-voto offerings not only ask for mercy or record thanks, but also leave a replica of *your* foot or *your* arm close to the shrine of the saint. Many pilgrims have literally left their mark on holy places, from the Piacenza pilgrim who in the late 6th century reverently wrote the names of his parents on a couch at Cana (*The Piacenza Pilgrim*, 4)[47] to the knights observed by Felix Fabri in the late 15th century who rather less reverently scrawled or scratched their names and other signs of their presence all over the Church of the Holy Sepulchre in Jerusalem.[48] The feet of statues such as those of St James at Santiago de Compostela or St Peter in Rome are worn by the very touch of devotion. Neither shrine nor worshipper remains unchanged.

The persistence of tactile piety

The power of tactile piety endured through the Middle Ages, although it was not unchallenged. In the 14th century *Piers Plowman*, the benefits of pilgrimage and the integrity of pilgrims are severely criticized (*Prologue*, 46–9). Anchoritic and mystical texts advocate staying still physically in order to journey inwardly. The writings of Richard Rolle and the Pseudo-Bonaventuran *Meditations on the Life of Christ* promote an imaginative exploration of the biblical narrative, rather than a physical trip to the Holy Land. And yet, curiously, alternatives to tactile piety tend to slip into recreating the tactile experience. Walter Hilton's use of pilgrimage to Jerusalem as a paradigm of the contemplative life is so concrete in its realization of pilgrim experience that the exemplum is in danger of overwhelming the application.[49] The virtual pilgrimages of the mind created by Rolle and others are in fact intensely tactile. In his *Meditations on the Passion*, Rolle writes: 'Lord, in my imagination I want to embrace the foot of the cross, prostrate on the ground as you were lying there, with the stench of dead mens' bones'.[50] Nicholas Love recommends: 'By devout imagination *as though thou were bodily present* [author's italics], comfort Our Lady'[51] and the Pseudo-Bonaventuran *Meditations on the Life of Christ*, focusing on the Nativity, suggests: 'Kneel and adore your Lord God … Kiss the beautiful little feet of the infant Jesus who lies in the manger … Pick him up and hold him in your arms' (38–9).[52]

Many of the problems inherent in the tactile piety that sprang up in the 4th century came to a head during the Reformation. Attempts were made to suppress pilgrimage and associated practices and to assert instead a word-based faith experience. Yet outside Protestantism tactile piety has always flourished, and in recent years the adoption of pilgrimage across most Christian traditions means that tactile piety has once again been strengthening its hold, although, as formerly, it is unclear whether this is driven by theology or experience.[53] All major faiths practise their own forms of tactile piety and in addition we now see a secular form active in tourist experience. 'Being there', seeing and touching for ourselves is now an experience available to more people than ever before. And what do we do when we get to a special place? We long to touch (even though conservators would rather we refrained) and we look around for what we can take home: objects that will capture the experience and enable us to re-live it and share it with others. We still acknowledge the power of place and of primary and secondary relics, whether in the context of personal relationships, or in relating to genuine heroes or more ephemeral celebrities. Why else would someone pay $4.6 million for a dress worn by Marilyn Monroe or £19,000 for the tooth of John Lennon? 'Tactile piety', whether manifested in religious experience or in emotional investment of a more secular kind, is still very much with us today.

Notes

1 The revulsion felt by pagans at the breaking down of the barrier between the living and the dead which had been carefully maintained in Roman law appears in the Emperor Julian's criticism of Christians carrying relics in procession: 'The carrying of the corpses of the dead through a great assembly of people … staining the eyesight of all with ill-omened sights of the dead. What day so touched with death could be lucky? How, after being present at such ceremonies, could anyone approach the gods and their temples?' *Epistulae et Leges*, cited in Brown 1981, 7.
2 See for example St Augustine's account of 'sacred earth' from Jerusalem in St Augustine 1972, XXII.8.
3 Wilken 1992, 115.
4 Kurath and Kuhn 1952–.
5 See Dyas 2001, ch. 1.
6 See Genesis 12:4–7; 28:10–22; Exodus 3:1–6.
7 For example Jesus touches a leper (Matthew 8:3) and takes children in his arms (Mark 10:16).
8 The Letter of St Clement to the Corinthians opens with the greeting, 'The Church of God which dwells as a pilgrim [παροικουσα] in Rome to the Church of God in pilgrimage at Corinth' (*The Apostolic Fathers* 1969, 9).
9 See for example *St Augustine* 1972, XIX.17.
10 Clement of Alexandria 1885, XII.
11 Origen 1885, VII:34.
12 Wilken 1992, 115.
13 Markus 1994, 259.
14 See the extensive analysis in Walker 1990.
15 See Elsner and Rutherford 2005 for the similarities and differences between pagan and Christian pilgrimage.
16 See MacCormack 1990.
17 'Custom called for a gift of thanksgiving to the god for the healing … a work of art showing the god and his family or the scene of the cure, an inscription commemorating the cure and/or the offering that was brought, a literary piece … or a reproduction of the part of the body that was healed' (Ferguson 1987, 176).
18 Lane Fox 1986, 66.
19 These can be seen clearly depicted in the St William window in York Minster (**Pl. 2**).
20 See n. 1.
21 *Against Vigilantius*, 4 in Jerome 1994.
22 Frank suggests that seeing the saints, 'embracing them with the eyes', is equated with a form of touching: 'seeing the holy provides an active, tactile encounter with it' (Frank 2000, 14).
23 *Religious History*, 26 in Theodoret of Cyrrhus 1992.
24 Walker 1990, 112.
25 *Catechesis* XIII.22, Cyril of Jerusalem 1970, 18.
26 *Egeria's Travels* 1971. See for example 5:10, 11.
27 Gregory of Nyssa 1954, Letter 2.
28 Jerome 1994, Letter 58, 2,3,4.
29 Jerome 1994, Letter 46, 10.
30 *Patrologia Graeca*, 1015C.
31 Hatwell *et al.* 2003, 20.
32 Hatwell *et al.*, 2003, 52.
33 Dale 1969.
34 Bagnoli *et al.* 2010, 113–14.
35 *The Itineraries of William Wey* 2010, 58.
36 *Western Pilgrims* 1952, 3.
37 Paulinus of Nola 1962, 49.14.

38 *The Itineraries of William Wey* 2010, 128.
39 Veronica (Latin *vera icon*, 'true image'): a cloth said to have been
   used to wipe blood and sweat from the face of Jesus on the way to
   Calvary and upon which his image was believed to have been
   miraculously imprinted. Also known as *Sudarium* (Latin, 'sweat') or
   Vernicle (Middle English).
40 Mandylion, also called the 'Holy Towel' of Edessa, a cloth believed
   to bear the miraculous imprint of Christ's face after a painter failed
   to capture His likeness.
41 *Homily on Psalm 115*, 4, *Patrologia Graeca*, 30.112c, cited in Wilken
   1992, 115.
42 *The Miracles of St James* 1996, 21.
43 Fabri 1896, I, 365.
44 Classen 2012, 29–30.
45 See Sarah Blick's chapter in this volume.
46 On pilgrim badges, flasks and other souvenirs see Spencer 1998;
   Blick and Tekippe 2004; Pentcheva 2010, 20–2; Kessler 2013, 235.
47 Wilkinson 1977, 79.
48 Fabri 1896, II.86–7.
49 Hilton 1991, vol. 2, 21–5.
50 Rolle 1989, 103.
51 For Love's reflections on the Nativity see Love 1992, 37–43.
52 *Meditations on the Life of Christ* 1977, 38–9.
53 See Dyas 2004.

Bibliography

Primary sources

The Apostolic Fathers 1969. *The Fathers of the Church*, vol. 1, trans. Francis
   X. Glimm, Joseph M.-F. Marique and Gerald G. Walsh.
   Washington, DC.
St Augustine 1972. *Concerning the City of God against the Pagans*, trans. H.
   Bettenson, Harmondsworth.
Clement of Alexandria 1885. *Stromata*, trans. W. Wilson, in *Ante-Nicene
   Fathers*, vol. 2, ed. A. Roberts, J. Donaldson and A. Cleveland Coxe,
   Buffalo, NY.
Cyril of Jerusalem 1970. *The Works of St Cyril of Jerusalem*, vol. 2, trans.
   L.P. McCauley, S.J. and A. Stephenson, *The Fathers of the Church*,
   vol. 64, Washington DC.
Egeria's Travels 1971. Ed. John Wilkinson, London.
Gregory of Nyssa 1954. *Select Writings and Letters of Gregory, Bishop of
   Nyssa*, ed. William Moore and Henry Austin Wilson, trans Philip
   Schaff and Henry Wace, *Select Library of the Nicene and Post-Nicene
   Fathers of the Christian Church*, vol. 5, Grand Rapids, MI.
Hilton, W., 1991. *The Scale of Perfection*, ed. J.P.H. Clark and R.
   Dorward, Classics of Western Spirituality, New York.
The Itineraries of William Wey 2010. Ed. and trans. F. Davey, Oxford.
Jerome 1994. *Letters and Selected Works*, trans. P. Schaff and H. Wace,
   Select Library of the Nicene and Post-Nicene Fathers of the Church, vol. 6,
   Grand Rapids, MI.
Love, N. 1992. *Mirror of the Blessed Life of Jesus Christ*, ed. Michael
   Sargent. New York.
Meditations on the Life of Christ 1977. Trans. I. Ragusa and R.B. Green,
   2nd edn, Princeton.
The Miracles of St James: Translations from the Liber Sancti Jacobi 1996. With
   introduction by T.F. Coffey, L.K. Davidson and M. Dunn, New
   York.
Origen 1885. *Against Celsus*, trans. Frederick Crombie, in *Ante-Nicene
   Fathers*, vol. 4, ed. A. Roberts, J. Donaldson and A. Cleveland
   Coxe, Buffalo, NY.
Patrologia Graeca 1857–. Ed. J.P. Migne, Paris.
Paulinus of Nola 1962. *Letters*, vol. 2, trans. P.G. Walsh, Ancient
   Christian Writers, Maryland.
Rolle, R. 1989. *Richard Rolle: The English Writings*, trans. and ed. by R.S.
   Allen, The Classics of Western Spirituality, London.
Theodoret of Cyrrhus 1992. *A History of the Monks of Syria*, trans. R.M.
   Price, Kalamazoo, MI.
Western Pilgrims 1952. *The Itineraries of Fr. Simon Fitzsimmons (1322–23), A
   Certain Englishman (1344–45), Thomas Brygg (1392)*, ed. Eugene
   Hoade, Publications of the Studium Biblicum Franciscanum, vol.
   18, Jerusalem.

Secondary sources

Badone, E. and Sharon, R. 2004. *Intersecting Journeys: The Anthropology of
   Pilgrimage and Tourism*, Urbana and Chicago.
Bagnoli, M., Klein, H.A., Mann, C.G. and Robinson, J. (eds) 2010.
   Treasures of Heaven: Saints, Relics and Devotion in Medieval Europe,
   Baltimore and London.
Blick, S. and Tekippe, R. (eds), 2004. *Art and Architecture of Late Medieval
   Pilgrimage in Northern Europe and the British Isles*, Studies in Medieval
   and Reformation Traditions: History, Culture, Religion, Ideas,
   Leiden.
Brown, P. 1981. *The Cult of the Saints: Its Rise and Function in Latin
   Christianity*, Chicago and London.
Classen, C. 2012. *The Deepest Sense: A History of Touch*, Urbana, Chicago
   and Springfield.
Dale, E. 1969. *Audio-Visual Methods in Teaching*, London.
Davies, P., Howard, D. and Pullan, W. (eds), 2013. *Architecture and
   Pilgrimage, 1000–1500*, Farnham and Burlington, VT.
Dyas, D. 2001. *Pilgrimage in Medieval English Literature 700–1500*,
   Cambridge.
Dyas, D. 2004. 'Medieval patterns of pilgrimage: a mirror for today?',
   in *Explorations in a Christian Theology of Pilgrimage*, ed. C.
   Bartholomew and F. Hughes, Aldershot, 92–109.
Elsner, J. and Rutherford, I. (eds), 2005. *Pilgrimage in Graeco-Roman and
   Early Christian Antiquity: Seeing the Gods*, Oxford.
Fabri, F. 1896. *The Book of the Wanderings of Brother Felix Fabri*. London:
   Palestine Pilgrims' Text Society.
Ferguson, E. 1987. *The Backgrounds of Christianity*, Grand Rapids, MI.
Frank, G. 2000. *The Memory of the Eyes: Pilgrims to Living Saints in
   Christian Late Antiquity*, Berkeley and London.
Hatwell, Y., Streri, A. and Gentaz, E. (eds), 2003. *Touching for Knowing:
   Cognitive Psychology of Haptic Manual Perception*, Amsterdam.
Kessler, H.L. 2013. 'Afterword: pilgrimage and transformation', in
   Davies *et al.* 2013, 231–42.
Kurath, H. and Kuhn, S. (eds) 1952–. *Middle English Dictionary*,
   Michigan.
Lane Fox, R. 1986. *Pagans and Christians*, Harmondsworth.
MacCormack, S. 1990. 'Loca sancta: the organisation of sacred
   topography in Late Antiquity', in *The Blessings of Pilgrimage*, ed. R.
   Ousterhout, Urbana.
Markus, R.A. 1990. *The End of Ancient Christianity*, Cambridge and New
   York.
Markus, R.A. 1994. 'How on earth could places become holy? Origins
   of the Christian idea of holy places', *Journal of Early Christian Studies*
   2 (3): 257–71.
Pentcheva, B.V. 2010. *The Sensual Icon: Space, Ritual and the Senses in
   Byzantium*. University Park, PA.
Spencer, B. 1998. *Pilgrim Souvenirs and Secular Badges*, Museum of
   London Medieval Finds from Excavations in London 7, London.
Walker, P. 1990. *Holy City, Holy Places? Christian Attitudes to Jerusalem and
   the Holy Land in the Fourth Century*, Oxford.
Wilken, R.L. 1992. *The Land Called Holy: Palestine in Christian History and
   Thought*, New Haven and London.
Wilkinson, J. (ed.) 1977. *Jerusalem Pilgrims before the Crusades*, Jerusalem.

Chapter 2
Vestiary Signs of Pilgrimage in Twelfth-century Europe

Janet E. Snyder

The First Crusade (1095–9), the campaign that combined practices of pilgrimage and holy war fought on behalf of the Christian religion, was initiated in 1095 as a response to the advance of the Seljuk Turks into Syria-Palestine. As Carl Erdman pointed out, without a clearly formulated definition of crusade, '. . . contemporaries used such words as *iter, expeditio,* or *peregrination. . .*'[1] The objective of this expedition of militant pilgrims was not only to worship at the Holy Sepulchre, but also to liberate Jerusalem by force from Muslim rule. Some warrior pilgrims never intended to return from this undertaking, while others meant to come home, having authorized delegates to maintain the status quo at home during their absence. By the end of the 11th century the Frankish population in the Christian states in Syria-Palestine had been recruited chiefly from pilgrims, but the number of Westerners who stayed in the Holy Land was never more than a fraction of the total, with the majority returning to the West.[2] It has been calculated that in 1180 the Frankish population of the Kingdom of Jerusalem was some 140,000 people[3] and there was about the same number in the northern states of Tripoli and Antioch.

Rather than considering those pilgrims who sold their earthly goods and gave away the proceeds before departing on a one-way journey, in this chapter I will look at those 12th-century pilgrims who came back from their expeditions to Palestine, examine evidence of textiles that they carried home and consider how appropriated textiles and elements of clothing were transformed by Europeans, thus altering their original significance. Vestiary elements conveyed meaning only if their significance was discernible. I propose that the imported textiles endowed their European owners with associations of prestige and signified power in the East.

Exotic and luxury materials like the silk shrouds of St Potentien and St Siviard (12th–13th century, Treasury of the Cathedral of Sens, Inv. B7 and B8), brought home by returning pilgrims, were transformed in their new contexts.[4] One way for returning pilgrims to advertise their close associations with the homeland of the Christian Messiah was by putting on textiles appropriated from eastern lands: Byzantine silk, Egyptian linen and especially *ṭirāz*.[5] Although in the 9th century Charles the Bald had favoured Byzantine ceremonial costume,[6] before 1100 textiles made of silk were exceptional treasures in northern Europe. The Council of Aachen of 836 encouraged European sovereigns who had received Byzantine imperial textile gifts to donate these silks to the churches.[7] Most famously the silk *sancta camisia* (believed to have been part of a garment worn by the Virgin Mary at the time of Christ's birth) that Charlemagne received from the Byzantine Empress Irene was given to Chartres Cathedral by his grandson Charles the Bald in 876.[8] Some 300 years later another Marian textile relic was one of the treasures brought home from the Holy Land by Maurice, Lord of Craon, when he returned in 1169 with '. . .a piece of our Lady's dress'.[9]

At the beginning of the 12th century the climate in northern France was unsuitable to sustain the mulberry trees required to feed silkworms, with the result that silk yardage could not be produced there. Utterly unlike native fabrics in substance, appearance and pattern, silk textiles were universally recognized and the names of their places of

Plate 1 Chartres Cathedral, west facade, left portal, left jamb, three column-figures, c. 1145–50, limestone with traces of pigment. Note neckline on the right column-figure (photo: Janet Snyder)

Plate 2 Chartres Cathedral, west facade, right portal, right jamb, centre column-figure, c. 1145–50, limestone with traces of pigment. This sculpture replicates the original column figure that is reserved in the cathedral crypt, including the armband and the open cuff (photo: Janet Snyder)

production were known in courtly and literary communities. In *Le Roman de Thèbes* the description of a royal garment made of *cendal d'Andre* suggests popular familiarity with specific fabrics.[10] Thebes, Andros and workshops in Central Asia produced specific types of silk or compound cloth.[11] References to and descriptions of particular textiles embedded in the *lais* and romances of Marie de France and Chrètien de Troyes demonstrate that the literate European elite recognized that luxury textiles like silk and compound furs like vair came from eastern lands, in regions associated with the Holy Land.[12]

It seems that by the 1130s European clothing makers working for the courtly elite selected and adapted textiles and elements of clothing rather than borrowing entire foreign costumes as souvenir outfits, evidently in ways that mirror medieval architectural practices of copying. New details such as the jewelled neckline cleft at the throat that can be seen on a bliaut in Chartres Cathedral, the *ṭirāz* armband and the open Islamic lower sleeve appeared for the first time in the West, adapted from Near Eastern or Mediterranean styles of clothing (**Pls 1–2**).[13] Appropriated details were represented in two and three-dimensional images, such as the over life-size high relief stone images of men and women in portal programmes of great churches.[14] Beginning in the 1140s, church facade sculpture schemes in northern Europe had been transformed with a new design

formula that featured ranks of personages dressed as courtiers standing along the doorjambs as if in reception lines.[15] The appearance of the textiles and clothing represented in this sculpture corresponds to similar depictions in manuscript illustrations, metalwork, seal images, paintings, embroideries and other decorative arts. It is these vestiary details that signal an association of the wearers with the Holy Land.

Textile weaving and embroidery workshops, known as *Dar al-ṭirāz* or *Dar al-Kiswa*, were maintained as a standard part of the Islamic communities from Afghanistan to Spain

Plate 3 Fragment of decorated linen, known as *ṭirāz*, Egypt, 11th century, length: 46cm, width 24.3cm. British Museum, London (ME OA 1901.3-4.55)

Plate 4 Abu Zayd, fritware bowl, painted with an enthroned ruler and his attendants, Mina'i ware, Kashan, Iran, 1187, diameter: 21.1cm. British Museum, London (ME OA 1945.10-17.261)

Plate 5 Bourges Cathedral, south lateral portal, left jamb, centre column figure, c. 1155, limestone with traces of pigment (photo: Janet Snyder)

from the 7th century until about the 13th century.[16] The term *ṭirāz* can refer to the workshop or to the textiles and embroideries produced by the workshop (**Pl. 3**). Typically a *ṭirāz* was a loom-woven cloth, with a line of embroidered or tapestry woven calligraphy inserted into the weaving, '… beginning with *bismillah* ['In the name of Allah'] then giving the ruler's name and titles, a salutary phrase, the place of manufacture and the date'.[17] Sometimes the inscription alone was used, but it could be combined with one or more narrow bands of abstract forms or stylized animal or bird motifs contained in cartouches. Near life-size stucco sculptures attributed to the Seljuk period in Iran or Afghanistan (1038–1194) illustrate courtly personages depicted in highly patterned clothing with bands of text applied to sleeves.[18] These inscribed bands carried the caliph's name, which was sacred and bestowed blessing upon those whom it touched.[19] Sacrality that was transferable through textiles was related by the 12th-century traveller Benjamin of Tudela in his *Itinerary*, when he reported how eagerly pilgrims kissed the corner of the caliph's garment that had been put out of the window to bestow a blessing.[20] Upper-arm bands decorated either with texts written in kufic lettering or with floral or schematic stripes typically appear depicted on figures painted on contemporary pottery (**Pl. 4**).[21] These textiles that incorporated sections of tapestry or embroidery into fields of loom-woven cloth appear to have been startling innovations for European visitors to the eastern Mediterranean. Their appropriation by Europeans reflects the impact of the Islamic world on travellers from the West.

Although some whole garments have been preserved as relics, such as the vestments of Thomas Becket in the Treasury of Sens Cathedral,[22] most extant fabric from the 12th century survives as textile fragments that once enveloped relics within reliquary containers in Western churches. Relics safeguarded in the reliquary head of St

Eustace from Basle Cathedral had been wrapped in a great variety of silk textiles.[23] Large *ṭirāz* such as the Veil of St Anne in Apt,[24] the Veil of Hisham (796–1013, Real Academia de la Historia, Madrid, Inv. 749)[25] and larger silk fragments such as the shrouds of St Potentien and St Siviard described above[26] were made sacred through their association with holy relics. Fabrics that enclosed relics had begun their travels from the East at the same time as the reliquary objects they enclosed, or they had been put into place in the reliquaries when they arrived in western Europe. Alternatively, they may have been added to the reliquary slightly later, during the course of inventions and translations. The result of this close association was that the precious textiles themselves were transformed to be valued as relics.[27]

In addition to reserving inscribed *ṭirāz* for personal use by the caliph, inscribed *ṭirāz* were also distributed to his close associates, high functionaries, ambassadors, foreign princes and to all persons whom he chose to honour or to thank.[28] There was more than a magical or wonderworking capacity involved; a strengthening and blessing effect was provided by these textile bands that had come in contact with the name of the lord. Upon their arrival from eastern Mediterranean lands, material goods such as these *ṭirāz* were appropriated by Europeans because the association of the textiles with the Holy Land endowed their owners with prestige. It seems likely that a belief in thaumaturgy provided motivation for Europeans to wear such bands on their right arms, as at Bourges (**Pl. 5**). The sculpted pattern decorating the band on the right arm of the central figure on the right jamb of the right portal at Chartres Cathedral forms a cross with equal arms, a sign of the Christian lord (**Pl. 2**).

According to L.T. Belgrano, Genoese participants in the First Crusade were described as 'The Genoese, wearing the cross on their right shoulders…'[29] and the *Gesta Francorum* reports that after Bohémond I, Prince of Taranto and later

Plate 6 Notre-Dame du Fort, Étampes, column figure, c. 1145, limestone with traces of pigment (photo: Janet Snyder)

Plate 7 Bronze ['Hansa'] bowl engraved with mythological scenes, probably German, 12th century. In the centre is Cadmus, 'CADAMUS GRECORUM SRUTATUR GRAMATA PRIMUM'; medallions depict the birth and Labours of Hercules. British Museum, London (1921, 0325,1)

of Antioch (c. 1058–3 March 1111), heard about the badges used to identify Frankish warrior pilgrims, he cut up a valuable cloak, perhaps Byzantine silk or a Sicilian *ṭirāz*, to mark his followers with armbands and crosses.[30] Bohémond's action – marking his partisans with personal textiles – follows the Islamic tradition (*khil'a*) by taking off a textile that had been worn by the leader to be given to his retainers, in the same way as the Prophet had given his mantle to the poet Ka'b ibn Zuhayr.[31] Once Prince of Antioch, Bohémond was imprisoned until ransomed in 1103. At the beginning of 1106 he went to France for a sensational visit, travelling from place to place, depositing pallia of silk on the altars and speaking vigorously in churches about his experiences as a warrior pilgrim, fulfilling a vow he had made while incarcerated.[32] According to Orderic Vitalis (1075–c. 1142),

during Bohémond's travels in Europe, throughout Lent, '. . . he reverently laid relics and silken palls and other desirable objects on the holy altars, delighted in the warm welcome given him'.[33] Just after Easter 1106, Bohémond married Constance (1078–January 1124/1126), daughter of Philippe I of France.[34] The wedding was celebrated in Chartres, hosted by Adèla of Blois, Countess of Blois-Champagne.[35] Certainly some of the 'silken palls' and luxury textiles Bohémond had brought from the East must have figured prominently in the wedding of this Christian Levantine prince and a princess of the Frankish court.

The clothing depicted in eastern figural sculpture and ceramics are depicted as having inscribed *ṭirāz* on both sleeves of open tunics. In European images decorative upper-arm bands can be seen only on the right arm, perhaps

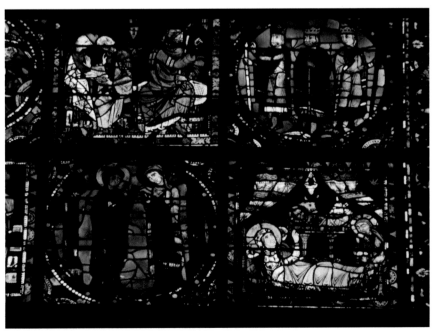

Plate 8 Detail of painted stained glass window depicting the childhood of Christ, lower section, interior of the west front, centre bay, Chartres Cathedral, c. 1150. Herod (with armband) is in the upper left square scene; Three Magi, upper right; the Visitation, lower left; the Nativity, lower right (photo: Janet Snyder)

Bibliography

Bagnoli, M., Klein, H.A., Mann, C.G. and Robinson, J. (eds) 2010. *Treasures of Heaven: Saints, Relics and Devotion in Medieval Europe*, Baltimore and London.

Baker, P.L. 1995. *Islamic Textiles*, London.

Belgrano, L.T. (ed.) 1890. *Annali genovesi di Caffaro e de' suoi continuatori dal MXCIX al MCCXCIII* (Rome: Fonti per la Storia d'Italia, no.1), in *Medieval Trade in the Mediterranean World*, trans. and ed. R.S. Lopez and I.W. Raymond, New York, 1995, 12–13.

Benjamin of Tudela 1173. *The Travels of Benjamin of Tudela* (http://www.sacred-texts.com/jud/mhl/mhl20.htm).

Benjamin, S. 1995. 'Letter from Baghdad,' in *The World of Benjamin of Tudela: A Medieval Mediterranean Travelogue*, Madison, NJ.

Bertrand de Brousillon 1893. *Etude historique accompagne du cartulaire de Craon* (vol. I, 100–5, nos 137–46), cited in Hamilton 1994.

Boehm, B.D. 2010. '"A brilliant resurrection": enamel shrines for relics', in Bagnoli *et al.* 2010, 149–61.

Crowfoot, E., Pritchard, F. and Staniland, K. 1992. *Textiles and Clothing, c.1150–c.1450*, London.

Delluc B. and Delluc, G. 2001. 'Le suaire de Cadouin et son frère: Le voile de sainte Anne d'Apt (Vaucluse). Deux pièces exceptionnelles d'archéologie textile', *Bulletin de la Société historique et archéologique du Périgord* 128/4, 607–26.

Durand, J. (ed.) 1992. *Byzance: l'art byzantin dans les collections publiques françaises*, Paris.

Elsberg, H.A. and Guest, R. 1934. 'Another silk fabric woven at Baghdad', *Burlington Magazine for Connoisseurs* 64/375 (June), 271–2.

Erdmann, C., 1977. *The Origin of the Idea of Crusade*, trans. Marshall W. Baldwin and Walter Goffart, Princeton (http://hdl.handle.net/2027/heb.01189).

Ettinghausen, R., Grabar, O. and Jenkins-Madina, M. 2001. *Islamic Art and Architecture 650–1250*, New Haven and London.

Fassler, M., 2010. *The Virgin of Chartres, Making History through Liturgy and the Arts*, New Haven and London.

Flury-Lemberg, M. 1987. *Au sujet de quatre vêtements sacerdotaux au Moyen-Age et de leur conservation*, Bern.

Geary, P. 1984. *Living with the Dead in the Middle Ages*, Ithaca, NY.

Gesta Francorum et aliorum Hierosolimitanorum (The Deeds of the Franks and the other Pilgrims to Jerusalem) 1962. Ed. R. Hill, London.

Goddard, E.R. 1927. *Women's Costume in French Texts of the Eleventh and Twelfth Centuries*, Baltimore and Paris.

Guibert of Nogent 1844–95. *Gesta Dei*, 7.37, in Académie des inscriptions & belles-lettres, 1844–95, *Recueil des historiens des croisades, historiens occidentaux*, 4, Paris.

Hamilton, B. 1994. 'The impact of Crusader Jerusalem on Western Christendom', *The Catholic Historical Review* 80/4 (Oct), 695–713 (http://www.jstor.org/stable/25024396).

Huyghe, R. 1958. *Larousse Encyclopedia of Byzantine and Medieval Art*, New York.

Institut du Monde Arabe 1992. *Terres secrètes de Samarcande, Ceramiques du VIII au XIII siècle*, Paris.

Le Roman de Thèbes 1968. Ed. G. Raynaud de Lage, 2 vols, Paris.

Lombard, M. 1978, *Études d'économie médiévale, III, Les textiles dans le monde musulman du VIIe au XIIe siècle*, Civilisations et Sociétés 61, Paris.

Lopez, R.S. and Raymond, I.W. 1955. *Medieval Trade in the Mediterranean World*, New York.

Luchaire, A. 1964. *Louis VI le Gros, Annales de sa vie et de son Règne (1081–1137)*, Brussels.

Martiniani-Reber, M. 1992. 'Les textiles IXe–XIIe siècle', in Durand 1992, 370–80.

Meyer, L. 2000. 'Textiles of Islamic Spain', *Complex Weavers' Medieval Textile Study Group Newsletter* 24 (June), 6.

Nelson, J. 1992. *Charles the Bald*, London, cited in L. Brubaker, 'The elephant and the ark: cultural and material interchange across the Mediterranean in the eighth and ninth centuries', *Dumbarton Oaks Papers* 58 (2004).

Orderic Vitalis 1978. *The Ecclesiastical History of Orderic Vitalis*, ed. and trans. M. Chibnall, 6 vols, Oxford.

Papadopoulo, A. 1979. *Islam and Muslim Art*, New York.

Pastoureau, M. 1976. *La vie quotidienne en France et en Angleterre au temps des chevaliers de la table ronde (XII–XII siècles)*, Paris.

Prawer, J. 1980. *Crusader Institutions*, Oxford.

Quicherat, J. 1875–7. *Histoire du Costume en France Depuis les Temps les plus reculés jusqu'a la fin du XVIIIe siècle*, Paris.

Riefstahl, R.M. 1931. 'Persian Islamic stucco sculpture', *The Art Bulletin* 13/1, 439–63.

Roberts, A. and Roberts, C. (eds) 1987. *Syria and Iran: Three Studies in Medieval Ceramics*, Oxford.

Sabbe, E. 1935. 'L'importation des tissus orientaux en Europe occidentale du haut Moyen Age IX–X siècles', in *Revue belge de philologie et d'histoire* (juillet-déc.), 1261–88.

Sanders, P. 2001. 'Robes of honor in Fatimid Egypt', in *Robes and Honor: The Medieval World of Investiture*, ed. S. Gordon, New York, 225–39.

Snyder, J.E. 2011. *Early Gothic Column-figure Sculpture in France: Appearance, Materials, and Significance*, Farnham.

Sokoly, J.A. 1997. 'Between life and death: the funerary context of tiraz textiles', *Islamische Textilkunst des Mittelalters: Aktuelle Probleme* Riggisberg 72.

Starensier, A. 1982. 'An art historical study of the Byzantine silk industry', PhD dissertation, Columbia University, New York.

Suger 1929. *Vita Ludovici Grossi regis*, in *Vie de Louis VI le Gros*, ed. and trans. H. Waquet, Paris.

Suger 1992. [*Vie de Louis VI, Le Gros*] *The Deeds of Louis the Fat*, trans. R. Cusimano and J. Moorhead, Washington, DC.

Suger 1994. *La Geste de Louis VI et autres œuvres*, ed. M. Bur, Paris.

Taburet-Delahaye, E. and Boehm, B.D. 1995. *Enamels of Limoges 1100–1350*, New York.

Taylor, P. 2000. 'Moral agency in crusade and colonization: Anselm of Havelberg and the Wendish Crusade of 1147', *The International History Review* 22/4 (Dec.), 757–84 (http://www.jstor.org/stable/40108524).

Thomas, T.K. 1990. *Textiles from Medieval Egypt AD 300–1300*, Pittsburgh, PA.

http://www.umich.edu/~kelseydb/Exhibits/Big_Textile/Tiraz_Other_Textiles.html accessed 28 September 2011

Watt, J.C.Y. and Wardwell, A.E. 1997. *When Silk Was Gold, Central Asian and Chinese Textiles*, New York.

Yoshida, M. 1972. *In Search of Persian Pottery*, New York.

Chapter 3
St George and Venice
The Rise of Imperial Culture

David M. Perry

Between 1283 and 1325, Venetian artisans constructed a new reliquary for their important relic of the arm of St George. The relic, probably sent from Constantinople in 1204 or 1205 in the aftermath of the Fourth Crusade, had resided in a simple silver sheath, but the new reliquary would be much more complicated. The artisans decorated the reliquary with enamel images of the apostles and evangelists, a silver-gilt Tree of Jesse and topped it with a mounted figure of St George (**Pl. 1**).[1] The iconography is unusual; these are not George's typical companions. The reliquary was not, of course, the first object or image related to the saint in Venice. In fact, at various moments from the 11th to the 13th centuries, medieval Venetians installed various, if scattered, images relating to the cult of St George on the outside and inside of the church of San Marco. Each image has been studied thoroughly, albeit rarely, but scholars have yet to define an overall programme of usage for St George in medieval Venetian hagiographic display and narrative. In this essay, I link the cult of St George and the display of his imagery to Venetian traditions of cultural appropriation found in two locations – 12th-century commemorative *translatio* narratives and a 13th-century iconographic display on the walls of San Marco – as a way of suggesting the

Plate 1 Reliquary arm of St George, interior Byzantine (before 1204), exterior Venetian (before 1325 and 16th century), silver gilt, enamels and glass, height of interior 31cm, height of exterior 51.9cm. Procuratoria della Basilica di San Marco, Venice (Santuario 159) (courtesy of La Procuratoria della Basilica di San Marco)

Plate 2 Marble relief of St Demetrios, installed between 1230–67, 166 x 99cm. Basilica of San Marco, Venice (photo © Cameraphoto Arte, Venice/Art Resource, NY)

Plate 3 Marble relief of St George, installed between 1230–67, 165.5 x 94cm. Basilica of San Marco, Venice (photo © Cameraphoto Arte, Venice/Art Resource, NY)

existence of such a scheme. I argue that the reliquary emerged as the culmination of a long, if scattered, programme of the use of St George as an intermediary saint who partnered foreign saints and objects and enabled the transformation of the foreign into the local.

Apotropaic relief icons

On the western facade of San Marco, a set of six relief icons ward the great doors. Two icons, 'St Demetrios' (**Pl. 2**) and 'Herakles and the Boar' (**Pl. 4**), are Byzantine spolia, plundered during the Fourth Crusade. Each Byzantine icon is matched by a Venetian icon inspired by the spolia. Otto Demus identified the Venetian icons as belonging to the workshop of a single innovative artist, dubbed the 'Heraclian Master', in which he located a new Venetian style that fused Byzantine and Adriatic norms.[2] The Byzantine icon of St Demetrios as *strategos*, or general, is re-imagined as St George (**Pl. 3**) sitting in a similar pose, while Herakles and the boar is re-fashioned as Herakles crushing the hydra (**Pl. 5**). Each of the icons would have projected multiple possible meanings to a medieval Venetian audience, most of them filtered through a general association with the cult of St George.

St Demetrios' presence on the walls, as the most widely venerated warrior-saint of the Greek empire, spoke of the ideas of *translatio imperii*, the concept that the imperial power of Rome had been transferred to the West. This notion had just begun to emerge within 13th-century Venetian culture as a result of the Fourth Crusade. He represented eastern Mediterranean Christian militarism which had now been appropriated by Venice. In the Venetian icon, Demetrios has been translated into St George, by this time a dominant

symbol of Latin Christian militarism and the Crusades.[3] With the two warrior saints, the impact of the addition of St George is clear. The Herakles set, on the other hand, requires closer analysis.

Demus argues that because one can read the hydra as the dragon, the Venetian Herakles not only invokes the many potential meanings of the classical hero, but also St George as a dragon killer.[4] This is a contested reading as images of St George and the dragon are rare in the West before the 1250s.[5] For Venice, however, with its links to Byzantine culture, the interpretation is credible. St George and the dragon can be found in Byzantine art as early as the 7th century.[6] In fact, some of these early scenes pair St George with St Theodore, Venice's first patron, adding to the polyvalent possibilities of the Herakles and hydra relief for Venetian viewers. With only one head, this hydra is iconographically rare, if not unprecedented, which makes it seem more draconian in appearance. If one accepts Demus' reading, the four Venetian icons present two representations of George: as a general and as a dragon-killer. The Herakles set is ever richer. Herakles can be seen as a Christ-precursor, but he can also represent Samson because of his strength, or even embody the classical concept of *virtus*. His name refers to Eraclea, the first site of political power in the lagoon, while his lion skin invokes St Mark.[7] Thus, within these four icons are all the themes of 13th-century Venetian cultural development – Christian militarism from East and West in Demetrios and George, a celebration of local origins and the protection of St Mark and the appropriation of the glory of three different Roman Empires – classical pagan, Constantine's Christian empire and the recently fallen Byzantium. It is therefore curious

Plate 4 Marble relief of Herakles and the Erymanthian Boar, installed between 1230–67, 59 x 88cm. Basilica of San Marco, Venice (photo © Cameraphoto Arte, Venice/Art Resource, NY)

Plate 5 Marble relief of Herakles and the Lernaean Hydra, installed between 1230–67, 174.2 x 93.5cm. Basilica of San Marco, Venice (photo © Cameraphoto Arte, Venice/Art Resource, NY)

that St George, a figure not particularly associated with Venice, stands at the centre of this transposition of the Byzantine into the Venetian.

Portale di San Alipio

By the mid-to-late 13th century, the relief plaques flanked a mosaic cycle of the *translatio* of the relics of St Mark from Alexandria to Venice. The design of the cycle and the construction of the Venetian relief icons were probably roughly contemporary, but the mosaics took some decades to install fully.[8] Only the final scene, located over the northernmost door, the Portale di San Alipio (**Pl. 6**), survives. The mosaic shows 13th-century Venetians outside their 13th-century church depicted as the 9th-century figures who actually received the relics before the modest ducal chapel of the time. Working in two time frames, this mosaic links the contemporary regime to the founding myth of the local state religion.[9] Below the mosaic, reliefs of the two Old Testament prophets have been placed at the north and south corners of an arch. These prophets watch over the reliefs of the four evangelists, depicted as a winged ox, lion, eagle and man. These reliefs were most likely placed there after the mosaics above were designed. The prophets and the evangelist Matthew were almost certainly made by the Heraclian Master's workshop, based on similarities between pieces.[10] The other three evangelists are Byzantine spolia probably brought to Venice after 1204, although their exact provenance is unclear.[11]

A square icon of St George occupies a spot just below the apex of the arch. The saint is mounted, his cloak billowing, and has the Greek inscription, 'Ο ΑΓΙΟΣ ΓΕΩΡΓΙΟΣ'.[12] This seems to be the earliest extant image of George on horseback in Venice. It is comparable to Byzantine mounted icons of military saints, mounted crusader icons of St George and copies of said icons in the West.[13] Based on the presence of the Greek caption, it is most likely to have come from Constantinople after 1204. George's position in relation to the evangelists seems to be unprecedented in medieval art.[14] Here, the mounted saint provides the transition from reliefs to mosaic, from the broader message of the Old and New testaments, prophets and evangelists, to the specific validating image of St Mark's blessing over Venice. Through the relatively innocuous, but central figure of St George – perhaps representing militant Christendom – the foreign is welcomed into Venice and the miracles of both the biblical and local past appropriated in support of a bright future.

Relief plaque and arm reliquary

In the 1260s, Venice marked the occasion of war with Genoa, a city famously dependent on the spiritual patronage of St George, by disseminating the news both to internal and external audiences that the relic of St George's arm was serving as a symbol of the unity between the secular and spiritual centres of Venice. The arm reliquary arrived in Venice after 1204 as one of a number of relics later linked to Doge Enrico Dandolo.[15] In 1265, at a moment of some peril

Plate 6 Portale di San Alipio, Basilica of San Marco, Venice (photo used by permission from Roman Bonnefoy)

for Venice after the Genoese allied with the Paleologi dynasty and together reconquered Constantinople, the arm relic was used as part of a propaganda campaign that included a diplomatic mission to Rome for recognition of a miracle involving related reliquaries, a preaching tour by friars and the commissioning of a relief plaque (**Pl. 7**).

The story begins on 13 January 1231, when a fire ripped through the Treasury of San Marco. In 1265, Doge Ranieri Zeno sent a letter to the papacy claiming that three relics, a piece of the True Cross, an ampulla containing the blood of Christ and the skull of John the Baptist had miraculously survived a fire in the Treasury of San Marco in 1231. He sought papal authentication of the miracle and commissioned a preaching tour by friars to follow the anticipated approval (in fact the Pope denied their petition). Around the same time, Zeno seems to have commissioned the relief plaque (**Pl. 7**).[16] The plaque displays the three surviving reliquaries, another Byzantine reliquary cross and finally the arm of St George in its pre-embellished state.[17] The two holy crosses, each signifying imperial Byzantine power, flank relics that symbolize saintly state patronage. One was Henry of Flanders' coronation cross, once allegedly

carried by Constantine himself; the other belonged to Empress Irene Doukas (c. 1066–1138), wife of Alexius Comnenus and ruler in her own right. The colour of the Holy Blood reflects the red robe of the Doge, thus serving as a symbol of the sacral aspects of the Venetian government. The other two relics point towards Venice's rivalry with Genoa. It is unlikely to be a coincidence that the plaque displays two relics of John the Baptist and St George, two patron saints of Venice's Italian foe.

As with the programme of relief icons outside the church, the multiple meanings of the images overlap and reinforce each other, speaking of major transformations of the Venetian state identity in the middle of the 13th century.[18] All five relics were acquired in the war of 1204 that cast down one empire. With the Latin Empire also fallen, as of 1261, Venice temporarily recognized no other legitimate heir to Constantine, a fact that bolstered Venetian imperial claims. Not coincidentally, this plaque was installed in the Andito Foscari, a passage that joined the ducal palace to San Marco, linking the sacred to the secular with its message of divinely backed *translatio imperii*.

Others

A few other images of St George can be found in the pre-1300 decoration of San Marco. On the Pala d'Oro, St George peers from various corners at the central panel of Christ in majesty. A martial relief of St George, of contested provenance, now hangs on the northern facade. It does bear similarities to other outputs from the Heraclian Master's workshop (Demus' argument), but could also be spolia that provided a model for local output.[19] The date of its installation on the facade is unclear. It may have been concurrent with the western reliefs (1230s–40s), which would wrap the apotropaic function of relief icons around the north-west corner of the facade from Herakles to this St George as a soldier. If this argument is correct, then the new facades of San Marco would display George as soldier, general, equestrian and perhaps dragon killer. F. Kieslinger, however, conjectured that the George relief, along with other northern facade reliefs of an armoured angel (perhaps St Michael), Christ and the four evangelists, were all part of

Plate 7 Marble relief of relics from the Treasury of San Marco, Venice, corridor to Palazzo Ducale, 1260s. Basilica of San Marco, Venice (photo: David M. Perry)

the 13th-century iconostasis inside the church that lasted until the late 14th century.[20] After the new screen was built, Venetians scattered the various reliefs across the northern facade. If Kieslinger is correct, then St George appeared in a key position among the evangelists, Christ and an angel, in a mode comparable to the Portale di San Alipio. Either way, the lonely relief on the northern facade potentially serves similar iconographic functions as the other images of St George discussed above.

Among the internal mosaics from earlier centuries, in three places one finds George portrayed as a martyr and partnered with a similarly portrayed St Theodore. Venetian mosaicists generally avoided military imagery in 12th-century iconography, instead re-casting military saints as 'mere' martyrs. Rather than elevate a partnering image, in the mosaics, George diminishes Theodore by demoting him from exalted patron – a patron dictated by Constantinople – to merely a member of an honoured group.[21]

Taken in isolation, these scattered images are about what one might expect to find of a major saint in a medieval city. But taken as a group, the malleable power of the icons to alter the significance of partnering symbols in whatever ways seemed useful to Venetian mythographers starts to emerge as a pattern. But why St George? This essay now turns away from visual representations and offers a new interpretation of the nature of the role played by St George in the transformation of medieval Venetian culture.

The monastery

There was another kind of three-dimensional invocation of St George in medieval Venice: the monastery of San Giorgio Maggiore. The origins of this institution probably date to not long before 829, just before the body of St Mark was brought to Venice, when the ducal Participazi family endowed a small church dedicated to St George on the island just across the water from the ducal palace (**Pl. 8**). They named it *maggiore* to distinguish it from a pre-existing church, San Giorgio in Alga. In 982, Doge Tribuno Memmo founded and generously endowed a Benedictine monastery on the island.[22] Thanks to generous donations from the elites of Venice, it gradually grew into a wealthy and powerful monastic institution with elite brethren and property abroad. From the perspective of a viewer of the western facade of San Marco, the monastery is just to the south, and the 13th-century viewer did not have to look past the pillars, the gothic facade of the Palazzo Ducale or the Palladian church in order to see it. This monastery gave the cult of St George a ritual and institutional presence in medieval Venice before 1100, even though the Doge invested his cultural capital chiefly on the martial symbol of Mark's lion, not George.[23]

In the year 1100, both Venetian civic religion and the role of San Giorgio Maggiore witnessed a sudden turn in fortune. In that year, the bishop of Castello and the son of the Doge claimed a great prize while on crusade – the body of St Nicholas of Myra, patron saint of sailors.[24] The body was given to the monks of San Giorgio Maggiore, who had recently built a church dedicated to St Nicholas on the Lido. The monks recorded the arrival of St Nicholas in a *translatio* narrative that presents an interpretation of the significance

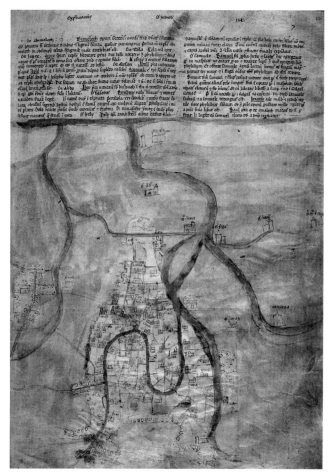

Plate 8 Earliest plan of Venice by Paolino da Venezia from the *Cronologia Magna*, 1346, indicating relative position of San Giorgio Maggiore and San Marco. Biblioteca Marciana, Venice (photo © Cameraphoto Arte, Venice/Art Resource, NY)

of the translation for Venice. At a key moment in the narrative, as the would-be relic thieves find themselves stymied in their initial attempt to locate the relic, the bishop of Castello addresses the saint directly in a prayer:

> Oh most holy Prelate Nicholas! Listen to our prayer. Deign to visit your city of Venice and the Occident. It is enough for the Orient and Greece, because they had you as their bishop and teacher, and because they have restrained you almost 700 years have passed. The Latins and Occidentals would rejoice to finally see your body in the present moment.[25]

The bishop places the moment in trans-regional terms and constructs Venice as the door to the Occident. The narrative thus presents the translation as a dramatic shift of prestige and saintly patronage not just from Greece to Venice, but from the East to the West, all filtered through the monastery of St George. Later in the *translatio*, the Venetian ships sail into port and are greeted by the leaders and populace of Venice. The narrative suggests that the Doge was tempted to claim the relic for himself and re-brand the Venetian state church as Santi Marco e Nicola. However, the entreaties and pious tears of the Abbot of San Giorgio and his whole congregation saved the Doge from his own folly.

In inviting St Nicholas into the ducal church, the doge threatened Venice's relationship with St Mark. Safely on the Lido, Nicholas' role as patron became clearly delineated. He operated as the maritime protector, while Mark's lion, the venerable Venetian military symbol, was its protector on land.[26] Gradually, the church of San Giorgio Maggiore and St Nicholas entered the ritual life of the city. Within a few years, the church became the location for an annual benediction in thanks for the blessings of the sea, a ritual that later evolved into the famed *sensa*, or ducal marriage to the sea. Venetians also celebrated St Nicholas' feast day, 6 December, as they certainly had done before they acquired the relics. However, like the benediction, this ritual came to take on greater and localized meanings over time. After the Fourth Crusade, Doge Pietro Ziani built a chapel dedicated to St Nicholas within the ducal palace in memory of his fallen predecessor, Enrico Dandolo. As the only chapel within the palace it became the key site of ritual veneration on the feast day for elites, and thus encompassed the annual celebration of the Mediterranean saint within the political culture of the region. Rather than celebrating St Nicholas and his maritime blessings generally, both rituals tied the presence of St Nicholas' body on the Lido to specific acts of political legitimacy (the *sensa*) and imperial expansion (the Fourth Crusade).[27] Both the actual movement of the alleged relics of St Nicholas to Venice and the more important civic memorialization of the *translatio*, relied upon San Giorgio to bring St Nicholas into Venetian culture and to negotiate Venice's relationship with its two patron saints.

This process reoccurs with other imported relics. Although a full study of each translation and hagiographical tradition would be beyond the scope of this essay, a few examples help illustrate the broader pattern.[28]

In 1107, a monk of San Giorgio first stole the body of St Stephen, famed for being the first of the apostles martyred, from Constantinople, then brought it to Venice with an escort of 72 leading Venetian citizens. After a miracle at sea, these citizens founded a confraternity in Stephen's honour, cementing the first martyr's position as a patron for the merchant class. They installed his relics in the monastery of San Giorgio. Stephen's position there enabled the gradual incorporation of the saint into the ritual life of the city's elites. Two centuries later, with Stephen no longer a newcomer to the Venetian pantheon, the Chiesa di Santo Stefano was built in Venice.[29]

The relics of St Lucy were donated to San Giorgio Maggiore after the Fourth Crusade by Doge Enrico Dandolo, where they remained until 1271. Her story has quite a few twists and turns, including a storm that drowned worshippers on their way across the water to the monastery on her feast day. She does not have an extant *translatio* tradition, but her case plays a transitional role between the relics of the 12th and 13th centuries.[30] For St Lucy, as with St Stephen, a new relic is installed in the monastery, becomes an object of local veneration and is eventually moved to an independent locale.

In 1222, the relics of St Paul the 'New' Martyr, who was martyred for defending icons during the period of iconoclasm, were translated from Constantinople to Venice in a relatively low-stakes action. The relic was not particularly important and his cult was not especially prominent. There was no risk involved in the translation itself and no post-translation liturgical or artistic innovation. In the crypt of San Giorgio, Paul joined a True Cross reliquary, the holy sponge and the relics of, quoting the

hagiographer, 'so many martyrs and virgins that we don't even have time to name them all!'. Paul became just another relic in the crypt with a lovely mosaic in San Marco. But the *translatio* treats us to drama on the high seas, stealth and deceit in the streets of Constantinople, long digressions on the nature of divine light and the occluding cloud of lies, prophecies and the assertion of great significance for all of Venice as a result of the relic's presence in the house of George. In one key moment the anonymous monk of San Giorgio explains why the monk asked a merchant friend to take the relic to Venice:

> He asked him [a friend and layman who would transport the relic] this [to translate the relic] so that he would convey the previous gem to his abbot, so that it might now adorn not only the monastery, but all of Venice. For, just as innumerable men and women arrive to visit the blessed Mark from nearly all parts of the world, so too it was the glorious custom to see the blessed Paul.[31]

The author is comparing veneration of Mark in Venice to the cult of Paul, and suggesting that Paul's cult will continue adorning 'all of Venice' once the relics are translated. More importantly, the *translatio* contains a retrospective prophecy, as follows:

> But just as the blessed martyr Paul's partner in name and race, the blessed Apostle Paul, called out to Caesar, knowing through the Holy Spirit that Rome would prosper greatly in the faith of Christ. So the blessed martyr allowed himself to be led to Venice, and if this happens, this is not a prediction, he will do many like miracles.[32]

This passage links the creation of the Christian Roman Empire to this translation of a minor relic, suggesting that the stakes are similar. Because this passage was written after Paul's relics had already arrived safely, the non-prediction must already be coming true, according to the internal logic. St Paul's presence in Venice suggests that a new Christian (and Rome-like) empire will rise on the Rialto, patterning itself after the glories of Constantine. Thus, according to the *Translation of St Paul*, Venice's triumph in 1204 enabled the emergence of a new imperial identity, all made possible by the arrival of a new relic encompassed within the monastery of St George.

Interpretations

The scholarship on the images of St George on the exterior of San Marco regularly mentions the presence of the monastery in order to note the pre-existing veneration of the saint in Venice.[33] The argument given is that considering the tradition of veneration and the new arrival of the arm reliquary after 1204, why not install an image of St George? But I suggest that one can locate deep connections between institution and iconography and the specific programmes of visual narratives in San Marco and textual narratives produced within the monastery. The centrality and malleability of the images of St George cannot easily be explained by mere casual correlation between venerative practice and display of spolia.

To find these deeper connections, I suggest that one must view the monastery not merely as an institution dedicated to the saint, but as a kind of super-reliquary of St George, a *locus* in which the saint is present within the local imaginary geography. From that position, the brethren of the monastery could control the potential reordering of the sacred landscape brought about by the arrival of a foreign relic. St George could contain, constrain, promote or partner with a newly arrived saint. Through the interlocution of San Giorgio, new relics could enhance the glory of the Venetian church without threatening Mark's pride of place. The monastery housed relics as needed and distributed them as appropriate. While within San Giorgio, the blessings of a newly arrived saint were accessible to all Venetians without favouring a specific parish or family. Monks produced narratives to shape collective memorialization of the acts of translation and subsequent *miracula*. The monastery sat across the *bacino* as a monastic reflection of the secular centre of Venice, inextricably tied to that centre, yet sufficiently apart to be malleable in its relationship with Venetian culture. When Venice received the arm reliquary, this tangible item sat in San Marco, hereby creating a new vector between monastery (seen as a super-reliquary) and the state church.[34]

Turn back to the opening image, with St George guarding the door and San Giorgio just across the *bacino*. In my view, it is not a coincidence that the representations of St George and his arm relic bind the foreign to the local in ways that are comparable to the traditions of the monastery that I have just outlined. Visually, the representations of St George and his reliquary open and control the paths by which foreign images and sacred objects enter Venetian political religion. St George – from the East but venerated heavily in the West, of unimpeachable pedigree but not a threat to St Mark's status – offered an iconographic bridge between East and West, old and new, sacred and secular. His image on the walls of San Marco kept him in service to the Republic of St Mark, always present, but on the margins or across the canal. He is significant, but no threat to the Venetian brand.

Conclusion

After the Fourth Crusade, the city of Venice experienced the pangs of a newfound maritime empire and the challenges of imperial rule. St George and the monastery of San Giorgio both played their roles in shaping the emergence of a new imperial culture in myth, ritual, image and text. But just as Doge Zeno was commissioning his relief plaque, the archbishop of Genoa, Jacobus de Voragine, was retelling the story of St George and the dragon in the *Golden Legend*.[35] As the legend proliferated, George lost his malleability, permanently mounting his horse and heading to combat. Venice followed the larger trend. Between 1283 and 1325, the arm reliquary of St George was adorned in its stunning form and crowned with a 'figure of St George riding a horse'.[36] If there was no dragon at the time, the newly designed arm represents the last major image of St George produced without a dragon in Venice. The arm is decorated with apostles and evangelists in enamel, alongside a silver-gilt Tree of Jesse. Just like the Portale San Alipio and perhaps the iconostasis, St George is being placed in conjunction with biblical figures.

By the middle of the 14th century, reliefs and paintings of St George on display throughout Venice all began to feature the dragon, as seen on the Scuola dedicated to him, in the baptistery of San Marco, in other scattered reliefs and later in important works by Carpaccio, Bordone and Tintoretto.[37] Venetian hagiographic narratives suddenly feature St George, such as in a famous story from 1341. With the city beset by terrible storms, Sts Mark, Nicholas and George appear as old men and compel a fisherman to sail out into the thick of the weather. There, the three saints triumph over demons bent on destroying Venice. Mark rewards the fisherman with a ring that subsequently becomes a major element of civic ritual.[38] George gets star billing, but his shape-shifting ways are over.

The end of St George's role as an intermediary suggests the limits of this type of cultural interlocution. Both the mechanisms and limits of St George's role raise questions that merit further study. Can we locate a new class of intermediary saints that function similarly in other cities? Or is this pattern limited to St George in Venice? The power of St George's images emerged out of a specific set of variables – the local traditions of cultural appropriation, the presence of this powerful monastery dedicated to a figure that transcends East and West and the spatial and institutional relationship between the state church of San Marco and San Giorgio. It is with that spatial relationship in mind that this chapter closes as it began, in the Piazza San Marco, waiting to enter the western doors and walk between the military saints that guard the portal. Today, as in the 13th century, one can look up at the relief icons, turn one's gaze across the water to the monastery and remember that there was an era in which for every lion in Venice, a George stood nearby in a supporting role.

Notes

1   Bagnoli *et al.* 2010, 51. Research for this essay was conducted in the Biblioteca Marciana and the Basilica of San Marco with the financial support of the Gladys Krieble Delmas Foundation and Dominican University, River Forest, IL. Ernie Krause served as the author's research assistant. Early drafts of this essay were read by Ludovico Geymonat, Jonathan Good, Rabia Gregory, Kathleen Kennedy and Elisabeth Perry. The author is grateful for their assistance.
2   Demus 1960, 125–37.
3   Perry forthcoming.
4   Demus 1960, 134–5.
5   Riches 2000, 24–7.
6   Walter 2003, 121–8, 140–2.
7   Demus 1960, 135.
8   Demus 1960, 137, 140–3; Demus 1984, vol. 2, 201–6.
9   Jacoff 2010 122–8; Dale 1994, 90–3; Demus 1984, vol. 2, 202. Dale argues that the scene reflects not 828–9, but 1094. This is possible, although this presents a chronological leap from the arrival of the relics in the neighbouring scene and an 11th-century act of rediscovery of the relics after they had been put in storage. The mosaic could, of course, operate in three time frames, rather than merely two.
10 Demus 1984, vol. 2, 201–6.
11 Dale 2010, 159–61; Tigler 1995, 100–1.
12 Tigler 1995, 102.
13 Riches 2000, 22–5.
14 Dale 2010,162. 'The juxtaposition with the evangelists appears to be unique.'
15 Klein 2010, 217. In the 14th century, Andrea Dandolo claimed that Doge Enrico Dandolo (from the same family but not a direct ancestor) had sent the relics to Venice after 1204. There is, however, no record of this link to Doge Enrico in the 13th century, and Klein believes that Andrea Dandolo may in fact have forged it.

16 Pincus 1984, 39–42.
17 Ibid., 41–2; Klein 2010, 216–17; Bagnoli *et al.* 2010, 92.
18 Perry forthcoming.
19 Tigler 1995, 75–6.
20 Kieslinger 1944, 57–61.
21 Demus 1984, vol. I, 162–3; Muir 1986, 96.
22 Damerini 1956, 5–12; Niero *et al.* 1972, 92.
23 Dale 2010, 161; Niero 1972, 203–4.
24 Pertusi 1978, 48–54 for the general overview.
25 Monk of the Lido 1895, vol. 5, 262. Author's translation.
   'Sanctissime praesul Nicolae! Votis fidelium acquiesce; dignare
   tuam Venetiam et Occidentem visitare. Sufficiat Orienti et
   Graecis, quod te pontificem et doctorem habuerunt, et quot te, post
   excessum, fere septingentis annis retinuerunt; gaudeant tandem
   Occidens et Latini tui corporis praesentia visitari.'
26 Ibid., vol. 5, 281. Author's translation. 'O felix Venetia! Et o beata
   Venetia! Quae beatum Marcum evangelistam, utpote leonem in
   bellis habes defensorem, et Nicolaum, patrem Graecorum, in
   navibus gubernatorum. In bello fortem leonem habes signiferum
   in tempestate maris graecum sapientem nauclerum. Cum tali
   leone metuendo hostium cuneos invades, cum tali nauclero secura
   per undas pelagi vadis.'
27 Muir 1986, 98–101.
28 Niero 1965, 181–208.
29 Damerini 1956, 19–24; Niero 1965, 205.
30 Polacco 1617; Musolino 1987, 41–4, 149.
31 Riant 1877–8, vol. 1, 144. Author's translation. 'Hunc rogavit, ut
   pretiosam gemmam suo abbati deferret, que non solum
   monasterium, sed & totam Venetiam sua presentia decoraret.
   Nam, sicut b. Marcum pene de universis partibus visitare
   adveniunt innumerabiles viri & femine, ita beatum Paulum facta
   est gloriosa consuetudo videndi.'
32 Ibid., vol. 1, 147. Author's translation. 'Beatus martyr Paulus sed
   sicut confors et gentium magister beatus apostolus Paulus Cesarem
   appellaverat, sciens per Spiritum, se Rome in fide Christi multis
   profuturum: ita beatus iste martyr, deduci se sinebat Venetias, et si,
   non predicatione, miraculis similia multis facturus.'
33 See, for example Dale 2010, 161.
34 For vectors, see Perry 2014.
35 Good 2009, 39–42.
36 Bagnoli *et al.* 2010, 51.
37 See, for example, *St George and the Dragon with Two Armorial Reliefs*,
   Victoria and Albert Museum, London (53B-1884).
38 Muir 1986, 132.

Bibliography

Bagnoli, M., Klein, H.A., Mann, C.G. and Robinson, J. (eds) 2010.
   Treasures of Heaven: Saints, Relics and Devotion in Medieval Europe,
   Baltimore and London.
Dale, T. 1994. 'Inventing a sacred past: pictorial narratives of St. Mark
   the Evangelist in Aquileia and Venice, ca. 1000–1300', *Dumbarton
   Oaks Papers* 48, 53–104.
Dale, T. 2010. 'Cultural hybridity in medieval Venice: reinventing the
   East at San Marco after the Fourth Crusade,' in Maguire and
   Nelson 2010, 151–92.
Damerini, G. 1956. *L'isola e il Cenobio di San Giorgio Maggiore*, Venice.
Demus, O. 1960. *The Church of San Marco in Venice*, Washington, DC.
Demus, O. 1984. *The Mosaics of San Marco in Venice*, 2 vols, Chicago.
Good, J. 2009. *The Cult of St George in Medieval England*, Woodbridge.
Kieslinger, F. 1944. 'Le transenne della basilica di San Marco del
   secolo XIII,' *Ateneo Veneto*, CXXXI, 57–61.
Klein, H. 2010. 'Refashioning Byzantium in Venice, ca. 1200–1400', in
   Maguire and Nelson 2010, 193–226.
Jacoff, M. 2010. 'Fashioning a façade: the construction of Venetian
   identity on the exterior of San Marco', in Maguire and Nelson
   2010, 113–50.
Maguire, H. and Nelson, R. (eds) 2010. *San Marco, Byzantium, and the
   Myths of Venice*, Washington, DC.
Monk of the Lido 1895. 'Historia de translatione Magni Nicolai',
   Recueil des historiens des croisades: Historiens occientaux 5, Paris.
Muir, E. 1986. *Civic Ritual in Renaissance Venice*, Princeton, NJ.
Musolino, G. 1987. *Santa Lucia a Venezia*, Venice.
Niero, A. 1965. 'Relique e corpi di santi,' in *Culto dei Santi a Venezia*, ed.
   S. Tramontin, Venice, 181–208.
Niero, A., Musolino, G., and Tramontin, S. 1972. *Santità a Venezia*,
   Venice.
Perry, D. 2014. 'The material culture of medieval Venetian identity', in
   Mediterranean Identities in the Premodern Era: Entrepôts, Islands, Empires,
   ed. K. Reyerson and J. Watkins, Aldershot, 15–34.
Perry, D. forthcoming. *Sacred Plunder: Venice and the Aftermath of the Fourth
   Crusade*, University Park, PA.
Pertusi, A. 1978. 'La contesa per le reliquie di S. Nicola tra Bari,
   Venezia e Genova,' *Quaderni Medievali* 5 (1978), 6–56.
Pincus, D. 1984. 'Christian relics and the body politic: a 13th-century
   relief plaque in the church of San Marco,' *Interpretazioni Veneziane*,
   ed. D. Rosand, Venice, 39–58.
Polacco, D.G. 1617. *Della Triplicata Traslazaione del corpo della gloriosa
   Vergine, & Martire S. Lucia*, Venice.
Riant, P. 1877–8. 'Translatio corporis beatissimi Pauli martyris de
   Constantinopoli Venetias,' in *Exuviae Sacrae Constantinopolitanae*,
   Geneva, vol. 1, 141–9.
Riches, S. 2000. *St George: Hero, Martyr and Myth*, Stroud.
Tigler, G. 1995. *Le sculture esterne di San Marco*, Milan.
Walter, C. 2003. *The Warrior Saints in Byzantine Art and Tradition*,
   Aldershot.

Chapter 4
Stones of St Michael
Venerating Fragments of Holy Ground in Medieval France and Italy

Lucy Donkin

This chapter considers relics not of the bodies of saints, but of the ground they had trodden. Relics of this kind were especially associated with those who had left few or no corporeal remains, such as Christ, Mary and the angels. Although this is a phenomenon usually discussed in relation to the *loca sancta* of Jerusalem and the Holy Land,[1] such relics were also taken from some places in western Europe. I focus here on locations associated with St Michael the Archangel, especially Monte Sant'Angelo in Apulia and Mont Saint-Michel in Normandy.[2] The former preserved the footprints or *vestigia* of the Archangel, left in confirmation of the vision which had established the sanctity of the site, while the latter, like other churches with the same dedication, claimed possession of a piece of the stone in which the imprints were set. Although Mont Saint-Michel had no angelic footprints of its own, the site more generally was conceived of as holy ground, fragments of which could be used to consecrate altars elsewhere. In asking how far the qualities of earthen relics overlap with those of bodily relics, and to what extent they had particular qualities that intersected with other aspects of the ground, emphasis will be placed on their materiality and on their capacity to represent and embody places.

The 6th-century *Sancta Sanctorum* reliquary box, containing stones and earth from key holy sites in Palestine, is well known.[3] Yet this is only the tip of the iceberg; relic lists throughout the Middle Ages include vast numbers of stones from a wide variety of *loca sancta*, which are often specifically described as places where figures had sat or stood: Angilbert's description of the relics of St Riquier includes one 'of the stone, where [Christ] sat, when he fed the 5,000';[4] the 12th-century description of the relic collection in the Lateran includes a relic 'of the rock in the River Jordan upon which Jesus sat when he was baptized';[5] the Waltham Abbey relic list, compiled in around 1204, includes a relic of 'the rock on which St Elizabeth was standing when the infant leapt in her womb';[6] a list of relics brought back by Abbot Martin of Pairis in 1205 after the Fourth Crusade includes 'a relic from the stone where John stood when he baptized the Lord'.[7] The Christological relics among them could be put at the top of the list, along with fragments of the True Cross or pieces of the Holy Sepulchre, challenging the humble status we might perhaps expect to adhere to secondary relics of stone.[8]

Outside the Holy Land, sites that gave rise to these kind of relics were fewer in number, but not unknown. In Rome, St Peter and St Paul were thought to have left their knee-prints in the spot on the Via Sacra where they had knelt to pray against Simon Magus during their battle with the magician. Imprints identified as those of St Peter are currently set into the wall of the church of Santa Francesca Romana (**Pl. 1**). In the *Liber pontificalis* the imprints are described as being set in the base of a tree,[9] but Gregory of Tours had understood them to be made in stone,[10] and the relic authentics at Sens include two 8th–9th century examples that relate to the site: one is explicitly labelled 'of that place where St Peter and St Paul prayed against Simon Magus'; the other simply reads 'of the stone where St Peter prayed' ('de petra ubi oravit s(an)c(tu)s Petrus').[11] In the latter case, it may be that Peter's name encouraged the description

Plate 1 Kneeprints of St Peter. Santa Francesca Romana, Rome (photo: author)

of the relic as 'petra' rather than 'lapidus'. Although Petrine relics of this kind are not common in later relic lists, around 1200 Anthony of Novgorod reported that the Church of the Apostles in Constantinople possessed a marble slab with the footprints of St Peter, brought from Rome.[12]

Elsewhere in Italy, the shrine of St Michael at Monte Sant'Angelo on the Gargano Peninsula in Apulia was marked by the footprints of the saint. According to the 7th or 8th-century foundation legend in the *Liber de apparitione sancti Michaelis*, the saint told the bishop of Siponto in a dream that the site was sacred, leaving his *vestigia* in the rock as a sign of his presence and confirmation of his words.[13] Subsequently when the citizens were in doubt as to whether they should consecrate the site, the archangel made another visionary appearance, and the next day they found an extensive church with a red cloth or cloak left on the altar. The place was a popular pilgrimage site, and a number of the relics of St Michael that feature in lists and authentics are likely to have come from the shrine. For example, a 7th- or 8th-century authentic from Sens names a number of relics including that 'de s(an)c(t)o a(n)gelo Michahel'.[14] Michael McCormick has argued that the relics are likely to have been collected in the course of a journey to the Holy Land via Monte Sant'Angelo, in which case this example must be either a fragment of ground or of the cloth left on the altar.[15] A record of the late 11th-century re-consecration of the church of St Michael at Fulda, however, is presumably referring specifically to the footprint when it mentions a relic 'de vestigio S. Michaelis', suggesting that a relic of St Michael which was included in Hrabanus Maurus' earlier dedication inscription was also from the rock in which the footprints were set.[16] More explicitly still, the 12th- or 13th-century list of the relics in the cave church or Spelunca of St Columbanus at Bobbio, close to one dedicated to the archangel, includes a relic of the rock where St Michael stood: 'de petra ubi sanctus Michael stetit'.[17] Although the location is not stated and links with other manifestations of the saint were possible – 12th-century Rheinau, for example, claimed possession of a relic 'of the place where St Michael killed the dragon' – the cave site is suggestive of an association with the shrine at Monte Sant'Angelo.[18] The late 12th-century *Ritus in ecclesia servandi* of Santa Reparata in

Florence shows the cathedral to have possessed a relic 'de lapide ubi archangelus Michael apparuit', which may relate to the shrine too.[19] A number of churches also claimed a relationship with Gargano and its relics as part of their foundation legends, not least Mont Saint-Michel in Normandy. The *Revelatio ecclesiae sancti Michaelis*, thought to have been composed in the early 9th century, recounts how the archangel thrice appeared in a dream to Aubert, bishop of Avranches, commanding him to build a church.[20] The bishop then sent monks to the shrine to collect tokens (*pignora*) of the saint: part of the red cloth he had left on the altar and part of the rock on which he had stood.

In considering what relationship such relics bear to others, the question of materiality is significant. Pieces of rock potentially shared with other relics a discrepancy between minimal visual impact and high spiritual value. The relationship between the substance of relics and that of their containers has recently been the subject of some discussion by art historians, and though these studies tend to focus on bodily relics, their conclusions apply equally to earthen ones.[21] These too could be enclosed in reliquaries of precious metals, which made apparent the significance of their contents. Well-known examples that contain pieces of the ground include the mid-12th-century Stavelot head reliquary of Pope Alexander I, which contains a stone from the site of the Ascension,[22] and the central part of the Zwiefalten True Cross reliquary, which contains small stones from Golgotha and the site of the Ascension.[23] Relics of the ground connected with St Michael could also be housed in high-status reliquaries. The silver-gilt processional cross of the collegiate church of St Michael, Beromünster (**Pls 2–3**), dated to *c.* 1300, contains a fragment 'de petra sancti Mychahelis', perhaps part of the 'magnum frustum de petra s. Michahelis' which a 15th-century relic list recorded as being kept in a chest.[24] Inscriptions on the back of the cross show the relic to be housed along with those of St Stephen and St Placidus in the right-hand arm (**Pl. 4**). Just as the subsidiary relics of the Zwiefalten True Cross reliquary are positioned behind precious stones at the ends of the central cross, the front of the Beromünster cross is liberally studded with gems, which take on additional significance in the light of the fragment

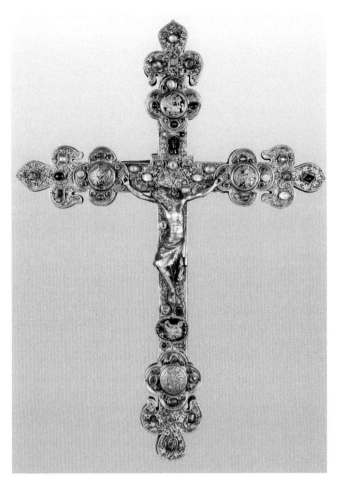

Plate 2 Processional cross, front, *c.* 1300, gilded silver over wooden core, cast silver, champlevé enamel, gems and intaglios, h. 700mm. Chorherrstift Beromünster (photo: Theres Bütler)

Plate 3 Back of processional cross (Pl. 2) (photo: Theres Bütler)

of rock within. Even miraculous *vestigia* – whether *in situ* or elsewhere – could be decorated and thereby authenticated by precious metals: the Piacenza Pilgrim described the footprint of Christ in the Praetorium in Jerusalem as being set in a block of stone decorated in gold and silver;[25] the Westminster *passus domini* relic of Christ's footprint from the Mount of Olives was set in silver;[26] and the footprint of Christ in the Templum Domini (the Dome of the Rock) was described by John of Würzburg as being reverently adorned.[27] Since classical cult *vestigia* were sometimes inlaid in metal,[28] it is possible that the early example in the Praetorium was inlaid too, but more probably the metal served to surround the imprints, rather in the manner of a portable altar.

At the same time, and in a similar way to bodily relics, the spiritual significance of earthen relics could also be expressed in terms of precious materials, with the value of the relics being said to outweigh or transcend that of conventionally prized materials. Famously, in the words of the 2nd-century *Martyrdom of St Polycarp*, relics were 'dearer … than precious stones and finer than gold'.[29] This attitude may well find an equivalent in the early 5th-century descriptions by Paulinus of Nola and Sulpicius Severus of the site of the Ascension, which – having been trodden by God – refused to accept marble paving.[30] In the late 10th century this idea was expanded on in the Blickling Homily on the Ascension, which states that 'no one has ever been able to

overlay the footsteps themselves, neither in gold, nor silver, nor with any worldly treasures'.[31]

However, the stone itself had the capacity to demonstrate worth, blurring the line between relic and reliquary. Stone was part of a spectrum, at one end of which was a material very much prized in worldly terms. Brigitte Buettner has asked whether a stone could be sacramental matter of the highest order, discussing an instance in which gems

Plate 4 Detail of the right-hand arm of the processional cross, as seen from the back, with inscription concerning relics, *c.* 1300, gilded silver over wooden core, h. 700mm. Chorherrstift Beromünster (photo: Theres Bütler)

Plate 5 Scene from the Stammheim Missal showing the Ascension, 1170s, tempera colours, gold leaf, silver leaf, and ink on parchment, 282 x 189mm. The J. Paul Getty Museum, Los Angeles, Ms. 64, fol. 115v (reproduced by kind permission of the J. Paul Getty Museum)

miraculously fall – meteor-like – from the heavens and are received as relics.[32] To precious stones such as these can be added marble. The extent to which marble and marble paving is associated with gold, silver and gems is evident both in medieval accounts of patronage and in rejections of lavish decoration: Agnellus of Ravenna reported building projects featuring 'stucco covered with gold' and 'wonderful marble cut pieces' in the same breath;[33] Aelred of Rievaulx asked whether the heavenly temple is wondrous 'in gold and silver or in precious stones? Or floors covered with marble?'.[34]

It is therefore significant that some *vestigia* sites and their associated relics are described as being marble. In the *Liber de apparitione sancti Michaelis*, for example, the rock into which the Archangel's imprints are set is twice described as such.[35] This is particularly interesting in light of the fact that the text contains an element of tension regarding the materiality of the site. The church took the form of a cave in the naked rock, with uneven walls and ceiling, prompting the author of the *Liber de apparitione* to conclude that the saint must prefer 'purity of heart' (*cordis … puritatem*) to 'adorned stone' (*ornatus lapidum*).[36] The fact that the uneven walls of the cave required justification suggests that the natural rock was viewed with

some ambivalence. The author sought the best of both worlds by casting a moralizing interpretation on the rock, while presenting it as a prestigious material that formed a suitable setting for the angelic prints. The prints were similarly viewed as made in marble in the writings from Mont Saint-Michel, both in the text of the *Revelatio* itself and in later descriptions of the arrival of the Gargano relics in the late 11th-century *Miracula sancti Michaelis* and the 12th-century *Roman du Mont Saint-Michel*.[37] Indeed, the relic continued to be identified as marble in inventories well into the early modern period.[38]

References to marble are clustered round imprint sites, rather than relics which had formed part of the ground more generally. As Andrea Worm has demonstrated, after the Crusades the Ascension site became shown as a separate stone slab, often veined marble; indeed the late 12th-century Stammheim Missal shows it as a red, porphyry-like stone akin to that used in decorated pavements (**Pl. 5**).[39] According to Matthew Paris, the 13th-century Westminster *passus domini* was white marble.[40] To a certain extent, surely the reference to marble rendered such a relic more miraculous, since the harder the stone, the more extraordinary any impression made on it. The stone can be seen to act as a reliquary for the relic impression – the form of the absent sacred body – as well as being itself a contact relic. However, the fact that the reference to marble extended to the description of relics from a *vestigia* site in the case of the Gargano relics is significant, and speaks of a possible continuum between the material of relics and the materials used to authenticate them and communicate their value. In this light, it is interesting that Eleonora Destefanis notes the existence of 'pietre colorate' among devotional items preserved at Bobbio, perhaps brought there from the eastern Mediterranean in common with the monastery's early medieval ampullae and terracotta tokens.[41] This suggests that the distinctive appearance of particular stones might have been a factor in their selection by pilgrims to the Holy Land, with the aesthetic qualities of the objects themselves rendering visible their spiritual significance and distant origin, quite apart from any role to this effect subsequently played by a container.

In possessing the potential to express worth when functioning as a relic by using the same properties as when it was used in a work of art or architecture, it could be argued that stone was not necessarily unique. Bones could potentially be seen as close in substance to whale bone and even ivory. However, these materials both look and feel different and I am not aware of instances in which saintly remains are described in such a way as to evoke the aesthetic of ivory.[42] Certainly, they do not seem to have been worked in a similar manner; the human skull once thought to have been engraved in the Middle Ages has since been revealed as a 16th-century fake.[43] The correspondence between container and contained was also not a direct one, since marble itself was not commonly used for reliquaries, although it was for portable altars and larger shrines and tombs. Furthermore, relics described in this way were not necessarily visible. The Mont Saint-Michel relics from Gargano were kept out of sight; indeed a miracle recorded in the late 11th century concerns the retribution taken by the Archangel on a monk who prized open the reliquary, doubting the existence of the relics inside.[44] But if texts and reliquary are combined, the invisibility of the marble does not necessarily render it redundant; rather preciousness and significance are expressed through matter and through faith.

The capacity of relics which had formed part of the ground to embody a particular place is another sphere in which they display correspondences both with relics and with pieces of stone used in other ways. Where the *Revelatio* traces the transfer of the relics from Gargano to Normandy, two miracle stories redacted at Mont Saint-Michel around 1080–95, and possibly reflecting events in the first two decades of that century, describe the taking of relics from Mont Saint-Michel in its turn. One concerns a man from Burgundy who visited the monastery, asking for a small stone ('minimum lapidem') from the Mont; this he took home and placed 'pro reliquiis' in the altar of a church he constructed in honour of St Michael.[45] The Burgundian requested the stone after having read a copy of the *Revelatio*, perhaps implying an emulation of the fetching of the Gargano relics. After his death, the church he built was neglected by his wife and children. As a result, when his wife paid a visit to Mont Saint-Michel, she was unable to ascend the mountain, being beset by a great pain as soon as she mounted the first step. Questioned by two monks, she realized her error and returned home to restore the church. This account is repeated and embellished in the *Roman du Mont Saint-Michel* by Guillaume de Saint-Pair, who rather downplays the pilgrim's 'pierrete' (little stone): being 'vile et petitete', it would likely not have been placed in the altar of the church had the man possessed better relics.[46] The other miracle story, which is not included in the *Roman du Mont Saint-Michel*, describes a man from Italy who was gravely ill and having been unsuccessful in finding a permanent cure through a pilgrimage to Monte Gargano, went to Mont Saint-Michel on the recommendation of two of the monks.[47] Here he took a small stone (again 'minimum lapidem') without permission, placing it in an altar, and fell ill again as a result. As a condition of his restoration to health, he had to return to the Mont with the stone, place it on the altar there and honour St Michael with worthy gifts. The stone was then given back to him by the monks for him to build a church in honour of St Michael.

In these two miracle accounts, the monks presented themselves as distributors as well as recipients of pieces of holy ground. It should be noted that there were a variety of grounds for seeing the terrain of Mont Saint-Michel as sacred; not least, the site of the abbey church was claimed in the *Revelatio* to have been marked out by miraculous means, firstly by the circumambulation of a bull and secondly by a fall of dew.[48] Additionally, the *Miracula* includes an account of a fire after which the relics of the saint were thought lost and then found safe on a stone at the bottom of the Mont.[49] This was subsequently venerated and healing miracles occurred in the vicinity, with the stone understood to derive its power from having come into contact with the relics. However, the small stones taken by the pilgrims are described as being from the Mont more generally, and there is a sense in which Mont Saint-Michel as a whole can be seen as sanctified by the fragment of Apulian marble, in a kind of chain reaction.

While the general structure of the second story corresponds to cautionary accounts of the unauthorized removal of any relics, with punishment by the saint concerned, it is noteworthy that removal itself is not the issue. This is all the more striking since there was a hagiographical precedent for stones, which had been trodden or sat on by a saint, refusing to be moved: Gregory of Tours reports the case of a man who tried – unsuccessfully – to move a stone on which St Martin had sat and was struck down dead a few days later.[50] Writing about the Holy Land earlier in the 6th century, Theodosius mentions a man who cut out the stone on which the Virgin Mary had sat and turned it into an altar, wanting to send it to Constantinople. Having failed to have it dragged more than a certain way, he too met his end and suffered additional retribution through the appropriate agency of the ground, which refused to accept his body for burial.[51]

In these cases, however, it is a question of the removal of the whole stone and thus the integrity and almost the *raison d'être* of the holy site is threatened. In the case of Mont Saint-Michel, they are only fragments of a wider expanse of holy ground, and thus it is the correct manner of removal and treatment that is at issue. In fact, the distribution of pieces of the Mont was of possible benefit to the monastic community, since it had the potential to place it at the centre of a nexus of sanctity. While the community sought to draw legitimacy from the possession of relics brought from Gargano, it also claimed a continuing relationship with and authority over places to which fragments of its own ground were taken. If the giving of a gift can be understood to set up an unequal relationship, this served to place Mont Saint-Michel in the middle of a sort of spatial hierarchy, below Monte Sant'Angelo but above any new churches. However, the fact that the stone in the second miracle is taken to Italy may be intended to express an equality of status regarding Gargano, reversing the effect of the initial transfer. Certainly this was a period in which the Normans were taking possession of southern Italy; indeed, the *Introductio monachorum* – thought to have been written at around the same time as the *Miracula* and perhaps by the same monk – notes the recent conquests.[52]

On one level, the transfer of the stones reflects what Robert Ousterhout has described as the 'belief that sanctity or spiritual value can be associated with persons, places, or objects, and that by being captured in matter, the numenous qualities can be carried away from the original location'.[53] Within this framework, fragments of the ground could be seen as having a particular, but far from exclusive, potential to embody and translate sacred place. At the same time, the mechanics and consequences of taking earthen relics strike me as having a connection with the way in which the ground was treated on other occasions. In particular, in the second Mont Saint-Michel miracle, the placing of the returned stone on the altar is reminiscent of the treatment of tokens used for land grants. Stones and even pieces of marble were among a large number of items that could serve as tokens of property transfer.[54] Clods of earth as well as vegetation from the site were also employed, while other objects used bore no physical relationship to the property concerned. In the context of investiture, such tokens might be placed in the

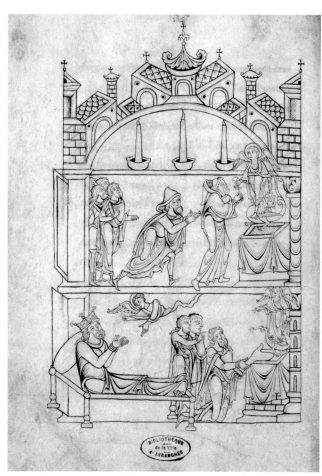

Plate 6 Donation scenes, Mont Saint-Michel cartulary, c. 1149–50. Bibliothèque Municipale, Avranches, MS 210, fol. 25v (Cliché Ville d'Avranches)

hand of the person being invested with the land. More unusually, a cult statue could be employed. In Peebles in 1462, when land belonging to the altar of St Michael in St Andrew's church was leased, a statue of the saint was taken there and 'erd and stan' ('earth and stone') placed in its hand before being delivered to the baillie and seriand – local officials – for them to bestow the property on the lessee.[55] In the case of gifts to ecclesiastical institutions, symbolic items were usually placed on the altar of a church, generally that of the recipients, in a public ritual incorporating those individuals with claims to the land. As Matthew Innes and Marguerite Ragnow have noted, the objects were thus brought into close proximity to the relics of the saint to whom the land was being given. The spiritual implications of the act could be heightened by the citation of biblical passages familiar from the liturgy and by parallels with other ceremonies of offering that focused on the altar, notably the Eucharist.[56] In the context of the present discussion, it should be added that, theoretically, both the relics within the altar and the tokens placed upon it could include pieces of stone.

If acts of donation and investiture could draw on liturgical practice and incorporate cult statues, heavenly, relic creating interventions in the foundation of a church could equally borrow aspects of donation ritual. The late 11th-century *Libellus de revelatione, aedificatione et autoritate Fiscanensis* gives an account of the consecration of the abbey church of La Trinité, Fécamp (Normandy), in which an angel appears in the guise of a pilgrim and decides the dedication of the church by placing on the altar a knife, on which is written 'In nomine sanctae et individuae Trinitatis' ('In the name of the holy and indivisible Trinity').[57] While the knife, subsequently enclosed in the altar cross, has been associated with the idea of sacrifice and related to Fécamp's relic of the Holy Blood, a possible connection with tokens of land transfer has also been suggested.[58] The latter interpretation seems particularly compelling since knives were not only commonly used as signs of donation, but might even be inscribed with texts noting the property with which they were associated.[59] According to the *Libellus*, the angel then vanished, leaving his footprints on a stone, a fragment of which was later incorporated into the foundations of the church when it was rebuilt. It is not stated what was done with the remaining part, although in the 15th century what was known as the 'pas de l'ange' would be venerated at the abbey.[60] Given the links between Fécamp and Mont Saint-Michel in the mid-11th century, including through their abbots,[61] it is possible that this angelic footprint and its role in the consecration of the church was in some way inspired by that of St Michael.

It remains to be asked how far the stones in the Mont Saint-Michel miracle story would have evoked associations with land transfer tokens used at the abbey. In her study of 11th-century Normandy, Emily Zack Tabuteau describes the 'prevalent dissociation of the act of donation from the land given', noting that symbolic objects rarely bear any relationship to the gift, and do not include something from the land itself.[62] While Tabuteau does cite exceptions and the practice was known elsewhere in France in the 11th and 12th centuries,[63] the mid-12th-century Mont Saint-Michel cartulary does not record any instances of the use of earthen tokens. Instead, from the 1130s, land grants were made by placing the arm reliquary of St Aubert on the altar of St Michael.[64] A drawing in the cartulary shows a kneeling man – perhaps Edward the Confessor – placing what has variously been identified as the reliquary or a glove on an altar above which is a representation of the archangel (**Pl. 6**).[65] This has sometimes been described as a statue, though there is no evidence for a cult statue in the abbey church until the 14th century,[66] and the image is as likely to denote the saint himself, whose relics were kept in the altar in this period. Only in the 15th century would gilded reliquary statues be made in which the figure of St Michael held the fragments of cloak and marble respectively.[67] In the upper tier of the cartulary drawing, a monk holds a branch – another token of land transfer – up to the hand of the saint or more likely receives it from him, in what has been seen to express the monks' claim to benefit from such gifts without restrictions.[68] Whether or not a statue is intended here, the action is suggestive of the later practice concerning the statue of St Michael in Peebles and both can be understood as visualizations of land transactions involving saintly proprietors.

Although evidence for the use of the arm reliquary postdates the *Miracula* by some decades, it is likely that the author was familiar with a ritual vocabulary that included placing tokens on the altar of St Michael and possibly also a conjunction of relics on and within it. This has various possible implications for the role and associations of the stone in the miracle story. The ritualized removal of a stone from Mont Saint-Michel clearly did not affect any actual transfer of the possession of the site; did it, however, act as a token of the sanctioned conveyance of the sanctity of holy ground, over and above more generally 'capturing in matter' the numinosity of the place? It is perhaps more probable that the stone placed on the altar represented the man's unspecified gifts, and therefore acted as a symbolic object which, while particularly resonant in the circumstances, did not bear a material relationship to what was given. Since he is allowed to return home with it, the stone may equally have acted as a kind of counter-gift. Nevertheless, the fact that a stone could express a transfer of property might well have informed the monks' desire for a public and consensual removal of fragments of their holy ground. Moreover, with the marble from Apulia within the altar and the stone from Mont Saint-Michel upon it (later to be enclosed in the altar of another church in its turn), that capacity to symbolize the transfer of property may also have enhanced a capacity to effect the sharing of sanctity.

In conclusion, while the stones of St Michael and other earthen relics discussed share many properties with other relics, they may have some distinctive qualities that speak partly of their origin in the ground. Although they shared the common potential discrepancy between material and spiritual worth, they could also be identified themselves as costly material. Similarly, while the movement of relics always had implications for the relationship between source and destination, fragments of ground could play a distinctive role in the creation of a hierarchical network of holy places, in the process perhaps evoking contemporary legal customs regarding the transfer of property. This association raises a possibility which requires more detailed discussion than it can receive here; nevertheless, it seems appropriate to mention it briefly, since it goes against the distinction just drawn between fragments of holy ground and other relics. Land transfer tokens that were taken from the site share correspondences with relics more generally, since both partake of a 'pars pro toto' logic. In the case of relics, a key text is the late 4th-century *De laude sanctorum* of Victricius of Rouen, who, speaking of relics that included 'blood and earth', famously said 'ubi est aliquid, ibi totum est' ('where the part is, there is the whole').[69] In the case of land transfer tokens, the logic may derive in part from Roman law. The 3rd-century *Institutes of Gaius* indicates that in cases of disputed ownership, the property in question should be brought into the court and touched by the disputing parties in turn. Where this was not possible, a part could be brought instead and the vindication would proceed 'just as if the whole had been present' ('et in eam partem proinde atque in totam rem praesentem fiebat').[70] In the case of a farm, a clod of earth fulfilled this function; for a house, a roof tile; for a flock of sheep, a single ewe or even a piece of wool from its fleece. Whether we are concerned with a fragment of a saint or the holy ground on which they had trod, this legal concept of presence may be worth taking into consideration.

Notes

1. Bagatti 1949; Hen 1999; Nagel 2010.
2. On these sites see now, Arnold 2013, esp. 68–76, 112–14 on the imprints.
3. Reudenbach 2005; Bagnoli *et al.* 2010, 36.
4. Waitz 1887, 176.
5. Cowdrey 1995, 741.
6. Rogers 1992, 178.
7. Orth 1994, 176; Andrea 1997, 126.
8. See, for example, the 14th-century Glastonbury relic list; Carley and Howley 1998, 94–5.
9. Duchesne 1955, vol. I, 465.
10. Krusch 1885a, 503.
11. Atsma 1987, 682, nos 71–2, 55.
12. Savvaitova 1872, col. 108–9.
13. Waitz 1878; Bouet, Otranto and Vauchez 2003, 1–4; for the dating see also Everett 2002. Arnold 2013, 70, suggests a first redaction in the mid-6th century.
14. Atsma 1987, 682, no. 9, 42.
15. McCormick 2001, 298, 304–5.
16. Ellger 1989, 82–3, 238, 242.
17. Cipolla and Buzzi 1918, 292; Destefanis 2002, 116–17; Saracco 2007, 229.
18. Hänggi 1957; Müller 1971, 409.
19. Toker 2009, 246, though see pp. 62 and 68 for the identification of the stone as a sculpted image; Tacconi 2005, 95, 97 n. 42, where the text is given as 'de lapide in quo sanctus Michael apparuit'.
20. Bouet and Desbordes 2009, 90–103.
21. For example, Toussaint 2003; Buettner 2005; Bagnoli 2010.
22. Wittekind 2004, 174.
23. Bagnoli *et al.* 2010, 88.
24. Lütolf 1918, 180–1; Reinle 1956, 80–7; Müller 1971, 410. I am most grateful to Jakob Bernet, Librarian of the Chorherrenstift Beromünster, for his assistance and to Theres Bütler for permission to reproduce her photographs of the cross.
25. Geyer 1965, 141.
26. Atkinson 1922, 413; Binski 1995, 142.
27. Huygens 1994, 90.
28. Dunbabin 1990, 94–6.
29. Musurillo 1972, 16–17.
30. de Hartel and Kamptner 1999, 271; Halm 1866, 86.
31. Kelly 2003, 88–9.
32. Buettner 2005, 55–6.
33. Mauskopf Deliyannis 2004, 200.
34. Talbot 1952, 123.
35. Bouet *et al.* 2003, 3.
36. Ibid., 3–4.
37. Bouet and Desbordes 2009, 99, 305; Bougy 2009, 145–7.
38. Bouet and Desbordes 2009, 292–5.
39. Worm 2003.
40. Luard 1880, 81–2.
41. Destefanis 2001, 347.
42. For discussion of comparisons drawn between worked ivory and the flesh of the martyrs, however, see Guérin 2013, 65–6.
43. Toussaint 2005, 89.
44. Bouet and Desbordes 2009, 305–7.
45. Ibid., 315–21.
46. Bougy 2009, 258–73.
47. Bouet and Desbordes 2009, 321–3.
48. Ibid., 97–9.
49. Ibid., 308–13.
50. Krusch 1885b, 753.
51. Geyer 1965, 123–4.
52. Bouet and Desbordes 2009, 150.
53. Ousterhout 1998, 394.
54. Du Cange 1885, 415–16.
55. Chambers 1872, 143; McRoberts 1971, 475.
56. Innes 2000, 31; Ragnow 2002.
57. Migne 1853, cols 715b–16b.
58. Beaune 1999, 714–15.
59. Tabuteau 1988, 128–30; Clanchy 1989, 175–7.
60. Guillouët 2004; I am most grateful to John McNeill for this reference.

61 Alexander 1970, 235–6.
62 Tabuteau 1988, 126–7, 344, n. 123.
63 Tabuteau 1988, 338, n. 42; Brittain Bouchard 1987, 38.
64 Keats-Rohan 2006, 24.
65 Maines 1986, 83; Nilgen 1999, 39–41; Dosdat 2006, 117.
66 Bouet and Desbordes 2009, 293.
67 Dubois 1966, 567–9.
68 Nilgen 1999, 41.
69 Mulders and Demeulenaere 1985, 85.
70 Gordon and Robinson 1988, 415.

Bibliography

Alexander, J.J.G. 1970. *Norman Illumination at Mont St Michel 966–1100*, Oxford.

Andrea, A.J. (ed.) 1997. *The Capture of Constantinople: The "Historia Constantinopolitana" of Gunther of Pairis*, Philadelphia.

Arnold, J.C. 2013. *The Footprints of Michael the Archangel: The Formation and Diffusion of a Saintly Cult, c. 300–c. 800*, New York.

Atkinson, A.G. (ed.) 1922. *Close Rolls of the Reign of Henry III Preserved in the Public Record Office*, 6, *AD 1247–1251*, London.

Atsma, H. *et al* (eds) 1987. *Chartae Latinae Antiquiores: Facsimile Edition of the Latin Charters Prior to the Ninth Century*, 19, France, 7, Dietikon, Zurich.

Bagatti, P.B. 1949. 'Eulogie Palestinesi', *Orientalia Christiana periodica*, 15, 166.

Bagnoli, M. 2010. 'The stuff of heaven. Materials and craftsmanship in medieval reliquaries', in Bagnoli *et al*. 2010, 137–47.

Bagnoli, M., Klein, H.A., Mann, C.G. and Robinson, J. (eds) 2010. *Treasures of Heaven: Saints, Relics and Devotion in Medieval Europe*, Baltimore and London.

Beaune, C. 1999. 'Les ducs, le roi et le Saint Sang', in *Saint-Denis et la royauté. Études offertes à Bernard Guenée*, Paris, 711–32.

Binski, P. 1995. *Westminster Abbey and the Plantagenets: Kingship and the Representation of Power, 1200–1400*, New Haven and London.

Bouchard, C. Brittain 1987. *Sword, Miter, and Cloister: Nobility and the Church in Burgundy, 980–1198*, Ithaca and London.

Bouet, P. and Desbordes, O. (eds) 2009. *Chroniques latines du Mont Saint-Michel (IXe-XIIe siècle)*, Avranches and Caen.

Bouet, P., Otranto, G., and Vauchez, A. (eds) 2003. *Culte et pèlerinages à Saint Michel en occident: Les trois monts dédiés à l'archange*, Rome.

Bouet, P., Otranto, G., and Vauchez, A. (eds) 2007. *Culto e santuari di san Michele nell'Europa medievale / Culte et sanctuaires de saint Michel dans l'Europe médiévale*, Bari.

Bougy, C. (ed.) 2009. *Le Roman du Mont Saint-Michel*, Avranches and Caen.

Buettner, B. 2005. 'From bones to stones: reflections on jeweled reliquaries', in *Reliquiare im Mittelalter*, ed. B. Reudenbach and G. Toussaint, Berlin, 43–59.

Carley, J.P. and Howley, M. 1998. 'Relics at Glastonbury in the fourteenth century: an annotated edition of British Library, Cotton Titus D.vii, fols. 2r–13v', *Arthurian Literature* 16.

Chambers, W. 1872. *Charters and Documents Relating to the Burgh of Peebles with Extracts from the Records of the Burgh, A.D. 1165–1710*, Edinburgh.

Cipolla, C. and Buzzi, G. (eds) 1918. *Codice diplomatico del monastero di S. Colombano di Bobbio fino all'anno MCCVIII*, 2, Rome.

Clanchy, M.. 1989. 'Reading the signs at Durham Cathedral', in *Literacy and Society*, ed. K. Schousboe and M. Trolle Larsen, Copenhagen, 171–82.

Cowdrey, H.E.J. 1995. 'Pope Urban II and the idea of Crusade', *Studi medievali*, 3rd ser. 36, 721–42.

de Hartel, W. and Kamptner, M. (eds) 1999. *Sancti Pontii Meropii Paulini Nolani opera*, vol. 1, *Epistulae*, CSEL 29, 2nd rev. edn, Vienna.

Deliyannis, D. Mauskopf (ed.) 2004. *The Book of Pontiffs of the Church of Ravenna*, Washington DC.

Destefanis, E. 2001. '*Sanctorum caenubia circuire*. Il monastero di Bobbio e il suo territorio sulle vie del pellegrinaggio altomedievale', *Bollettino storico-bibliografico subalpino* 99, 337–62.

Destefanis, E. 2002. *Il monastero di Bobbio in età altomedievale*, Florence.

Dosdat, M. 2006. *L'Enluminure romane au Mont-Saint-Michel*, Rennes.

Du Cange *et al*. (ed.) 1885. *Glossarium mediae et infimae latinitatis*, vol. 4, Niort.

Dubois, J. 1966. 'Le trésor des reliques de l'Abbaye du Mont Saint-Michel', in *Millénaire monastique du Mont Saint-Michel*, vol. I, *Histoire et vie monastiques*, ed. J. Laporte, Paris, 501–93.

Duchesne, L. (ed.) 1955. *Le Liber pontificalis: Texte, introduction et commentaire*, 3 vols, rev. edn, Paris.

Dunbabin, K. 1990. '*Ipsa deae vestigia* … Footprints divine and human on Graeco-Roman monuments', *Journal of Roman Archaeology* 3, 85–109.

Ellger, O. 1989. *Die Michaelskirche zu Fulda als Zeugnis der Totensorge: Zur Konzeption einer Friedhofs- und Grabkirche im karolingischen Kloster Fulda*, Fulda.

Everett, N. 2002. 'The *Liber de apparitione Sancti Michelis de monte Gargano* and the hagiography of dispossession', *Analecta Bollandiana* 120, 364–91.

Geyer, P. (ed.) 1965. *Itineraria et alia geographica*, CCSL 175, Turnhout.

Gordon, W.M. and Robinson, O.F. (trans) 1988. *The Institutes of Gaius*, London.

Guérin, S.M. 2013. 'Meaningful spectacles: Gothic ivories staging the divine', *Art Bulletin* 95/1, 53–77.

Guillouët, J.-M. 2004. 'Une sculpture du XVe siècle et son contrat. Le "Pas de l'ange" à La Trinité de Fécamp', *Bibliothèque de l'École des chartes* 162, 133–61.

Halm, K. (ed.) 1866. *Sulpicii Severi libri qui supersunt*, CSEL 1, Vienna.

Hänggi, A. 1957. *Der Rheinauer Liber Ordinarius (Zürich Rh 80, Anfang 12. Jh.)*, Freiburg.

Hen, Y. 1999. 'Les authentiques des reliques de la Terre Sainte en Gaule franque', *Le Moyen Âge: Revue de'histoire et de philologie* 105/1, 71–90.

Huygens, R.B.C. (ed.) 1994. *Peregrinationes tres: Saewulf, Iohannes Wirzibgurgensis, Theodericus*, CCCM 139, Turnhout.

Innes, M. 2000. *State and Society in the Early Middle Ages: The Middle Rhine Valley, 400–1000*, Cambridge.

Keats-Rohan, K.S.B. (ed.) 2006. *The Cartulary of the Abbey of Mont-Saint-Michel*, Donington.

Kelly, R.J. (ed.) 2003. *The Blickling Homilies*, London.

Krusch, B. (ed.) 1885a. 'Liber in Gloria Martyrum', in *Gregorii Turonensis opera*, vol. 2, *Miracula et opera minora*, MGH, SRM 1.2, Hannover, 484–561.

Krusch, B. (ed.) 1885b. 'Liber in gloria confessorum', in *Gregorii Turonensis opera*, vol. 2, *Miracula et opera minora*, MGH, SRM 1.2, Hannover, 744–820.

Luard, H. Richards 1880. *Matthaei Parisiensis, monachi Sancti Albani Chronica majora*, vol. 5, *AD 1248–AD 1259*, London.

Lütolf, K. 1918. 'Dörflingers Reliquienverzeichnis von Beromünster', *Zeitschrift für schweizerische Kirchengeschichte* 12, 157–97.

Maines, C. 1986. 'Good works, social ties, and the hope for salvation: Abbot Suger and Saint-Denis', in *Abbot Suger and Saint-Denis: A Symposium*, ed. P. Lieber Gerson, 76–94.

McCormick, M. 2001. *Origins of the European Economy: Communications and Commerce, A.D. 300–900*, Cambridge.

McRoberts, D. 1971. 'The cult of St Michael in Scotland', in *Millénaire monastique du Mont Saint-Michel*, vol. III, *Culte de Saint Michel et pèlerinages au Mont*, ed. M. Baudot, Paris, 471–9.

Migne, J.-P. (ed.) 1853. 'Libellus de revelatione, aedificatione et auctoritate Fiscannensis monasterii', *Patrologia Latina* 151, cols 699–724.

Mulders, I., and Demeulenaere, R. (eds) 1985. 'Victricius. De laude sanctorum', in *Foebadius, Victricius, Leporius, Vincentius Lerinensis, Evagrius, Ruricius*, CCSL 64, Turnhout, 51–93.

Müller, I. 1971. 'Zum Frühmittelalterlichen Michaelskult in der Schweiz', in *Millénaire monastique du Mont Saint-Michel*, vol. III, *Culte de Saint Michel et pèlerinages au Mont*, ed. M. Baudot, Paris, 393–420.

Musurillo, H. (ed. and trans.) 1972. *The Acts of the Christian Martyrs*, Oxford.

Nagel, A. 2010. 'The afterlife of the reliquary', in Bagnoli *et al*. 2010, 211–22.

Neveux, F. 2003. 'Les reliques du Mont-Saint-Michel', in *Culte et pèlerinages à Saint Michel en occident: Les trois monts dédiés à l'archange*, ed. P. Bouet, G. Otranto and A. Vauchez, Rome, 245–69.

Nilgen, U. 1999. 'Le *Cartulaire du Mont-Saint-Michel* et la miniature anglaise', in *Manuscrits et enluminures dans le monde normand (Xe-Xve siècles)*, ed. P. Bouet and M. Dosdat, Caen, 29–49.

Orth, P. (ed.) 1994. *Gunther von Pairis, Hystoria Constantinopolitana*, Hildesheim.

Ousterhout, R. 1998. 'Flexible geography and transportable topography', in *The Real and the Ideal in Jewish, Christian and Islamic Art*, ed. B. Kühnel, Jerusalem, 393–404.

Ragnow, M. 2002. 'Ritual before the altar: legal satisfaction and spiritual reconciliation in eleventh-century Anjou', in *Medieval and Early Modern Ritual: Formalized Behavior in Europe, China and Japan*, ed. J. Rollo-Koster, Leiden, 57–79.

Reinle, A. 1956, *Die Kunstdenkmäler des Kantons Luzern*, vol. 4, *Das Amt Sursee*, Basel.

Reudenbach, B. 2005. 'Reliquien von Orten. Ein frühchristliches Reliquiar als Gedächtnisort', in *Reliquiare im Mittelalter*, ed. B. Reudenbach and G. Toussaint, Berlin, 21–41.

Rogers, N. 1992. 'The Waltham Abbey relic-list', in *England in the Eleventh Century*, ed. C. Hicks, Stamford, 157–81.

Saracco, M. 2007. 'Il culto di San Michele nell'Italia settentrionale: sondaggi e prospettive d'indagine', in *Culto e santuari di san Michele nell'Europa medievale / Culte et sanctuaires de saint Michel dans l'Europa médiévale*, ed. P. Bouet, G. Otranto, and A. Vauchez, Bari, 219–39.

Savvaitova, P. (ed.) 1872. *Kniga Palomnik, Puteshestvie Novgorodskogo Archiepiscopa Antoniya v Tsargrad v Kontse 12-go Stoletiya*, St Petersburg.

Tabuteau, E. Zack 1988. *Transfers of Property in Eleventh-Century Norman Law*, Chapel Hill and London.

Tacconi, M. 2005. *Cathedral and Civic Ritual in Late Medieval and Renaissance Florence: The Service Books of Santa Maria del Fiore*, Cambridge Studies in Palaeography and Codicology 12, Cambridge.

Talbot, C.H. (ed.) 1952. *Sermones inediti B. Aelredi abbatis Rievallensis*, Series Scriptorum S. Ordinis Cisterciensis 1, Rome.

Toker, F. 2009. *On Holy Ground: Liturgy, Architecture, and Urbanism in the Cathedral and the Streets of Medieval Florence*, London and Turnhout.

Toussaint, G. 2003. 'Heiliges Gebein und edler Stein. Der Edelsteinschmuck von Reliquiaren im Spiegel mittelalterlicher Wahrnehmung', *Das Mittelalter* 8, 41–66.

Toussaint, G. 2005. 'Die Sichtbarkeit des Gebeins im Reliquiar – eine Folge der Plünderung Konstantinopels?', in *Reliquiare im Mittelalter*, ed. B. Reudenbach and G. Toussaint, Berlin, 89–106.

Waitz, G. (ed.) 1878. 'Liber de apparitione sancti Michaelis in Monte Gargano', MGH, *Scriptores rerum Langobardicarum et Italicarum saec. VI–IX*, Hannover, 540–3.

Waitz, G. (ed.) 1887. 'Angilberti abbatis de ecclesiae Censulensi libellus', MGH, Scriptores 15.1, Hannover, 173–9.

Wittekind, S. 2004. *Altar – Reliquiar – Retabel: Kunst und Liturgie bei Wibald von Stablo*, Cologne.

Worm, A. 2003. 'Steine und Fußspuren Christi auf dem Ölberg. Zu zwei ungewöhnlichen Motiven bei Darstellung der Himmelfahrt Christi', *Zeitschrift für Kunstgeschichte* 66, 297–320.

Chapter 5
The Saint and the King
Relics, Reliquaries and Late Medieval Coronation in Aachen and Székesfehérvár[1]

Scott B. Montgomery

Upon his arrival at Aachen for his coronation as *Rex Romanorum* (King of the Romans) on 8 November 1414, King Sigismund of Hungary was greeted at the Kölntor – the city's eastern gate – by a procession of civic officials, clerics and dignitaries, including Charlemagne himself in the form of his massive reliquary bust:

> And at about the fifth hour, when the king was entering the gate with his queen following him directly, the king dismounted from his horse and humbly kissed the cross, which the deacon was holding in his hands and which he respectfully held up to the mouth of the king, and then bowing his head the king showed his reverence for the head of blessed Charles, which had been carried there and was being held by two canons.[2]

Given the impressive size and weight of the larger-than-life reliquary bust, it is hardly surprising that it took two canons to hold it (**Pl. 1**). More noteworthy is the way in which the reliquary is described as the head of Charlemagne himself – 'capiti beati caroli'. Equally describing the shape, subject and contents of the reliquary, such fluid terminology evidences the way in which the reliquary itself is held to be the metallic epidermis of the saint himself.[3] Saint and figural reliquary fuse into a single entity; a sacred person whose presence is signalled by the familiar form of the reliquary and whose active agency is facilitated through its portage by the two, presumably struggling, canons. In being thus processed to the city gate, Charlemagne, as both saint and quintessential German 'Roman' emperor, personally greeted his successor at the point of entry to the coronation city.[4] After dismounting and venerating the head, Sigismund followed it to the coronation ceremony in the cathedral, the former palace chapel of Charlemagne:

> The king mounted his horse and his queen followed him directly on her horse, and directly in front of the king, the Lord Duke of Saxony, the only other mounted person, carried (the king's) sword. The head of the blessed Charles was carried immediately in front of this duke, and in front of the head was a procession which proceeded toward the monastery....[5]

The new emperor was thus welcomed by his forebear who literally led him to his coronation as saint, patron of the chapel and hallowed predecessor to the throne. In venerating the relics of his forebear who so actively participated in the ceremony, Sigismund was directly and closely connected with the grand tradition of imperial lineage stemming from Charlemagne. This ritual practice underscores the central role played by reliquaries (particularly figural ones that visualize venerable, holy predecessors) in the process of asserting rightful succession by legitimizing new kings through the means of saintly blessing.

The continuation of this practice is evidenced in the *ordo* of the entrance and coronation of Emperor Frederick III on 15 June 1442.[6] Sigismund's 1414 coronation appears to have served as the template for the *ordo* for the coronation of Frederick III. Upon his arrival at Aachen, Frederick was met by a procession that escorted him to the cathedral. 'Before the Emperor and the princes...are carried the head of St Charles the Emperor and other relics in the afore-mentioned procession, which then proceeds to the cathedral of St Mary in the city.'[7] Johann Bürn von Mohnhausen's account goes on to elaborate:

... after that the great head of St Charles the Emperor on which sits a golden crown, which has an arch on the top and a cross on the front, as an emperor would wear. Before it come twelve men, bearing horns made from bell metal, playing in praise and honour of the relics and the new king. Pilgrims and other folk also sound horns, in accordance with tradition in Aachen, that a new king is greeted with a great sound.[8]

Observing the imposing scale of the bust, Bürn also pays particular attention to its crown, possibly even obliquely alluding to the crown's use in the actual coronation of Frederick, as appears to have been the case at other coronations, which will be discussed below. Regardless of whether this was on Bürn's mind or not, he clearly indicates the importance of the reliquary, its crown and the fanfare with which it was processed.

This tradition carried on into the 16th century, as attested by a number of sources.[9] In the guise of his reliquary bust, Charlemagne personally greeted his successor, Charles V, who dismounted and with great humility kissed the reliquary in 1520.[10] Similarly, the proceedings for the coronation of Ferdinand I on 11 January 1531 began as all the priests and clergy gathered and waited at the city gate to greet the emperor. Among other relics, they brought with them 'the head of Emperor Charles the Great' with which they escorted the emperor and empress to the church of Our Lady.[11] It seems that through the imposing presence asserted in the form of his massive reliquary bust, Charlemagne both oversaw and participated in the crowning of his successors.

While numerous relics were carried in these coronation processions, each account singles out the head of Charlemagne for special mention. The impressive size of the reliquary bust boldly asserts Charlemagne's grandeur and importance, as he literally appears greater (in size) than other reliquary figures in the Aachen treasury alongside which it would have been displayed. While the imposing scale of the Charlemagne reliquary allows it to be more visible in processional use as discussed above, the inordinately large size also fashioned an image of Charlemagne as greater, more important and more visually dominant than other saints visibly juxtaposed through their presence in smaller, more life-sized reliquary heads. Charlemagne dominates the nexus of sacrality and kingship that is concentrated in his palace chapel in the centre of the coronation city. Through his reliquary bust Charlemagne played a central and active role in the coronation rituals, his huge reliquary visage dominating the proceedings. On some occasions the crown from the bust played an even more active and crucial role in the crowning itself. Eigil von Sassen's account of the 1414 crowning of Sigismund states that Sigismund was crowned with the crown from the head of Charlemagne while '...the king remained seated on the throne. Thereupon the king was given the Gospels and garbed in the alb, stole and the crown from the head of Emperor Charles.'[12] By this, I suggest that he means the reliquary bust – which literally contained the head of Charlemagne and was perceived and described as the actual head of Charlemagne ('capiti beati caroli'). The placement of the crown on the new emperor's head during the coronation itself is described specifically as using 'the crown from the head of Emperor Charles'. While this could be

Plate 1 Reliquary bust of Charlemagne, c. 1349, silver, partially gilded, semi-precious stones, antique gems and cameos. Cathedral Treasury, Aachen (photo: Art Resource, NY)

understood as a rhetorical flourish denoting the symbolic origin of the crown used in the 1414 coronation, a more literal reading suggests that the crown might have been physically lifted from the reliquary bust – thus Charlemagne's actual head – and placed upon the head of the new ruler. The crown sat atop the head of the reliquary bust, directly above the relic cavity and thus literally sitting atop the real cranium of the saint.[13] Given the common reference to the reliquary bust as the actual head of Charlemagne and the Savoyard ambassador's 1414 description of the archbishop setting the 'coronam de capite Karoli Magni' upon Sigismund's head, it seems highly likely that the ceremony involved the passage of crown from saint to king through the participation of the reliquary bust.[14] In being thus crowned with the very crown from the head of Charlemagne, the king's legitimacy as the heir to the throne of his illustrious and holy predecessor is brilliantly and effectively proclaimed. Not only is it proclaimed, but it is also sanctioned and indeed enacted by the saintly king through his relics. The role of the reliquary bust of Charlemagne is central to these coronation rituals, from the moment of the king's entry into the coronation city to the very act of handing his crown to his successor.

The crowning of Charles IV as *Rex Romanorum* on 25 July 1349 involved similar imperial relic veneration and may have been the first instance of the ritualized use of the Carolingian

Plate 2 Scenes of Charles IV acquiring relics, mid-14th century. Mural in St Mary's Church, Karlštejn Castle (photo: Erich Lessing/ Art Resource, NY)

emperor's relics to valorize the Holy Roman Emperor. The timing of the coronation – on the feast of St James – seems to have been by design, as St James and Charlemagne are closely linked in hagiography and legend, such as the widely circulated Pseudo-Turpin chronicle of Charlemagne's exploits in Spain.[15] Furthermore, it seems equally by design that Charles IV's coronation coincided with the initiation of the septennial ostensions of relics at Aachen, Maastricht and Cornelimünster – itself a ritualized display of the most potent relics in the region.[16] Indeed, as Koldeweij notes, the ostension is first documented at Aachen in 1349 and may have been initiated in conjunction with Charles IV's coronation.[17] The coincidence of coronation, the public display of substantial relic collections and possibly the first appearance and coronation use of the Charlemagne reliquary bust seems by design to legitimize Charles IV's rule as both holy and Roman, cast in the model of his saintly namesake.

However, Charles placed particular emphasis on linking himself to Charlemagne, to whom he claimed a blood relationship through his grandmother, Margaret of Brabant. Charles fostered such comparison through a series of ecclesiastical foundations and relic donations.[18] As Iva Rosario has noted, Charles was 'keen to demonstrate that he belonged to an imperial tradition' in part to legitimize his rule in light of his rather troubled ascendancy following the dispute with, and death of, Ludwig the Bavarian.[19] In the extensive decoration of his residence at Karlštejn Castle in Bohemia, Charles IV is regularly paired and compared with his great namesake. To bolster his claims, Charles IV pushed the parallel with Charlemagne further by having himself and Charlemagne depicted wearing identical crowns in paintings in the St Mary and St Katherine chapels at Karlštejn (**Pl. 2**). Indeed, a very similar crown is worn by the reliquary bust in Aachen. In drawing this connection between Charles IV and his sainted namesake's reliquary, the Karlštejn paintings further the notion of Charles as a new Charlemagne. Hilger has gone so far as to suggest that Charles IV had his own features used for the face of Charlemagne on the Aachen reliquary bust.[20] While it is clear that Charles drew parallels between himself and his

saintly namesake, I am not wholly convinced that the reliquary bust of Charlemagne literally bears the features of Charles IV. Nonetheless, this would be in keeping with the abundant evidence that Charles clearly fashioned himself as a 'New Charlemagne' and strategically used visual culture to underscore this parallel. This visual parallel may have included the active participation of Charlemagne's relics through the means of the reliquary bust in the coronation of Charles IV. Given the evidence of the bust's prominent role in later coronation rituals, both in the *adventus* procession and the physical coronation itself, it is possible that the coronation of Charles IV set the precedent by initiating these practices.

Ernst Günther Grimme has suggested that the reliquary bust was created and donated after Charles IV's 1349 coronation.[21] This would echo his earlier donation of the crown from his 1347 coronation as king of Bohemia to the reliquary bust of St Wenceslas in the cathedral of St Vitus in Prague.[22] While the subsequent processional activity of the bust is well documented as a standard feature of Aachen coronations, as noted above, the origin of this practice is not certain and may actually stem from Charles IV. This would not be surprising, given that Charles IV's 1347 *Ordo ad coronandum regem Boemorum* essentially codified the rituals for the crowning of the kings of Bohemia.[23] Given Charles' interest in establishing normative rituals of coronation, we might look here for the origin of the use of the Charlemagne reliquary bust in Aachen. Certainly, the 1349 coronation was unusual, given the absence of the imperial crown due to opposition from supporters of Ludwig the Bavarian. Might it have been unusual enough to prompt the exigency of conscripting the sainted emperor into legitimizing the proceedings? Is it possible that the reliquary bust of Charlemagne and its massive crown that appears to have been used in the coronation were actually fashioned for this occasion and not as a post-coronation donation? It is generally accepted that the crown which Charles IV had created for his coronation was subsequently donated to the reliquary bust.[24] However, it is also possible that Charles' coronation crown and the reliquary bust were fashioned together prior to, and even for, the coronation ceremony. In this scenario, Charles IV literally gave his coronation crown in advance to Charlemagne's reliquary, and in doing so received it from him, in an astute political move that linked the two rulers whose two heads bore the same crown. A ceremonial exchange is enacted between saint and emperor who trade blessings and veneration. In accepting the gift, Charlemagne's head would demonstrate the saint's approval of his successor's reign, clearly manifested by him allowing his crown to be used for the coronation. In such a case, the reliquary and its crown would be the key props in the ritual performance of this holy mandate, essentially the role that they play in later coronations.

The practice of royalty donating crown-bearing reliquary heads to important religious institutions was certainly not new in the 14th century. Indeed, this can be traced back to the earliest documented head reliquary – that of St Maurice which was given to his titular cathedral in Vienne by King Boso of Burgundy (879–87).[25] This golden head, adorned with precious gems and wearing a jewel-encrusted metal crown, was lost in the 17th century, but is depicted in two 1612 drawings by Nicolas-Claude Fabri de Peirsec.[26] The importance of this donation is attested by its inscription as well as its inclusion in Boso's epitaph, both of which specifically mention the crown.[27] This is but the first recorded instance of a king giving a crown-bearing reliquary head, a practice that was widely followed throughout the Middle Ages. Ritual donation of crowned reliquaries of saints seems to have been a most effective means of drawing associations between the reign of the donor and the sanctity of the holy predecessors, thereby bolstering the ruler's claim to legitimate power. While this was a common practice with a then nearly 500-year-old tradition, Charles IV's possible donation of the Aachen Charlemagne reliquary seems to have consciously pushed the association further. The unusually massive size of the Charlemagne reliquary emphasizes its importance, as he literally appears larger than other saints – truly Charles the Great. Similarities in their crowns, as discussed above, and the active use of the reliquary bust in subsequent coronations suggests that Charles (or his followers) initiated a more dynamic, performative and tightly linked connection between royal donations of reliquary busts and the legitimization of the donor's right to rule. By linking the bust to coronation ritual and emphasizing the 'sharing' of the same crown by ruler and saint, the practice at Aachen elevated and activated the role of crowned, royal reliquary busts in royal propaganda. Whether it was fashioned as Charles' post-coronation votive offering or as an actual prop for his coronation, the Charlemagne reliquary bust subsequently became a key player in German coronation ritual, serving to validate the reign of a new king. Given his established interest in linking himself to Charlemagne, it is at least worth giving consideration to the possibility that the coronation use of the Charlemagne bust was, in fact, initiated by Charles himself.

Charles IV further pursued the connection to his saintly predecessor with the relocation of relics of Charlemagne to Prague in 1351, where they were placed in the Augustinian abbey dedicated to Charlemagne and the Assumption of the Virgin Mary in Prague Neustadt.[28] In both shape and dedication, the octagonal chapel was intended to invoke the German coronation church in Aachen.[29] Just as Charles IV had journeyed west to Charlemagne's 'court' for his coronation, this relic *translatio* carried the sainted emperor eastwards to Charles' realm. It seems that Charles IV and Charlemagne engaged in an ongoing practice of ritualized gift exchange and patronage – an interface that bolstered Charles' claims to imperial legitimacy.

The perceived success of such ritualized propagandistic use of the Charlemagne reliquary in the coronation ceremony seems to have prompted similar practices in the kingdom of Hungary. The modelling of Hungarian rituals after those in Germany demonstrates the symbolic potency of the German practices, revealing the status of the German coronations as worthy of association by imitation. Knowledge of the form of German coronation rituals is extremely likely in Hungary, given the large numbers of Hungarian pilgrims documented at Aachen and Cologne during the later Middle Ages.[30] Hungarian kings performed coronation rituals that aligned themselves with the older,

venerable and successful German model, and in doing so used Hungary's own saintly royal past to validate them in much the same way as German kings did with Charlemagne. This emulation of the use of reliquaries in coronation ritual to self-legitimize was doubtless prompted by a desire to harness the history of sainted Hungarian kings in much the same way as Charlemagne's legacy had been co-opted in the service of the German rulers. The careful orchestration of Charlemagne's relics (and reliquaries) in the service of his heirs to the imperial throne appears to have been an important determining factor in the selection of this model for emulation. It is interesting that it was neither French nor Byzantine coronation models that were the main source of influence for the Hungarian ones. Hungarian kingship aligned itself with a Germanic model in terms of holy and pious rule asserted through the use of relics and reliquaries in coronation ritual, as had been effectively practised at Aachen for a century.

Coronation practices very similar to those enacted at Aachen can be seen in the crowning of the kings of Hungary, particularly in the 15th century. During the coronation of Wladislaus I of Hungary on 17 July 1440 in the coronation basilica of Székesfehérvár, the crown was literally lifted from the head reliquary of St Stephen of Hungary and placed on the new king's head, as clearly described by canon Dlugosz of Krakow: '…the golden crown was taken from the head of King Stephen and placed on the head of the king… '.[31] As may have been the case with the Aachen coronation of Charles IV, extenuating circumstances seem to have prompted this use of an alternate crown:

> … seeing nonetheless that this kingdom could not do without the swift protection of a suitable king, that the same most serene lord King Wladislaus (was) of equal devotion and shared our desire, we have established, disposed and decreed that he should be crowned with the other golden crown, an ancient work, of the most blessed Stephan, Apostolic king and our patron, which is in the case of the head reliquary of the same man and has thus been preserved with much veneration.[32]

The importance placed on the fact that the crown from the reliquary bust of the saintly founder of Hungarian Christian kingship was specifically used might be explained by the absence of the actual Crown of St Stephen which the Hapsburgs would not relinquish for the ceremony.[33] The crown of St Stephen was necessary for a legitimate coronation performed at the saint's titular church in Székesfehérvár. In its absence, this critical piece of coronation regalia was replaced by the repurposed crown lifted directly from the head of St Stephen himself, by means of his reliquary bust.[34] Through contact with the relic, made possible through the relic's public face – the reliquary bust – the replacement crown was tantamount to the actual crown of St Stephen, as it was literally worn by the saint. Dlugosz describes the ritual as 'in…modum coronatione perfecta', implying that nothing was amiss and the surrogate crown was every bit as legitimate as the traditional coronation crown.[35] The substitute crown – worn by the reliquary, and thus St Stephen himself – proved more than sufficient in legitimizing the reign of Wladislaus as a rightful successor to the crown of Stephen. Although it is not clear whether or not

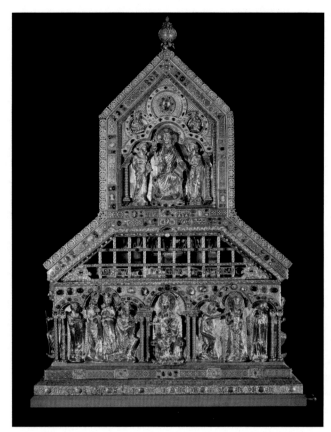

Plate 3 Nicholas of Verdun, shrine of the Three Magi, short side with grate for relic viewing and scenes of the Adoration of the Magi with donor Emperor Otto IV and Christ's Baptism, begun in 1181, gold, enamel, precious stones, cameos and antique gems. Cologne Cathedral (photo: Erich Lessing/Art Resource, NY)

Plate 4 Reliquary bust of St Ladislaus, between 1357 and 1378, silver, partially gilded, and enamel. Györ Cathedral, Hungary (photo: author)

this practice had been initiated with the 1349 coronation of Charles IV, as discussed above, given the conscious modelling of some of the Hungarian coronation rituals on those held at Aachen it is worth considering that this might be the case, particularly given Charles' familial connections to Hungary. Regardless, the active use of a crowned reliquary bust of a saintly regal predecessor to legitimize a potentially challenged accession to the throne offers a parallelism that at least reveals the widely acknowledged and accepted propagandistic potential of such royal reliquaries.

In coronations, both normative and exceptional, relics played a key role in sanctifying the proceedings and furthering political agendas. Both the Aachen and Székesfehérvár coronations were followed by pilgrimage to, and ritual veneration of, the relics of saintly kings. German emperors travelled to Cologne to pray before the relics of the Three Magi in Cologne Cathedral. The emperor's first act of venerating the head of his sainted predecessor Charlemagne in Aachen was followed by his honouring of the quintessential and prototypical saintly kings: the Three Magi in Cologne.[36] This practice is documented as early as the coronation of Henry VII as *Rex Romanorum* on 6 January 1309.[37] The timing of the event on the feast of the Epiphany emphasized this connection between Christian kings as Henry VII travelled to venerate his holy regal predecessors on the feast day celebrating the Three Kings' own sacred journey to venerate another king. The representation of Otto IV essentially as a fourth magus on the short side of the Shrine of the Three Magi further visualizes the ongoing connection between

saintly kings, Christian emperors, relic veneration and regal legitimacy (**Pl. 3**).[38] The ritualized act of post-coronation pilgrimage and veneration conscripts the Three Magi as essentially proto-German kings, whose benediction further bestows a holy mandate to rule upon the new king.

Hungarian kings travelled considerably further from the coronation city of St Stephen – Székesfehérvár – to the relics of the other great Hungarian king – St Ladislaus – enshrined in the cathedral of Nagyvárad far to the east in the Kingdom of Hungary.[39] By the 14th century this was standard practice for Hungarian coronations.[40] While the rituals in Hungary and Germany are not exactly parallel, they are most decidedly conceptually concordant. In Germany the ritual began with the reliquary bust of Charlemage and ended with the relics of the Three Magi in their shrine in Cologne. In Hungary, it began with the reliquary bust of St Stephen in Székesfehérvár and ended with the relics of St Ladislaus in his shrine and the reliquary bust in the cathedral of Nagyvárad. As I have discussed elsewhere, the late 14th-century reliquary bust of St Ladislaus, which was the culminating focus of the pilgrimage to Nagyvárad, appears to have been at least conceptually modelled upon the mid 14th-century reliquary bust of Charlemagne, which served as the opening focus in German coronation ritual (**Pl. 4**).[41] In both cases, venerating relics of saintly predecessors served as bookends to the actual crowning, literally placing the new ruler's ascendance within a clearly demarcated tradition of holy rule. The heads, crowns and head reliquaries of sainted regal predecessors provided the alpha and omega of the inaugural ceremonies of their earthly successors. In his coronation peregrination, the new king moved through space and time between the defining parameters established by relics, especially the gilded, bejewelled and crowned heads of his saintly regal predecessors. It seems that the success of the ritualized performance in Aachen prompted the modelling of Hungarian coronation ritual after that practised in the Holy Roman Empire. Indeed, as Fügedi has established, the coronation city of Székesfehérvár was itself at least partially based on Aachen.[42] Given that the Hungarian coronation city was fashioned as something of a 'new Aachen', it is not surprising that the coronation rituals which were enacted at Székesfehérvár were equally inspired by those at Aachen.

In 1352, Nagylajos (Louis the Great/Louis I of Hungary) performed a votive pilgrimage to Nagyvárad whereupon he donated a silver crown to the shrine of St Ladislaus, an act that paralleled the recent donations of crowns to reliquaries of Charlemagne and St Wenceslas in Aachen and Prague respectively.[43] The most extensive and adamant linking of the Hungarian and German (Holy Roman) post-coronation pilgrimage practices occurred in 1357 with the ritualized peregrination of Charles IV (along with the Hungarian Queen Mother, Elizabeth) from Hungary to Prague to the Rhineland – specifically to Aachen and then Cologne. This last section of his journey essentially traced the path of the German kings' post-coronation pilgrimage. At Aachen, a Hungarian chapel was founded in the former palace chapel of Charlemagne, further asserting the strong German-Hungarian connection that was at least partially developed by linking royal saints with the Charlemagne legacy. This chapel would receive generous gifts of relics of the three sainted Hungarian kings of the Árpád dynasty: Stephen, Imre and Ladislaus. Like the transfer of relics of Charlemagne to Prague in 1351, the translation of the Hungarian relics united the holy kings of Hungary and Germany both literally and symbolically, as they rested in accord under one vault. From the resting place of the prototypical German king in Aachen, the imperial pilgrimage travelled to Cologne to venerate the prototypical Christian kings – the Three Magi. Here too a Hungarian chapel was founded and dedicated to Hungary's own three kings (Stephen, Imre and Ladislaus). As such, it would appear as though Hungarian royal rituals and related regal pilgrimage of both coronation and sacro-political votive offerings were modelled upon those practised in the Holy Roman Empire, at least in terms of the propagandistic use of relics.

Medieval coronations and the rituals of dynastic cults have been thoroughly and brilliantly examined by Ernst Kantorowicz, Percy Schramm, János Bak, Gábor Klaniczay and many others.[44] My intent here is to further this discussion by noting the central, active and even performative role played by relics – and specifically reliquaries – within these profoundly symbolic rituals. There is still much work that needs to be done in order to understand the larger picture, but I have aimed to highlight both the role of reliquaries and the effectiveness of such practices which prompted emulation in other kingdoms. As demonstrated by the examples discussed herein, relics and

their reliquaries were often among the most significant and active agents in this process of political legitimization. These reliquaries were not so much props but active participants in the coronation ritual, literally framing and validating the event. This was effective enough propagandistically so that when the traditional coronation insignia were not available, an alternate crown, lifted directly from the reliquary of a sainted royal predecessor, could effectively serve to legitimize an otherwise potentially questionable coronation, as was the case with Wladislaus I of Hungary in 1440. The validity of the replacement crown was directly resultant from the belief that the relics of the saint constituted the presence of the saint and the reliquary bust was tantamount to the saint's flesh. A crown worn by a reliquary was *ipso facto* a crown worn directly by the saint. Hence, it was the direct involvement of the saint's body through the means of the metallic skin that performed the requisite connection between sainted royal forebear and newly crowned king. The active performance of the reliquary bust in the coronation ceremony, such as at Aachen and Székesfehérvár, articulated this image of legitimacy and continuity. Post-coronation peregrination to heads and bodies of saintly regal predecessors at Cologne and Nagyvárad provided the omega to the alpha role played by the reliquary busts at the actual coronation proceedings held at Aachen and Székesfehérvár. The use of, and movement between, royal relics and reliquaries fashioned a four-dimensional nexus of visualizing the legitimacy of new rule, as the recipient of the crown moved through space and time to suitably honour his predecessors whose own active participation demonstrated approval of the new reign. From Aachen to Cologne, Székesfehérvár to Nagyvárad, and from saint to king, relics of holy regal predecessors served as key players in legitimizing the coronation of a new ruler.

Notes

1   I would like to thank James Robinson and Anna Harnden in particular for orchestrating such a superb and stimulating conference and for inviting me to include this paper alongside the excellent work of the august contributors to the conference and this volume. Thanks to Sarah Faulks for her superb editing of this volume. I am delighted to have the opportunity to revisit and rethink this material, some of which found its origin in my doctoral dissertation, 'The use and perception of reliquary busts in the late Middle Ages' (PhD dissertation, Rutgers University, 1996). For helpful insight and discussion regarding this material I thank Alice Bauer, Elizabeth McLachlan, Sarah McHam, Laura Gelfand, Vibeke Olson, Janet Snyder, Sally Cornelison, Erik Inglis, Elizabeth Pasten and doubtless others whose names are only omitted due to my own memory malfunctions. For splendid help with bibliography, I thank my research assistant Katherine Rousseau. Profound thanks to my wonderful wife – Alice – and our three darling girls – Francesca, Gabriella and Serafina – for always making it all worthwhile.
2   '…et hora quasi quinta rege portam imtrante cum regina eum immediate sequente, rex de equo descendit et crucem, quam decanus in minibus suis tenebat et ori regis reverenter applicuit, humiliter osculabatur et deinde inclinando caput reverentiam exhibuit capiti beati caroli, quod ibi per duos canonicos portatum tenebtauer' (Aachen Reichstagakten 7, 245 f., Nr. 168). Printed in Kaemmerer 1961, 76.
3   Grimme notes that in the reliquary bust the form and the contents (relic and reliquary) fused into an inseparable unity – the image and actual presence of Charlemagne. See Grimme 1992–3, 66. Regarding the conflation of reliquary images and relics in general, see Montgomery 1996.

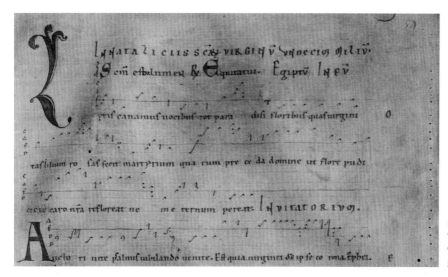

Plate 2 Ursuline office (chants for first Vespers and Matins: 'Letis canamus' and 'Auctori vite'), c. 1167. Bayerische Staatsbibliothek, Munich, Clm 9921, f. 54

Group 5
- Abbey of Villers-en-Brabant, Cistercian abbey, church province of Cologne: Source D.
- Abbey of Rupertsberg/Bingen, Benedictine abbey, church province of Mainz: Source R.

Essen (Source E: Düsseldorf, Universitätsbibliothek D3)

The oldest source discussed here comes from the imperial abbey of Essen, a community of *sanctimoniales* situated approximately 60km from Cologne where the cult started. The abbey was founded for women from Saxon nobility by Bishop Altfrid around 850. In the 10th century, the community became an Ottonian family abbey, governed consecutively and for a considerable period by abbesses such as Mathilde II (973–1011), Sophia (1011–39) and Theophanu (1039–58), all members of the imperial family. It was probably during Mathilde's reign that the sacramentary, a book with texts recited by the officiating priest during the Mass and written originally in the middle of the 10th century, received additions in the margins, including Lauds in honour of Cologne's virgins. According to the calendars and hagiographic sources, this took place when Pinnosa still occupied Ursula's place as the leader of the group of virgins.[25]

Therefore, this earliest source of the office of St Ursula only offers us the possibility of studying the text, since there is no musical notation. One might consider it the beginning of an office tradition, and the chant texts from this oldest source remain unchanged during several centuries; Lauds in particular would become the core of the new offices in honour of Cologne's virgins.

Quedlinburg (Source Q: Berlin, Staatsbibliothek Preussischer Kulturbesitz Mus. Ms. 40047)

The second oldest source comes from the imperial abbey of Quedlinburg,[26] founded by Emperor Otto I in 936, in one of the Ottonian empire's political, spiritual and cultural centres. Queen Mathilde was succeeded as the abbey's ruler by Otto's daughter Mathilde II (966–99) and then by Adelheid (999–1044), sister of Otto III. The abbey was an important part of the inner circle of Ottonian power for over 100 years and it is during this period when the antiphoner, one of the oldest German liturgical manuscripts with musical notation, was written (most probably at the abbey's own scriptorium).[27]

Elements of the virgins' cult are to be found in the calendar that was written at the same time as the antiphoner, but by another scribe. S*anctarum virginum* has been notated there for the date of 21 October. The *Chronica et historiae aevi Saxonici* from 1039 relates how in 1021, when the new abbey church was dedicated, relics of *sanctarum virginum de Colonia* were kept in at least one of the altars of the church.[28] One might imagine that the cult had been introduced to Quedlinburg from the imperial abbey of Essen, both Ottonian and closely related.

Comparing the calendar and the antiphoner of source Q, we see the more specific rubric *In nativitate sanctarum virgines* on folios 110v–111 containing the same Lauds as in source E and an additional Vespers antiphon. The texts of the chants are inspired by the *Sermo in natali* not using the name of Ursula but still that of Pinnosa.

This source gives us the opportunity to study an early office in a neumatic notation without any staff lines. There are so-called adiastematic neumes (*neuma*, Greek for 'gesture', used as a melodic sign, and *diastema*, Greek for 'interval') with no precise interval or pitch indication readable only in comparison to later versions. The melodic signs in the Quedlinburg antiphoner can be considered as so-called German neumes.

Ottobeuren (Source O: Munich, Bayerische Staatsbibliothek Clm 9921)

In the 12th century the imperial abbey of Ottobeuren was a flourishing spiritual and intellectual centre in south-west Germany, especially under the abbots Rupert (1102–45) and Isingrim (1145–80). Rupert introduced the Benedictine Hirsau Reform,[29] transformed the abbey into a double convent and built a new abbey church in Ottobeuren, while his successor Isingrim concentrated on improving the cultural environment, including the abbey's library and scriptorium. In the course of their liturgical reform, a substantial number of manuscripts were produced in the abbey's scriptorium.

In 1167, only a few years after the discovery of the skeletons in Cologne, the translation of relics (five whole bodies, three halves and two fragments)[30] of St Ursula to

Ottobeuren led to the establishment of the St Ursula feast day. The miscellaneous manuscript Clm 9921, probably written at the same time, contains various music-related texts and treatises, as well as a complete versified office which is considered to be one of the most compelling sources of Ursuline offices. Ottobeuren's Lauds have their origins in the earlier non-prose tradition composed about 100 years previously, as we have seen in the Essen and Quedlinburg antiphoners. These prose Lauds have been compiled with the new versified parts of the office and they are undoubtedly an interesting example of how old and new elements became part of a dynamic liturgy throughout the centuries.

The musical notation of the complete Ursuline office cycle appears in this manuscript with so-called Lotharingian neumes, signs originating from the Metz region which give relatively precise information about the number of notes to be sung to a syllable and the melodic movement. These neumes are written on a four-line staff carved into the parchment with the tip of a knife, the F-line being coloured with red ink. All lines begin with a clef letter; clefs do not designate an absolute pitch, they only establish half and whole steps of the melody indicating its tonality (**Pl. 2**).

Zwiefalten (Source Zw: Karlsruhe, Badische Landesbibliothek, KA Aug. 60)

Another antiphoner comes from the Benedictine abbey of Zwiefalten, founded in 1089 by monks from Hirsau and situated at this point on the southern boundary of the Mainz church province. Virtually no medieval remnants have survived, except for those from the reconstruction of the baroque period. Between the 11th and 14th centuries the community functioned as a double monastery, above all for members of noble families from the surrounding area, especially to those from the county of Achalm. Under the direction of Abbot Berthold, two bodies of the Eleven Thousand Virgins were translated from Cologne to Zwiefalten in 1145.[31] Zwiefalten had a close relationship to Hildegard's abbey at Rupertsberg and so monks, including Berthold, assisted in the copying of Hildegard's work.

The antiphoner from the 12th century, possibly used by the female community, contains an almost complete Ursuline office, specifically three chants for first Vespers, complete Matins and Lauds and a Magnificat antiphon for the second Vespers. The older Lauds chants might have been imported with the relics from Cologne, while the other chants are almost identical to those from Ottobeuren.

The 13th-century musical notation is a palimpsest notation over so-called German neumes (from the 11th century); early gothic neumes are carefully executed on a four-line staff with C and F clefs. Psalm tones are not specified, whereas melodic modes are indicated by numbers.

Himmerode (Source H: Trier, Stadtbibliothek, Hs. 412/1737 4°)

Himmerode, a Cistercian abbey near Trier, was founded by Bernard of Clairvaux in 1134. Shortly after, in the second half of the 12th century, its first abbot, Randolph, started to construct the abbey church in the Romanesque style. Around 1171 the monastery, closely related to Hildegard of

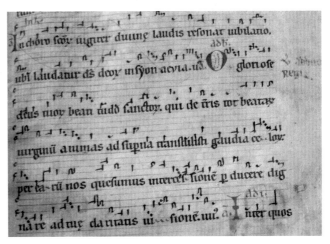

Plate 3 Ursuline office (chants for Lauds: 'In choro sanctorum' and 'O gloriose deus'), late 12th century. Stadtbibliothek, Trier, Hs. 412/1737 4° f. 100

Bingen and her convents, was a flourishing location for manuscript production. It is possible that the skeleton discovery in Cologne or the exchange between the monks and Hildegard could have inspired the introduction of the Ursuline office found in source H (**Pl. 3**).

The antiphoner, handed down from the Municipal Library of Trier, presents a complete Ursuline office on folios 96v–100v as well as a hymn and a second incomplete office on the first folio (in another hand). The neumatic notation is early gothic from the 12th–13th century, written on a four-line staff with clefs C, F and G. In some passages, a red F-line has been used, but only when necessary for the melody.

Abbey of St Cassius, Bonn (Source Bo: Cologne, Historisches Archiv des Erzbistums Köln, St Severin A II 3)

For a long time, it was believed that this manuscript came from the Benedictine abbey of St Severin in Cologne. However, thanks to the recent work of Andreas Odenthal and Albert Gerhards,[32] we know that before coming to Cologne, the book had been produced and used at the St Cassius Abbey in nearby Bonn. This abbey, a canons' community founded in the 7th century, was one of the most important abbeys in the medieval archdiocese of Cologne and was situated on a direct road leading from Bonn to St Ursula in Cologne. In addition to the presence of the *Liber Ordinarius* of the St Cassius abbey in the manuscript, the patrons' feast of St Cassius and St Florentius has the most solemn initials in the antiphoner, followed by offices for St Ursula and St Severin which are clearly celebrated in Bonn as well. How exactly the manuscript came to the abbey of St Severin, most probably in the 16th century, cannot be explained yet. As both abbeys have very similar liturgical traditions, the book could have been used in Cologne as well by this date.

The antiphoner dates from late 12th to early 13th century, with some later additions. In the earlier *Sanctorale* section that dates from the late 12th century, there are parts of an Ursuline office with an antiphon and responsories for Matins and the complete earlier Lauds, notated in gothic notation on a four-line staff, with a red F line and a yellow C line.

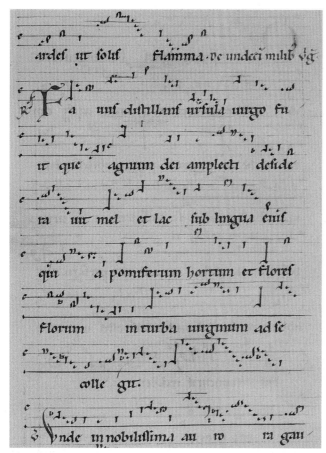

Plate 4 Hildegard's Ursuline chants (responsory 'Favus distillans'), second half of 12th century. Hessische Landesbibliothek, Wiesbaden, Hs. 2 f. 471v

Tongeren (Source To: Den Haag, Koninklijke Bibliotheek 70 E 4)

The Ursuline cult extended from monastic to urban communities such as the canons of the Church of Our Lady in Tongeren, which during the entire Middle Ages was part of the church province of Cologne. This manuscript, 70 E 4 with liturgical fragments, is considered to be part of the canon's oldest liturgical writings, the Ursuline office being notated around the year 1300 when the Church of Our Lady attracted many pilgrims, especially from Cologne. Several fires destroyed the chapter's library, which might explain why only a few fragments of liturgical manuscripts have been preserved over the centuries.

On folios 105–106v one discovers chants for first Vespers, incomplete Lauds – almost all of the chants are to be found in the earlier Lauds tradition – and some chants for the second Vespers. The notation is a gracefully written early gothic notation, on a five-line staff including a red F line.

Zutphen (Source Zu: Zutphen, Gemeentearchief, ZU a 6)

An antiphoner from Zutphen fully notated with neumes, partly written in the 15th and then the 16th century, is still to be found in the town's archives. In the 11th century, the town was part of the diocese of Utrecht and the church province of Cologne. By then, the first church dedicated to St Walburga had been constructed where, from the early 12th century onwards, a canons' community assured the chant of the daily liturgy. In the 15th and 16th centuries, the same community collected a fine library, the *librije*.

The large antiphoner could have been used in the daily Liturgy of the Hours of the 15th and 16th centuries, since by then the oral tradition of chant transmission had been replaced by sight-reading from often large choir books on two-sided lecterns. Only the manuscript's summer part (late medieval liturgical books are often split into two parts, summer and winter) from the 15th century survives, which contains offices in honour of St Walburga and St Ursula and the Eleven Thousand Virgins. For a long time relics of the virgins had been venerated in this church before being translated to Antwerp in the 16th century.

The Ursuline office is presented on folios 144r–147v with chants for first and second Vespers and for Matins and Lauds, notated in late gothic neumes on a four-line staff.

Villers-en-Brabant (Source D: Dendermonde – Abdij S. Pieter en Paulus, Codex 9)

The two major manuscripts with Hildegard of Bingen's compositions also include parts of an Ursuline office. The highly unique chants could have been completed by chants of other 'Benedictine offices' during the feast in honour of St Ursula, but at present there is no evidence to suggest that Hildegard's chants were inserted into the liturgy at one of her convents.

There is a clear temporal link between the skeleton excavations in Cologne (1155–63) and Hildegard's composition of Ursuline chants. The manuscript destined for the Cistercian abbey of Villers-en-Brabant also contained Hildegard's visionary work *Liber vitae meritorum* and Elisabeth of Schönau's *Liber Viarum Dei* and can be dated to after 1163. Almost all of Hildegard's chants, except for the *Ordo Virtutum* and some possibly later composed chants, are united in this 'quasi-liturgical' part of the manuscript. Although the chants are ordered with rubrics and follow different feasts and saints, it is not entirely comparable to the *sanctorale* part of an antiphoner. The collection forms a kind of anthology for certain feasts, from which one could select one or more chants to complete the 'usual' office.

Hildegard seemed to have been particularly inspired by St Ursula as she composed entire Lauds offices, Matins' responsories, a hymn and even a sequence in her honour. It is possible to speculate that it was the sensational discovery of bones, accompanied by the commissioned visions of Elisabeth of Schönau[33] that revealed the names of hundreds of Ursula's companions or the following traffic with the relics which inspired her to compose these chants. With relics comes liturgy, and so the feast day of 21 October must have been introduced into both of Hildegard's abbeys soon after. Even if this chant collection was destined for Villers-en-Brabant, it could possibly reflect the chant practice of Hildegard's own convents.

The notation is early gothic on a four-line staff, including a red F line and a C clef.

Rupertsberg (Source R: Wiesbaden, Hessische Landesbibliothek Hs. 2)

It may seem surprising that as an abbess of the elite convent of Rupertsberg, Hildegard was clearly inspired by this expression of mass piety driven by the discovery of Ursula's relics and the subsequent boom of the cult of the saint and her companions. With her liturgical compositions she indubitably helped to spread the cult of St Ursula during the 12th century.

As previously discussed, two of the surviving manuscripts with Hildegard's chants contain complete Ursuline Lauds and other chants for the Liturgy of Hours. The Rupertsberg manuscript, called Riesenkodex, had been compiled in Hildegard's own scriptorium, shortly after her death in 1178. Moreover, this collection contains Hildegard's visionary writings *Scivias*, *Liber vitae meritorum*, *Liber divinorum operum*, her *vita*, as well as most of her correspondence and compositions. It is probable that the older chant section was notated during Hildegard's lifetime.[34] It is highly possible that the codex was destined after Hildegard's death to be part of her canonization process, which was only achieved in 2012.[35]

Almost all of Hildegard's chants, including the *Ordo Virtutum* are put together in this 'quasi-liturgical' fascicle. As in the Villers manuscript (Source D), the chants are notated in an anthological order with rubrics, following different feasts and saints. Most certainly, this collection of chants offers reliable insight into the musical and liturgical practice of Hildegard's convents at Rupertsberg and Eibingen.

The notation is very similar to that of the Villers manuscript, early gothic on a four-line staff, including a red F line and a C clef (**Pl. 4**).

Conclusion

It has been noted that there was a strong relationship between the development of the cult of St Ursula and hagiographic texts mentioning the names and numbers of St Ursula and her group of companions, calendars, the existence of relics in a monastery or a church and specific local or regional liturgical traditions at these locations.

The early transmission of the cult can be observed within Ottonian monasteries (Essen and Quedlinburg) in the 10th and 11th centuries, mostly inspired by relic translation and hagiographic texts. It was during this time when the core Lauds were composed, which would be integrated almost unchanged into new offices over the following centuries.

The surge in the following of the cult of St Ursula in the 12th century resulted in its expansion to south-western German Benedictine monasteries founded or transformed during the Hirsau Reform. Despite their rather centralized approach to the veneration of saints, they do appear to have tolerated specific local traditions, often supported by relic translations accompanied by new hagiographic texts such as the Ursula Passions, which then led to the composition of a specific versified office joining the earlier Lauds. Cistercian monasteries such as the abbey of Himmerode also received relics and in addition to the core Lauds imported from Cologne, they established a further new Ursuline office in the 13th century. Over the following centuries the cult spread to urban communities such as those in Bonn, Tongeren and Zutphen – all situated in the church province of Cologne – where new Ursuline chants were also composed.

Hildegard can be considered a special case. It is clear that Hildegard was directly inspired by the large scale excavations in Cologne and by Elisabeth of Schönau's revelations, and so supported a veneration of Ursula and the virgin saints of Cologne in her Benedictine communities, as can be seen in her own liturgical chants.

In conclusion, one sees how Ursuline offices are, in addition to the art works and relics of St Ursula, an intriguing example of the growth of a local saint cult in the Middle Ages. The life cycle of a saint's popularity could develop over a period of years, even hundreds of years, and sometimes their cult eventually disappeared. In this way St Ursula is a very good example of a cult's cyclical evolution. The Ursuline repertoire was undoubtedly part of a rich liturgical and musical tradition which travelled across medieval Christian Europe and remained part of the *sanctorale* for several centuries. Even if her feast day is no longer celebrated, the many art works representing Ursula or the Eleven Thousand Virgins keep her present in our memories still today.

Notes

1 De Voragine 1850, 701–5.
2 'Das älteste Denkmal und den festen Kern der Ursula-Legende bildet die Inschrift des Clematius' ('The Clematius inscription forms the oldest monument and the core of the legend') Levison 1928, 3.
3 'monasterium sanctarum virginum extra muros Colonia' (de Buck 1858, 215).
4 According to the *Sermo in natali*, Pinnosa or Winnosa was the daughter of Brittania's king. See also Schubel 1941.
5 Peter Brown observes how 'the careful noting of the anniversaries of the deaths of martyrs and bishops gave the Christian community a perpetual responsibility for maintaining the memory of its heroes and leaders.' Brown 1982, 31.
6 Calendar from Herfurt: Milan, Bibl. Pinacoteca Ambr. M 12 sup.
7 Litany from Cologne: Köln Erzbischöfl. Diözesan und Dombibl. Ms.106 f. 74r.
8 See the Latin text edition of the *Sermo in natali* in de Buck 1858, 154–5 and the English translation in Sheingorn and Thiébaux 1996, 45–54.
9 A litany from Cologne mentions Martha, Saula, Paula, Brittola and Ursula and the calendar of the same manuscript which can be dated to the end of the 10th century. *In Colonia XI milia sanctarum virginum*: Köln Erzbischöfl. Diözesan und Dombibl. Ms.88 f.10r.
10 See the Latin text edition of the first Passion *Fuit Tempore* in Levison 1928, 145–57.
11 Dahmen 1953, 26.
12 See the Latin text edition of the second Passion *Regnante Domino* in de Buck 1858, 157–63 and the English translation in Sheingorn and Thiébaux 1996, 15–37.
13 The Passion *Regnante Domino* mentions a *martyrium sanctarum undecim milium virginum* (see previous note).
14 This work took place outside Cologne's ancient city wall when they wanted to enlarge the city *intra muros*. Peter Brown states: 'The rise of the Christian cult of saints took place in the great cemeteries outside the cities of the Roman world: and, as for handling of dead bodies, the Christian cult of saints rapidly came to involve the digging up, the moving, the dismemberment (…) of the bones of the dead, and frequently, the placing of these in areas from which the dead had once been excluded.' Brown 1982, 4. Individual excavations of skeletons had already begun in 1105, but it was only the larger excavations that took place between 1155 and 1164 which led to the substantial traffic of relics related to St Ursula.
15 See Theoderich of Deutz (*c.* 1164), *Revelationes titulorum*, in Holger-Egger 1883, 569–70. The only copy of the manuscript with the lists of names has been lost since the Second World War.
16 See Elisabeth of Schönau between 1157–8 in *Liber Revelationum*, edited in de Buck 1858, 163–73.
17 See Schmitz and Wirbelauer 1991 for an excellent discussion of the tituli and the revelation of names in the 12th century.
18 Holger-Egger 1883, 570.
19 I would prefer not to place St Ursula and the Eleven Thousand Virgins in a specific liturgical group, but rather as patron saints

since we know that Hildegard's community had received relics of the virgins after the excavations in Cologne. All Eleven Thousand Virgins' chants, which may reflect Hildegard's own liturgical practice, are notated among chants of patron saints (Disibod, Rupert or the Virgin Mary) in the Riesenkodex manuscript. See also Newman 1988.

20 In my opinion, there was no erroneous reading of *XI milium*, but rather a wish to establish a strong cult in Cologne with the 11,000 female martyrs fulfilling the role of protector of the town. As Arnold Angenendt writes: 'Das Mittelalter hat die eigenen Märtyrer gefeiert und zugleich das Martyrium der Alten noch weiter gesteigert. Die Zahl der Märtyrer erhöhte sich wie die Grausamkeit ihrer Leiden. Ein besonders eindrückliches Beispiel bietet die heilige Ursula mit ihren elftausend Jungfrauen in Köln, deren bis in die Spätantike zurückreichende Kirche dort auf dem nördlichen Gräberfeld steht.' ('The Middle Ages celebrated their own martyrs and amplified the martyrdom of earlier martyrs. The number of martyrs was raised as well as the cruelty of their sufferings. St Ursula with her 11,000 virgins of Cologne, whose Late Antique church is located on a northern burial site, offers a particularly impressive example.') (Angenendt 1997, 37). See also Montgomery 2009, where he thoroughly reviews different opinions concerning the history of names and numbers.

21 'Mit der Untersuchung der Clematius-Inschrift greift er bis in das christliche Altertum zurück; er macht Halt am Ende des 12. Jahrhunderts, als die Legende zum Abschluss gekommen war und die Gestalt erreicht hatte, in der sie so oft von Künstlerhand klassischen Ausdruck gefunden hat.' ('With his research about the Clematius inscription he goes back to the antique Christianity and he only ends at the turn of the 12th century when the legend was fully formed as we can see in many artworks of an almost "classical" expression.') Levison 1928, 2.

22 Scott Montgomery speaks of 'the corporate nature of the cult in the Middle Ages' in Montgomery 2009, 4.

23 Double monasteries were composed of a male and a female community, living in different buildings and celebrating the divine office either collectively in a common church or in separate churches. They were ruled together by an abbot, sometimes also by an abbess.

24 Rules for *sanctimoniales* are less strict than for sisters, as they may keep private property and leave the convent while sisters have to give up all their property and take eternal vows of chastity and *stabilitas* (i.e. commitment to a particular monastery).

25 In the calendar, written at the same time as the addition, we find on 28 February the mention of *Translacio sancte Pinnose*.

26 This text has been part of the Berlin Staatsbibliothek collection since the 19th century.

27 See Fliege 1978; Möller 1990, 44.

28 Pertz 1839, 87.

29 The Hirsau Reform was inspired by the 11th-century Cluny Reform and initiated by Wilhelm of Hirsau in 1069, firstly in his own Benedictine abbey of Hirsau and followed by more than 120 mostly German abbeys including Ottobeuren and Zwiefalten.

30 See a parchment fragment containing a list of relics in Ottobeuren's abbey in the second half of the 12th century, now kept in Munich, Hauptstaatsarchiv, Urk. Kl. Ottobeuren 1a.

31 '*Translatio duarum virginum* – Heae sanctorum reliquiae pio labore domni Bertolfi, patris huius loci quarti, nobis sunt acquisitae: Duo integra corpora sanctarum XI milium virginum Coloniae pro Christi passarum …' ('Translation of two virgins – the following holy relics have been aquired by the pious effort of Lord Bertolf, fourth abbot of this place: two entire bodies out of the holy XI thousand virgins of Cologne, who gave their lives for Christ…'); Pertz 1852, 92.

32 Odenthal and Gerhards 2008.

33 In 1156 Abbot Gerlach of Deutz, who led the excavations in Cologne, sent two relics to Schönau as well as the tituli (inscriptions of martyrs' names which were said to be found with the bodies) in order for Elisabeth to prove their authenticity through her visions and add new names to the list. See Levison 1923, 115–20.

34 Many thanks to Michael Embach from the Stadtbibliothek in Trier for having suggested this earlier dating based on codicological research.

35 It is worth mentioning that more than 800 years later in 2012, Hildegard was canonized and since October 2012 she has been officially recognized as one of the very few female *doctores ecclesiae*. See 'The sybil of the Rhine doctor of the Church', *La Stampa*, 16 December 2012. Her canonization took place by decree, not by a process, on 10 May 2012. See *Litterae decretales de peracta Canonizatione aequipollente Hildegardis Bingensis. Benedictus Episcopus Servus Servorum Dei, ad perpetuam rei memoriam*: 'Itaque ad Dei gloriam, ad exaltationem fidei et vitae christianae incrementum, apostolica Nostra ex auctoritate decernimus ut Hildegardis Bingensis, monacha professa Ordinis sancti Benedicti sancta sit et Sanctorum Catalogo adscribatur ac pia devotione recoli et inter Sanctos Ecclesiae Universalis invocari debeat.' ('With apostolical authority for God's honour, the increase of faith and Christian life, we canonize Hildegard of Bingen, nun of the order of St Benedict, and inscribe her in the catalogue of saints to be piously venerated and invoked among the saints of the Holy Universal Church.').

Bibliography

Angenendt, A. 1997. *Heilige und Reliquien*, Munich.

Brown, P. 1982. *The Cult of the Saints*, Chicago.

Dahmen, O. 1953. *Das Kölner Sankt-Ursula-Problem auf Grund der Ausgrabungen in den Kriegsjahren 1942 und 1943*, Aachen.

De Buck, W. 1858. *Acta Sanctorum Octobris Tome IX*, Antwerp, Brussels, Tongerlo and Paris.

De Voragine, J. 1850. *Legenda Aurea*, ed. T. Graesse, Leipzig (2nd edn).

Fliege, J. 1978. 'Die Handschriften der ehemaligen Stifts- und Gymnasialbibliothek Quedlinburg in der Universitäts- und Landesbibliothek Sachsen-Anhalt in Halle (Saale)', dissertation, Berlin.

Holger-Egger, O. (ed.) 1883. *Monumenta Germaniae Historica*, Scriptores 14, Hannover.

Levison, W. 1928. *Das Werden der Ursula-Legende*, Bonn.

Möller, H. 1990. *Quedlinburger Antiphonar I*, Tutzing.

Montgomery, S. 2009. *St Ursula and the Eleven Thousand Virgins of Cologne*, Oxford.

Newman, B. 1988. *Saint Hildegard of Bingen Symphonia*, Ithaca.

Odenthal, A. and Gerhards, A. (eds) 2008. *Märtyrergrab – Kirchenraum – Gottesdienst* II, Interdisziplinäre Studien zum Bonner Cassiusstift (SKKG 36), Siegburg.

Pertz, G.H. (ed.) 1839. *Monumenta Germaniae Historica*, Scriptores 3, Hannover.

Pertz, G.H. (ed.) 1852. *Monumenta Germaniae Historica*, Scriptores 10, Hannover.

Schmitz, W. and Wirbelauer, E. 1999. 'Auf antiken Spuren? Theoderich, das Benediktinerkloster in Köln-Deutz und die Legende der heiligen Ursula', in *Colonia Romanica* 14, 67–76.

Schubel, F. 1941. 'Die heilige Pinnosa', in *Anglia – Zeitschrift für englische Philologie* 65, 64–80.

Sheingorn, P. and Thiébaux, M. 1996. *The Passion of Saint Ursula and the Sermon on the Birthday of the 11,000 Holy Virgins*, Toronto.

Wallach, L., König, E. and Müller, K.O. 1978. *Die Zwiefaltener Chroniken Ortliebs und Bertholds*, Sigmaringen, 132.

Chapter 7
Picturing Narrative and Promoting Cult
Hagiographic Illumination at Three English Cult Centres

Kathryn Gerry

Accounts of the lives and miracles of the saints, rich with information on the roles played by relics, have provided us with a starting point for investigating the medieval cult of saints and the monumental structures and magnificent reliquaries that were part and parcel of that phenomenon.[1] More often than not, the contents of these *Lives* have been studied as edited texts, disembodied from the manuscripts through which they have been transmitted. Over the last several decades, the manuscripts themselves have received more attention, with a particular focus on the iconographic content of their illustrations and the relationship of iconography to text and historical context.[2] This art-historical focus on illustrated saints' *Lives* has expanded our understanding of how cults were established and promoted, and how visual arts could be used to direct the interpretation of text. Nevertheless, we run the risk of treating pictures as we have previously treated texts, in isolation from the physical matrix of the book. Through an examination of three manuscripts, this essay will demonstrate the fundamental importance of considering the technical and codicological aspects of individual books, alongside their iconographic content and historical context, when seeking to understand how meaning was conveyed through copies of saints' *Lives* and to clarify what that meaning was. By questioning why certain styles and techniques were selected, we can gain a fuller understanding of how those responsible for producing illustrated saints *Lives* sought to situate their products within historical or regional contexts. Furthermore, a consideration of the original structure of a given manuscript and subsequent changes made to that structure can enrich our knowledge of the motivations for producing and keeping those particular books which have survived to the present day.

The three manuscripts in question are the *Life of St Cuthbert*, most likely made in Durham at the start of the 12th century, perhaps in 1104, and now in Oxford (University College, MS 165; **Pls 1–3**); the *Life of St Alexis*, commonly called the Alexis Quire, a booklet consisting of a single gathering that has been bound together with other materials to create the celebrated St Albans Psalter, now at Hildesheim (Dombibliothek, MS St Godehard 1; **Pls 4–7**); and the *Life and Miracles of St Edmund* made for the community of Bury St Edmunds in the 1130s, though perhaps not made entirely at Bury St Edmunds (Pierpont Morgan Library, New York, MS M.736; **Pls 8–9**).[3] Commonly called *libelli* since Francis Wormald's 1952 article put them on the map in the world of medieval studies, manuscripts containing saints' *Lives* as the main text can take a variety of forms, and each of the three discussed in this chapter represents a different approach to arranging and grouping the illustrations and texts associated with a given saint.[4] In this paper I place the Alexis Quire within its proper context as an illuminated saint's *Life*, specifically as one of only three surviving illustrated *Lives* produced in England in the first half of the 12th century. All three of these manuscripts have received a good deal of scholarly attention, but the relationships between them have not. In addition to offering some further comments on the circumstances of and intentions behind their production, my contribution here is to reframe these three as a group and to explore the connections between them. These books should

Plate 2 *Life of St Cuthbert*, early 12th century, chapter 18. University College, Oxford, MS 165, p. 58 (courtesy of The Master and Fellows of University College, Oxford)

Plate 1 *Life of St Cuthbert*, early 12th century, chapter 38. University College, Oxford, MS 165, p. 108 (courtesy of The Master and Fellows of University College, Oxford)

Plate 3 *Life of St Cuthbert*, early 12th century, chapter 55. University College, Oxford, MS 165, p. 163 (courtesy of The Master and Fellows of University College, Oxford)

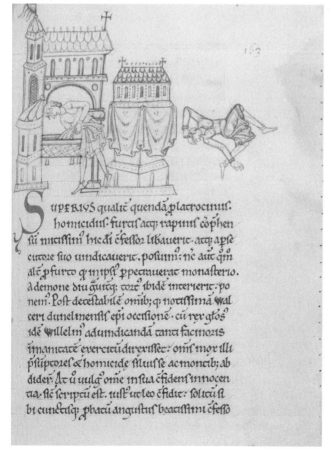

certainly be taken as a group in so far as they provide the only evidence we have of the earliest phases of a developing tradition that would thrive in the 13th century in England. However, as will be demonstrated below, there are closer connections between the three individual books than one might expect, and this in turn offers evidence of how ideas moved between English monastic institutions and their scriptoria in the 12th century.

All three of these manuscripts have been examined and published by a host of familiar names and are often included in discussions of medieval manuscript illumination.[5] But despite the attention researchers have given these books, questions of who first owned them, where they were made and how they were used have not been fully resolved. It has been proposed that all three might have been made for the use of private, individual persons, rather than corporate monastic groups. The question of lay ownership as opposed to religious, whether collective or individual, could easily provide the content for an entire paper; for the moment, it must suffice to point out that the proposals made for lay ownership of these books, while not entirely implausible, are based on tenuous evidence and a fair amount of special pleading.[6] In all three cases, we are confronted with manuscripts that appear to have been made at monasteries containing the lives of saints associated with those monasteries – in the lack of clear and compelling evidence that they were created to be given to individuals outside of those houses, it seems to make the most sense to consider them within a corporate monastic sphere.

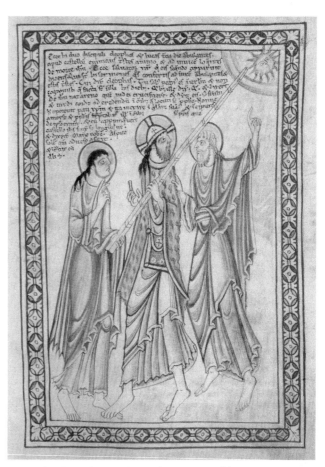

Plate 4 St Albans Psalter, Alexis Quire, *c.* 1120s(?), three scenes from the *Life of Alexis*. Dombibliothek, Hildesheim, MS St Godehard 1, p. 57 (property of the Basilica of St Godehard, Hildesheim, © Dombibliothek)

Plate 5 St Albans Psalter, Alexis Quire, *c.* 1120s(?), Christ on the Road to Emmaus. Dombibliothek, Hildesheim, MS St Godehard 1, p. 69 (property of the Basilica of St Godehard, Hildesheim, © Dombibliothek)

Plate 6 St Albans Psalter, Alexis Quire, *c.* 1120s(?), the Supper at Emmaus. Dombibliothek, Hildesheim, MS St Godehard 1, p. 70 (property of the Basilica of St Godehard, Hildesheim, © Dombibliothek)

Plate 7 St Albans Psalter, Alexis Quire, *c.* 1120s(?), the Disappearance from Emmaus. Dombibliothek, Hildesheim, MS St Godehard 1, p. 71 (property of the Basilica of St Godehard, Hildesheim, © Dombibliothek)

I would like to start with the odd-man-out in this group, the Alexis Quire. Edmund and Cuthbert were both saints with solid established cults in England around the turn of the 12th century, while Alexis, a continental saint, is more often associated with Rome or with the Norman reform movement in north-western Europe.[7] The Alexis Quire is also an outlier in the group because it does not conform to what we have come to expect from hagiographic *libelli*, even in consideration of the great deal of variation usually acknowledged within this group.

Our understanding of the Alexis Quire as an illustrated saint's *Life* has been somewhat muddied by its current position as a part of the St Albans Psalter, a large and richly illustrated manuscript with, as its name suggests, the Psalms and associated material as its core content. The Alexis Quire was first made to stand on its own, but since the middle of the 12th century it has been bound together with the other components of this larger volume. Building on the work of Adolph Goldschmidt and Kristine Haney, I have elsewhere pointed to a number of features that demonstrate that this gathering spent some time as an independent booklet, not bound with the rest of the St Albans Psalter and not intended to be part of a psalter at all until a later phase of adaptation. Furthermore, I have also suggested that it is best considered as a hagiographic *libellus*.[8]

The hagiographic *libellus*, as Francis Wormald defined it, has the *Life* of the saint in question as its core text, and this is often grouped with other texts related to the celebration of that saint, usually in the form of offices, prayers or hymns.[9] The examples Wormald discussed were characterized as being 'smallish quartos, rather square, and [...] usually written in a good hand which frequently resembles the hand of the liturgical books'.[10] The Alexis Quire is smallish, but not tending towards the square and when compared with contemporary manuscripts from St Albans, it is clear that the Alexis Quire was not written in the finest liturgical hand available.[11] However, I think the main obstacle in grouping this small illustrated saint's *Life* with the manuscripts discussed by Wormald, Cynthia Hahn and others, has not been its format but its contents. Although its core is an illustrated hagiographic text, this text is grouped with several other elements, including full-page tinted line drawings of the episode of Christ at Emmaus, a commentary on the importance of spiritual battle with an accompanying illustration, and a large initial B introducing Psalm 1. These components have often been considered as a piece, but in fact the Beatus initial and the marginal text and drawing on the subject of spiritual battle are later additions, and there are clear material indications that they were not part of the original plan for this quire.[12] This leaves us with the three scenes of Christ at Emmaus. Although these depictions are not taken from the Alexis *Life*, I think we should nevertheless understand them as illustrations accompanying that text: their style, format and pictorial content can be seen as a completion of and indeed an expansion of the Alexis narrative. The three-part illustration depicting Alexis at the start of the text depicts the saint departing from home and family to live as an anonymous eremite, unrecognized even by his parents until the moment of his death (**Pl. 4**). The three pictures of Christ represent a key moment in the

recognition of the human Jesus as the divine Messiah, and thus offer an interpretative layer to Alexis's life of anonymity (**Pls 5–7**).[13] Wormald made a point of emphasizing that many of the pictorial cycles used to illustrate saints' *Lives* were modelled on Christological Passion cycles in order to imply that the saints in question were following in the footsteps of Christ.[14] Implicit in the manuscripts Wormald described, this relationship between the saint and his ultimate exemplar is made explicit in the Alexis Quire, where a direct pictorial link is established between Alexis and Christ.

The other two manuscripts considered in this paper, the *Lives* of Cuthbert and Edmund now in Oxford and New York respectively, were part of Wormald's core group, and Barbara Abou-El-Haj, Malcolm Baker and Cynthia Hahn, among others, have explored the roles that these two manuscripts played in the promotion of the cults of Cuthbert and Edmund. English examples of illustrated saints' *Lives* blossomed in the later 12th and 13th centuries, perhaps most notably in the work of Matthew Paris, a monk of St Albans Abbey. However, the Cuthbert and Edmund manuscripts have been discussed as the first surviving examples made in England, and the only two to survive from the first half, even the first two thirds, of the 12th century. The Alexis Quire was produced at St Albans Abbey; it is often dated to the 1120s – I might put it a little earlier, perhaps in the late teens – and therefore it should be considered alongside these other two books.[15]

The Cuthbert manuscript is the earliest of the three and conforms most closely to what we might expect of an illustrated saint's *Life* based on continental examples. The principal text of the manuscript is a copy of Bede's *Life* of Cuthbert that also includes excerpts from the *Ecclesiastical History* and a group of later miracles recorded in the 10th and 11th centuries; a copy of the metrical *Life* of Cuthbert has been included at the end of the manuscript.[16] Each chapter of the text is prefaced with an illustration related to the content of that chapter, executed in the technique of tinted line drawing (**Pls 1–3**).[17]

The use of this technique offers an important point of comparison with the Alexis Quire, which is also illustrated with tinted line drawings. Although not unique to England, the technique was often employed in Anglo-Saxon scriptoria and can be found in many of the manuscripts associated with the 10th-century monastic reform movement led by Dunstan, Aethelwold and Oswald. Early 12th-century examples were made at St Albans and other English monasteries, but I think it would be fair to say that the technique might have appeared old fashioned by this time.[18] It has been noted that this particular copy of the *Life* of Cuthbert would have been complete by the time of the translation of the saint's relics in 1104, and I think it is possible, perhaps even likely, that the production of this booklet was intended to coincide with that event.[19] The monastic community at Durham was relatively new at this point, having been founded only in 1083, but the monks considered themselves to be members of Cuthbert's own community at Lindisfarne, re-establishing that house after a long exile.[20] Faced with the imposed authority of a Norman bishop, the monks sought to assert the strength of their patron saint and the close ties that Cuthbert had with members of his community.[21] The first of these aims can be traced in scenes of the potency of the saint's relics, as in the episode in which a Norman knight is struck down after attempting to pillage the shrine (Chapter 55, p. 163; **Pl. 3**).[22] The second goal, highlighting Cuthbert's special relationship with this community of monks, is in part accomplished through a pictorial strategy that emphasizes Cuthbert's reliance on his brethren, as seen in the illustration for Chapter 38, where the monks of Lindisfarne help Cuthbert to his oratory on Farne Island (Chapter 38, p. 108; **Pl. 1**).[23] I think it is likely that the tinted line drawing technique was selected for this manuscript because of its potential to trigger an association with a distant and glorious past, thereby collapsing the temporal distance between Cuthbert's heyday on Lindisfarne and the attempts to revitalize his cult after the community re-established itself at Durham.[24] The use of a technique so often encountered in pre-Conquest manuscripts would emphasize Cuthbert's status as a venerable saint and particularly as a venerable Anglo-Saxon saint.

We find the same technique used in the Alexis Quire, but the background of Alexis is hardly comparable with that of Cuthbert. Alexis had no long-standing ties to the St Albans community and no other local connection, either in the region of St Albans or anywhere else in England. Rather than being a venerable English saint, he was a continental saint, introduced by the newly arrived Norman masters. However, perhaps we should see the same intent here. Anyone steeped in the traditions of Anglo-Saxon monastic book production might well have associated tinted line drawings with the accomplishments of a pre-Norman past. We know that attempts were made to introduce a cult of Alexis at St Albans in the first half of the 12th century; if Alexis's foreignness, and his association with the Normans, was a point of dispute at the monastery, perhaps depicting him in the stylistic guise of a local saint was seen as a way to mitigate such disputes.[25] The Alexis Quire contained new information in a new language about a new saint, but it would have looked, at first glance, like many of the older books in an English monastery.

If the tinted line drawing technique was indeed used for such a similar purpose in both the Cuthbert and Alexis manuscripts, then we must ask whether or not the makers of the later Alexis manuscript were aware of the earlier Cuthbert manuscript. I do not think a direct model would have been absolutely necessary – the tinted line drawing technique appears in several of the manuscripts then in the St Albans library[26] – but there is in fact a direct connection between the two manuscripts that deserves some consideration. The attempts to install a cult of Alexis at St Albans appear to have commenced under Abbot Richard, abbot from 1097 to 1119, who dedicated a chapel to Alexis during his time in office, perhaps when the newly reconstructed church was consecrated in 1115.[27] This same Abbot Richard attended the translation of Cuthbert's relics at Durham in 1104. This was apparently a moving occasion for Richard: the *Gesta abbatum monasterii sancti Albani*, the main historical record for the abbey, records that Richard's arm was healed while he was in Durham, and when he

returned he dedicated a chapel in St Albans to Cuthbert.[28] If the Cuthbert manuscript was in fact displayed at the events surrounding the saint's translation, it seems likely that Richard, and anyone travelling with him, would have seen it. Could he or members of his retinue have been so impressed with this small manuscript of the *Life* of Cuthbert that they decided to produce a similar book to promote their own cult of Alexis? In addition to the same technique, the format of the illustration introducing the Alexis *Life* is notably similar to many of the illustrations in the Cuthbert manuscript. In the Alexis Quire illustration, several scenes divided by an architectural device represent several moments in a narrative, and this compositional arrangement is found in several of the Cuthbert illustrations, where consecutive events within a short span of time are depicted within the same picture (for example, Chapter 18, p. 58; **Pl. 2**). The Alexis picture, executed without a border, takes up about half of the page, and serves as a preface to the text; the same format is found in the Cuthbert manuscript, where each chapter is opened with an unframed drawing which occupies about one-third to one-half of the page. We might even see a similarity in the willingness to break the implied border of the ruled page, extending the pictorial narrative into the margin: in the Alexis Quire, Alexis boards a boat waiting in the margin, and in the Cuthbert *Life*, the twisted body of a Norman knight, stricken after attempting to pillage Cuthbert's shrine, lies in the margin (**Pls 3–4**).

Connections between St Albans and the *Life* of Edmund have been more widely recognized and accepted. Here the connection is not directly between the Alexis Quire itself and the Edmund manuscript, but between the production of manuscripts at St Albans and at Bury St Edmunds. The *Life* of Edmund is usually dated to around 1130, slightly later than the Alexis Quire and a generation or so after the Cuthbert manuscript. This volume contains a pictorial cycle illustrating a version of the saint's *Life* as well as two texts recording the life and miracles of Edmund, lessons for the office of Edmund and hymns. Historiated initials punctuate the textual portions of the book.

Like the St Albans Psalter, the *Life* of Edmund appears to be a composite volume, as Elizabeth Parker McLachlan pointed out in 1965.[29] The prefatory miniatures are not conjoined with the rest of the manuscript – that is, the two sections share no leaves or gatherings – and the colour, texture and thickness of the parchment differ between the pictorial and textual segments. The proportions of the miniatures also differ from the ruled areas of the text.[30] The pictorial cycle is not only codicologically distinct from the rest of the manuscript, but there is a clear disjuncture in both the style and content of the prefatory miniatures and the historiated initials of the text. As C.M. Kauffmann has argued, the version of the narrative followed in the pictorial cycle differs from that of the text copied within the manuscript (**Pls 8–9**).[31] The pictorial cycle was almost certainly intended to preface a copy of Edmund's *Life*, but these discrepancies imply that those responsible for producing the pictorial cycle were not using the Bury text as a guide and were not working in close collaboration with those responsible for the main textual portion of the copy of the *Life* of Edmund now in New York.

Chapter 8
Presentation of Relics in Late Medieval Siena
The Cappella delle Reliquie in Siena Cathedral

Wolfgang Loseries*

In 1359 the large hospital in Siena (**Pl. 1**), Santa Maria della Scala, purchased a treasure of relics from the collection of the Byzantine emperors in Constantinople for the enormous sum of 3,000 gold florins. Siena's government believed that the acquisition would increase the prestige of the city and therefore financed its transfer to Siena and commissioned the head of the cathedral's administration, the rector of the Opera del Duomo, to build a chapel in the hospital where the relics could be stored in a dignified fashion.[1] A pulpit was placed outside the chapel on the hospital's facade where the relics were presented to the assembled faithful once a year. However, the piazza in front of the hospital soon proved to be too small for this occasion and was enlarged in 1371.[2]

This presentation took place on 25 March, the feast day of the Annunciation of the Virgin who was the patron saint of the church of Santa Maria della Scala. This date marked the beginning of the new year in the Sienese calendar. Ever since Siena had dedicated the city to the Mother of God in 1260 (after which date it began to call itself the *Civitas Virginis*), the promotion of the cult of the Virgin had become an affair of the state in which religion and politics were intertwined. As the relics were presented on the important feast day of the Virgin in the presence of government officials, the cult of the relics was closely connected with that of the Mother of God. The feast day of the Annunciation acquired additional glory as a result of the relics, whose significance in turn was increased by this association with the cult of the Virgin.

The purchase invoice of 1359 contains a list of the relics.[3] Those of the Passion of Christ were listed first: a nail and a piece of the Cross, a sponge, a lance, a pole, hairs from Christ's beard and his blood. These items were followed by a list of pieces of the Virgin's clothing and then by the relics of a variety of saints. The intact nail that supposedly held Christ to the Cross was considered the most important relic. A large cult formed around this *Santissimo Sacro Chiodo* (Holiest Sacred Nail); an altar in Santa Maria della Scala was donated to the cause and a fraternity of that name was founded.

The new cult surrounding the hospital's relics grew under the supervision of the bishop, the canons of the cathedral and the rector of the Opera del Duomo. The cathedral and

Plate 1 The Santa Maria della Scala hospital (left) and the cathedral, west facade (right), Siena

Plate 2 (left) Siena Cathedral, east facade (left) and house with sacristy in the upper storey

Plate 3 (above) Sacristy with chapels, Cappella delle Reliquie (left)

the hospital were the two most important religious institutions in Siena, both controlled by the municipal government. In 1383 after a dispute concerning the piazza on which both institutions were located, a marble strip was laid in the piazza to mark precisely the boundary between the cathedral and the hospital.[4] The relationship of these two institutions was therefore also marked by competition, and in many ways the cult of the hospital's relics represented a challenge for the cathedral: at the time the relics from Constantinople were acquired, the cathedral already had similar items. However, they were not stored in as lavish a fashion; they were in the cathedral's sacristy, which at the time was anything but imposing. In 1407 the rector of the Opera del Duomo reproached the members of the government, saying that the sacristy was 'not sufficient [even] for [the chapel of] a little castle and a great shame for the entire city', and called for it to be rebuilt and specifically made 'honourable and beautiful, as the much praiseworthy and venerated church demands'.[5]

A new sacristy building was erected within a few years (**Pl. 2**). In 1408–9, an arch was constructed over the street north of the cathedral so that the sacristy could be expanded from the cathedral to the upper storey of the house on the opposite side of the street. On the northern end of the resulting large room, three vaulted chapels were built (**Pl. 3**). As soon as construction was completed, the sacristy was decorated with stained glass windows, sculptures, paintings, frescoes, furniture and further embellishments. By 1413 the site had already been selected by the municipal government as a prestigious location for the reception of a cardinal.[6] Within a very short period of time, a magnificent late medieval *Gesamtkunstwerk* had been created which the city of Siena could proudly present to its important guests.

In the large hall of the sacristy stood the enormous cabinet for the vestments.[7] The central one of the three chapels was dedicated to the Virgin Mary.[8] The one to the right was furnished as a library with bookshelves, writing desks and furniture for sitting, and the chapel to the left was

intended for the storage of the relics, the Cappella delle Reliquie. All three chapels were decorated with frescoes by Benedetto di Bindo in 1411–12 and their iconography alludes to the function of the room in question.[9]

The unpretentious architecture of the exterior of the sacristy has remained largely intact for more than six centuries. However, its interior has suffered from considerable changes, which also applies to the relic chapel. This space has lost its original function and its poorly preserved frescoes are all that remain of its original decoration. The grille and the furniture were removed; many of the precious gold and silver works of the Gothic, Renaissance and Baroque eras were melted down after the earthquake of 1798 to pay for the repairs to the church. Most of what still remained of the cathedral's treasures after this date was seized shortly afterwards by Napoleon's troops.[10]

Nevertheless, with the aid of documents and pieces of the decoration that survive in the cathedral museum, it is possible to reconstruct the relic chapel. The earliest inventory dates from 1420 and calls the chapel 'richly decorated and beautiful'.[11] Further inventories followed in 1429, 1435, 1439 and later.[12] They list well over 100 different objects in the chapel, beginning with the furnishings, many of which are recorded in the account books of the Opera. The first thing we learn from the early inventories written between 1420 and 1439 is that the area was protected by a beautiful iron grille with a lockable door.[13] The grille was forged by Niccolò di Paolo in 1415,[14] composed of quatrefoils and decorated with candlesticks. Two decades later, the same smith produced the grille for the Cappella dei Signori in the Palazzo Pubblico of Siena. Completed in 1445 after Niccolò di Paolo's death in 1437, it also featured quatrefoil ornaments and mounted candlesticks so it may convey some elements of the lost grille of the chapel for the relics in Siena Cathedral.[15] The relic chapel was lit by a handsome six-armed brass chandelier, bought in 1412, which hung from the centre of the vault.[16] The four inventories mentioned above list it after the grill as the second item, followed by the

Plate 4 Benedetto di Bindo, panels of the Arliquiera (verso, before restoration in early 20th century), 1412, tempera on wood. Museo dell'Opera della Metropolitana, Siena

Plate 5 Benedetto di Bindo and assistant, panel of the Arliquiera (recto, before restoration in early 20th century), 1412, tempera on wood. Museo dell'Opera della Metropolitana, Siena

furniture, beginning with the most important piece, a gilded and painted cabinet for the relics – the so-called Arliquiera (**Pls 4–5, 9–10, 12**), which presumably stood on the wall beneath the window. A walnut table and chairs had been placed in front of the Arliquiera, with benches built along the two side walls. Next in the inventories is a list of relics, figures, altar furnishings and many other items, much of it made of gold and silver, as rings with pearls and precious

Plate 6 Lorenzo Vecchietta, Arliquiera of Santa Maria della Scala (recto, photo early 20th century), 1445–6, tempera on wood. Pinacoteca Nazionale, Siena

stones which were used to decorate a figure of the Madonna, and other treasured objects.

It was not a chapel in the liturgical sense. In place of an altar stood the large cabinet for the relics, and like an altar this Arliquiera had a silk baldachin above it. Its gilded and painted doors survive in the cathedral museum, painted in 1412 by Benedetto di Bindo and his assistant Giovanni di Bindino.[17] In the 20th century, the panels of the Arliquiera, which were painted on both sides, were joined to form eight large cabinet doors and given new frames in a medieval style. It remains uncertain how closely this reconstruction corresponds to the historical reality. It would be helpful for any reconstruction to compare it to the reliquary cabinet built for the hospital in Siena in 1445, which was also painted on two sides by Lorenzo Vecchietta (**Pl. 6**).[18] The Arliquiera in the hospital was made by someone very familiar with the one in the cathedral, and in this case the original frame and structure have been largely preserved. Given space constraints, however, I will not discuss the problem of reconstruction and limit myself to the iconography of the Arliquiera in the cathedral.

The gilded exterior of the cathedral Arliquiera was divided into 32 painted fields, each of which depicts a half-length figure of an angel holding a scroll identifying a relic (**Pl. 5**). On six of these banderoles, the text has entirely or largely disappeared. Text is also fragmentary on the 26 remaining ones, but they are nevertheless sufficiently conserved for them to be assigned to Christ or a saint. Nine relics of Christ are mentioned, and seven of these refer to the

Plate 7 Duccio, *Maestà* (recto), 1308–11, tempera on wood, 370 x 450cm. Museo dell'Opera della Metropolitana, Siena

Passion: the knife with which Peter cut off Malchus's ear during the arrest of Christ, pieces of the column of the flagellation, the wood of the Cross, the sponge, the tombstone and Christ's blood. A piece of a nail from the Cross was also there. The Mother of God appears on four of the scrolls, but in this case damage prevents the identification of all but the milk relic.[19] One of the three illegible Mariological scrolls probably referred to Mary's veil, listed in the inventory of 1420.[20] According to the banderoles, the cathedral had the bodies of the city's four patron saints, previously mentioned in the oldest inventory of 1389: Ansanus, Victor, Savinus and Crescentius (**Pl. 5**).[21] In reality these relics were not – as the scrolls suggest – the preserved corpses of the patrons, but what remained of them after a fire had destroyed the old sacristy probably in the 13th century.[22] Finally, the banderoles name relics of Sts John the Baptist, Agnes and six others.[23]

The list of the relics on the painted exterior of the Arliquiera reflects the cults and the hierarchy of the saints who were especially venerated in Siena. This becomes clear from looking at the painting Duccio produced for the high altar of the cathedral in 1308–11 (**Pl. 7**). Most of the ten saints standing or kneeling at the throne of the Queen of Heaven and her son, surrounded by angels, also appear on the banderoles of the Arliquiera built a century later. Only three saints who appear in Duccio's painting – Catherine, Paul and John the Evangelist – are not represented on the Arliquiera. It is, however, possible that their names were written on the six scrolls whose texts have disappeared. Of the 26 legible banderoles, 20 refer to Christ, the Virgin Mary or the saints at the throne.

Duccio's *Maestà* highlights the four patron saints of the city, kneeling in the foreground. The special significance of these four saints is also evident from the decorations of the sacristy and the Cappella delle Reliquie. Once a year their relics were placed on the high altar in front of the *Maestà*.[24] In 1408, life-size wooden sculptures were commissioned

from Francesco di Valdambrino for this purpose (**Pl. 8**). The four patron saints, gilded and painted by Benedetto di Bindo and Andrea di Bartolo, were depicted as seated and holding gilded boxes containing their own relics. On the anniversary of the cathedral's consecration, the figures were placed on the high altar; otherwise they were found in the relic chapel. Unfortunately, one of these figures has been lost entirely; the other three were sawn up (probably in 1795) and reduced to busts, which are on view today in the cathedral museum.[25] By 1381 the Opera del Duomo had commissioned four silver figures of the patron saints of the city, but only the one of St Ansanus had been finished two years later. In 1413, the municipality decreed that from then on the feast days of the four patron saints would be observed like Sundays when shops were closed and work forbidden.[26] In the same year the

Plate 8 Francesco di Valdambrino, *St Victor*, 1409, wood, h. 35.5 cm. Museo dell'Opera della Metropolitana, Siena

Plate 9 Benedetto di Bindo, panels of the Arliquiera (verso, before restoration in early 20th century), 1412, tempera on wood. Museo dell'Opera della Metropolitana, Siena

Plate 10 *Emperor Heraclius with the True Cross in Front of Jerusalem's Closed City Gate*, detail of Pl. 9 (in its current state)

missing three silver figures were commissioned and Francesco di Valdambrino provided the design for one of them, the statue of St Savinus.[27] The large gilded silver figures, approximately 80cm high, were produced in the years that followed and treasured alongside the figure of St Ansanus in the relic chapel, but have since been lost. The importance of the city patrons, to whom the four chapels next to the high altar of the cathedral were dedicated, and which were furnished with paintings by the Lorenzetti brothers, Simone Martini, Lippo Memmi and Bartolomeo Bulgarini, becomes evident also in the decoration of the sacristy. In 1411–12 four of the sacristy windows received stained glass depictions of the city patrons, created by the Dominican Ambrogio di Bindo, brother of the painter Benedetto di Bindo, possibly after designs by Andrea di Bartolo.[28] Furthermore in 1435–9, Domenico di Bartolo covered the walls of the sacristy with an important fresco cycle dedicated to the same four saints, of which unfortunately only a few fragments survive.[29]

Whereas the outer sides of the doors on the Arliquiera present a list of 32 relics, the inner sides of the doors feature only one: the Cross, the noblest relic of Christianity and its very symbol. The backs of the doors are divided not into 32 fields like the front, but eight larger ones instead.[30] They depict the Finding of the Cross and the Elevation of the Cross – both of which correspond to feast days in the Christian calendar. Benedetto's depictions follow the two stories as told in the *Legenda Aurea* in eight scenes.[31] Scene one:

the Jews of Jerusalem come to an agreement not to assist Empress Helena in the search for the True Cross, out of fear that their religion could be harmed if the Cross is found (**Pl. 4**). Scene two: after Helena threatened to burn the Jews if they did not provide information, they revealed that one of their number, Judas, was the one who knew where the True Cross could be found. However Judas refused to reveal his information. Scene three: the empress had him thrown in a dry well and left him to starve. Scene four: after being tortured in this manner for six days, Judas revealed the place where the Cross was buried. Scene five: The crosses of the two thieves were also found at this location. The power of the crosses was tested on a recently deceased youth to identify the true relic (**Pl. 9**): Christ's Cross brought the dead man back to life. Scene six: Judas took the Cross to the empress and, having been impressed by the miracle, converted to Christianity. He received the baptismal name Quiriacus and became bishop of Jerusalem. The legend further relates that at Helena's request, he searched for and found the nails of the Cross as well. However this part of the story, which would have been interesting for the hospital's relics of which the *Sacro Chiodo* was the most venerated, is not depicted on the cathedral's Arliquiera. Instead, this scene is followed by two episodes from the Elevation of the Cross. Scene seven: after the Persian King Khosrau II had conquered Jerusalem in 615 and looted the True Cross, the Byzantine Emperor Heraclius defeated the Persians in 627 and reclaimed the Cross (**Pl. 10**). When the victorious

Plate 11 Duccio, *Christ and the Samaritan Woman* (originally part of the *Maestà* in Siena Cathedral), 1308–11, 43.5 x 46cm. Museo Thyssen-Bornemisza, Madrid

Plate 12 *Heraclius Bears the Cross as a Penitent through the Gate of Jerusalem*, detail of Pl. 9 (in its current state)

emperor, accompanied by two cardinals and a bishop, wanted to ride into Jerusalem with the Cross in triumph, the gate to the city closed into an impenetrable wall and an angel appeared and spoke: 'CHRISTUS HINC AD PASSIONEM * EGRESSVS * EST * CVM * / * HUMILITATE * ET MANSVETUDINE' ('From here Christ went out to his Passion in humility and tameness'). With this reference to Christ's last walk through the gate out of Jerusalem on his way to be crucified on Golgotha, the story as depicted by Benedetto di Bindo differs from the *Golden Legend* where the angel refers to Christ's entry into the town on Palm Sunday: 'When the king of heaven went to his Passion by this gate, he was not arrayed like a king, ne on horseback, but came humbly upon an ass, in showing the example of humility, which he left to them that honour him.'[32] However, the effect of the angel's speech shown in the painting is the same as described in the *Golden Legend*. Scene 8: Heraclius removed his clothes and all of his imperial insignia and bore the Cross as a penitent through the gate, which then opened for him (**Pl. 12**). Benedetto di Bindo depicted the entry into Jerusalem as a procession of penitents, in which even the singing clerics – identifiable by their tonsures – with bare feet and in underclothes are following the Cross carried by the emperor. The cycle of the True Cross thus ends with a Via Crucis procession in which this most important of relics is borne as a sign of the *Imitatio Christi*.[33] For the setting of these two last scenes, Benedetto di Bindo was inspired by Duccio's depiction of Christ and the Samaritan woman (**Pl. 11**), originally part of the complex altarpiece of the *Maestà* which at this time was on the high altar of Siena Cathedral. Duccio's architectural setting of the Samaritan town of Sychar was copied (and slightly simplified) by Benedetto di Bindo to illustrate Jerusalem.

The frescoes on the walls of the Cappella delle Reliquie supplement and extend the subject of relics. Whereas in the

decoration of the Arliquiera the emphasis is placed on the most important relic of Christ, in the programme for the murals a relic of the Virgin Mary is placed in the foreground. Here too a procession is depicted, and again the power of a relic is demonstrated before our eyes (**Pl. 13**). The miracle, illustrated on the east wall, is recounted in the *Legenda Aurea*: to end the plague in Rome, Pope Gregory the Great organized a large rogation procession, carrying the portrait of the Mother of God painted by the Apostle Luke. The icon caused the epidemic to recede, and from the heavens the angels were heard singing the hymn *Regina Coeli* for the first time. As a divine sign of the end of the epidemic, the Archangel Michael appeared above Hadrian's mausoleum, putting his bloody sword back in its scabbard.[34]

This apparition above the mausoleum – which has been known ever since as the Castel Sant'Angelo – is still quite visible in Benedetto di Bindo's fresco, and below it is a depiction of the procession carrying the icon of the Virgin without the Child in a gesture of intercession (**Pl. 16**). The icon is held by a cleric on a pole high above the heads of the participants, much as it was in a later painting of the same miracle by Giovanni di Paolo around 1465 (**Pl. 14**).[35] However, the painting in the procession depicted by Giovanni di Paolo is a Madonna and Child and therefore a different icon than the one painted by Benedetto di Bindo.

There was a bitter debate in late medieval Rome on precisely this subject: what painting was carried in Gregory the Great's procession against the plague? Three Roman churches claimed to own the icon painted by the Apostle Luke.[36] For a long time, it was identified with the Madonna di Santa Maria Maggiore, known as the Salus Populi

Plate 13 Benedetto di Bindo, *The Miracle of Pope Gregory's Rogation Procession*, 1411–12, fresco. Cappella delle Reliquie, Siena Cathedral

Romani, which shows the Madonna and Child. By contrast, on the other two competing Roman icons, the Madonna di San Sisto and the Madonna di Santa Maria in Aracoeli (**Pl. 15**), the Virgin is depicted without the Child as an intercessor or *advocata*. The painting in the procession depicted by Benedetto di Bindo corresponds to these *advocatae* (**Pl. 16**). As the Madonna di Santa Maria in Aracoeli is a copy of the Madonna di San Sisto, it cannot be determined from the depiction of Gregory's procession alone which of the two icons the painter intended to show. However, in Siena it seems that it was considered important not to leave the viewer uncertain about this. The answer is provided by the fresco on the opposite wall on the west side

Plate 14 Giovanni di Paolo, *The Miracle of Pope Gregory's Rogation Procession*, c. 1465, predella scene, tempera on wood. Musée du Louvre, Paris

of the relic chapel. It also depicts a story told in the *Legenda Aurea*:[37] on the day of Christ's birth, Emperor Augustus asked the Tiburtine Sibyl whether one day someone more powerful than he would be born (**Pl. 17**). The Virgin and Child appeared in the sun surrounded by a golden circle, above an altar, and a voice was heard saying: 'This is the altar of heaven', whereupon the Sibyl pronounced to the emperor the words, which Benedetto di Bindo has written on a scroll: 'ILLE PVER MAIOR TE EST / IDEO IPSVM ADORA'.[38] Augustus arranged for an altar to be built for the Son of God on the Capitol hill, the site of this apparition and according to legend, this is where the church of Santa Maria in Aracoeli now stands.

For an illustration of this extremely rare subject in Sienese painting, Benedetto di Bindo had studied the mural created by Andrea Vanni in the last third of the 14th century for the Compagnia di Santa Maria sotto le Volte in the hospital of Santa Maria della Scala in Siena (**Pl. 18**). In this version, the Sibyl is also depicted as holding on to a banderole with the citation given in the *Legenda Aurea*.[39] The appearance of the Virgin and Child in the golden circle on the fresco in Santa Maria della Scala is a prefiguration of the roundel in the Cappella delle Reliquie. Andrea Vanni's Christ Child holds a scroll with the abbreviated words of Isaiah 45:6: 'EGO DOMINUS ET NON EST A[lter]' ('I am the Lord, and there is no other'). It is possible that the mutilated text on the Child's scroll in the relic chapel, which also starts with 'Ego', was an identical citation of Isaiah.

The connection between the scenes on the facing walls in the relic chapel is obvious. The icon carried through Rome in Pope Gregory's procession against the plague was therefore not from the Dominican church of San Sisto, but from Santa Maria in Aracoeli, the church of the competing Franciscan order.[40] With this concrete reference to one of the

Plate 15 (left) *Madonna di Santa Maria in Aracoeli*, probably third quarter of 11th century, tempera on wood. Santa Maria in Aracoeli church, Rome

Plate 16 (right) Benedetto di Bindo, depiction of the Aracoeli Madonna, detail of *The Miracle of Pope Gregory's Rogation Procession* (Pl. 13)

Roman icons by Luke, the programme of the relic chapel represents an extraordinary rare, perhaps even unique, example of the iconography of the procession of Gregory from the 14th to 16th century.

It remains to be considered why the decoration of the relic chapel in Siena Cathedral would have referred so explicitly to this Roman icon. Perhaps it was considered the most effective *advocata* who could be called upon when plague threatened. The icon had this reputation among the Romans, whose money donated during the Great Plague of 1348 had paid for the grand stairway that still leads up to the church of Santa Maria in Aracoeli.[41] An outbreak of plague in Siena in 1411 was probably decisive in the choice of this theme.[42]

On 12 July 1411, the municipality ordered 'in praise and honour of all-powerful God and his most sacred mother, the Virgin Mary, intercessor and protector of the city of Siena [...] to make a large, beautiful and pious procession through

the city [...] so that the Lord God in his grace and mercy will be lenient [...] and rescind this terrible plague'.[43] This great procession, which started and ended at the cathedral, had to be repeated on the following two days. Benedetto di Bindo's fresco depicts just such a procession against the plague with a happy conclusion. It can be understood as a votive image, and at the same time it illustrates the power of relics, in this case the icon painted by the Apostle Luke.

One further allusion could be to the situation in ecclesiastical politics at the time. The contemporary viewer could not have seen this depiction of Rome and the Pope's procession through the city without thinking of the pathetic situation in which the Church, torn apart by schism, had found itself. Three popes were competing over Peter's throne, which had long stood empty in Rome as the city was occupied by the king of Naples, Ladislaus, with whom Siena and Florence were at war. It was not until 12 April 1411 that John XXIII was permitted to enter Rome, but the city

Plate 17 Benedetto di Bindo, *Emperor Augustus and the Tiburtine Sibyl*, 1411–12, fresco. Cappella delle Reliquie, Siena Cathedral

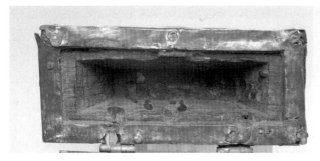

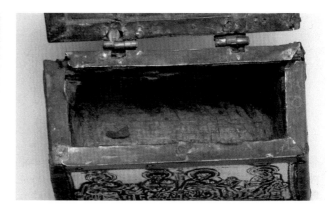

Plate 5a–b (above and right) Interior views of chrismatory; a) lid; b) base (photos: British Museum)

undecorated copper sheet. These were all originally held in place by silver bindings, some of which still survive. A sheet from one of the gable ends is missing, but the decorative panels are otherwise remarkably complete and in good condition, although begrimed with wax and dirt.

The ridge-pole is made of a gilded copper alloy and its composition as well as its decoration differs from that of the panels. It is cast and inlaid with silver strips, originally set with three precious stones or pearls, which also bear two inscriptions. The technical and stylistic differences from the rest of the box indicate that this is a later replacement for an original fitting.

There is also considerable evidence of ancient repairs: these include many secondary rivet holes in the wood and metal, later medieval or early post-medieval brass hinges and iron replacement bindings of uncertain, but evidently ancient, date. As with the modifications to the wooden core mentioned above, these changes are evidence of a long history of repair and alteration. It must have been during the course of one of these refurbishments when the two end panels were exchanged, so that the keyhole noted above no longer sits in front of the hole in the wooden core. At some stage in its existence the box appears to have been converted into a reliquary, as the little chamber cut into the underside of the base and the enlarging of the interior may suggest. Although the sequence of these modifications is uncertain, the later history of the box may hint at a context for the reshaping of the interior and the carving of the relic cavity on the underside which will be discussed below.

The original surfaces of the wooden core are dark with age; a brown waxy substance with some traces of shellac is also visible in the interior and around the small chamber cut

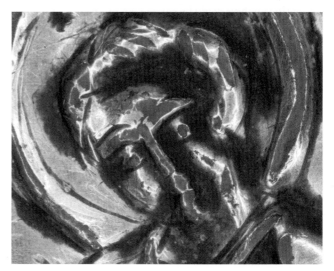

Plate 6 Front of chrismatory, close-up of head of an evangelist showing incised detail (photo: British Museum)

into the base, and may be filler or a repair. The exterior of the box is coated with a dark brown fatty deposit, the analysis of which at various points shows traces of resin, beeswax and tallow; the last two elements are consistent with periods of exposure to candle smoke, from both church (beeswax) and domestic (tallow) candles.

Decoration and inscriptions

The front of the box, its principal face, is decorated with figures of Christ and the four evangelists. On the base, the four evangelists are depicted seated with their gospels in a variety of positions; on the lid is the risen Christ, holding the Cross and book, flanked by berried vine scrolls (**Pl. 7a–b**).

Plate 7a–b Front of chrismatory; a) lid panel with the Risen Christ flanked by vines; b) base panel with the four evangelists. St John is second from the left (photos: British Museum)

Plate 8 Back of chrismatory, with above, a vine springing from a chalice, and below, a similar vine springing from a chalice, with deer-like animals disporting in it (photo: British Museum)

The individual evangelists are not identified by inscriptions or their symbols, but it is noteworthy that one figure has a more elaborate halo and is unlike the other evangelists who are all depicted in the act of writing. He presents his Gospel to the viewer, revealing the Word of God, and also seems to be marked out from the others by the cross held by Christ on the lid above, which points directly to his head. This may signify that this figure is John, in whose Gospel Christ's divine nature is most fully treated.

The back of the box is decorated on the base with two long-necked deer flanking a chalice from which a fruiting vine springs; the lid has a similar image without the animals (**Pl. 8**). The end panels have images of sprightly winged creatures, perhaps lions, on both the base and the surviving lid gable (**Pls 4a–b, 9**).

The gilded copper-alloy ridge-pole is inlaid with bands of silver, bearing inscriptions separated by settings for gems, as noted above (**Pl. 10a–c**). Along the front there are two panels of tight regular interlace, each containing six quatrefoil elements, while its back is plain, but divided into two equal parts by the central inscribed band. Each end face of the ridge-pole has a cross with expanded arms inscribed in a circle intersected by a four-lobed knot (**Pl. 4a**).

Two separate but linked inscriptions, twelve letters in all, run along and across the ridge-pole, carefully executed in

Plate 9 Right end of chrismatory, lower panel with winged creature (the gable panel is missing) (photo: British Museum)

Plate 10a–c Three views of the ridge-pole, showing decoration and inscriptions; a) front; b) back; c) top (photos: British Museum)

neat seriffed capitals. First along the ridge-pole run two contracted words, KA-P and BA-P, separated by a gem setting (**Pl. 10c**). Across this runs the second tripartite inscription, also with contraction marks, each element punctuated by the gem settings. These all begin at the front of the ridge-pole and end on the back (**Pl. 10a–b**). From left to right, they read:

K-C Θ-C   I-C X-C   C-O T-P

Although these are at first sight confusing – not least because of their layout across the ridge, which requires them to be read in instalments – these mini-texts are clearly in Greek, albeit in what John Higgitt has called 'rather round and Roman-looking lettering';[7] they represent the names of Christ: *Kyrios Theos, Iesos Christos, Soter:* 'Lord God, Jesus Christ, Saviour'. The abbreviated title I-C X-C starts immediately above the head of Christ on the lid panel below. The lengthways inscription at first resisted interpretation, until Richard Camber recognized that this inscription is not in Greek, but in Latin. He has proposed for this to be read as *kapsa* or *kapsella baptismalis* – literally, a baptismal box.

Plate 11a–d (from top to bottom) a–b) the Mortain chrismal, front and back views, Anglo-Saxon, late 8th or early 9th century, gilded copper-alloy on a wooden base, h. 135mm. Collegial church of St Evroult, Mortain (photo: British Museum); c) the Gandersheim chrismal, front view, Anglo-Saxon, late 8th century, whale-bone, with copper alloy mounts, h. 126mm. Herzog Anton Ulrich-Museum, Braunschweig (photo: Herzog Anton Ulrich-Museum); d) the Winchester reliquary, back view, Carolingian, first half of 9th century, gilded copper-alloy on a wooden base, h. 175mm. Winchester City Museums (photo: Winchester Museums Service)

Function

What do these inscriptions imply for the function of this container? I would argue that this is an example of an early medieval chrismal, or chrismatory, usually defined as a container for oils used in administering the sacraments, of which baptism is the first.[8] The Latin inscription is indeed quite specific in stating that the box is associated with baptism, and the Greek inscription also refers to Christ as Saviour, reinforcing the idea of salvation through the sacrament of baptism. However, these are on the ridge-pole which as we shall see is probably a later addition. Was the box originally designed for this purpose? I believe the answer to this question must be yes. The iconography of the front panel shows the triumphant risen Christ, the saviour flanked by vine scrolls evoking Christ as the *vitis vera*, the true vine that represents Christ nourishing his church, and in the early medieval period an image of the Eucharist itself.[9] The presumed figure of St John, in whose Gospel Christ declares that he is 'the true vine', seems, as we have seen, to have been marked out both by his special halo and Christ's Cross pointing directly at his head. The back panels show the image of deer feeding on the true vine, the fruiting Tree of Life, which is also associated with baptism; here the Eucharistic symbolism is reinforced by the chalice from which the fruiting vine springs, which is also a reference to the Fountain of Life. The winged lion-like creatures of the end panels appear in early medieval art as symbols of the risen Christ as king, and so also represent salvation.

Finally, the construction of the box, which allows it to be opened and locked as well as making it easily transportable, also relates it to the other two objects that have been identified as Anglo-Saxon chrismals or chrismatories (**Pl. 11a–c**). The late 8th or early 9th-century Mortain Casket bears an explicit runic inscription in Old English – 'God bless Æadda who made this chrismal' – as well as an appropriately Eucharistic iconography, in which the archangels Michael and Gabriel hold the host in the form of round loaves.[10] This has also been adapted as a reliquary at some later stage, as a glass-covered hole cut into its roof indicates. The second Anglo-Saxon exemplar is the 8th-century Gandersheim Casket, with its elegant and densely textured cosmological imagery, again playing on the *vitis vera* (Tree of Life) and other Christological symbolism.[11] That this form of container was specifically identified with a chrismal finds support from one of the Latin riddles composed by the Anglo-Saxon scholar Aldhelm (*c.* 639–709);[12] number 55, entitled *Crismal*, describes a specifically house-shaped container, which none can open, except by removing its roof to gain access to the *species…Christi* (the form of Christ, i.e. the host) within. Therefore its construction, imagery and inscription all point to the original use of this container as a chrismal.

Date and place of manufacture

In size and type, the chrismal is related to small surviving house-shaped shrines of Insular – mainly Irish and Pictish – origin, such as the Abbadia San Salvatore, Emly and Copenhagen shrines, some of which, as mentioned already, share the distinctive locking mechanism affording ready access to the contents, which appears to be confined to

Plate 12 a–b; a) detail of the Bischofshofen cross, Anglo-Saxon, late 8th century, gilded copper-alloy with glass insets, on a wooden base, height of the whole 158cm. Diocesan Museum, Salzburg (photo: O. Anrather); b) the Ormside bowl, exterior of the base, Anglo-Saxon, late 8th century, gilded silver and copper-alloy with glass settings, diameter 138mm. Yorkshire Museum, York (photo: Yorkshire Museum)

Insular examples.[13] It may well be that some of these accessible and portable containers were also originally intended as chrismals. However, these differ from the newly discovered chrismatory in that they are mostly made of yew, not oak, and the proportions of the latter are steeper and more slender, closer to some of the continental 'purse' reliquaries, so-called due to their purse-like form; these however differ from the chrismatory in that they are usually sealed containers, designed to enshrine precious relics.

The use of decorated gilded copper-alloy sheeting is also very common on continental early medieval reliquaries, such as those from Sitten, Chur and Enger, but is also seen on the Anglo-Saxon Mortain chrismal and the 9th-century Anglo-Carolingian reliquary excavated at Winchester (**Pl. 11d**).[14] It is also stylistically distinct from both the Irish and continental examples. The decoration of the ends and back is characteristically Anglo-Saxon in style, being closely related to vine scroll and animal ornament on two of the few surviving pieces of Anglo-Saxon 8th-century church metalwork – the Ormside bowl and the great *crux gemmata* from Bischofshofen, near Salzburg, which was probably made for the abbey church at Salzburg which had strong Insular associations (**Pl. 12a–b**).[15] These both date to the later 8th century and have very similar decoration. The bowl comes from a Viking grave in Ormside churchyard, Cumbria, but its inhabited vine scroll decoration, gilded interior, suitable for holy water or other liquids, and the prominent cross motifs both inside and out suggest that it was intended for liturgical use. In addition to the animal and Tree of Life ornament on its surviving face, the cross, which is associated with a centre of 8th-century Anglo-Saxon missionary activity, also carries interlace and tightly coiled vine scroll decoration on its sides and inset glass roundels with running spirals of Insular type. It must be either an export from England, or made by an Anglo-Saxon craftsman working in the monastic community at Salzburg. The striking similarity of the plant and animal decoration of the

chrismal to the decoration of these two ecclesiastical objects suggests that it too should be dated to the later 8th century.

The decoration of the front, however, is harder to find comparisons with for the good reason that so little Anglo-Saxon ecclesiastical metalwork survives from this period and there are very few decorated copies of the Gospels to offer comparisons. Nevertheless, the front panels have the same metal composition and use the same techniques as the rest of the panels, indicating production in the same workshop and at the same time. The vine scrolls flanking Christ are certainly Anglo-Saxon in appearance and congruent with

Plate 13 Flavigny Gospels, Carolingian, late 8th century. Bibilothèque Municipale Autun, MS 4, f.8r, canon table (after Hubert, Porcher and Volbach 1969)

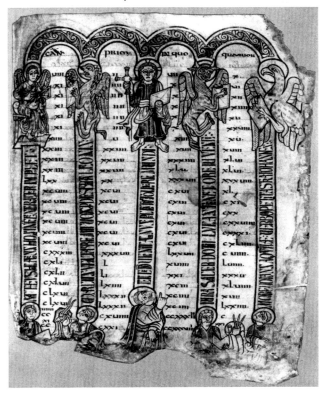

Plate 14a–c a) Second Bible of Charles the Bald, Carolingian, 871–7, h. 430mm, w. 335mm. Bibliothèque Nationale, Paris, Ms Lat. 2, f.11 (photo: Bibliothèque Nationale); b) detail of end of ridge-pole; c) detail of front of ridge-pole

the vine scrolls on the back of the chrismal. The realistically modelled evangelist figures, however, clearly show an association with continental models. For instance, details such as the single-legged lectern and the attitudes of some of the evangelists echo images in Carolingian manuscripts;[16] however, seen as a quartet, the evangelists have no precise parallel. An early 9th-century Carolingian Gospel from the Paris region suggests one kind of model from which this arrangement could have derived; here the portraits of the evangelists are lined up in the usual order of Matthew, Mark, Luke and John, under arcades on two facing pages of the manuscript; all but Matthew are depicted in the act of writing.[17] The attitude of Luke is similar to that of the second figure from the right on the chrismatory, but there is otherwise little direct correspondence between the two sets of figures, and if John has been correctly identified on the chrismal, the order is different. Some hint of Anglo-Saxon tradition appears in their elongated, beardless faces with prominent chins and the elaborate bun-like coiffure of the John figure, which recalls some examples of Mercian sculpture from the late 8th and early 9th centuries, such as the Breedon and Lichfield archangels, which were themselves influenced by Carolingian models.[18]

The risen Christ is a striking and dynamic image which also has its strongest parallel in a Carolingian source in one of the canon tables of the Flavigny Gospels dating to the later 8th century (**Pl. 13**).[19] Here a very similar image of the risen Christ stands at the centre of the canon table just below the arcades; it is flanked by the four evangelist symbols. At the bottom of the page, the evangelist portraits look up at their respective symbols, while in the centre the figure of John the Baptist points up to Christ directly above him. Along each column runs a text from the *Carmen Paschale*,[20] except for the one that extends between this figure and that of Christ, which has a text derived from the words of the Baptist in the Gospel of St John 1.29: *ecce Dei venit agnus peccatum tollere mundi*,[21] 'summing up in one line', as Jean Hubert puts it, 'the message of the evangelists and the detailed account they give of the Redemption'.[22] This visual connexion between St John's Gospel and the risen Christ also appears to occur on the chrismatory, reinforcing the

impression that it shares a model with the Flavigny manuscript, albeit at some distance. Interestingly, some of the pages of the manuscript have animal ornament showing a very strong Anglo-Saxon influence, a further indication of the Anglo-Carolingian connexions shared by these two objects.

Carolingian manuscripts, metalwork and ivories were certainly circulating in England in the late 8th century and could have served as models for the chrismal front. Alternatively, it could have been made abroad by an Anglo-Saxon monastic craftsman working in a Carolingian context. The Anglo-Saxon Bischofshofen cross, which as we have seen was probably made in Salzburg in the later 8th century, suggests one sort of context in which such an object might have been produced. Indeed, given its French connexions (see below), the chrismal could have been just the sort of fine ecclesiastical metalwork to have been made at Tours in Alcuin's time, alongside the great bibles produced there during his abbacy;[23] we know that many Anglo-Saxons travelled to France to join him there.

However, what is certain is that the chrismal was in a prominent monastery in Francia by the last quarter of the 9th century at the point when the ridge-pole was replaced. The distinctive decoration of this addition is very close in style to a number of later 9th-century Franco-Saxon manuscripts, attributed to the monastery of St Amand in northern France (**Pl. 14a–c**). The fine, tightly organized interlace, quatrefoils and the distinctive interlaced cross motifs on the terminals have close parallels in a number of Franco-Saxon manuscripts such as the Le Mans Sacramentary (Mediathèque Louis Aragon, Le Mans, ms 77, f 7v, f 8r, f 9r), a Gospel book from Quedlinburg (Universitäts- und Landesbibliothek Sachsen-Anhalt, Halle (Saale), Qu.Cod.83, f 144v, f 145 r) and the Prague Gospels (Metropolitan Chapter Library, Prague, ms Cim.2, f 25r).[24] Two of the grandest Franco-Saxon manuscripts are associated with Charles the Bald and his patronage of the royal abbey of St Denis, where he was lay abbot: the St Denis Sacramentary (*c.* 867–77) and the great Second Bible of Charles the Bald (*c.* 871–7);[25] they both contain decorative elements seen on the chrismal ridge-pole. Perhaps even more suggestive of this link is the fact that these manuscripts, both associated with imperial patronage, also contain texts in Greek. In the St Denis Sacramentary, the name of St Denis appears in Greek letters in the calendar and the manuscript also contains a *missa graeca*;[26] while a part of the dedicatory poem by Hucbald of St Amand in the Second Bible of Charles the Bald is also written in Greek. Although evidence of Carolingian acquaintance with Greek makes an occasional appearance in earlier examples, such as Hrabanus Maurus' *De laudibus sanctae Crucis*, it is amongst the circle of Charles the Bald that the systematic translation and study of Greek was first actively pursued in Carolingian circles, most prominently by the Irishman John Scottus. This therefore supplies a context for the ridge-pole's decoration and a possible explanation for the unusual use of Greek in the inscriptions which cross it.

It should also be noted that there is a possible numerological element to the inscription and the decoration of the ridge-pole. The abbreviated Latin inscription has six letters and the Greek one twelve, both significant numbers in Christian numerology for their association with the six days of creation, the hours of the day and the months of the year, as well as the number of the apostles. Could it also be noteworthy that the quatrefoils in the interlace on the front of the ridge-pole also number twelve?

Provenance and history

Finally, what of the chrismal's provenance prior to its recent appearance? It seems likely that it was for many years, perhaps for much of its existence, in France. A paper note, written in French and dated 'Moissac, 16 août 1801', is said to have been inside the box when it came to light (**Pl. 15**). This survives and appears to be genuine. The text reads:

> Je declare avoir placé moimeme dans cette espece de chasse les reliques qui y sont contenues je les trouverai parmi les effets de ma tante alpinienne de bessou [?]née Lespinasse qui certainement les tenait des personnes tres pieuses je crois meme que celles de St pierre, St julien, et St cyprian lui avait été données par le sacristan, L'abbé castanier, qui les avait extraittes lui meme des reliquaries du chapitre. A moissac ce 16 aout 1801, Lespinasse fils ainé.

> I declare that I have myself placed in this kind of chasse the relics which are contained in it. I found them among the effects of my aunt Alpinienne de Bessou[?], neé Lespinasse, who certainly had them from very pious persons I believe, even though those of St Peter, St Julien and St Cyprien had been given to her by the sacristan, Abbé Castanier, who had extracted them himself from the reliquaries in the chapter house. At Moissac, 16 August 1801, Lespinasse the elder son.

Note that the text does not say or imply that the 'chasse' itself came from the abbey at Moissac (although it certainly possesses a chapter house), nor indeed is there any independent evidence to suggest that the present object is the 'chasse' mentioned in the text. However, Richard Camber has drawn my attention to an inventory of the Moissac treasury dated 1669, which lists an 'autre reliquaire en pyramide, de cuivre doré';[27] this could well describe a house-shaped shrine or chrismal – perhaps indeed this very object.[28]

Whatever its true history, it is likely that it had been taken out of a church for safe keeping in the troubled times of

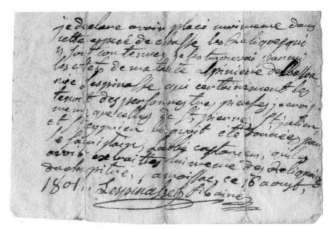

Plate 15 Paper note associated with the chrismatory (photo: Galerie Ladrière)

1793–4 when church treasures in France were ordered to be destroyed or collected and taken to Paris to be melted down. Many objects were quietly preserved from the melting pot at this time, and like this piece their fate through the ensuing years is sometimes obscure. The Franks Casket, formerly in the church of St Julien at Brioude and now in the British Museum, only re-emerged to public view in the 1850s and others came to light later still. A small object such as this could quite possibly have remained forgotten and unrecognized in a French attic until it passed into the hands of art-dealers in the later 20th century.

We may never know for certain the true history of this remarkable object, but I believe that it is possible to demonstrate that it was made in the late 8th century as a chrismal or chrismatory in an Anglo-Saxon context with access to Carolingian models. Whether this was in England or in a continental centre with a significant Anglo-Saxon presence, perhaps in France (Tours, for instance) is uncertain. About a century later, it was fitted with a new ridge-pole with Franco-Saxon decoration and inscriptions in Greek and Latin; the ridge-pole's stylistic relationship to the St Amand manuscripts, including some associated with the court of Charles the Bald, suggests that the chrismal was in northern France during this period. It may even have been kept in a monastery favoured by the emperor, such as St Denis or St Amand itself. After that, the trail goes cold. However, the apparent link to Moissac is a plausible one and if true, may indicate that it was there from at least the 17th century. The presence of beeswax on its surface suggests that it has spent some time in a church context, and the later repairs and adaptations, probably to facilitate its use as a reliquary, could be consistent with the history indicated by the 1801 note. What is certain, however, is that there is certainly more to be discovered about this remarkable object, its more recent history and its origins and context.

Notes

1   Bagnoli *et al.* 2010, cat. no. 56. It has also since been briefly discussed in Webster 2012, 164–6.

2   Fogg 2007, 16–21. The entry draws on the work of Richard Camber and the author.

3   I would like to thank a number of scholars who have contributed valuable comments and observations on the chrismatory, in particular Anna Gannon, Richard Gem, Jane Hawkes, the late John Higgitt, David Hinton, Raghnall Ó Floinn, Lawrence Nees,

Susan La Niece and her colleagues in the British Museum Department of Conservation and Scientific Research, Elisabeth Okasha, Michael Peter and Susan Youngs. A special debt is due to my former colleague Richard Camber, who first brought the chrismatory to my attention, acted as mediator with its then owner and whose researches on the Moissac archive have suggested important lines of enquiry concerning the provenance of the object; to him also goes the credit for recognizing the Latin inscription for what it is and for cracking its meaning. It is hoped that important input from specialists into what has so far been a series of informal discussions will lead to a joint collaborative publication.

4   The additional hope had been that the British Museum might acquire such an outstandingly important piece, given its significance for the study of Anglo-Saxon and Carolingian art and ecclesiastical relations between England and the continent in the later 8th and 9th centuries. However, although the French authorities did not classify the chrismatory as *patrimoine*, thus removing one obstacle to its acquisition, the gap in its recent history meant that there could be no certainty that a restitution claim might not arise, thus making its acquisition by the Museum impossible at the time. The reliquary has since passed into a private collection, and I would like to record my thanks to the owner for his encouragement and for permission to publish it here.

5   See Quast 2012 for a valuable survey of early medieval reliquaries and chrismals.

6   Youngs 1989, cat. no. 129; Bourke 2001–2; Bourke 2013. For the Emly shrine, see the Boston Museum of Fine Arts website: www. mfa.org/collections/object/reliquary-casket-emly-shrine-552287.

7   Pers. comm.

8   The term is also used in the early medieval period to refer to a container for the host: see Cabrol and Leclercq 1913, 1478–81.

9   John 15: 1–7

10 Webster and Backhouse 1991, cat. no. 137, where it is suggested on the basis of its iconography that this chrismal may have been intended to hold the host.

11 Webster 2000; Elbern 2000.

12 Lapidge and Rosier 2009, 'Enigmata', 81.

13 For these and other Insular house-shaped shrines, see Youngs 1989 and Bourke 2001–2. The origin of the form has been much debated, but Bourke has made a strong claim for the Irish shrines to be a reflex of continental forms of the second half of the 7th century.

14 Hinton, Keene and Qualmann 1981.

15 See Webster 2012, figs 93, 71, 123.

16 For example, the writing desk in the Matthew image in the Vienna Coronation Gospels (Kunsthistorisches Museum, Vienna, Schatzkammer, Inv. XIII 18, f15r) and the attitudes of Matthew and Luke in the Ada Gospels (Stadtbibliothek, Trier, Codex 22).

17 Bibliotheque Nationale, Paris, ms lat. 11959, f.19v., f 20r; Lafitte and Denoël 2007, cat. no. 30.

18 See Webster 2012, figs 9 and 85.

19 Bibliothèque Municipale, Autun, ms 4; Hubert, Porcher and Volbach 1969, fig. 192. I am very grateful to Lawrence Nees for drawing this image to my attention. A canon table is a table of concordance for two or more parallel texts of the Gospels.

20 A poem by the 5th-century Christian writer, Sedulius.

21 'Behold the Lamb of God [who] comes to take away the sins of the world'.

22 Hubert, Porcher and Volbach 1969, 182.

23 Alcuin of York (*c.* 735–804) was an Anglo-Saxon churchman, scholar and teacher who became one of Charlemagne's chief advisors, ending his career as abbot of Tours.

24 For these see Stiegemann and Wemhoff 1999, XI.4; Puhle 2001, vol. 2, III.33; vol. 1, 232.

25 Bibliothèque Nationale, Paris, ms lat. 9387, ms lat. 2290 and ms lat. 2; Lafitte and Denoël 2007, cat. nos 57 and 14.

26 These are chants of the Roman ordinary of the mass with Greek texts written in Latin manuscripts in Latin characters.

27 'Another reliquary in the form of a pyramid, of gilded copper'.

28 Lagrèze-Fossat 1870; Lagrèze-Fossat 1875.

Bibliography

Bagnoli, M., Klein, H.A., Mann, C.G. and Robinson, J. (eds) 2010. *Treasures of Heaven: Saints, Relics and Devotion in Medieval Europe*, Baltimore and London.

Bourke, C. 2001–2. 'Clonmore and Bobbio: two seventh-century Irish shrines', *Dúiche Néill* 14, 24–34.

Bourke, C. 2013. 'Der Schrein von Clonmore', in *CREDO, Christianisierung Europas im Mittelalter*, ed. C. Stiegemann, M. Kroker and W. Walter, Petersburg, cat. no. 182, 223–4.

Cabrol, F. and Leclercq, H. 1913. *Dictionnaire d'archeologie chretienne et de liturgie*, vol. 3, part 1, Paris.

Elbern, V. 2000. 'Das Gandersheimer Runenkästchen – Versuch einer Ikonographischen Synthese', in Marth 2000, 83–90.

Fogg, S. 2007. *Art of the Middle Ages*, London.

Hinton, D., Keene, S. and Qualmann, K. 1981. 'The Winchester reliquary', *Medieval Archaeology*, 25, 45–77.

Hubert, J., Porcher, J. and Volbach, W.F. 1969. *The Carolingian Renaissance*, London.

Lafitte, M-P. and Denoël, C. 2007. *Trésors Carolingiens. Livres Manuscrits de Charlemagne à Charles le Chauve*, Paris.

Lagrèze-Fossat, A. 1870. 'Inventaire du Trésor de l'Abbaye de Moissac en 1669, extrait d'un procès – verbal de l'état de l'église de l'abbaye de Moissac en 1669', *Études historiques de Moissac* 1, 258.

Lagrèze-Fossat, A. 1875. 'Inventaire du Trésor de l'Abbaye de Moissac en 1669, extrait d'un procès – verbal de l'état de l'église de l'abbaye de Moissac en 1669', *Revue des Sociétés Savantes* (sixième série), 232–6.

Lapidge, M. and Rosier, J. (trans.) 2009. *Aldhelm: The Poetic Works*, Cambridge.

Marth, R. (ed.) 2000. *Das Gandersheimer Runenkästchen. Internationales Kolloquium Braunschweig 24–26 Marz 1999*, Braunschweig.

Puhle, M. (ed.) 2001. *Otto der Grosse, Magdeburg und Europa*, Mainz.

Quast, D. 2012. *Das merowingerzeitliche Reliquienkästchen aus Ennabeuren: eine Studie zu den frühmittelalterlichen Reisereliquiaren und Chrismalia* (Römisch-Germanisches Zentralmuseum, Kataloge Vor- und Frühgeschichtlicher Altertümer, 43), Mainz.

Stiegemann, C. and Wemhoff, M. (eds) 1999. *799 Kunst und Kultur der Karolingerzeit: Karl der Grosse und Papst Leo in Paderborn*, Mainz.

Webster, L. 2000. 'Style and function of the Gandersheim Casket', in Marth 2000, 63–72.

Webster, L. 2012. *Anglo-Saxon Art: A New History*, London.

Webster, L. and Backhouse, J. (eds) 1991. *The Making of England: Anglo-Saxon Art and Culture AD 600–900*, London.

Youngs, S. (ed.) 1989. *The Work of Angels*, London.

Chapter 10
Grist for the Mill
A Newly Discovered Bust Reliquary from Saint-Flour[1]

Barbara Drake Boehm

In June 2010, the bust of a saint, long kept in the attic of a house at 40 rue Sorel in the French city of Saint-Flour, was brought to the attention of Mme Pascale Moulier (**Pl. 1**). As the archivist of the diocese and a principal of the Association Cantal Patrimoine, she immediately identified it as a work of the 12th century. Mme Moulier's remarkable discovery serves yet again as a reminder of the rich artistic heritage of the Auvergne region, and offers an opportunity to review the state of research of the study of image reliquaries of the Massif Central region[2] and provides an occasion to trace the history of one city's artistic treasures through the vicissitudes of the French Revolution.

Carved from the burl (the knotty, rounded outgrowth of the trunk of a tree), perhaps black poplar or the local maple that grows along the banks of the Ander River near Saint-Flour,[3] the bust of a man in liturgical vestments is just under life-size, measuring 68cm high, 50cm wide and 45cm deep. His head is lost, and the neck, partly covered by a metal collar, has been broken in an irregular and abrupt manner. The right arm is bent at the elbow; the right hand of metal, with its fingers broken, is apparently extended in blessing. The left hand is missing.

The vestments of the Saint-Flour bust had been painted red, except around the neck and the middle of the torso, which are covered with metal.[4] The removal of the later paint revealed a handsomely and confidently carved bust, characterized by a strong, rhythmic pattern of drapery. At the same time, cleaning revealed a delicately patterned repoussé sheathing of mercury-gilded copper that decorates

Plate 1 Reliquary bust, current state after restoration, mid-12th century. Musée diocésain, Saint-Flour

the chest and central back of the figure's vestment. The delicacy of the gilded copper has been compromised by the later, thick and heavy strips of iron that band the neck and front of the garment. The later paint obscured a number of nails that still hold small fragments of silver which were originally juxtaposed to the gilded copper, sheathing the saint's robe completely in metal. There are additional torn strips of silver caught along the edges of the heavy metal neckband, both on the front and back.[5] The wood itself bears the marks of the forcible removal of the silver sheets.[6]

While the losses are regrettable, the bust found in Saint-Flour is not the only sculpture from Auvergne to survive in a compromised condition. Other examples include the isolated heads of a Virgin and Child from Notre-Dame-du-Port, preserved in the treasury of the cathedral at Clermont-Ferrand;[7] or the Notre-Dame de Sion, on which the head of the Child was replaced at an unknown date, well before the theft of the sculpture from the church of Bredons in 1958;[8] the headless and armless torso of Christ said to be from the convent of Lavaudieu;[9] or a silvered hand from the Alphonse Kann collection preserved in the Metropolitan Museum of Art, New York, arguably from an Auvergnat saint.[10]

In order to reconstruct the history of the bust, it is necessary to look both to the history of the city of Saint-Flour and other examples of this type of sculpture, surviving or documented. It is likely that the bust has been at Saint-Flour since the Middle Ages. The city, poised majestically atop a great, extinct volcanic plug, was strategically important, and ecclesiastical foundations grew alongside its civilian population. A Benedictine priory under the authority of the Abbey of Cluny was established in the early 11th century.[11] In 1095, Pope Urban II, who was in Clermont-Ferrand to preach the First Crusade, consecrated the church dedicated to St Flour (*Florus*), evangelizer of the region, and St Peter.[12] It is clear that, from the time of the church's dedication, a great chasse with the relics of the patron saint was located above the altar, as Pope Urban's *Vita* mentions the relics of St Flour. It specifies that 'the bones of the saint, gathered in a large chasse secured by three locks, were placed on a support raised behind the altar'.[13] More than 500 years later, the church historian Dominique de Jésus mentioned a chasse of St Flour in the same location, adding that no previous bishop had dared to open it before the current one, Charles de Nouailles, bishop of Saint-Flour from 1609 to 1647.[14]

There are a few surviving medieval works of art from the church and some additional information to be gleaned from documentary sources. Two Romanesque wood sculptures survive from Saint-Flour, both representative of the fine artistic heritage that one expects from the medieval Auvergne. A polychromed Virgin and Child from the cathedral, of the 'Throne of Wisdom' type for which the region is famous, is preserved in the collection of the Musée de Lyon.[15] A magnificent, over life-size 12th-century crucifix dominates the interior of the cathedral of Saint-Flour today, its quality manifest despite its successive painting and repainting. Unfortunately somewhat neglected in the literature, and occasionally mistakenly attributed to the 15th century,[16] the sculpture merits comparison to other examples

preserved at the nearby churches of Auzon, Lavoûte-Chilhac and Valuéjols.

Two documentary sources bear witness to an ensemble of substantial, three-dimensional images on the altar at Saint-Flour. The first is a record of payment made in 1396 (in wine and bread rather than coin) to woodworkers for taking down the 'Crucifix and other images' from the altar at the time of repairs to the church.[17] The second is in a 1666 annotation of the cathedral inventory of 1657 that refers to two pieces of purple velvet enhanced with faux-silver threads that were placed 'derrière les images de l'autel' ('behind the images of the altar'), a clear indication that the images were sculptures and not paintings.[18] Such tantalizing references are neither abundant nor contemporary with the bust found by Mme Moulier, but are typical of the kind of records from which one must carefully draw inferences in an effort to visualize and understand medieval reliquaries.[19]

The same mid-17th century inventory also mentions a number of reliquaries, and although the descriptions are summary, focusing on the material and the subject, it would appear that several of them were image reliquaries. Near the beginning of the 1657 inventory, just after the listing of a 'recently remade' great silver cross, five silver chalices and the ivory oliphant[20] of 'Monsieur St Flour', is a reference to 'une chasse de l'imaige de monsieur Sainct Flour, laquelle chasse est decorée au bord avec la crosse de cuivre esmailhée et surdorée…' ('a chasse of the image of Monsieur St Flour, which is decorated along the edge, with the crozier of enamelled and gilded copper'). Here the mention of the chasse as 'of the image' of 'Mister St Flour' suggests that the image is a personification. The mention of an affiliated oliphant and a gilded copper and enamel crozier additionally suggest a three-dimensional object. The material of the object itself is not mentioned, though its pre-eminence in the inventory may be taken as a reflection of the reliquary's importance to the religious devotions of the community, in addition to its monetary value. Second is a silver chasse of the image of the Virgin. Later in the inventory there is a description of the dress that was placed on 'Notre Dame', as well as on 'the Magdalene', indicating that these were both statuettes of some kind.[21] Third is another chasse, of 'Monsieur Sainct pierre', patron of the church along with St Flour. The description indicates that this reliquary is made of both silver and copper, as is the case with the recently found reliquary and the contemporary bust of St Césaire in the church dedicated to him at Maurs (**Pl. 2**), also in the Auvergne region of France.[22] In addition, there was also a gilded silver chasse of 'Monsieur St Jehan baptiste'.[23]

Following the list of additional silver objects (notably a gilded dove set on a column at the high altar),[24] the inventory notes the presence of a chasse of the head of St Sylvester of gilded copper, clearly distinguished from a listing at the end of the inventory of a large silver chasse of St Sylvester with its case.

Church inventories, such as the 1382 inventory of the Abbey of Cluny[25] or the 1354 inventory of St Vitus Cathedral in Prague, often begin with image reliquaries, a function of their large size and relative preciousness. In the 1657 inventory of the cathedral at Saint-Flour, additional

Plate 2 (left) Reliquary bust of St Césaire, mid-12th century with 13th century and later additions. L'abbatiale Saint-Césaire, Maurs

Plate 3 (right) Enthroned bishop (St Flour?), first half of 14th century. Musée de la Haute-Auvergne, Saint-Flour

reliquaries, not apparently in the form of busts or images, appear later in the list of precious objects, referred to as 'reliquaires' not 'châsses', and further identified by the phrase 'ou sont les relicques de saint' ('in which are the relics of saint …').[26] In this inventory, 'châsse' seems to be used exclusively to describe image reliquaries.

Judging from the inventory descriptions, it would therefore appear that by the mid-17th century, the cathedral at Saint-Flour possessed a number of three-dimensional images of the saints, embellished with metal and containing relics: 1) a reliquary of St Flour, of unspecified material, but holding a gilded and enamelled copper crozier; 2) an image of the Virgin in silver (probably containing relics as well); 3) a silver and copper reliquary of St Peter; 4) a reliquary of St John the Baptist in gilded silver; and 5) a gilded copper reliquary for the head of St Sylvester. Is it possible to link any of these to the bust found on the rue Sorel?

Before further investigation, one more work of art needs to be brought into consideration: the final medieval sculpture associated with the cathedral of Saint-Flour, a 14th-century carved wood image of a seated bishop (**Pl. 3**). Thought to represent the patron St Flour, this wood sculpture has a niche for relics at the back, now open, and a second, which is plugged, in his head.[27] While later in date than the newly found bust, this statue of an enthroned bishop is, in one specific detail, tantalizingly linked to the recently discovered bust. A tiny clue suggests at the very least that the two wood sculptures were once in the same place – a single, decorative nail found on the newly discovered bust is used with some frequency on the seated bishop. Had the earlier bust somehow been damaged, or might it have been simply already out of fashion in the 14th century? [28] Perhaps the enthroned figure was created around 1317, when the

church of Saint-Flour was raised to a bishopric.[29] Might it therefore have been made as a replacement for the newly discovered bust, which could also represent St Flour?

We will return to the question of the 14th-century image. First, a review of the history of other surviving saints' images in the region may suggest circumstances that could account for the current state of the Saint-Flour bust. The bust of St Chaffre at Le Monastier, south of le Puy en Velay, provides a first point of reference (**Pl. 4**).[30] Like the newly discovered bust, it has a carved wood core. After carving, the trunk of the saint's body and his head were sheathed in silver, with gilding used to accent the vestment as well as the tonsure of the saint, who was the patron and second abbot of Le Monastier. Only the hands of St Chaffre are painted, the original hands reputedly having been detached in 1793 and replaced at the beginning of the 19th century.[31] A text in the cartulary of the abbey of Le Monastier indicates that the bust contained many relics wrapped in a Byzantine silk: the skull of the saint, but also a piece of the True Cross. Furthermore, the relics of the saint were divided between two containers: an *arca* (box-shaped reliquary) and an *imago* (three-dimensional image).[32] Remarkably, however, the cartulary, dating to the abbacy of Guillaume IV (1087–1136), reveals that this 12th-century image is not the first version of the bust of St Chaffre. In fact, the precious metal exterior of the original had been removed, and the profit derived from the sale of its silver sheathing, along with his crown of pure gold and precious gems, had been used to fund the voyage of pilgrims to Jerusalem. This had been agreed on the understanding that an appropriate sum would be returned to the church for a refurbished image, presumably this one, graced not with a golden crown, but with the Byzantine silk and a relic of the Cross secreted inside. Might metal

Plate 4 Reliquary bust of St Chaffre, mid-12th century. L'abbatiale Saint-Chaffre du Monastier, Monastier-sur-Gazeille (photo: Francis Debaisieux)

sheathing from the bust recently found in Saint-Flour have similarly been taken to fund a medieval pilgrimage?

The lost bust of St Privatus of Mende (south of Saint-Flour in the Lozère region), which had been made before 1036 (when it had been carried in procession to a synod convened by the bishop of Le Puy), suffered a worse fate than St Chaffre in the medieval period. Before 1151, the gold head and the right arm of the image, as well as gems and gold from his garment were stolen by two thieves (each of them named Guido!).[33] The inherent monetary value of the busts of St Chaffre and St Privatus put them at risk, whether to fulfill lofty or mundane goals.

Documentation concerning the bizarre post-medieval history of the statuette of St Peter from Bredons was discovered with the sculpture. A detailed and apologetic letter written by the church vicar in 1707, tucked inside the cavity at the back of the sculpture, explained how he had intended to destroy the sculpture with an axe, only to discover the relics inside with his first blows. Subsequently it was hidden behind the retable of the church, and uncovered only in 1953.[34]

The 13th-century bust of St Yrieix in the Metropolitan Museum of Art, New York, which comes from the monastic church that bears his name south of Limoges, was described and weighed in 1791 as officials of the French Revolution prepared to melt it down (**Pl. 5**).[35] By unknown means, it was ultimately preserved.

Not unlike these examples from elsewhere in the Auvergne and the Limousin regions, the precious contents of the cathedral of Saint-Flour were threatened at several points in the city's history, any one of which could account for the compromised condition of the recently discovered bust. While the city was not captured during the Hundred Years War, the condition of the cathedral of Saint-Flour declined during the 14th century[36] to such an extent that in 1393 it was described as being on the verge of ruin. Three years later, the choir collapsed; more than 52 pages of payments for repairs are recorded in this critical period.[37] Centuries later, around 1776, certain renovations were put into effect, with the ancient choir screen being destroyed and the church painted white throughout.[38] In the 18th century, a goldsmith of Saint-Flour was charged with the theft of a reliquary from the cathedral and was put to death.[39] But, such events notwithstanding, it seems most likely that the bust found in Saint-Flour was both damaged, and ultimately saved, during the French Revolution.

The threat posed to works of art by the republican and anti-clerical fervour that swept France during the French Revolution mounted gradually. A nationwide decision that all church property should be sold was taken on 9 July 1790,[40] just short of a year after the storming of the Bastille. By the 26th of that month, the Municipal Council of Saint-Flour ordered that the inventory of all the churches be conducted, starting with its cathedral, as soon as possible.[41] It is clear from a thorough listing of important documents prepared in 1793 that the inventory of the 'meubles, effets or et argenterie' ('furniture, gold objects and silverware'), as well as papers of the collegiate church, was taken the following day, but that inventory has not, alas, been found.[42]

Following the law instituted on 27 March 1791 concerning 'Matieres d'or et d'argent des Communautés et Eglises supprimées' ('material of gold and silver from suppressed communities and churches'), and instructions on 1 August that it be done without delay,[43] a number of items were confiscated from the cathedral of Saint-Flour to be sent to the mint where they would be melted down. (This was the moment when the bust of St Yrieix was seized in the Limousin.) In fact, instructions had already been passed on in July from the 'comités réunis d'administrations ecclésiastiques et d'aliénation des biens nationaux' ('Assembled board for ecclesiastic administration and conveyance of national goods') as to how to write proper descriptions (*notices*) of works of art. On the list from Saint-Flour, accordingly, we can recognize a number of objects described in the 1657 inventory, and already mentioned here, beginning with the large crucifix. On the front of the document, under 'observasions', it is noted that it was necessary to take down and break two large crosses (not mentioned in the inventory), as well as the great crucifix from the high altar and six of its large candlesticks, in order to remove wood and iron supports before weighing the precious metals of which they were composed.[44] The silver statue of the Virgin also appears in the list, as does a 'representation de St Silvestre', curiously described as having been taken 'avec son casque' (presumably a papal tiara, not mentioned specifically in the 1657 inventory), and the arm of St Flour 'avec toutes ses garnitures' (shorthand, presumably for its being on a silver base supported by two angels as noted in 1657). The list also includes a representation of St Anthony 'avec sa garniture partie en cuivre' ('with its decoration partly of copper') that is not listed in the 1657 inventory.

In April, some 'old tapestries and coffrets' were sold from the 'sale capitulaire' (Chapter house), and a few wood altars from the Dominican church 'of no use to the parishes or national oratories' were sold.[45] By 30 September 1791, it was reported that inventories of suppressed ecclesiastical buildings in Saint-Flour yielded 'aucun monument de sculpture, peinture, gravure et dessin qui méritât d'être conservé' ('no sculpture, painting, engraving or drawing worthy of preservation').[46]

Two years later, matters intensified dramatically. The president of the 'Société populaire de Saint-Flour',[47] M. Daude, presided at a dramatic and raucous ceremony in the square in the newly established place de la République in front of the cathedral on 30 November 1793.[48] The populace was alerted by the sound of a tambour (in lieu of the oliphant of the medieval period). Images, in bust form, of 'Lepeletier, Marat, Chalier and Beauvais' were presented as 'martyrs of the Revolution' on a raised 'altar'. The four were among the most celebrated revolutionaries of the time: Louis Michel Le Peletier, Jean-Paul Marat, Joseph Chalier and Charles Nicolas Beauvais de Préau.[49] In fact, the festival in Saint-Flour of the presentation of the busts of revolutionary heroes reflects a wider phenomenon emanating from the capital. Prominent artists in Paris created images of the four and their compatriots in various media. The best known is David's *Death of Marat*, but there were plans for other heroic painted portraits, as well as busts in porcelain, images to be placed on the curtain of the theatre in Paris and printed images for wide circulation.[50] The martyrs of the Revolution became perfect substitutions for the saints of the Christian faith. The celebration of the Revolution, held in the square before the cathedral at Saint-Flour, is eerily reminiscent of the tradition of the public procession of saints' relics and indeed of image reliquaries in bust form, which ultimately traces back to the Middle Ages.[51]

The Société populaire of Saint-Flour unequivocally and unabashedly rejected the traditional saints venerated by their ancestors. Indeed, on 14 December the Société closed its meeting with a hymn praising the fact that saints had been turned into coin.[52] It had been a lively meeting, full of applause for the various readings and propositions. These culminated in the request made by 'un des frères des bataillons' ('one of the brothers of the batallions' – a fellow revolutionary) that, in order to root out the remnants of fanaticism and to allow all reason to triumph, it was necessary to hold another 'autodafé' (a public ritual to root out 'heresy') at which all the 'cult objects' that were of no use would be burned. Such a proposition had been made earlier, but delayed until any useful objects could be separated from the rest. As the Société populaire now deemed that the matter could be delayed no longer, the date was set for two days hence, on 16 December.[53]

Word of the impending 'autodafé' seems to have spread, for the following day, a member of the local council voiced concern that the troops stationed in Saint-Flour were planning to pillage the churches the very next day and to make a bonfire 'de tous les saints en Bois et tableaux qui pourraient être dans les églises' ('of all the saints in wood and

Plate 5 Reliquary bust of St Yrieix, *c.* 1220–40 with later grill. Metropolitan Museum of Art, New York (17.190.352a, b)

paintings that might be in the churches'). Indeed, it was said that some of the 'volunteers' were already in the cathedral, chopping up works into pieces. Immediately the order was given, in order to protect 'the interest of the Nation', to dispatch members of the city administration to the cathedral and the Convent of the Visitation and Our Lady, in order to remove any 'gold, silver, cloth, ornaments and other precious objects' that might still be there, and to place them promptly in a secure depot. This was established in the episcopal palace, under the direction of a commissaire.[54]

Alas, the written record in the immediate aftermath of this decision falls silent, whether through loss or perhaps due to officials' focus on other, even more pressing concerns. A year and a half later, on 25 June 1795, beginning at 6 am, an inventory was taken of objects held in the large storeroom (the 'grand magasin'). In that list '5 bustes de saints de différents plaquets, de différentes tailles' ('5 busts of saints of different plates [metal coverings], of different sizes') are recorded. These are followed by 24 candlesticks of different sizes, a fountain, a large silvered candlestick, 7 old tapestries and various other pieces of wood furniture and textiles. The items are described as requiring urgent sale in order to avoid their dispersal.[55] Do these five busts relate to the four described in the 1657 inventory? We have already seen that the fourth bust in the pre-Revolutionary inventory, the bust of St Sylvester 'avec sa casque', was confiscated to be melted down in accordance with the law instituted on 27 March 1791, along with a St Anthony that had not appeared in the 1657 inventory. That means that three of the busts in the 1657 inventory of the cathedral are not recorded as having been sent to the font: the St Flour, listed first; the St Peter, of copper and silver, and the John the Baptist, of gilded silver. Might they be among the five listed as in storage in 1795?

Is it possible that they escaped attention, or were somehow rescued, like the bust of St Yrieix? In fact, one

Plate 6 (left) Reliquary statue of St Peter, mid-12th century. Église Saint-Pierre de Bredons, Albepierre-Bredons (photo: municipalitè d'Albepierre)

Plate 7 (right) Reliquary bust of St Baudime, mid-12th century. Église Saint-Nectaire, Saint-Nectaire (photo: Francis Debaisieux)

senses that some of the citizens of Saint-Flour were less ardent revolutionaries than the members of the Société populaire. At the very least they were slow to meet their obligations. A report for the Département du Cantal concerning the state of copper, bronze and bell metal belonging to the Republic prepared in December 1795 gives specific weights for Aurillac and Murat, whereas Saint-Flour 'did not provide information'.[56] In any event, it is clear that, notwithstanding the various efforts to rid the city of any vestiges of religion, and the effort of the nation to wrest any value from church property, the job was not complete.

On 26 March 1797, the council of Saint-Flour wrote to 'citoyen Palis, commissaire de l'administration' ('Citizen Palis, commissioner of the administration') from Aurillac concerning the 'grande quantité d'ornements et le plus riche de la cathédrale de St Flour' ('a large quantity of ornament and the most valuable from the cathedral of saint Flour') that were under the control of M. Lavalette, the guard of the storage depot. They expressed concern that, in lieu of carefully itemized accounting, M. Lavalette might intend to provide them only with a total weight and value for the material and that he might accordingly be able surreptitiously to remove some valuable material for himself without being detected. The council therefore charged citizen Palis with assessing the situation and providing a report.[57] In response, M. Palis wrote an account of his visit, and, in particular, he remarked that some of the 'statues of saints were also made of copper'. Consequently, 'as it appeared to us that some of these were covered partly with silver and partly with copper plaques, we had all the silver material removed in our presence by the goldsmith'.[58] This document therefore speaks of a specific historic episode at Saint-Flour, when an officer of the government noted the materials used in the creation of certain statues of saints and took the decision to remove the silver, while leaving the less

valuable copper in place. It provides a highly plausible explanation of the denuded condition of the bust recently found on rue Sorel.

The same circumstances could likewise account for the current condition of the 14th-century statue of a seated bishop in the Museum of Saint-Flour (**Pl. 3**). As noted above, that sculpture has distinctive silver nails with tiny floral heads of the same type that are found on the recently discovered bust, evidence that the two objects, although created two centuries apart from one another, were together at least once, apparently in the workshop of a goldsmith or restorer. The image of the seated bishop also shows evidence of having had silver sheathing that had been pulled off from the wood core. Moreover, there are original nails set in a regular pattern along the hem of the bishop's gown, indicating that it was once decorated with metal. The proper left hand of the bishop, which has been repaired, appears to have held a crozier. In these critical respects, the now somewhat humble, painted wooden statuette of the bishop in the Museum of Saint-Flour appears to conform to the 'image of Monsieur St Flour', holding a gilded and enamelled crozier and decorated along the edge (or hem), as described in the 1655 inventory.

Returning to that inventory, we see that we have now accounted for the loss of the silver Virgin and the image of St Sylvester, and we theorize that the St Flour listed in the inventory survives as the sculpture in the museum – beautiful, but more humble in materials than when it was created. This leaves the image of John the Baptist in gilded silver, almost certainly from the cathedral's parish of John the Baptist and therefore created no earlier than the late 14th century, and the image identified as St Peter 'in silver and copper'.

It is not impossible that a 12th-century image of St Flour was replaced when the church was raised to a cathedral in

the 14th century, and that the earlier image was only subsequently associated with St Peter. It is likewise possible that the recently discovered bust was originally carved to represent St Peter, co-patron of the monastic community at Saint-Flour. Other early images of St Peter recorded in French churches support this possibility. A silver image reliquary of St Peter was recorded at the abbey of Cluny before 1023.[59] While the reliquary of St Peter from Saint-Pierre-de-Bredons, near Saint-Flour, is the only surviving example in the Auvergne (**Pl. 6**), the report of a parish visit in 1652 to Saint-Nectaire indicates that an image of St Peter was one of three set on the high altar – the second, of St Baudime (**Pl. 7**), is unquestionably of the 12th century and the third, of the Virgin, is likely to be the 12th-century polychromed image also still in the church today.[60]

If the bust recently found on rue Sorel represents the image of St Peter stripped of its silver by M. Palis in 1797, how might one explain its preservation in the attic there for a little more than two centuries? The ownership of the house can be traced to within a decade of M. Palis' removal of silver from statues of saints in 1797. In 1809, the house was purchased for 2,050 francs by Jean Pagès, who is described in the recorded transaction as a 'menuisier', a worker of wood.[61] The house, sold by a family of bakers named Tiabut who retained other property nearby, had a 'boutique' on the street level, two bedrooms on the first floor, two more above them and a 'grenier' ('attic'), where the bust was found, above those rooms.

At the time of the sale, Catholicism had been reinstituted in France, according to the terms of the Concordat signed by Napoleon and Pope Pius VII in 1801. In Saint-Flour, the keys to the cathedral had been handed over to a priest in July 1802; the new bishop was installed in November of that year.[62] Efforts to restore the cathedral and to provide it with all necessary and appropriate furnishings commanded the attention of church officials for much of the 19th century. Had the recently found bust of a saint, largely stripped of its monetary value, been sold or offered to M. Pagès, the woodworker, as raw material, something which is known to have happened during the French Revolution, in the same way as stonemasons acquired vestiges of stone sculpture and metalworkers purchased old copper? Or might the bust have been turned over to him after the Concordat with a view to its restoration? Was he responsible for painting the raw wood uncovered when it was stripped of its silver? Was the head already lost, having been forcibly removed? Were the heavy iron bands now set at the neck and around the base of the statue provided by Antoine Jubelein, his next-door neighbor on the rue Sorel, a member of a prominent family of iron workers in Saint-Flour?[63]

The bust was painted, with iron bands and, I believe, a new base added, but the restoration of the bust was not completed. M. Pagès became ill during the winter of 1815 and died on 23 April 1815; later that year the ownership of the house passed to his widow, Françoise Clavières[64] following the terms of his will.[65] The couple was childless,[66] and there was no one to assume Jean Pagès' woodworking trade. Françoise Clavières remained in the house until her death in 1839. Subsequently the property passed to her niece Marguerite, who was Jean Pagès' goddaughter;[67] then it

passed through the hands of female relatives until the 1950s. No woodworker, artist or sculptor owned the property after M. Pagès. I believe that the bust found on the rue Sorel represents a 12th-century reliquary of St Peter, described in the inventory of 1655, stripped of its silver in 1797, and turned over to M. Pagès, woodworker of Saint-Flour, prior to his death in 1815. This remains, however, speculation. What is unquestionable is that this bust represents a significant addition to the patrimony of the Auvergne and the corpus of image reliquaries.

Notes

1 I am deeply grateful to M and Mme Moulier, who brought the reliquary to my attention on the recommendation of Jean-René Gaborit and who have repeatedly welcomed me to Saint-Flour. My appreciation for the city and its artistic heritage is rivalled only by my thankfulness for their friendship.

2 See Gaborit-Chopin 2005a and the entries for objects lent to the exhibition *La France romane*; Boehm 1990.

3 This suggestion was made by M. Jeannot, a local expert, and communicated to me by Pascale Moulier.

4 With the advice of Jean-René Gaborit, the sculpture was cleaned by Agnès Gall-Ortlik and Jennifer Batelot, restaurateurs du Patrimoine in Lyon, who removed some of the later paint and cleaned the metal.

5 Observed during examination with Pascale Moulier, September 2011. The conservators' report notes only the presence of such fragments in the back, leading her to suggest that the face may have been in gilded copper, like the hands.

6 Noted in the restoration report of Gall-Ortlik and Batelot.

7 Illustrated and discussed recently in Leroy and Debaisieux 2009, 62–3.

8 See Beaufrère 1964, 48.

9 The provenance is apparently Auvergnat and purportedly from Lavaudieu. See Gaborit *et al.* 2005, 114–16.

10 Metropolitan Museum of Art, Rogers Fund, 1927, 27.14.18, from the Alphonse Kann collection (sold Paris, 1927, no. 484).

11 The date is variously given, but in any case it was before the death of Odilon of Cluny in 1049.

12 The history is well summarized in Moulier 2001, 19.

13 Ruinart 1853, CCXXX. See Boudet 1902, CCVI, 'les ossements du saint, réunis dans une grande châsse fermée de trois serrures, furent placés sur un support élevé en arrière de l'autel'.

14 See de Jésus 1635, 255–6. In 1647 he became bishop of Rodez.

15 See Forsyth 1972, no. 33, 171–2; Gaborit 2005, 114–17.

16 See for example, Fouilheron 1965, 493–7. Because of its exceptionally large size, the Christ was not requested for the exhibition *La France romane* in Paris in 2005. I am grateful to Jean René Gaborit for this information.

17 'item ont donnat los senhors cossels a cels que davalaront lo Crosefit e a las alstras emagos…' Archives de la commune de Saint-Flour, compte de 1396, cited in *Documents d'histoire et art religieux* 1966, no. 99, 34. The same document has another listing for raising the chasse of St Flour up above the altar.

18 Bardol, royal notary at Saint-Flour, *Inventaire des ornements de la Sacristie de Messieurs du Chappitre cathedrale de St Flour* in *Minutes des notaires de Saint-Flour avant 1730*. The document is preserved in the Archives départementales du Cantal à Aurillac; a transcription by Roger Caullet can be consulted in the Archives municipales de Saint-Flour.

19 A document of 1319 created when Henri de Fauthières, abbot of Cluny, became the second bishop of Saint-Flour lists the objects he took with him to his new post in the Auvergne. No relics or reliquaries are mentioned, only items needed for the liturgy and the bishop's personal adornment, including an episcopal ring, a jewelled mitre, chalices and liturgical straws.

20 This mention appears to be the first to link the oliphant preserved at Saint-Flour to its patron saint, a link that Marcellin Boudet believed to be of more recent date.

21 The inventory also includes 'le Manteau de l'imaige Sainct Benoict de soye noire', as well as a red mitre, all of which are described as

very worn. As the image itself is not described in the inventory of works in precious materials, it may have been a wood or stone sculpture in the cathedral.

22 Bagnoli *et al.* 2010, no. 107, 193.

23 Perhaps from the Dominican chapel of John the Baptist in Saint-Flour, which became the parish church of the cathedral. It had been endowed by Jean, duc de Berry and begun in 1367. The duke provided the relic of an ear of the saint. While popularly, and erroneously, known as the church of St Vincent, its dedication was always to John the Baptist. See Chassang 2011, 69–70.

24 The description recalls the dove preserved at Saint-Yrieix in the Limousin. The dove at Saint-Flour, had its own 'ornemants', in colours appropriate to each liturgical season; the one at Saint-Yrieix has a single, richly embroidered cover. See *Les Trésors des églises de France* 1965, no. 378, p. 205, pl. 227.

25 Bénet 1888; Podlaha and Šittler 1903.

26 The reliquary of the Magdalene, listed on the third page, is called a 'reliquaire', although the fact that it had a dress associated with it suggests that it was a statuette. It follows the mention of several small reliquaries, one of them of enamelled copper, perhaps of Limoges work.

27 The niches have not been opened, and the sculpture has not been x-rayed.

28 The statue's history is undocumented. Legendarily it was once associated with a family of butchers, and thus it has been suggested that it might originally have belonged to the corporation of butchers of Saint-Flour, which had pre-empted the other corporations and reserved the saint as its exclusive patron. See *Documents d'histoire et art religieux*, no. 96, 93. Pascale Moulier recently told me that the purported donation of the statue by a family of butchers is unsubstantiated

29 A possible patron may have been the third bishop of Saint-Flour, Archambaud, who served from 1320 to 1347. Unlike many of the city's bishops over the centuries, he was resident in the diocese throughout his episcopacy. During his tenure, he granted permission to the chapter of Saint-Flour to build a new church. Archives départementales du Cantal, I G1.

30 See Gaborit-Chopin 2005b, no. 295, 385.

31 *Les Trésors des églises de France* 1965, no. 428, 236. No documentation is provided for this statement.

32 See Boehm 1990, for the same phenomenon at St Martial, Limoges, St Foy, Conques and St-Yrieix.

33 Forsyth 1972, 79; Hubert and Hubert 1982, 269; Boehm 1990, 329–30.

34 See Gaborit-Chopin 2005b, no. 294, 382, 384. Its history is also summarized in Moulier 2001, 37.

35 Limoges, Archives départementales de la Haute-Vienne, 1Q521; Boehm 1990, 240, 247.

36 Pierre Moulier discusses the effects of depopulation and emigration during the Hundred Years' War and the Plague. See Moulier 2001, 19.

37 It seems that the confraternities were founded at this time as a way of increasing the cathedral's revenues. Later documents indicate that confraternities offered money annually for masses and offices. See Archives nationales, F 19 7872, no. 81, budget for the cathedral in April 1821.

38 Mentioned in a document of 1836 as having happened 60 years earlier. See *Documents d'histoire et art religieux* 1966.

39 Chassang 2011.

40 The Revolution as it pertained to Saint-Flour is thoroughly discussed in Chassang 2008.

41 *Délibérations du conseil municipal, 1790–1791*, D1, no. 1, fol. 20. In addition to the mayor and two officers, the abbé de Rochebrun was one of those charged with this task.

42 It is listed in the Inventaire des Titres et Papiers de la Municipalité de St Flour, Archives municipales de Saint-Flour, D3, no. 4, p. 22, no. 7. The required inventory seems finally to have been conducted on 4 October 1791, and was referred to on 23 January 1793 by the Municipal council.

43 Archives départementales du Cantal, L593, fol. 155 (summarized in L, vol. 2, p. 388).

44 'On observe que dans les matieres d'or, et d'argent provenant du cij devant Chapitre cathedral on a ete oblige de démonter et casser les deux grandes croix, le grand crucifix du maître autel, et les six grand chandeillors dudit autel pour en extraire les matieres etrangeres tells que Bois et fer, et de procurer par là une certitude du poids des matieres envoyées. [n.b. transcribed as written, with irregular use of accents] Archives départementales du Cantal, Aurillac, 1Q428, no. 3. The six large candlesticks were listed in the inventory of 1657 as being of 'loton' (brass or latten), not precious metal, perhaps useful for the military in the revolutionary period.

45 Archives départementales du Cantal, L593, fol. 118v, 120. The sale from the sale capitulaire yielded 113 livres, 6 sous; the altar of St Anne from the Dominican church 48 livres.

46 Archives départementales du Cantal, L593, fol. 172.

47 On this society, see Belard 1913.

48 The 'calendrier republicain' was instituted on 22 September 1793. Dates are given in the text according to the standard calendar.

49 Charles Nicolas Beauvais de Préau was still alive in November 1793, but he had fallen into ill health as a result of his imprisonment earlier that year. He died on 28 March 1794.

50 In addition to David's famous *Death of Marat*, there is a drawing of the death of Lepelletier, as well as drawings of Charles Beauvais de Préau with Pierre Baille. A letter of 1860 indicates that David also drew portraits of both Beauvais and Chalier, but they have not been identified. Pajou made a bust of Beauvais de Préau. See Mongan and Stewart 1996, 56. A Sèvres bust of Lepelletier is preserved at the Château de Vizille, Isère. A number of print images are preserved in the collection of the British Museum and can be seen on the website by searching the names of the four. BM 1898,0527.207, not illustrated, represents designs for a finger ring commemorating three martyrs, Marat, Chalier and Lepelletier; BM 1891,0713.201 is a mounted fan leaf with Marat, Lepelletier and Chalier. The notion of substituting 'martyrs' of the Revolution for Christian martyrs is discussed specifically in the case of Lepelletier by Vanden Berghe and Plesca 2005, esp. 16–21.

51 Adding to the festivities at Saint-Flour, a bonfire was made of both documents of the ancient regime, and any 'Crosses, images or outside chapels' that had been found in the streets of the town, around which the people danced and sang. The text is partly transcribed in Chassang 2008, 523. *Registre des Délibérations du conseil general de la Commune du 22 novembre 1792 au 15 avril 1794 (22 germinal an 2)*, Archives municipales de Saint-Flour, D 1, part 2, p. 152v and 154v, 155v–156, 6 et 10 frimaire (26 and 30 November 1793).

52 Recorded in the *Registre des deliberations de la Société populaire de St Flour du 15 Frimaire an II au 7 Prairial an III*, Archives municipales de Saint-Flour, I2, no. 133. This is also noted in passing in Chassang 2008, 507.

53 Le 26 frimaire. See Belard 1913, 17.

54 Procès verbaux des séances du district de Saint-Flour, Archives Départementales du Cantal, described in Série L, vol. II, p. 282, original text L588, fol. 17v, 24 frimaire an II (15 Dec. 1793): 'Sur l'observation d'un membre que les troupes qui étoient ici avoient témoigné le désir de faire un autodafé de tous les saints en Bois et tableaux qui pourraient être dans les églises, et qu'elle se proposaient de la faire demain, que plusieurs volontaires étoient même déjà dans l'église ci-devant cathédrale, où ils mettoient tout en pieces et en morceaux, le conseil craignant qu'ils ne s'emparent aussi des linges et ornements qui servaient ci-devant au culte, et considérant que l'intérêt de la Nation à qui ces objets appartiennent exuge que l'on prenne les mesures convenables pour les mettres en lieux de sureté, arête le vice procureur syndic entendu, que les sieurs Marsal et Teissandier, membres de l'Administration de ville et Richard, autre membre, se rendront de suite, savoir: les deux premiers à la ci-devant cathédrale et le second au ci-devant couvent de la Visitation et de Notre Dame, après s'être adjointes d'un officier municipal de la Commune de St Flour à l'effet de faire transporter au District les matières d'or et d'argent et autres effets précieux qui pourraient encore s'iy trouver, et mettre en lieu de sureté et à l'abri de tout pillage, les ornements et linges ci-devant à l'usage du culte, de tout quoi sera dressé l'inventaire dont les minutes seront deposés aux archives du District' (M. Teissandier appears to have been promoted, having earlier been charged with the delivery of 14 pigs to Mauriac on le 9 frimaire an III, as described in serie L vol. II p. 124 – L493, fol. 52); he would later be put in charge of gathering the property of emigrés, L 588, fol. 60.

55 Archives départementales du Cantal, 1Q386, Biens de 1ere origine, mobilier national, District de St Flour, 12 frimaire an II, fols 7–7v.

56 Archives départementales du Cantal, Aurillac, Q447, no. 7, 27 frimaire an V.

57 Archives départementales du Cantal, Aurillac, L91, no. 1713: 'il reste encore une grande quantité à vendre…la dite [commission] du ci-devant district ne voulut pas lors d'un récolement des inventaires de marger de ces ornements attend q'uil les avoit fait degalloner sans autorisation, qu'il le presentoit en bloc et qu'ayant perdu leur forme il n'etoit pas facile de verifier s'il manquait quelque chose.' The letter makes reference to two letters from Palis to the council, dated 20 and 22 ventôse, but I have not been able to find these in the archives, either at Aurillac or in Saint-Flour.

58 'Et nous ayant paru que certaines d'elles [les statues de saints] étaient plaqués partie en argent partie en cuivre, nous avons fait extraire en notre presence par le dit orfèvre toutes les matières d'argent.' Archives départementales du Cantal, 1Q429, no. 6. The goldsmith was either Pierre or Antoine Andrieu, sons of Jean-Baptiste Andrieu, also a goldsmith at Aurillac. See L'Orfèvrerie en Haute-Auvergne 1996, 97–100.

59 Mentioned in the Consuetidines Farfensis; see Boehm 1990, 355. The first item listed in the 1382 inventory of the abbey is described as follows: 'Une statue de saint Pierre, dorée, avec une couronne d'argent sans diadème, garnie de pierres prétieuses, mais il y en manque une à la cime; ensemble un chef d'argent doré et une chaîne de fer.' Unlike some of the other descriptions in the inventory, there are no details in this one that betray the date of the object.

60 Saint-Flour was a dependency of Cluny, but neither Saint-Nectaire nor Bredons was. The dedication of the church at Saint-Flour to St Peter, rather than imitation of Cluny, seems to have been the determining factor in the church having a reliquary of St Peter.

61 I am grateful to Mme Vernier of the Archives départementales du Cantal for having found this reference for me. 4QS6U6. Transcription d'Actes de mutation 20.7794. M. Pagès is distinct from the eponymous 'garcon menuisier' who married on 25 Flor….an XII (15 mai …1804), and from his older brothers, also named Jean (one of whom had survived to adulthood), and his father.

62 Archives municipals de Saint-Flour, P1, nos 43, 44bis.

63 Jubelein was one of the witnesses of Jean Pagès will, along with other neighbours. Archives municipals de Saint-Flour, 3E274, art. 1352.

64 Recorded in the Tables des successions du Canton, 3Q9429.

65 Per the terms of his will of 17 January 1815, registered on 20 July of that year. The Testament was given before M. Richard; it included some furniture, valued at 100 francs, the house and an annual revenue of 60 francs 'capital au dernier vingt douze cent francs'. Archives départementales du Cantal, 3Q8920, Déclaration des mutations par decès, 145, no. 945. The declaration of the widow was made on 17 October 1815.

66 An earlier will was prepared on 7 May 1793, which similarly named his widow as his heir, unless he had a child born posthumously.

67 Recorded in the Registre de Naissances 1810–12, Archives municipales de Saint-Flour, 1E31. Her subsequent marriage to Jean Beral, named with her as owner of the house, is recorded in the same archives, 1E32, no. 24.

Bibliography

Bagnoli, M., Klein, H.A., Mann, C.G. and Robinson, J. (eds) 2010. Treasures of Heaven: Saints, Relics and Devotion in Medieval Europe, Baltimore and London.

Beaufrère, A. 1964. Bredons et ses Trésors d'Art, Aurillac.

Belard, L. 1913. La Société Populaire de St-Flour et la Mission de Châteauneuf-Randon dans cette ville, Aurillac.

Bénet, A. 1888. 'Le trésor de l'abbaye de Cluny, Inventaire de 1382', Revue de l'art chrétien, vol. CVI, 195–205.

Boehm, B.D. 1990. Medieval Head Reliquaries of the Massif Central, Michigan.

Boudet, M. 1902. Cartulaire de Saint-Flour, Monaco.

Chassang, P. 2011. Saint-Flour. Histoire d'une forteresse, Histoire d'une cité, des origins au début du XXIe siècle, Brioude.

Chassang, P. 2008. La Révolution dans les Districts de Saint-Flour et de Murat, Clamecy.

de Jésus, D. 1635. Histoire paraenetique des trois saincts protecteurs du haut Auvergne, Paris.

Documents d'histoire et art religieux, 1966. Exh. cat., Saint-Flour.

Forsyth, I.H. 1972. The Throne of Wisdom: Wood Sculptures of the Madonna in Romanesque France, Princeton.

Fouilheron, J. 1965. 'Du Bon Dieu de Saint-Flour au Christ noir de la cathédrale', Revue de la Haute-Auvergne, 493–7.

Gaborit, J.-R. 2005. 'Les Images de Culte', in Gaborit et al. 2005, 111–17.

Gaborit, J.-R., Gaborit-Chopin, D. and Durand, J. (eds) 2005. L'art roman au Louvre, Paris.

Gaborit-Chopin, D. 2005a. 'Les statues-reliquaires et la renaissance de la ronde-bosse. Les Majestés romanes', in Gaborit-Chopin 2005b, 378–85.

Gaborit-Chopin, D. 2005b. La France romane au temps des premiers capétiens (987–1152), Paris.

Hubert, J. and Hubert, M-C. 1982. 'Chrétienne ou paganism: Les statues-reliquaires de l'europe carolingienne', in Cristianizzazione ed organizzazione ecclisiastica della champagne nell'alto medioevo: espansione e resistenze, Spoleto, 235–75.

Leroy, H. and Debaisieux, F. 2009. Vierges romanes, Beaumont.

L'Orfèvrerie en Haute-Auvergne, 1996. Exh. cat., Aurillac.

Les Trésors des églises de France, 1965. Exh. cat., Paris, Musée des arts décoratifs.

Mongan, A. and Stewart, M. 1996. David to Corot: French Drawings in the Fogg Art Museum, Cambridge, MA.

Moulier, P. 2001. Eglises romanes de Haute-Auvergne, III: La region de Saint-Flour, Madrid.

Podlaha, A. and Šittler, E. 1903. Chrámový Poklad u Sv. Víta v Praze, Prague.

Ruinart, T. 1853. Vita B. Urbani II (Patrologiae cursus completes: series latina…), ed. J.-P. Migne, vol. 151, Paris.

Vanden Berghe, M. and Plesca, I. 2005. Lepelletier de Saint-Fargeau sur son lit de mort par Jacques-Louis David: saint Sébastien révolutionnaire, miroir multiréférencé de Rome, Brussels.

Chapter 11
New Dating of the Limoges Reliquaries of the Stigmatization of St Francis

Elisabeth Antoine-König

Two Limoges quatrefoil reliquaries depicting the stigmatization of St Francis have long been famous for showing what is believed to be the first representation of this crucial event in Franciscan spirituality, and more widely in western medieval spirituality. The early dating of the reliquaries to around 1228–30 has been repeatedly proposed up to the modern day,[1] although in 1993 Chiara Frugoni suggested a later date for these two pieces in a footnote in her magisterial book *Francesco e l'invenzione delle stimmate*.[2] Over the last century historians and theologians have debated the issue of the stigmata as one of the main problems of *la question franciscaine*: what is the significance of this event (symbolic or real?) and to what extent should Francis be considered as an *alter Christus*? While this paper will not consider this question from a spiritual perspective, the progress made in these studies must be taken into consideration, particularly with reference to the publications in 2009 celebrating the 800th anniversary of the foundation of the order. In France this provided the opportunity to publish a remarkable complete edition of the sources on St Francis[3] and an extremely stimulating biography of the saint by André Vauchez.[4] Based on this new material and on the doubts of historians concerning the precedence of these two enamels in the iconography of the stigmatization, it is timely to reconsider them and to take into account the analyses of Chiara Frugoni.

Two unique reliquaries

A plaque is all that remains for one of the two pieces, with the rest of the reliquary now lost.[5] It is part of the Louvre's collection, but is on loan to the Cluny museum and will therefore be referred to as the Cluny plaque for practical purposes (**Pl. 3**). The Louvre also has a remarkably well-preserved complete reliquary of the same form, with its foot still intact (this will be termed the Louvre reliquary).[6] On this complete reliquary, one can see that the stigmatization plaque is in fact the back plate of the reliquary, with the front side decorated with glass cabochons and five crystals (**Pl. 1**).

The enamelled scene stands out against a guilloché-patterned background, with small motifs in reserve: there are quatrefoils on three of the foils, with stars, the sun and the moon surrounding the seraph in the upper foil. In the lower foil stands St Francis (**Pl. 2**). He is represented with a halo, which therefore means that the enamelled plaque was made after his canonization in 1228 (as stated above, the plaque has usually been dated to around 1228–30, immediately after this event). With his face raised towards the sky, the saint opens his hands, revealing inside two red spots, the stigmata, also visible on his feet; a slit in his robe allows the viewer to see the wound on his side. Above him stands a seraph, two wings folded in the upper part, with another pair spread out in a cross shape and the third pair covering its body. This is a very restrained representation of the miracle of the stigmatization, which according to the official Franciscan tradition occurred in September 1224, and as Tommaso da Celano described it in his *Vita* of 1229.[7]

The other side of the Louvre reliquary, the major one, is decorated with five large crystal cabochons, allowing the viewer to look into the body of the reliquary which contains

Plate 1 Reliquary of the stigmatization of St Francis of Assisi (major side), Limoges, third quarter of the 13th century, copper: punched, chased and gilt; rock crystal and glass cabochons; turquoise enamelled beads; wood core, 36.2 x 20.6cm; diam. of base: 15.2cm. Musée du Louvre, département des Objets d'art, Paris (photo © RMN-Grand Palais (musée du Louvre)/Daniel Arnaudet)

Plate 2 Reliquary of the stigmatization of St Francis of Assisi (reverse): the stigmatization, Limoges, third quarter of the 13th century, copper: punched, chased and gilt; champlevé enamel; wood core, 36.2 x 20.6cm; diam. of base: 15.2cm. Musée du Louvre, département des Objets d'art Paris (photo © RMN-Grand Palais (musée du Louvre)/Daniel Arnaudet)

the relics, and are surrounded by blue and yellow glass cabochons on a copper gilt background. This reliquary has a rather complex structure: the plaque, which is held by a hinge, can be lifted to reveal another copper plaque, with five openings shaped like Greek crosses. Inside the cavities in the wooden core are the relics, hidden behind a red textile. On the foot, two pairs of confronted peacocks are drinking from the Fountain of Life: this return to early Christian iconography is rather rare in Limoges enamels, although confronted peacocks can be seen on a few gemellions, for example the pair of gemellions in Baltimore, which Marquet de Vasselot dated to between 1250 and 1280.[8]

As for the Cluny reliquary, it has lost its wooden core, its front plaque, its relics and its foot. In the catalogue of the exhibition *L'Œuvre de Limoges*,[9] Élisabeth Taburet-Delahaye argued that it was extremely likely that an enamelled reliquary foot from the Bargello[10] was originally part of the Cluny reliquary. On a dark blue background there are four medallions: three with a peacock, and on the fourth medallion stands St Francis with a halo, holding a book and blessing a donor kneeling in front of him (**Pl. 4**). The five stigmata are clearly represented. The costume of the donor, as well as his long hair, is that of a layman. However, one has to question why the features on the foot appear against a

blue enamelled background, whereas on the Cluny quatrefoil the features appear against a gilt background (and likewise on the Louvre reliquary, the foot and quatrefoil have a gilt background). Therefore it is possible that this foot may correspond to a third reliquary connected with St Francis.

Although the Louvre and Cluny quatrefoil plaques have exactly the same dimensions, there are slight differences in their composition and manner, as is usual with Limoges enamels. In summary, the enameller of the Louvre piece seems to have slightly enlarged most of the elements of the composition: the composition on the Cluny plaque is more elegant, refined and mastered in a superior fashion, while the execution of the Louvre example is slightly less elegant. Is it just a question of mastery, with one enameller being more skilled than the other? Or is it a matter of evolution, with the Cluny reliquary being an earlier version and the Louvre one a later version?

Strangely enough, only these two examples survive of the production of Limoges enamels of this shape with this specific iconography: why are there not others? They seem to have been rather particular commissions, but for which church? The problem is that little is known about their original destination. The Cluny plaque was bought in 1851

Plate 3 (above) Plaque from a reliquary of St Francis: the stigmatization of St Francis, Limoges, third quarter of the 13th century, copper: punched, chased and gilt; champlevé enamel; wood core, 20 x 20cm. Musée de Cluny, Paris (photo © RMN-Grand Palais musée de Cluny – musée national du Moyen-Âge)/Jean-Gilles Berizzi)

Plate 4 (right) Foot of a reliquary (?), Limoges, third quarter of the 13th century, copper: punched, chased and gilt; champlevé enamel, h. 17.5cm, diam. of base 17.5cm. Museo del Bargello, Florence (su concessione del Ministero dei Beni e delle Attività Culturali e del Turismo)

from the master of the choir school (*maîtrise*) of the cathedral of Rodez, which may imply a local provenance, as Rodez in 1851 was not a major centre for the art market. In addition, the Franciscans were already established in Rodez as early as 1232.[11] As for the Louvre reliquary, it was acquired in 1899 from the Michel Boy collection. Boy purchased it in 1890 from the sale of the Charles Ducatel collection in Paris:[12] according to Émile Molinier and an annotated sale catalogue, it had been purchased in Spain, and was reputed to have come from a convent in Las Palmas, Majorca.[13] Las Palmas was reconquered by the Crown of Aragon on 31 December 1229. Soon after, in 1232, the Franciscans arrived and built a small chapel at Las Palmas, followed by a larger church in 1244. According to Joaquin Yarca Luaces, if this reliquary was made for the Franciscans of Majorca, it could not have been made before 1240–5 on account of the modesty of the first Franciscan chapel there.[14] This raises an important consideration for both pieces: which Franciscan church would commission such a splendid and rich reliquary so soon after the death of St Francis, the lover of Lady Poverty? One must keep in mind that it was only in 1253 that Pope Innocent IV authorized the Franciscans to receive golden or silver sacred vases as gifts for their churches.

A very particular iconography

Despite the lack of certainty regarding their origin or destination, these two pieces have been very precisely dated by most art historians. As soon as the Cluny plaque was acquired, Laborde published it and dated it to immediately after the canonization in 1228.[15] The same date was adopted by Labarte in 1865,[16] who intended to date it even earlier (to the time of stigmatization on the Alverna), but had to admit

that on account of the halo, it must have been made after 1228. In 1906, Henri Matrod wrote an article in the *Miscellanea Francescana*, entitled 'Deux émaux franciscains au Louvre. Les stigmates de saint François. Leur plus ancienne représentation connue',[17] in which he argued that the two enamelled plaques of the stigmatization were perfectly faithful to the account given in the first *Vita* of St Francis by Tommaso da Celano, and were therefore strictly contemporary with this text of 1229. This article was adopted as the authority on these pieces, and Matrod's conclusions were faithfully repeated by art historians, including Marie-Madeleine Gauthier (who was also inclined to date them earlier).[18]

The two plaques correspond to Tommaso da Celano's account as far as the careful description of the seraph and its wings as well as the precise moment of the event are concerned: Francis has to arise in order to try to understand the meaning of the vision, feeling both sad and happy at the same time. It is this very moment that is depicted on these pieces, when the vision, on first entering his heart, makes the stigmata appear on his body. However, it is noteworthy that the enamellers have not represented the cross on which the seraph is fixed, which is mentioned twice in the text. The representation is therefore not as faithful as Matrod stated. Therefore, are these two plaques really the illustration of this *Vita*, or of something else?

In order to understand the iconography of the two plaques, one must first recall the main steps in the construction of the Franciscan story of the stigmata.[19] St Francis died in the chapel of the Transito[20] during the night of 3–4 October 1226. On 4 October, Brother Elia, Vicar General of the Franciscan Order, sent an encyclical letter announcing the death of Francis to the order, in which he described the stigmata and attested to their miraculous nature. Less than two years after his death, Pope Gregory IX on 28 July 1228 officially canonized St Francis. But, in the *bulla*, the pope did not mention the stigmata.

In 1229, at the request of Gregory IX, Tommaso da Celano wrote the *Vita* of St Francis, which gave a more precise account of the event on the Alverna than the letter of Brother Elia. Da Celano's *Vita* would remain the main source for the hagiography of St Francis for over thirty years.

In 1230, the body of St Francis was transferred to the new basilica built in his honour in Assisi. Enclosed behind a wall, it remained there until the beginning of the 19th century. The body remained intact, which therefore means that all reliquaries of St Francis contain relics from his lifetime, such as parts of his tunic, blood or water which had been been in contact with his wounds, nails, hair and so forth, but absolutely no bones. In another *bulla* in 1237, the same pope, Gregory IX, asserted the existence and holiness of the stigmata and, contrary to the canonization *bulla*, declared that it was mainly on account of the stigmata that Francis had been canonized. In 1250 a church was built on the Alverna, which became a place of pilgrimage, with pilgrimages to the Alverna soon receiving indulgences from the papacy. In 1255, a further *bulla* issued by Alexander IV asserted again the truth of the stigmata, referring particularly to the wound in the side. The wound in the side had special significance since in the Gospels this was the last wound inflicted on Christ's body and the single act that clearly showed the fulfilment of the Scriptures and revealed Christ as the Messiah. Therefore, its presence on Francis's side (strictly hidden during his lifetime) was an important issue in the process of identification between Francis and Christ.

In 1263 the *Legenda Maior* of St Bonaventura was approved, provoking a big shift in the perception and the iconography of St Francis: in 1266 the General Chapter of Paris ordered that all previous *vitae* of the saint be destroyed. From this time onwards, the *Legenda Maior* became the official version of the life of St Francis, from which artists could take inspiration. In this text, Bonaventura related for example that one night Gregory IX had a dream as he still doubted the existence of the wound in St Francis's side: St Francis appeared to him with his side bleeding and the pope filled a whole cup with his blood; following this vision, Pope Gregory was most devoted to the side wound of St Francis.[21]

Eventually, in 1282 an enquiry was conducted on the stigmatization, with the result that a date was officially set for the commemoration of this event; the 14th of September, the very day of the feast of the Exaltation of the Cross. Over the course of approximately half a century, this miraculous event had been questioned, reinterpreted and theologically re-elaborated.[22] Between 1237 and 1291, the popes proclaimed no fewer than nine *bullae* in order to assert the veracity of the stigmata, and especially the wound in the side, in defence against their detractors.[23]

In parallel with the written sources, we must also look at the iconography of St Francis, the first saint in Western spirituality whose cult was so largely and quickly connected

Plate 5 The Master of St Francis, *The Stigmatization of St Francis*, c. 1260–70, stained glass. Basilica of San Francesco, window A1, panels a9–10, Assisi (after F. Martin, *Die Glasmalereien von San Francesco in Assisi*)

to images.[24] The first known image of St Francis is the fresco at Subiaco in which he has no halo, is termed 'Brother Francis' and does not display the stigmata; it may therefore have been painted before the canonization, probably in 1227 or 1228.[25] The first dated painting of the stigmatization appears on the large altarpiece by Bonaventura Berlinghieri in Pescia, dated 1235. The founder of the order stands in the centre of the altarpiece, surrounded by episodes from his life and his miracles. The stigmatization appears on the upper left scene, which closely parallels the story told by Tommaso da Celano, but with one rather important difference from the scene on the Limoges reliquaries: St Francis is not standing (as Tommaso described), but kneeling. This is an obvious pictorial way of assimilating the scene to Christ's prayer on the Mount of Olives. Around 1250–60, the workshop of Margaritone of Arezzo had painted a considerable number of 'pseudo-portraits' of St Francis. They do not show the stigmatization, but represent the stigmata: only four of them, without the wound on the side.

At about the same time, in the lower church of Assisi, the so-called Maestro di San Francesco was the first to dedicate a whole cycle to the life of the saint, in exact parallel with the life of Christ. Unfortunately, the image of St Francis in the stigmatization scene has been destroyed and so the representation cannot be considered here. However, it is still

Plate 6 Quatrefoil reliquary (major side), Limoges, last third of the 13th century, copper: punched, chased and gilt; rock crystal and glass cabochons; wood core, 21.5 x 17.7cm. Musée du Louvre, département des Objets d'art, Paris (photo © RMN-Grand Palais (musée du Louvre) / Daniel Arnaudet)

possible to see the stained glass window attributed to the same master in the upper church (**Pl. 5**). Its iconography is quite close to our two reliquaries, with the exception of the saint's position: he is kneeling and not standing, as noted above on the Berlinghieri altarpiece. The tunic is slit in order to show the wound on the side.

Therefore, according to Chiara Frugoni, in the 1250s, as a result of the popes' actions, a new iconography was established through the innovations of the large Assisi workshop. This iconography insisted on the exposure of the wound on St Francis's side. After that, the *Legenda Maior* would foster another shift, as illustrated by Giotto in Assisi and on other major works: the seraph clearly takes Christ's face, with the rays connecting him to St Francis, and Brother Leo is present as a witness of the event.[26] Therefore, it is clear that the Limoges reliquaries precede the Bonaventura iconography. However, it is my opinion that, following Frugoni's analyses, they seem to fit perfectly in the middle of the century (1250–60), when the debate was at its height and the exposure of the side wound was so significant. The construction of the basilica of Assisi also introduced a change of scale in the Franciscan churches and their décor, as can be seen for example in the Franciscan churches of the Holy Roman Empire with their huge stained glass windows. The Limoges reliquaries, with their vibrant colours and gold background, are more appropriate to this setting rather than that of the first small, modest constructions that characterized the beginnings of the Franciscan Order. One must also keep in mind the authorization of 1253 that

permitted the receipt of precious vases, which fits perfectly with this chronology.

Another matter for consideration is the question of where these two reliquaries were made. They have not always been attributed to Limoges,[27] but sometimes to Spain,[28] a Limoges workshop working in Italy[29] or an Italian workshop working 'à la manière de Limoges'.[30] Nevertheless, several factors suggest that these reliquaries were made in Limoges by enamellers from Limoges. A first line of argument is provided by the iconography, primarily through the way in which the Alverna is represented. It is shown as a site with blossoming trees, in a poetic atmosphere redolent of the Franciscan spirit, evoking the *Canticle of Creatures* (which Francis wrote after his encounter with the seraph). This, however, is very far from the reality of the Alverna, a wild and rocky area in the Abruzzo region, which at the time was considered a desert where Francis had retired in order to meditate, in the same way as Christ had done in the desert. The enameller apparently had no idea of the nature of the Alverna, nor had he seen how other artists (mostly painters) had represented it, using rocks, grottoes and sometimes even bears to suggest the wilderness of the place.

A second iconographical argument originates from the Berlinghieri altarpiece: following its example, Italian artists represented the stigmatization with St Francis kneeling in a rocky landscape, as a reference to the prayer of Christ on the Mount of Olives.[31] If a Limoges enameller had made the reliquaries in Italy, with strong connections to Franciscan circles, he would have known one of these altarpieces, which adorned most Franciscan churches, and would have taken their composition as a model. The representation of the stigmatization on these reliquaries is totally disconnected from the iconographical tradition soon established and retained in Italy. The enameller was working outside of this tradition, and appears to have no visual point of reference to represent this event.

A third argument in favour of Limoges as the production centre is that the Cluny plaque emerged in Rodez in 1851. As stated above, Rodez was not an important player in the art market and it is difficult to conceive how it would have come from Italy to Rodez at this early date. It is much more likely that it was made in Limoges for Rodez or a nearby church.

The quatrefoil reliquaries in Limoges production

It is now interesting to examine how the proposed later date of execution of these two pieces fits into the 'œuvre de Limoges'. Although the quatrefoil shape is quite common in the Rhine-Meuse area and Lower Saxony in the second half of the 13th century, the shape seems to be very new in Limoges in either 1230 or 1250. There is no known reliquary of this shape from Limoges in the 12th century or from around 1200. Limoges had chosen the sarcophagus shape for its shrines, and stubbornly stuck to this form for a long period. If our two reliquaries date from around 1230, they are unique and without immediate successors, which is very unusual in Limoges. However, if they date to around 1250–60, they are not quite so unusual since their shape encountered a certain success in Limoges during the second half of the 13th century. A small group of quatrefoil Limoges

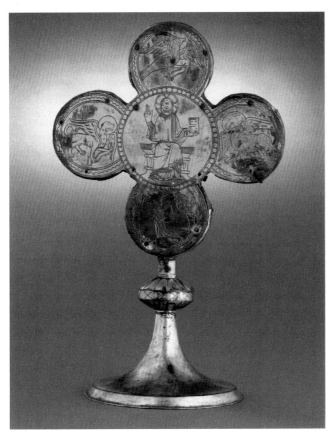

Plate 7 Quatrefoil reliquary (reverse): Christ in Majesty; symbols of the evangelists and a donor, Limoges, second half of the 13th century, copper: punched, chased and gilt; wood core, 28.2 x 17.4cm; diam. of base: 12.4cm. Musée de Cluny, Paris (photo © RMN-Grand Palais musée de Cluny – musée national du Moyen-Âge)/Stéphane Maréchalle)

Plate 8 Cross (reverse): the stigmatization of St Francis, Limoges, third quarter of the 13th century, copper: punched, chased and gilt; champlevé enamel; wood core, dimensions unknown. Current location unknown (© Département des Objets d'art, Musée du Louvre)

reliquaries can be gathered, all of which have been dated to about 1250 or the third quarter of the 13th century. These reliquaries are more sober than those depicting St Francis as they are not enamelled, but have only engraved decoration on a guilloché background. This group of quatrefoil Limoges reliquaries includes:

1. A reliquary acquired by the Louvre in 1989 (**Pl. 6**), which also has five large crystal cabochons on the major side, as well as the same system of double copper plates covering the relics as on the St Francis reliquary. On its reverse, there is an engraved plaque representing Christ in majesty and the four evangelists at work, with small quatrefoiled reserves on a guilloché background.[32]
2. A quatrefoil reliquary in the Cluny museum, with rather similar decoration (**Pl. 7**): five big crystal cabochons are on the major side, and depicted on the reverse are the engraved figures of Christ in Majesty in the centre surrounded by only three symbols of the evangelists, the angel of St Matthew having been replaced in the lower foil by the figure of a donor kneeling between two trees (a composition similar to that used on the St Francis reliquaries), who in this instance is shown to be a cleric.[33]
3. A quatrefoil reliquary from the Walters Art Museum in Baltimore adorned with crystal cabochons on both sides.[34]
4. The Brooklyn Museum also owns a reliquary of this type, which is most probably the reliquary published by Rupin as coming from the hospital of Limoges.[35]

5. Equally of interest is the reliquary from the True Cross of Balledent (originally from the Grandmont Treasury), which has the same structure, although the head of an ivory Virgin has been inserted in place of the central crystal.[36] The motifs engraved on the background of the foot of the Balledent reliquary are exactly the same as the ones on the edge of our St Francis reliquary.

Together, these quatrefoil reliquaries represent a coherent group, if we consider the St Francis reliquaries as the leading pieces, with the others being more modest in their execution. Therefore, it is my belief that rather than the reliquaries of St Francis appearing suddenly around 1230 without precedent or later imitators for the next 20 years, with a second generation of quatrefoils appearing in the middle of the 13th century, it is more plausible to date all of them to between the middle and the third quarter of the 13th century.

The St Francis reliquaries should also be compared with other Limoges works from the middle of the 13th century that demonstrate the same elegant knot with turquoise pearls, such as the monstrance reliquary of Saint-Georges-les-Landes (also from the Grandmont Treasury)[37] or the cross with double arms from Saint-Priest-Taurion.[38]

In order to complete the survey of stylistically similar works, it is necessary to mention two further 'Franciscan' Limoges pieces, Firstly, there is the mandorla-shaped reliquary from the collegiate church Saint-Martin of Brive, dated to around 1260,[39] which represents on the upper part

Chapter 12
Christus crystallus
Rock Crystal, Theology and Materiality in the Medieval West

Stefania Gerevini

This chapter focuses on the interactions between theoretical knowledge and material choices in the arts of the Middle Ages in the West.[1] It considers a widely employed artistic medium – rock crystal – and it explores the multiple symbolic meanings associated with this stone as well as examining its employment specifically in relation to a cross reliquary preserved in Borghorst, Germany, until its recent theft. Due to its physical properties of hardness and transparency and its widely accepted associations with congealed water, rock crystal was approached in the medieval West as a metaphor for a variety of theological notions: angelic natures, the Incarnation of Christ, the sacrament of baptism and the miraculous conversion of souls hardened by sin. Knowledge of these theological implications assists in explaining the popularity of rock crystal in the liturgical arts of the Middle Ages and allows a better understanding of its specific artistic meanings, particularly in the manufacture of reliquaries. However, rock crystal was just one of the many gemstones invested with metaphorical implications in the Middle Ages. The enigmatic and ambivalent nature of rock crystal, which encompassed the opposing qualities of liquid and solid bodies, provided visual substantiation to otherwise elusive notions concerning the ontological status of created beings and their participation in the divine. Thus, it offers us a privileged standpoint from which to analyse medieval attitudes towards matter and its connection with the spiritual world.

Rock crystal belongs to the family of quartzes and is a very hard stone.[2] Its carving was practised throughout the Mediterranean in antiquity and the Middle Ages. Seals, amulets, intaglios and sculpted objects of various shapes and sizes were produced until Late Antiquity in Egypt, Greece and the Roman Empire.[3] A good number of pendants, seals and intaglios have also survived from Byzantium; mostly, these date between the 5th and 8th centuries and attest to the appreciation of this stone in the early empire.[4] After this time rock-crystal production seems to have dwindled in Byzantium, whilst after poorly attested beginnings in Umayyad and Abbasid Islam it reached its medieval zenith between the 9th and 11th centuries in the Fatimid caliphate.[5] Rock crystal was also a popular artistic medium in the medieval West. Early attestations there include a number of unengraved quartz pebbles or spheres, many of which have been excavated from 6th-century Saxon and Merovingian cemeteries, where they were probably used as amulets.[6] Starting in the 9th century, lapidary workshops supplied polished rock-crystal cabochons and globes that were employed along with other precious stones and metalwork as adornments for altars, liturgical crosses, book covers and, most frequently, reliquaries, which preserved the association of the semi-precious stone with funerary contexts. The most sophisticated rock-crystal artefacts to have survived from this period are a group of intaglios of varying dimensions produced in the Carolingian Empire in the 9th century, a testament to the refined skills of Carolingian engravers.[7] At this time, Western lapidary workshops seem to have chiefly executed small-scale, non-sculpted rock-crystal objects. Artefacts of larger size and more sophisticated workmanship, such as relief-cut vessels, were instead imported from the Islamic world, particularly from Fatimid

Egypt, and were frequently reused as liturgical furnishings and relic holders in ecclesiastical treasuries throughout Europe.[8] In the course of the 13th and early 14th centuries, however, the production of rock-crystal artefacts by Western lapidaries grew in quality and variety: objects manufactured at this time include sizeable liturgical vessels of different shapes, liturgical crosses and elaborate reliquaries of various forms and dimensions.[9] The production of rock-crystal artworks in western Europe continued during the Renaissance, although from the mid-15th century the newly invented *vetro cristallo* (transparent Venetian glass) began to provide a cheaper, but aesthetically equivalent alternative to rock crystal.[10]

While the specific uses and techniques of rock-crystal carving evolved over the course of the Middle Ages, its popularity was enduring. Practicality certainly contributed to the propagation of its use. The stone is perfectly transparent and much harder than glass; thus, it afforded greater durability to precious artworks and reliquaries, while also granting visibility and protection to the relics or images placed inside them.[11] In addition, quartz has significant refracting and magnifying properties. Although these characteristics were only systematically investigated by scholars of optics from the mid-13th century onwards, the magnifying properties of rock crystal were exploited artistically long before they became the object of scientific enquiry.[12] As Genevra Kornbluth has demonstrated, Carolingian engravings provide a good case in point. The engraver of the cabochon known as the St Denis Crystal, now preserved at the British Museum, incised the scene of the Crucifixion on the reverse of the stone leaving a margin of 7mm between the engraving and the edges of the stone. However, seen from the obverse, the image is magnified precisely so that it fills the margins of the cabochon, demonstrating that the artist had full awareness of, and could cleverly manipulate, the optical properties of rock crystal (**Pl. 1**).[13] In other examples the magnifying properties

Plate 1 St Denis Crystal, 9th century, rock crystal, l. 155mm, w. 110mm, d. 45mm. British Museum, London (1855,0305.1)

of rock crystal were exploited to increase visually the size of relics, as is the case with a number of 12th- and 13th-century jewelled cross reliquaries or to emphasize the lavishness – and perceived preciousness – of the containers. The so-called Ninian Reliquary at the British Museum is a suitable example of this type (**Pl. 2**).[14] A polished cabochon is set on the lid of the reliquary pendant against a background of diminutive pearls that surrounds a minute wooden cross (an allusion to the relics held within the pendant). Both the

Plate 2 The Ninian Reliquary, c. 1200, human bone (?), horn, gold, rock crystal, pearls and wood, h. 54.5mm, w. 52mm, diam. 52mm, depth 28mm. British Museum, London (1946,0407.1.a)

pearls and the cross are magnified by the crystal and look larger than their actual size, making the pendant appear even more precious.

However, the popularity of rock crystal was not only due to practical convenience. This material had long been invested with complex theological and symbolic meanings, which influenced its use and application throughout the Middle Ages. Christianity had inherited from antiquity the belief that transparent quartz was the product of the prolonged congealment of water that could no longer be turned to liquid.[15] This belief, although occasionally the target of scepticism, survived until the end of the Middle Ages and the association of the stone with water, as well as its transparency (and thus its alleged purity), triggered imaginative interpretations of the medical properties and metaphorical implications of rock crystal.

The medical efficacy attributed to rock crystal depended on its associations with liquids: powdered and mixed with honey, it was believed to increase the quantity of breast milk, and placed under the tongue, it was believed to quench thirst.[16] The medical properties listed by lapidary treatises help to explain the popularity of rock crystal in the manufacture of amulets, and may indicate that this stone retained a prophylactic function when it was employed for the creation of jewel reliquaries, such as the Ninian Reliquary. However, medieval artistic uses of rock crystal are best understood against the background of contemporary theological writings. As was the case with other gemstones, theological interest in rock crystal was primarily triggered by references made to it in the Bible, and more specifically in the Book of Ezekiel (Ez. 1:22), the Book of Psalms (Ps. 147:17) and the Book of Revelation (Rev. 4:6; 21:11; 22:1).

In the opening chapter of the Book of Ezekiel, the prophet is confronted with the glorious vision of God. Having described the cherubic creatures supporting the throne of God, the prophet notes: 'Spread out above the heads of the living creatures was what looked something like a vault, sparkling like crystal, and awesome' (Ez. 1:22).[17]

Gregory the Great's gloss on this passage provided a framework of interpretation that remained valid in subsequent centuries. The crystal firmament, Gregory proposed, could represent angelic natures: in the same way that rock crystal was once water but then became solid stone, such was the case with angelic natures. When they were first created, angels were given the freedom to decide whether they wished to be humble and remain in the presence of God or to give in to pride and fall from their blessed state. Those who decided to stand by God would fall no more: their mutable natures were made incorruptible in the same way as water was congealed into unbreakable crystal. Secondly, Gregory argued that the crystal vault might be understood as a metaphor of Christ. Rock crystal was unbreakable, but derived from liquid water; similarly, the body of Christ was subject to human corruptibility and change until his death, but was transformed into incorruptible matter through the Resurrection. From this perspective, Gregory added, the rock-crystal firmament is correctly described in the biblical passage as awesome, because Christ is a judge who appears beautiful to the righteous, but fearful to those who have sinned.[18]

Later exegetes further expanded Gregory's established associations between rock crystal, angelic natures and the person of Christ, additionally connecting the precious stone with the Holy Spirit and the Sacrament of Baptism. These associations were derived from the Book of Revelation, wherein rock crystal is mentioned three times. Chapter 4, which draws on the Book of Ezekiel to describe John's vision of the throne of God, observes that 'also in front of the throne [of God] was what looked like a sea of glass, clear as crystal' (Rev. 4:6).[19] Several authors commented on this passage, explaining that the sea of glass was to be understood as the sacrament of Baptism, which purifies the human soul and makes it transparent. The *mare vitreum* of the biblical passage, however, is said in the text to be clear as crystal. Various explanations were provided for this simile, some of which revolved around the different qualities of glass and crystal, namely the fragility of the former and the strength of the latter. Haymo of Auxerre (or Haymo of Halberstadt) proposed that in this context rock crystal was a simile for the saints who, purified by baptism, were made steadier by the sufferings of their lives, in the same way as the rigour of winter caused water to solidify into crystal.[20] Rupert of Deutz explained instead that the biblical passage delineated the progressive transformations of the human soul: the sea of the apocalyptic text was first said to be like glass, which is transparent but fragile, and then like crystal, transparent and firm. Similarly, men are purified by the water of baptism, but their corruptible bodies remain fragile; this fragility will be dissolved with the glory of Resurrection, when their souls will be blessed and their bodies made as incorruptible as crystal.[21]

The exegetical tracts mentioned above seem to suggest that rock crystal was a particularly convenient visual substitute for theological notions which, like the Incarnation of Christ, the resurrection of men and the nature of angels, entailed enigmatic transmutations of matter or the concomitance of different ontological states. This is confirmed by medieval readings of other passages from the Book of Revelation. In Chapter 21:11, John's spirit is lifted by an angel to see the Heavenly Jerusalem. The city, whose foundations were made of 12 different precious stones, 'shone with the glory of God, and its brilliance was like that of a very precious jewel, like a jasper, clear as crystal'.[22] In this context, the brilliancy of crystal was most commonly understood as pertaining to the resurrected Christ, as Richard of St Victor tersely stated in his commentary of this passage: 'Christ is [like] crystal, because rising from the dead he shone, gleaming with the glory of immortality'.[23]

The associations between rock crystal and the person of Christ (as per Ez. 1:22 and Rev. 21:11) as well as with the Holy Spirit and the sacrament of Baptism (Ez. 1:22) all converged into medieval interpretations of Rev. 22:1. Here, the clarity of crystal is mentioned in relation to the River of Life that John sees flowing from the throne of God: 'Then the angel showed me the river of the water of life, as clear as crystal, flowing from the throne of God and of the Lamb'.[24] Most medieval authors understood the crystal clear river as an image of the Holy Spirit that proceeds similarly from the

Plate 3a–b Cross of St Nikomedes of Borghorst, *c.* 1050, gold and copper gilt over a core of wood, precious stones, rock crystal and pearls, h. 41.1 cm, w. 28.4cm. Location unknown, formerly (until 2013) Pfarrgemeinde St-Nikomedes, Steinfurt-Borghorst, Germany (photo: Mr Stephan Kube)

Lord and from Christ, and thus employed it to allude to the Trinitarian mystery.[25] Alternatively, the river was taken to represent the vivifying water of the Holy Scripture and the sacramental descent of the Holy Spirit onto the human soul – baptism – which purifies and makes the souls of men resplendent.[26]

Lastly, medieval exegesis associated rock crystal with the miraculous conversion of human souls hardened by sin, particularly with the conversion of St Paul. This correlation was based on St Jerome's *Iuxta Septuaginta* translation of Psalm 147:17.[27] This psalm evokes a number of awe-inspiring activities performed by God, including the phrase: 'He sendeth his crystal like morsels: who shall stand before the face of his cold?'

St Augustine discussed this cryptic verse at length, and his interpretation was largely followed by later commentators. Rock crystal, he reminds us, is snow made harder by numerous winters that can no longer be melted. This property makes crystal a suitable metaphor of *duritia*, the exceptional hardness of the soul of sinners. Psalm 147 suggests that God sends out this hard crystal as if it were pieces of bread (*frusta panis*). According to St Augustine, the bread evoked in the psalm is the body of Christ, of which we all partake and to which we all belong. Thus, the passage signifies that God is capable of transforming the hardest of souls into morsels of Christ's life-giving bread, and thus into

spiritual nourishment that can feed and be beneficial to other souls.[28]

St Augustine furthermore proposed that the passage most directly applied to the figure of St Paul and his miraculous transformation from prosecutor of Christians to fervent believer: 'Crystal was the apostle Paul: hard, striving against the truth, shouting against the Gospel as if hardening against the sun'.[29] God, however, dissolved Paul's hardness of heart: 'no matter how hard he had been, no matter how cold, He … called him passionately from the heaven – Saul, Saul, why do you persecute me? – A call from that voice, and all the hardness of crystal was dissolved.'[30]

Medieval exegetical literature thus attributed to rock crystal a set of interrelated theological connotations. Such associations provide, in turn, a rich template to investigate the significance of this artistic medium in medieval art. At the simplest level, the symbolic associations of rock crystal were exploited to reinforce or mirror the messages conveyed by images. As already noted by Genevra Kornbluth, this was the case for Carolingian intaglios, which were most often engraved with scenes of the Crucifixion, the Baptism of Christ and the Angels, suggesting a close interaction between the symbolism of the material and the iconography that it supported.[31] Furthermore, quartz plaques were often applied to reliquaries and other liturgical artefacts to protect relics or miniatures on parchment. In the first case, the symbolic associations between rock crystal, the Incarnation, the Resurrection and sainthood would highlight the significance of the holy tokens. Likewise, the symbolism of rock crystal would complement the iconographic messages conveyed by miniatures on parchment, especially those bearing images of the Crucifixion, Christ in Majesty or portraits of saints.[32] Finally, rock crystal could convey meaning even in the absence of images. A number of jewelled crosses and saints' reliquaries survive from the early and central Middle Ages that incorporate rock-crystal cabochons and intaglios placed in prominent locations, employed alone or alongside other gemstones. In keeping with exegetical literature, quartz cabochons could articulate messages concerning sainthood, the Incarnation and the Resurrection. Combined with other stones, they furthermore alluded to notions of the Heavenly Jerusalem and its precious foundations and adornments, as described in Rev. 21:9–27.[33]

A more complex and ambivalent example of the interactions between pictorial iconography and material symbolism in medieval artworks is provided by the cross reliquary which until its recent theft was preserved in the parish church of St Nikomedes in Steinfurt-Borghorst, Germany (**Pl. 3a–b**).[34] The Borghorst Cross was manufactured in the mid-11th century to shelter a group of relics of Christ, the Virgin and numerous saints, all identified by a lengthy inscription that runs around the reverse of the cross.[35] The artefact consists of a core of wood covered in gold (front) and gilded copper (back). The relics, wrapped in red cloth,[36] are arranged inside two Fatimid rock-crystal flasks that are visible from both sides of the cross.[37] The larger flask is set at the crossing of the arms, in the position elsewhere occupied by the Crucifix, while the smaller ampulla is housed inside the lower arm. A large oval cabochon of the same material, also visible from the obverse and reverse of the cross, is inserted in the upper shaft, while a second, smaller cabochon is applied to the extremity of the right arm and is only visible from the front of the reliquary. The obverse is also adorned with a variety of precious stones and reused intaglios. A repoussé image of the Crucifixion is placed on the upper arm above the larger rock-crystal flask, while the effigies of Sts Cosmas and Damian and Sts Peter and Paul, executed in the same technique, are arranged along the horizontal axis to the left and right of the central flask. Finally, a kneeling figure approached by two angels, identified by the accompanying inscription as Emperor Henry (most likely the Holy Roman Emperor Henry III, r. 1046–56), occupies the space between the two rock-crystal flasks in the lower arm.[38] The decoration on the reverse of the Borghorst Cross is simpler. In addition to the above-mentioned inscription running around the border, this side features a motif of vegetal scrolls engraved in the upper and side arms, around the rock-crystal flasks and cabochon. The image of a second kneeling figure, inscribed as Abbess Bertha, is placed in the lower arm, between the two rock-crystal vessels, in the same position occupied by the emperor on the obverse.

On one level, the rock-crystal elements employed in the Borghorst Cross may be understood in terms of a visual metaphor. The central rock-crystal flask occupies the position generally taken by the Crucifix and, although occasionally understood by scholarship as an allusion to the chalice that caught the blood of the crucified Christ, it may be more appropriately interpreted as a substitute for the body of Christ itself.[39] The visual analogy between the rock-crystal ampulla and the crucified Christ is suggested by the elongated shape of the vessel, which evokes the image of a body, and by the presence of red cloth inside the crystal. Together, the textile and the transparent container would visually allude to the blood and water shed by the Saviour upon his death. The interaction between the bloodlike redness of the cloth and the transparency of crystal would reveal to the beholders the dual nature of Christ, fully human and fully divine. It would furthermore remind them of the crucial role of the Crucifixion, which simultaneously marked the fulfilment of Christ's human existence and his triumph over death. In contrast to the central flask, whose transparency is partly obscured by the fragment of cloth, and whose surface is made uneven by the relief-cut motifs that decorate it, the crystal cabochon that occupies the summit of the cross is impeccably polished and gleams with light. The two rock-crystal elements appear to work in concert: the reddened flask, filled with relics, manifests the coexistence of humanity and divinity in the person of Christ on the cross. The translucent cabochon, on the other hand, visualizes his perfect glory after the Resurrection, while at the same time it may also evoke the presence of God and of the Holy Spirit at the Crucifixion. The shape and position of the small Fatimid flask placed in the lower arm (rather than the larger flask above) would be reminiscent of the chalice that gathered the blood of the Saviour. This small ampulla is roughly shaped like a drinking vessel; it is filled with the same red cloth that fills the larger container, implying a relationship between the two, and it is located at the foot of the cross in the position usually occupied by the chalice in figurative representations of the Crucifixion. Situated next to the kneeling figures of the emperor (front) and the abbess (back), it would suitably advertise the centrality of Christ's sacrifice in human history, while also performing an intercessory function for the two patrons whose bodies are in close proximity.[40]

Rock crystal evokes enticing associations on the back of the cross as well. The vegetal motifs that decorate this side allude to the *lignum vitae*, the Tree of Life which the cross of Christ was understood to represent throughout the Middle Ages. The Tree of Life, it should be recalled, appears in the same passage of the Book of Revelation that describes the River of Life as 'clear as crystal' (Rev. 22: 1). More specifically, the river (which, as mentioned above, medieval exegetes identified as the Holy Spirit and the sacrament of baptism) is said in the Bible to flow through the Tree of Life, which grows on either side of it. The vegetal motifs and the rock-crystal elements on the Borghorst Cross replicate the relative positions of the biblical Tree of Life and crystal clear river. The quartz elements are neatly arranged along the vertical axis and reach the kneeling figure of Abbess Bertha, bringing to her the vivifying waters of divine grace. The vegetal scrolls, in turn, blossom around the crystal flasks in the same way as the biblical Tree of Life grows on both sides of the riverbanks in the Book of Revelation.

The arrangement of the rock-crystal components on the Borghorst Cross, inserted so as to be visible from both sides, enhances the iconographic contiguity between the two sides of the artefact, thus emphasizing the correlation between the sacrifice of Christ represented on the front and the saving descent of the Holy Spirit onto humankind on the reverse. The presence of rock crystal, however, does not only encourage a holistic approach to the Borghorst Cross. The interaction between rock crystal, metalwork, gemstones and textile fragments also produces an accumulation of visual contrasts (among transparent, reflective and opaque surfaces, between translucency and colour, and so forth) that draws the attention of viewers to the materiality of the reliquary. These unresolved visual tensions, in turn, reinforce the Christological and eschatological messages conveyed by the iconography of the reliquary and the symbolism of its materials, for they physically manifest and replicate the enigmatic concomitance of divine and human natures in Christ, the unfathomable descent of the Holy Spirit onto human beings and the ambivalent role of relics as glorified earthly matter.

The Borghorst Cross is illustrative of the multiple ways in which rock crystal engaged its viewers. Because exegetical tradition explicitly associated it with a cluster of theological concepts (the Incarnation of Christ, the Resurrection, angelic natures and so forth), these notions became, so to speak, permanent iconographic attributes of this stone. Therefore, on one level the Borghorst Cross conveys a set of iconographic messages that rely on the preordained metaphorical meanings of rock crystal and its iconographic interaction with the other constituents of the artefact. However, on another level, the rock-crystal cabochons and flasks do not only iconographically signify the Incarnation and the Resurrection. Instead, they offer the beholder the possibility of visually experiencing those enigmas of the Christian faith. Transparent quartz aroused the interest of medieval authors because it was believed to have formed from congealed water and thus integrated the contrasting properties of liquids and solid minerals. This extraordinary quality, alongside the transparency and the exceptional hardness of rock crystal, made this substance the ideal means to visually articulate a set of theological notions. Such concepts, however diverse, nevertheless shared one essential feature. They were difficult to apprehend because they implied the concomitance of different ontological states, or entailed an extraordinary transformation of matter. The nature of angels was difficult to define, for they were incorporeal and yet created beings, intermediaries between men and God. The Incarnation posed even greater problems, for Christ was at the same time uncreated and created, eternal and finite. The cleansing function of the sacrament of Baptism, by which men could reach eternal life, posed profound questions concerning the nature of sin and redemption in addition to the relationship between good and evil. Finally, saints and their venerated earthly remains prompted questions about the state of just souls and their bodies before the final Resurrection, the relationship between created and uncreated matter and the participation of created beings in the divine. In brief, the theological concepts that crystal was made to embody on objects like the Borghorst Cross were mysteries that, by definition, implied physical and spiritual paradoxes.

Rock crystal was chosen to approach these theological enigmas because as a substance it was itself paradoxical and inexplicable. Rock crystal simultaneously partook of liquidity and solidity, of change and immutability, and for this reason it could be employed as the physical substitute for the concomitance of human mutability and divine unchangeability that characterized the Incarnation. Rock crystal was solid but, unlike most solid bodies, it was also fully transparent and posed no resistance to light. Thus, it mirrored the enlightenment of the human soul by divine grace achieved through baptism, the miraculous conversion produced by God in sinful souls celebrated by Psalm 147: 17–18 and it forecast the glorification of all bodies on the day of the Resurrection. In addition, its material hardness reverberated with theological notions of incorruptibility, providing a visual gloss on the nature of sainthood. In all these cases, rock crystal did not just symbolically point to a set of theological ideas. Rather, by means of its physical properties and visual appearance, it offered corporeal evidence of how those imponderable theological conundrums operated spiritually and of the way in which created matter participated in the mystery – and the history – of salvation.

Notes

1 These issues have received growing attention in recent years. On issues of medieval materiality, see Bynum 2011, with comprehensive bibliography. For an introduction to the notion of materiality and materials, see particularly Ingold 2007, and all other essays in the same volume. For discussions of specific artistic media in the middle ages, see especially Dell'Acqua 2008 and Kessler 2011. Although frequently referred to in specialist literature, rock crystal has not yet been the subject of a dedicated study. However, see Henze 1991 for an introduction to its allegorical meanings and for some useful observations on its iconographic interaction with images and relics.

2 The hardness of minerals is commonly measured following the Mohs scale, a comparative ranking of minerals that measures their relative scratch resistance. Rock crystal measures 7/10 on the Mohs scale, ranking among hard minerals that cannot be scratched with iron.

3 For a brief introduction to the physical properties of rock crystal, as well as to its applications throughout history, see Kornbluth 1996.

4 Kornbluth 1994–5.

5 For a recent survey of rock-crystal carving in Fatimid Egypt, see Contadini 1998.

6 On Anglo Saxon uses of rock crystal in funerary contexts see Wilson 1992, 113. Merovingian crystal amulets and spheres are mentioned in Kornbluth 1995, 13, 16.

7 These have been comprehensively examined in Kornbluth 1995.

8 For a comprehensive survey of extant Islamic artefacts in Western treasury collections and an interpretation of this phenomenon, see Shalem 1998.

9 The most comprehensive catalogue of Western medieval rock-crystal artefacts is Hahnloser and Brugger-Koch 1985.

10 On the invention of *vetro cristallo* in Venice and on its implications, see Turner 1999. For an introduction to Renaissance rock-crystal carvings, see Raggio 1952.

11 As mentioned above, rock crystal measures 7 on the Mohs scale, while most glasses measure 5.5–6 on the same scale. See Trench 2000, 415.

12 On medieval optics and theories of vision, see amongst others Denery 2005; Akbari Conkin 2004, esp. 21–44; Gilson 2000, 7–39; Lindberg 1983; and Lindberg 1976. On medieval notions of refraction, see Lindberg 1968.

13 Kornbluth 1995, 20.

14 British Museum, 1946,0407.1. The object was most recently

discussed in Bagnoli *et al.* 2010, cat. 72, 131 with further references. For a full bibliographical record, including a restoration report (2009), see the relevant page of the British Museum Collection Online database (http://www.britishmuseum.org/research/collection_online/search.aspx).

15 Pliny the Elder, *Natural History*, Book 37, Chapter 9: 23–9, vol. 10, 180–5; On the inherited tradition of rock crystal originating from congealed water, see, amongst others, Isidore of Seville *Etymologiae*, Patrologia Latina (hereafter PL), 82: 577; Hrabanus Maurus, *De Universo*, PL, 111: 472.

16 Marbode of Rennes, *De Lapidibus*, 550–1, 77–8; Albert the Great, *Libri Mineralium*, vol. 5, 34; Arnold of Saxony, *De Virtutibus Lapidum*, vol. 18, 433; Cecco d'Ascoli, *Acerba Aetas*, 273.

17 Unless otherwise specified, this essay follows the New International Edition of the Bible. This passage is rendered in the Vulgate edition as follows: 'Et similitudo super caput animalium firmamenti quasi aspectus cristalli horribilis et extenti super capita eorum desuper'.

18 Gregory I, *Homiliae in Ezechielem*, PL, 76: 848–50. See also Hrabanus Maurus, *De Universo*, PL, 111: 472–3; Hrabanus Maurus, *Commentaria in Ezechielem*, PL, 110:535–6; Rupert of Deutz, *De Trinitate et operibus ejus*, PL, 167:1435.

19 Latin Vulgate: 'Et in conspectu sedis tamquam mare vitreum simile cristallo'.

20 The text appears in the *PL*, where it is attributed to Haymo of Halberstadt, *Expositio in Apocalypsim*, PL, 117:1008. The online database *Alcuin. Autoren und Texte der Denkgeschichte des Mittelalters (500–1500 n. Chr.)* of the University of Regensburg, reports that the work has been reattributed to Haymo of Auxerre in Gansweidt 1989. See http://www-app.uni-regensburg.de/Fakultaeten/PKGG/Philosophie/Gesch_Phil/alcuin/philosopher.php?id=906 (accessed 27 April 2012).

21 Rupert of Deutz, *Commentaria in Apocalypsim*, PL, 169: 910–11.

22 Latin Vulgate: '[Civitatem sanctam Hierusalem] habentem claritatem Dei lumen eius simile lapidi pretioso tamquam lapidi iaspidis sicut cristallum'. Interestingly, the clarity of rock crystal is a visual property of the Heavenly Jerusalem, but this gemstone is not one of the 12 precious stones upon which the holy city is built. These are jasper, sapphire, agate, emerald, onyx, ruby, chrysolite, beryl, topaz, turquoise, jacinth and amethyst, and are all described in the passages that follow, Rev. 21:18–20.

23 'Christus crystallus, quia ex mortuis resurgens gloria immortalitatis clarus effulsit'. Richard of St Victor, *In Apocalypsim Iohannis*, PL, 196:865.

24 Latin Vulgate: 'Et ostendit mihi fluvium aquae vitae splendidum tamquam cristallum procedentem de sede Dei et agni'.

25 Ambrose of Milan, *De Spiritu Sancto*, PL, 16: 812; Theodulf of Orleans, *De Spiritu Sancto*, PL, 105: 252–3; Rupert of Deutz, *Commentaria in Apocalypsim*, PL, 169:1206; Richard of St Victor, *In Apocalypsim Iohannis*, PL, 196: 875.

26 On the river as baptism, see Anselm of Laon, *Enarrationes in Apocalypsim*, PL, 162:1583; as Holy Scripture, Haymo of Auxerre, *Expositio in Apocalypsim*, PL 117:1211.

27 Two different Latin translations of this passage were available in the Middle Ages. Both provided by St Jerome, they respectively derived from the Hebrew Bible and from the Greek Septuagint, and read: 'proicit glaciem suam quasi buccellas ante faciem frigoris eius quis stabit' (*iuxta Hebreos*), and 'mittit cristallum suum sicut buccellas ante faciem frigoris eius quis sustinebit' (*iuxta Septuaginta*). Modern English translations of the Bible alternate the two versions. I have employed here the Douay-Rheims edition of the Psalms, closest to the *iuxta Septuaginta* version and to the readings of the passage provided by the exegetical texts discussed below.

28 Augustine of Hippo, *Enarrationes in Psalmos*, PL, 37: 1133–4; Hrabanus Maurus, *Allegoriae in Universam Sacram Scripturam*, PL, 112:896; Peter Lombard, *Commentaria in Psalmos*, PL, 191: 1282; Peter of Blois, *De Conversione Sancti Pauli*, PL, 207:796; Alain of Lille, *Liber Distinctionibus Dictionum Theologicalium*, PL, 210:755. Richard of St Victor understood the crystal for morsels as the tokens of divine wisdom ministered by God to men through angelic intermediation, see Richard of St Victor, *Adnotationes mysticae in Psalmos*, PL, 196: 326. Augustine's commentary is also discussed in Meier 1977, 96–9.

29 'Ecce crystallum erat apostolus Paulus, durus, obnitens veritati, clamans adversus Evangelium, tanquam indurans adversus solem'. Augustine of Hippo, *Enarrationes in Psalmos*, PL, 37:1134. See also Peter Lombard, *Commentaria in Psalmos*, PL: 191: 1282; Peter of Blois, *De Conversione Sancti Pauli*, PL, 207: 796.

30 'Sed quanquam esset durus, quanquam gelidus, ecce ille … clamavit de coelo fervidus, Saule, Saule, quid me persequeris (Act. IX, 1–4)? Una illa voce, tanta illa duritia crystalli resoluta est.' Augustine of Hippo, *Enarrationes in Psalmos*, PL, 37: 1935.

31 Kornbluth 1995, 17.

32 For examples, see Henze 1991, 428–51; with regard to the interaction between rock crystal, parchment and figurative representation of the Crucifixion in an unusual quartz cabochon held at the National Museum in Copenhagen, see Kessler 2004, 33. Objects incorporating miniatures under crystal became particularly popular in 13th-century Venice, whence they were exported throughout Europe. The most comprehensive catalogue of these objects is Hahnloser and Brugger-Koch 1985; see also Hahnloser 1956 and more recently Caselli 2007; specifically on crosses, see Caselli 2002.

33 The most comprehensive study of the allegorical meanings of stones is Meier 1977. For an introduction to the symbolic associations of precious stones in relation to the Heavenly Jerusalem, see Sedinova 2000; on the origins and modern interpretations of such symbolism, see Reader 1981.

34 Bagnoli *et al.* 2010, 138 and cat. 77, 174–5; Toussaint 2011, 102–4; Toussaint 2010; De Castro Valdes 2008, cat. 45, 247–9 (with further bibliography); Stiegemann and Wemhoff 2006, vol. 2, cat. 362, 255–7 (with further bibliography); Shalem 1998, cat. 5, 179–80 and cat. 26, 192; Forsyth 1995; Legner 1985, vol. 3, cat. H 28, 106–8 (with further bibliography). I am grateful to Michaela Zoeschg for her support in obtaining the permission to publish **Plates 3a–b**.

35 The inscription runs clockwise along the border of the cross, and begins at the bottom left. It reads: 'HEC SUNT NOMINA ISTORUM SANCTORUM DE LIGNO DNI DE SPONDIA DNI DE LECTO MARIE MATRIS DNI DE CORPORE SCI PETRI APL S ANDREE APL SCI BARTHOLOMEI APL SCI STEPHANI M S NICOMEDIS S MAURICII S PANCRACII S LAURENTII S CRISTOFORI S CLEMENTIS S NICOLAI DE SCAPULA S SIMEONIS S MARIA MAGDAL S AGATHE V ISTI ET OMNES SANCTI INTERCEDANT PRO ME PECCATRICE ET PRO OMNIBUS ILLIS QUI ALIQUID BONI AD HOC SIGNACULO FECERUNT.' Edited in Legner 1985, vol. 3, cat. H 28, 106.

36 Bagnoli *et al.* 2010, cat. 77, 174.

37 On the Fatimid flasks and the meaning of their artistic reuse on the Borghorst Cross, see especially Forsyth 1995, 154–5 and Shalem 1998, 134.

38 The figure has been identified as Henry III in all recent exhibition catalogues. For a discussion of dating, see Forsyth 1995, 155; and Althoff 1978, 283–98 (cited in Shalem 1998, 180).

39 The flask has been associated with the chalice that caught the blood of Christ due to its location below the figurative representation of the Crucifixion in the upper arm, which it would complete (Bagnoli *et al.* 2010, cat. 77, 174; Shalem 1998, 134; Forsyth 1995, 154; Legner 1985, cat. H 28, 106). However, the inverted proportions between the diminutive representation of the Crucifixion and the large crystal vessel (twice the size of the repoussé work) seem to suggest that the image and the quartz container might have functioned as visual analogues rather than being iconographically complementary.

40 The idea that the Borghorst Cross conveyed messages regarding the salvific and intercessory role of the sacrifice of Christ and of saints is directly implied by the inscriptions on the reverse of the cross, and has also been advanced by Martina Bagnoli in Bagnoli *et al.* 2010, 138.

Bibliography

Primary sources (editions and translations)

Alain of Lille (d. 1203), *Liber Distinctionibus Dictionum Theologicalium*, PL, 210: 685–1011.

Albert the Great (*c.* 1200–80), *Libri Mineralium* (1890, *Alberti Magni Opera Omnia*, ed. Auguste Borgnet, Paris, vol. 5, 1–103).

Ambrose of Milan (c. 339–97), *De Spiritu Sancto*, PL, 16: 703–816.

Anselm of Laon (d. 1117), *Enarrationes in Apocalypsim*, PL, 162: 1499–1586.

Arnold of Saxony, *De Virtutibus Lapidum* (1875, 'Aristoteles *De Lapidibus* und Arnoldus Saxo', *Zeitschrift zur Deutsches Alterthum*, ed. V.Rose, vol. 18, 321–455).

Augustine of Hippo (354–430), *Enarrationes in Psalmos*, PL, 37: 1033–1967.

Cecco d'Ascoli, *Acerba Aetas* (2005, *L'Acerba. Acerba Aetas*, ed. Marco Albertazzi, Lavis).

Gregory I (c. 540–604), *Homiliae in Ezechielem*, PL, 76: 785–1072.

Haymo of Auxerre (d. 855, attr. Haymo of Halberstadt, d.853), *Expositio in Apocalypsim*, PL, 117: 937–1220.

Hrabanus Maurus (c. 780–856), *Allegoriae in Universam Sacram Scripturam*, PL, 112: 849–1088.

Hrabanus Maurus, *De Universo*, PL, 111: 9–614.

Hrabanus Maurus, *Commentaria in Ezechielem*, PL, 110: 497–1084.

Isidore of Seville (c. 570–636), *Etymologiae*, PL, 82: 73–728.

Marbode of Rennes (1035–1123) *De Lapidibus* (1977, *Marbode of Renne's (1035–1123) De Lapidibus Considered as a Medical Treatise; with Text, Commentary and C. W. King's Translation; together with Text and Translation of Marbode's Minor Works on Stones by John Riddle*, ed. and trans. C.W. King, Wiesbaden).

Peter Lombard (c. 1100–60), *Commentaria in Psalmos*, PL, 191: 31–1296.

Peter of Blois (c. 1130–1212), *De Conversione Sancti Pauli*, PL, 207: 791–6.

Pliny the Elder (23–79 AD), *Natural History* (1958–63, ed. J. Anderson, 10 vols, Cambridge, MA and London).

Richard of St Victor (d. 1173), *In Apocalypsim Iohannis*, PL, 196: 683–888.

Richard of St Victor, *Adnotationes Mysticae in Psalmos*, PL, 196: 265–404.

Rupert of Deutz (c. 1075/80–1129), *De Trinitate et Operibus Ejus*, PL, 167: 197–1827.

Rupert of Deutz, *Commentaria in Apocalypsim*, PL, 169: 825–1214.

Theodulf of Orleans (c. 760–821), *De Spiritu Sancto*, PL, 105: 239–76.

Secondary sources

Akbari Conkin, S. 2004. *Seeing Through the Veil. Optical Theory and Medieval Allegory*, Toronto.

Althoff, G. 1978. *Das Necrolog von Borghorst: Edition und Untersuchung*, Münster.

Bagnoli, M., Klein, H.A., Mann, C.G. and Robinson, J. (eds) 2010. *Treasures of Heaven: Saints, Relics and Devotion in Medieval Europe*, Baltimore and London.

Bynum, C.W. 2011. *Christian Materiality. An Essay on Religion in Late Medieval Europe*, New York.

Caselli, L. 2002. *La Croce di Chiaravalle Milanese e le Croci Veneziane in Cristallo di Rocca*, Padua.

Caselli, L. 2007. 'L'ornamento dei santi: arte orafa e miniature sotto cristallo nel '200 e '300 veneziano', in *Oreficeria Sacra a Venezia e nel Veneto*, ed. L. Caselli and E. Merkel, Treviso, 85–101.

Contadini, A. 1998. *Fatimid Art at the Victoria and Albert Museum*, London.

De Castro Valdés, C. (ed.) 2008. *Signum Salutis. Cruces de Orfebrería de los Siglos V al XII*, Oviedo.

Dell'Acqua, F. 2008. 'Between nature and artifice. "Transparent streams of new liquid"', *RES* 53/54, 93–103.

Denery, D.G. 2005. *Seeing and Being Seen in the Medieval World*, Cambridge.

Forsyth, E.H. 1995. 'Art with history: the role of spolia in the cumulative work of art', in *Byzantine East, Latin West: Art Historical Studies in Honour of Kurt Weitzmann*, ed. C. Moss and K. Kiefer, Princeton, 153–62.

Gansweidt, B. 1989. 'Haimo von Auxerre', in *LexMA*, vol. 4, 1864.

Gilson, S.A. 2000. *Medieval Optics and Theories of Light in the Works of Dante*, Lewiston, Queenston and Lampeter.

Hahnloser, H. 1956. 'Opus venetum ad filum. Schola et arte cristellariorum de Veneciis, 1284–1319', in *Venezia e l'Europa*, International Congress of the History of Art, Venice, 157–65.

Hahnloser, H.R. and Brugger-Koch, S. 1985. *Corpus der Hartsteinschliffe des 12.-15. Jahrhunderts*, Berlin.

Henze, U. 1991. 'Edelsteinallegorese im Lichte mittelalterlicher Bild- und Reliquienverehrung', *Zeitschrift für Kunstgeschichte* 54, 428–51.

Ingold, T. 2007. 'Materials against materiality', *Archaeological Dialogues* 14, 1–16.

Kessler, H. 2004. *Seeing Medieval Art*, Peterborough.

Kessler, H. 2011. 'The eloquence of silver. More on the allegorization of matter', in *L'Allégorie dans l'Art du Moyen Âge*, ed. C. Heck, Turnhout, 49–64.

Kornbluth, G. 1994–5. '"Early Byzantine" crystals: an assessment', *The Journal of the Walters Art Gallery* 52/53, 23–32.

Kornbluth, G. 1995. *Engraved Gems of the Carolingian Empire*, University Park.

Kornbluth, G. 1996. 'Rock crystal', in *Dictionary of Art*, ed. J. Turner, New York, 484–7.

Legner, A. 1985. *Ornamenta Ecclesiae. Kunst und Künstler der Romanik*, Cologne.

Lindberg, D. 1968. 'The cause of refraction in medieval optics', *The British Journal of the History of Science* 4, 23–38.

Lindberg, D. 1976. *Theories of Vision from Alkindi to Kepler*, Chicago.

Lindberg, D. (ed.) 1983. *Studies in the History of Medieval Optics*, London.

Meier, C. 1977. *Gemma Spiritalis. Methode und Gebrauch der Edelsteinallegorese vom frühen Christentum bis ins 18. Jahrhundert*, Munich.

Raggio, O. 1952. 'Light and line in Renaissance crystal engravings', *The Metropolitan Museum of Art Bulletin*, New Series, 10/7, 193–202.

Reader, W.W. 1981. 'The twelve jewels of Revelation 21:19–20: tradition, history and modern interpretations', *Journal of Biblical Literature* 100/3, 433–57.

Sedinova, H. 2000. 'The precious stones of Heavenly Jerusalem in the medieval book illustration and their comparison with the wall incrustation in St. Wenceslas Chapel', *Artibus et Historiae* 21/41, esp. 33–6.

Shalem, A. 1998. *Islam Christianised. Islamic Portable Objects in the Medieval Church Treasuries of the Latin West*, Frankfurt.

Stiegemann, C. and Wemhoff, M. 2006. *Canossa 1077. Erschütterung der Welt; Geschichte, Kunst und Kultur am Aufgang der Romanik*, Munich.

Toussaint, G., 2010. 'Grosser Schatz auf kleinem Raum. Die Kreuzvierung als Reliquienbuhne', in *Le Trésor au Moyen Age. Discours, Pratiques, et Objets*, ed. L. Burkart, P. Cordez, P.A. Mariaux and Y. Potin, Florence, 283–96.

Toussaint, G. 2011. *Kreuz und Knochen. Reliquien zur Zeit der Kreuzzuge*, Berlin.

Trench, L. (ed.) 2000. *Materials and Techniques in the Decorative Arts. An Illustrated Dictionary*, London.

Turner, G. 1999. '"Allume catina" and the aesthetics of Venetian "cristallo"', *Journal of Design History* 12, 111–22.

Wilson, D. 1992. *Anglo Saxon Paganism*, London.

Chapter 13
Dressing the Relics
Some Thoughts on the Custom of Relic Wrapping in Medieval Christianity

Martina Bagnoli

For quite some time now, scholars have drawn attention to the shift that occurred in the later Middle Ages from materiality to visuality. There is an ever increasing body of work dedicated to this subject, in particular to the way in which the sense of sight contributed to the devotional experience. Indeed, much has been said about the relationship between seeing and believing. In my essay for the catalogue that accompanied the *Treasures of Heaven* exhibition, I too expounded on this subject and discussed the impact that an increasing reliance on physical sight had on the design of reliquaries.[1] Indeed, this concept was one of the main narratives of the exhibition. Those who visited the show in Baltimore will recall that strolling through the galleries one moved from impenetrable marble sarcophagi to luminous rock-crystal containers and finally to two-dimensional pictures. Reliquaries such as the magnificent Man of Sorrows from Santa Croce were instrumental in mediating the passage from materials to image.[2] The micromosaic image of the Man of Sorrows was gifted to the Roman church of Santa Croce in Gerusalemme by an aristocrat who had acquired it in Constantinople. Sometime after its arrival, the icon (perhaps because of its wondrous technique) began to be venerated as a relic. It was believed that it was the testimony of Pope Gregory I's vision, when an image (thought to be this very image) of the suffering Christ appeared on the altar of Santa Croce as the pope was celebrating the Eucharist. A later local legend maintained that the icon was made with the bones of the saints. Presumably, such an association was triggered by the multitude of relics visible around the picture, itself a relic: the bones underscoring the sacred nature of the image. Caroline Walker Bynum has argued that visual presentation

Plate 1 Portable altar, 1190–1200, copper gilt over a wood core, limestone, painted vellum, rock crystal and ivory, 35.4 x 25.1cm. British Museum, London (1902,0625.1)

of relics was crucial to anchor the devotional powers of images in the later Middle Ages.[4] Bynum argues that the display of body parts in reliquaries was a way to refute the corruption of the flesh.[5] But were the relics really visible? In a large number of medieval 'transparent' reliquaries, the relics are not displayed in a naked form but are instead wrapped up in precious little pouches, the same way in which they would be when concealed inside reliquaries (**Pls 1–2**).[6] The perceived visibility of relics in the face of their apparent invisibility is the subject of this article. I shall start my discussion with a brief survey of the Christian tradition of relic wrapping and will pay special attention to silk as the material of choice to protect and conserve relics.

Since the beginning of the veneration of relics, material remains were wrapped in reverence. We are told that notable figures such as St Anthony the Great (d. 356) abhorred the Egyptian habit 'to wrap in linen cloths at death the bodies of good men, and especially of the holy martyrs; and not to bury them underground, but to place them on couches, and to keep them in their houses, thinking in this to honor the departed'.[7] The 4th-century priest Vigilantius also complained that 'heaps of tapers are lighted, and everywhere a paltry bit of powder, wrapped up in a costly cloth, is kissed and worshipped'.[8] In response to this, Jerome sharply replied: 'It is nothing less than the relics of the martyrs which he [Vigilantius] is vexed to see covered with a costly veil, and not bound up with rags or hair-cloth, or thrown on the midden'.[9] In the late 7th-century *vita* of St Eligius written by Dado of Rouen, Eligius who had been tasked to find the remains of St Quentin, found first 'the wrapping of the holy body'.[10] When the tomb of the saint was opened, some of the bones were withheld for distribution and then 'he brought the body to the altar wrapped in the most precious silk and decently laid out'. In the early

13th-century account of the translation of Gilbert of Sempringham we read how 'the revered relics were wrapped in spotless linen within a precious silk cloth', both items given by Hubert Walter, Archbishop of Canterbury, for this purpose, and only then were they placed within the consecrated vessel.[11] The evidence from the textual sources is substantiated by archaeological findings. Indeed, most of the surviving textiles from the medieval period were used as wrapping material for relics. The dating and provenance of these pieces of cloth is becoming clearer thanks to the studies of Regula Schorta, Annemarie Stauffer, Marielle Martiniani-Reber and others.[12] Some may be as old as the relics, such as the 5th-century Near Eastern silk with Dionysian images from the cathedral of Sens, while others are later but still medieval, such as the 11th-century Byzantine silk wrapped around the remains of St Germain of Auxerre (d. 448), recently identified with one of the precious clothes given at the time of Bishop Hugh of Chalon around 1030.[13] Another example is the Amandus shroud from the Cleveland Museum of Art (**Pl. 3**), an 11th- or 12th-century Near Eastern silk that became integrated into the shrine of St Amandus in Salzburg.[14] The material evidence confirms what the sources tell us: bodies were wrapped at burial and then rewrapped every time the tomb was opened to translate the relics, to obtain a relic, to insert a new relic into a shrine or even to verify its contents. This practice continued well into the modern era. For example, of the relics contained in the Grande Chasse of Sion, Switzerland, 18 were laid out in a sealed box, wrapped and tied in a large piece of taffeta silk cloth. An enclosed document dated 1832 established the nature of the contents and another dated 1923 certified a new opening and closing of the reliquary.[15] This brief analysis shows that whereas it was common for early modern reliquaries to revel in the

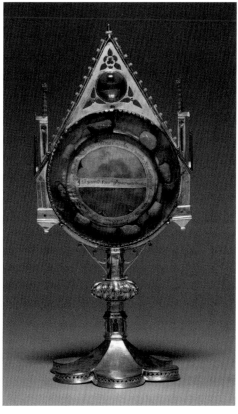

Plate 2a–b Front and reverse of *ostensorium* with 'Paten of St Bernard', paten *c.* 1180–90, silver, silver gilt and niello, diam. 13.4cm, monstrance *c.* 1350–1400, silver, silver gilt and rock crystal, 34.5 x 15.9 x 14cm. The Cleveland Museum of Art, purchase from the J.H. Wade Fund with additional gift from Mrs R. Henry Norweb (1930.505)

Plate 3 Amandus shroud, 11th or 12th century, silk and gold, 46.4 x 54.6cm. Cleveland Museum of Art, purchase from the J.H. Wade Fund

Plate 4 Book of Hours, 1470, French, Burial Service, Office of the Dead. Walters Art Museum, Baltimore, MS. W. 249, fol. 119r

exhibition of gnarled bones, such as the 1682 St Titus reliquary in the Treasury of San Marco, Venice, medieval reliquaries are much more reticent and, more often than not, the chambers of relics present but a handful of fabric pouches.[16] There are notable exceptions of course, the most famous being the hand of St Attala in Strasbourg which is not wrapped and the reliquary consists of a rock-crystal vase containing one bony hand. The custom of wrapping relics in precious fabrics is certainly not to be taken as a rule, but the

Plate 5 Book of Hours, c. 1430s, French, Burial Service, Office of the Dead. Walters Museum of Art, Baltimore, MS. W. 262 fol. 90

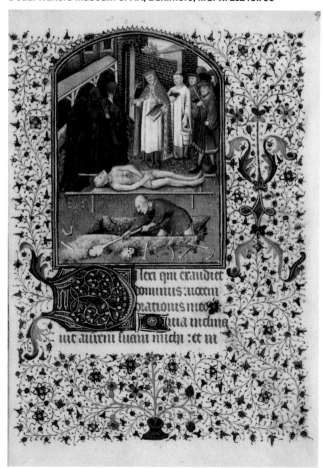

number of examples is significant enough that we can talk of it being a common practice.[17]

While the bones of saints were wrapped up and concealed, those of normal human beings were often left exposed.[18] Illustrations of the office of the dead (cycle of prayers recited throughout the nine canonical hours for the soul of the deceased) in late medieval Book of Hours offer visual evidence of medieval funerary practices.[19] The bodies of the deceased were washed and then sewn into a shroud (**Pl. 4**). They were then placed in a coffin for transportation to the church and the cemetery. Coffins became common from the 13th century onwards mostly for transport as the dead were laid directly into the earth (**Pl. 5**). As is evident from these images, and many others like them, the deceased left the world as he or she had entered it: naked. After the body had been consumed by decay, the burial spot of an individual could be used for another, while the remaining bones would be kept in a charnel house (**Pl. 6**).

Despite the claims of theologians, especially Thiodfrid of Echternach, that beautiful reliquaries were a necessity in order to mask the disgusting nature of sacred matter, medieval men and women seemed to be quite unaffected by the exhibition of human bones.[20] So why were relics wrapped? There are a number of reasons why this was done. The most obvious is the veneration that relics were due. As with all sacred things, relics were not to be touched by human hands. In the 12th-century Limoges Chasse of St Valerie, Valerie holds her own severed head with covered hands (**Pl. 7**), while in Rogier van der Weyden's *Exhumation*

Plate 6 Book of Hours, *c.* 1460, Bruges, Burial Service, Office of the Dead. Walters Art Museum, Baltimore, MS. W. 197, fol. 175v

Plate 7 Reliquary chasse with St Valerie, *c.* 1170–2, copper, gold and enamel, 16.5 x 29.2cm. British Museum, London (WB.19)

of St Hubert, the body of the saint is lifted out of the tomb by a cleric whose hands are reverently covered with a precious blue cloth (**Pl. 8**). Reliquaries themselves, as *vasa sacra* and containers of the holy were not to be touched with bare hands. The 1396 inventory of the church of Il Santo in Padua mentions 19 silk clothes to handle relics, while the 1382 inventory of the relics at the shrine of St Cuthbert in Durham Cathedral included 'five napkins for carrying the relics'.[21]

This type of reverence expressed the desire to shield sacred matter from human touch and its association with carnality. Although pilgrimage was dictated by the desire to gain physical knowledge of sacred sites, as a rule pilgrims could not touch the actual relics with their bare hands. In his extensive travel accounts, Egeria describes how before a relic of the True Cross, pilgrims would 'stoop down, touch the Holy Wood, first with their forehead and then with their eyes, and then kiss it but no one puts out his hands to touch it'.[22] In Augustine's narration of Ambrose's procession of the bodies of the martyrs Gervasius and Protasius through the streets of Milan, a blind man who had approached the coffins of the saints and touched them with his handkerchief is cured when the same handkerchief is put on his eyes. Ambrose himself is quick to sanction the sacred nature of *brandea*, equal to relics acting as miracle workers. In Ambrose's narrative there is plenty of touching, but the saints are always shielded from human hands by pieces of

cloth, a sign of their intangible nature. Ambrose implicitly acknowledges this notion when he says: 'you see that the miracles of old time are renewed, when through the coming of the Lord Jesus grace was more largely shed forth upon the earth, and that many bodies are healed as it were by the shadow of the holy bodies'. It is the shadow of the holy bodies that the *brandea* seem to absorb. The proscription or at least the difficulty of touching relics directly continued into the later Middle Ages. In the *Anonymous Book of St Gilbert*, we read that during the canonization of St Gilbert his relics were paraded inside his reliquary and when some people approached the 'consecrated chest' and touched it, they were delivered from their illnesses.[23]

For the most part, if touching occurred then the act was described almost as an illegitimate pleasure, even if the person did not touch the body directly. During the transfer of St Edmund's body from his sepulchre to a more ornate

Plate 8 Rogier van der Weyden, *The Exhumation of St Hubert*, late 1430s, oil with egg tempera on oak, 88.2 x 81.2cm. National Gallery, London (NG783)

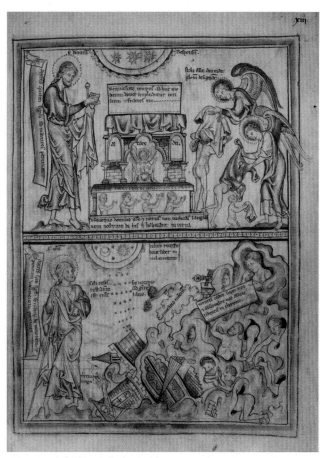

Plate 9 Apocalypse. Opening of the Fifth Seal (bottom) and souls of the martyrs under the altar (top). Morgan Library and Museum, New York, MS PM 524, fol. 3

shrine, the enthralled Jocelin of Brakelond standing before the spectacle of the saint's coffin, confesses of putting his 'sinful hand' on it (the coffin), although the abbot had forbidden anyone to 'come forward unless summoned.'[24] In the same text, we read that upon opening the sepulchre, Abbot Samson undid all of the wrapping that protected the body of the saint with the exception of the last layer of fine linen.[25] This puzzling passage reads as follows:

> And so the abbot looking near, found after this a silken cloth which covered the whole body, and then a linen cloth of wonderful whiteness; and over the head a little linen cloth and another small and skillfully made silken cloth, as it were the veil of some holy woman. And then they found the body wrapped in a linen cloth, and so at last all the lines of the holy body were clearly *traceable*. Here the abbot stopped, saying that he *dared not go further, and behold the naked body of the saint*. Therefore, he held his head between his hands, and said with a groan, 'Glorious martyr, holy Edmund, blessed be the hour in which you were born. Glorious martyr, turn not my daring to my hurt, in that I, who am a sinner and wretched, *touch you*. You know my devotion and my intention.' And then he touched the eyes and nose, the latter being thick and very large, and afterwards touched the breast and arms, and raising the left hand touched the fingers and placed his own fingers between those of the saint. And going further, he found the feet standing upright as though they had been the feet of a man but lately dead, and he touched the toes, and counted them as he touched them.[26]

The evocative description of the abbot's exploration of Edmund's face and torso is one of rapture and akin to a lover's caress. Reading it, one is made aware of the

languorous longing for physical contact, a desire bound to remain frustrated. Note that Abbot Samson is only touching the body of the saint through the protective layer of the linen shroud. He is not stroking his actual skin. Samson does not see the saint's body (his naked flesh), and while he feels it with his hands, his touch is also a non-touch because the body is shielded by a thin veil. By protecting the relics from human contact, the wrappings of relics proclaimed the intangible nature of the divine.

In addition, relic wrappings conferred a certain degree of security. Theft of relics was certainly a concern, especially when relics were exhibited to the public. It was harder to steal relics from a tightly wound body or parcel. In the late 9th-century *vita* of St Theodora of Thessaloniki, we read that when her relics were moved from a communal tomb to an individual tomb, her body was 'securely wrapped in a shroud so that no one could steal any part of the relics'.[27] In western Europe, the protective function of funerary shrouds is highlighted by the story of Hugh, bishop of Lincoln. According to his *vita*, Hugh went to the abbey of Fécamp and asked to see the relics of Mary Magdalene. The body of the saint was sewn in three different cloths and nobody had ever seen it. Since the clerics guarding the relics did not accede to Hugh's request to see the bones, he took a knife and cut through the wrappings, after which he admired the relics so much that he bit off one of the saint's fingers.[28] In this case, the tight shroud could do nothing against Hugh's ferocious devotion; however the abbot of Fécamp clearly thought that it would provide adequate protection.

Wrapping conferred protection not just from thieves, but also and, more importantly, from uninitiated people. The act of wrapping, tying and sealing relics in small precious pouches was part of a series of rituals restricted to the clergy. These rituals were tightly controlled and included the translations, examinations and the bestowing of relics as gifts, when relics could be handled by the chosen few and then withdrawn from view. The recourse to wrapping rituals in order to create some distance between a thing and ordinary life is encountered in cultures across time.[29] Consequently, observations drawn from other contexts can enhance the discussion of the wrappings of relics in Christianity. Among the ancient people of Hawaii, for example, objects considered to be the manifestation of gods were wrapped in bark cloths at the time of consecration. Valerio Valeri discusses this procedure as a way of manifesting the god's presence in these objects. Valeri argues that 'the act of removing the object from sight favors the implantation of the belief in the god's invisible presence because it creates the experience of a passage from a concrete reality to an invisible one, from a thing of perception to a thing of the mind, and therefore from an individual object to a general concept. In other words, wrapping has become a sign of consecration because it reproduces the concept by which the mind reaches the idea of the god.'[30] The Christian custom of wrapping relics manifests similar ideas. In their pouches, relics were kept at a distance even when exhibited to the faithful. It was precisely by removing the relics from sight that they became visible to one's mind alone and thus a symbol of God's invisible presence. Contrary to the image gods of Hawaii, relics did not need to become activated through ceremonial wrapping: they did not need to be consecrated as, according to Christian doctrine, they already held the immanence of God. Yet, it is clear that the action of enclosing them in carefully constructed pouches confirmed and enhanced their special status as objects of divine power.

As a result of the relationships that they engendered (of power, control and the invisibility of God's presence), the wrappings of relics established an interesting parallel between the earthly remains of saints and their heavenly lives. According to scripture, on the day of Judgement, the martyrs would be given white robes to wear: 'And when He had opened the fifth seal, I saw under the altar the souls of them that were slain for the Word of God, and for the testimony which they held: and they cried with a loud voice, saying, How long, O Lord, Holy and True, dost Thou not judge and avenge our blood on them that dwell on the earth? And white robes were given unto every one of them' (Rev. 6). The passage was frequently illustrated in medieval art, for example in a 13th-century English apocalypse (**Pl. 9**).

The scriptural trope appears early on in hagiographic narratives and continues throughout the medieval period. In the 3rd-century account of Saurus' vision of his and Perpetua's martyrdom, we read that after death, the saints arrived at a palace made with shining walls and upon entering it they were given white raiment to wear by four angels.[31] In the 13th-century *Lives of the Brethren of the Order of the Preacher*, we read that before dying, one of them, John of Serlin, 'told a companion how he dreamt he was dwelling in a grand palace and in the company of a goodly throng of exalted personages, and there he heard this melody sung by voices of ravishing sweetness: "This is the man who, having trodden under foot all earthly life and gains, has attained onto heavenly kingdoms: he has been clothed with the stole of glory by the tight hand of the most High, and his place is numbered among the saints."'[32] The stole of glory mentioned in this passage is to be understood as the white robes of chapter six of the Book of Revelation. It is true that in medieval exegesis the white robes distributed to the martyrs were commonly associated with the blissful state that the souls of the elect will achieve after death. A second reward, or stole, would, according to common exegetical thought, await them at the Second Coming when the bodies would be resurrected.[33] A beautiful illustration of this idea appears on one of the long sides of the 12th-century St Servais shrine in Maastricht (**Pl. 10**) where we see the robing of the elect at the Last Judgement.[34]

The association of white robes with spiritual beauty was also applied to church symbolism and in particular to the nature of liturgical vestments. Durandus of Mendes, author of important and popular treatises on ecclesiastical symbolism, distinguished the dress for common use from that for the service of the Lord.[35] The distinction is made in order that 'the Priest, doth off the old man with his doing, and putteth on the new man, made in the image of God'.[36] In this context, priestly robes are compared to those which God commanded Aaron and his sons to wear: 'holy garments for Glory and for Beauty' (Ex. 28:2) that were 'taken to signify virtues and express the mystery of the incarnation'.[37] This concept also appears in the 12th-century *Mytrale* by Sicardus

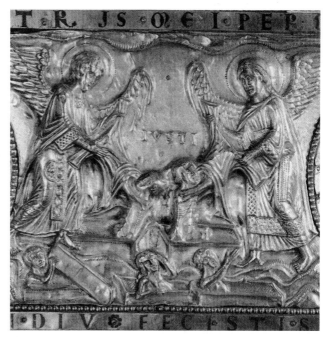

Plate 10 Shrine of St Servais, Church of St Servais, Maastricht

of Cremona, a classic manual of Church symbolism.[38] Liturgical vestments were thus like a new skin, one not tainted by the original sin.

Saints straddled both the realm of the dead and the living in as much as their remains were imbued with the power of God. Their bodies were signs of their heavenly souls as they were able to discard the robe of the flesh and wear instead that of the spirit. They were made in the image of God, hence the incorruptibility of their remains. The Catalonian painter Jaume Serra painted a vivid rendition of this idea in his 1385 retable of St Peter. The discovery of the saint's body is illustrated in the bottom right corner, where Peter is found beautifully dressed and preserved next to two decomposing skeletons (**Pl. 11**). Since the body of a saint was a sign of his soul, it stands to reason that presenting his remains wrapped in precious textiles reinforced the identity of the relics by evoking visions of the saint's soul as it would have appeared in paradise: dressed with the reward of divine bliss. The fact that relic packaging was often made out of priestly garments strengthens the notion that these textile shells alluded to the prelapsarian state of grace enjoyed by the saints in paradise.

In this context, the nature of the materials chosen to wrap relics is interesting. The medium of choice seems to have been silk, even though parchment was also used. Scripture is quite precise about the polluting nature of animal byproducts. In the Bible, Adam and Eve are clothed with tunics made with animal skins when they are chased from paradise as a sign of their fall from grace (Gen. 3:21). In contrast, Moses took off his leather sandals before encountering God as the burning bush (Ex. 3:4). From a theological point of view, materials made from animals were impure as they had been polluted by carnality. Indeed, in scripture and exegetical literature purity of soul is always identified with robes made of fine white linen. The Book of Revelation does not mention what type of fabric the stoles given by God to the martyrs were made of, but we can assume that they would be of the finest linen. Why then are the overwhelming majority of relics wrapped in silk? As with

Plate 11 Jaume Serra, *St Peter*, 1385, tempera on wood. Museo Nacional de Arte de Catalunya, Barcelona (003947-CJT)

Plate 12 Silk of Dioscurides, Byzantine, 7th or 8th century. Church of St Servais, Maastricht

gold and silver, materials often used in crafting medieval reliquaries, silk had notions of preciousness and monetary value and was thus used as a metaphor for the spiritual value of the relics and hence their authenticity. Silk was a very precious commodity whose price and output was tightly controlled.[39] Until the later Middle Ages most silk came from the Byzantine Empire or the Near East whence many relics also originated, thus silk manufacture itself was a sign of good provenance. Still, the value of silk alone is not enough to justify the possible contamination of sacred matter with an animal material.

How can this paradox be solved? With typical medieval ingenuity, a means was found to justify the taste and desire for luxurious textiles. Durandus explained that silk was acceptable for episcopal vestments instead of linen because it was made from worms, which are born from flesh without intercourse. This was a commonly held idea in the medieval period and is mentioned in medieval bestiaries.[40] It is possibly for this reason that in his *Decretum*, Gratian is careful to articulate how after the fall Adam and Eve were dressed with tunics made of animal skins and not of silk.[41] Silk here is a symbol of being in a state of grace.

What of the wrappings made of parchment? Was animal skin not the epitome of uncleanliness? This clearly seemed to have been the case for furs and leather. Parchment, on the other hand, being the material of sacred books had been long associated with the flesh of Christ. Scripture on parchment became a metaphor of the mystery of the incarnation: the word made flesh.[42]

This notion is of interest when considering the role of *cedulae* in relics wrapping. *Cedulae* or *authentiques* were small strips of parchment attached to the pouches to identify the relics. They provided a sort of 'proof' of the authenticity of relics. In his treatise against relic veneration, Guibert of Nogent mentioned this practice as a symptom of foolish credulity. Guibert's exasperated tone alone is evidence that the custom was thought to be credible.[43] To be sure, the significance of these labels was beyond that of confounding the simple minded. Judging from the collections of *cedulae*

preserved without their relics, it is clear that they were (or later became) meaningful in and of themselves. Among the collection of *authentiques* from the Sancta Sanctorum (the Pope's private chapel in the Lateran Palace, Rome), one with a large reddish brown stain at the centre could have itself been a relic perhaps of the blood of a certain Luplireni.[44] These inscriptions were significant not only because they had been in contact with sacred matter, but also and mostly because they incarnated the presence of the saints, and their names, so to speak, were inscribed on the flesh of Christ (parchment). *Cedulae* also evoked the saints through speech. The invocation of saints' names was an important part of liturgical performances and exegetical sources testify to the power of saints' names as equal to that of the relics themselves.[45] Since the relics were hidden in their pouches, the strips of parchments with the saints' names served to make their presence tangible: they substituted the saints for the relics. In this way a pinch of sacred dust or the splinter of a bone hidden from view conjured through the labels the image of the saint, not as a man but as a dweller of paradise. In the same way, we know that words uttered by holy people could be kept as verbal relics, for example those of St Francis. His biographer St Bonaventure, tells us that a piece of paper containing prayers written by St Francis was kept as a keepsake and performed miracles.[46]

Given the reliance on materials in the art of the Middle Ages to evoke and, indeed, invoke the sacred, one would be tempted to argue that reliquaries with transparent chambers still relied on materials to reconstruct the visible, as much as those that hid the relics completely. Yet, some distinctions must be made. Relics and their casings worked in parallel to create a visual metaphor pointing to the lives of the blessed in their heavenly dwelling. In fact, relics and their shells were interchangeable. The importance of textiles as relics is a good case in point. The shroud in which the body of a saint was wrapped or the dress in which he or she was buried often became a relic in its own right. The examples are legion; a famous instance is that of the 7th- or 8th-century Byzantine silk in Maastricht, known as the silk of the Dioscurides (**Pl. 12**).[47] The fabric was identified as the dress of St Servatius when in fact its date and provenance indicate that it could be the precious silk cloth that the archbishop of Worms donated to the saint's shrine in 826.[48] With time, the princely donation used to cover the shrine became identified as a piece of the saint's clothing. Hugh of Lincoln managed to obtain a relic of the tooth of St Benedict, this time without resorting to violence to acquire it. Hugh got the relic from the abbot of Fleury together with another coveted possession: a piece of the cloth in which Benedict's remains had been buried. Later Hugh distributed fragments of this cloth to the monks and abbots of his house 'out of his unbound generosity'.[49] The relics of the Three Magi in the church of St Gregory in Ribeauvillé (Alsace) are but fragments of a 1st- or 2nd-century Syrian textile that arrived in Cologne with the so-called relics of the Three Magi.[50] The blurring of boundaries between relic textiles and wrappings is exemplified at best by the custom of sewing new cloth onto the original shrouds in order to protect them.[51]

To conclude, wrappings and inscriptions complicate the idea of transparency in medieval reliquaries by creating a self-referential enshrinement. Following Seeta Chaganti, I use enshrinement not to refer 'to acts of enclosure but instead to the more complex effect whereby contained and container are interchangeable'.[52] At play is the paradox between the relic and its packaging. The latter conceals the former to highlight the absence of the sacred (the soul of the saint in heaven), but at the same time reveals itself as the saint (his or her material presence). The invisibility of relics in transparent chambers means that their objecthood is absolved first by the wrappings and then by the reliquary. The latter therefore did not merely act as a framing device, but rather as the embodiment of the relics: it personified them. Fifteenth-century *Heiltumbücher* (relic books) are a perfect expression of this notion,[53] whereby relics were illustrated by images of their reliquaries. Consequently, it is not surprising to find bits of old reliquaries often reused in newer ones: the material scraps calling back the memory of the previous container and maintaining the presence of the old and sacred in the new.[54] Here, one needs to consider what constitutes a relic. Patrica Cox Miller and Julia Smith have recently invited us to reconsider the long-held distinction between primary relics and contact relics, a differentiation that, albeit normative, was not followed in popular devotion.[55] There was little perceived difference between the value and efficacy of a so-called contact relic and a 'real' piece of bone. In the same way, ampullae filled with the oils collected at pilgrim sites were themselves relics and not just containers of the holy. One appears as such encased in the frame of the icon of St Demetrios, now in Sassoferrato.[56] The shift of identity between relics and their wrappings follows similar ideas, indicating that the visibility of bones was not a prerequisite for experiencing sacred matter.

Notes

1 Bagnoli 2010.
2 H.L. Kessler in Bagnoli *et al.* 2010, cat. no. 116 (202). With further bibliography.
3 The legend is reported by Carlo Bertelli in his magisterial study of the icon, Bertelli 1967.
4 Bynum 2011.
5 Ibid., 70.
6 N.C. Speakman in Bagnoli *et al.* 2010, cat. no. 66 (127). H.A. Klein in Bagnoli *et al.* 2010, cat. no. 44 (87).
7 The quote is taken from Athanasius of Alexandria's *vita* of St Antony, see Athanasius of Alexandria 1892, 220 (also available online in the University of Fordham Medieval sourcebook: http://www.fordham.edu/halsall/basis/vita-antony.asp).
8 Jerome, 'Against Vigilantium', *Nicene and Post-Nicene Fathers*, vol. 6, 417–23 (also available online at http://www.fordham.edu/Halsall/source/jerome-againstvigilantius.asp).
9 Ibid.
10 Dado of Rouen 1902, 699: 25 (now available online on the site of the Bayerische Staatsbibliothek: http://www.mgh.de/dmgh/resolving/MGH_SS_rer._Merov._4_S._699. I here use the translation by Jo Ann McNamara, available on the Internet Medieval Sourcebook, Fordham University at http://www.fordham.edu/halsall/basis/eligius.html.
11 Anonymous, *The Canonization*, in *The Book of St Gilbert* 1987, 185–95.
12 Schmedding 1978; Stauffer 1991; Marielle Martiniani-Reber in *Byzance* 1992, 148–55, 192–9, 370–81; Schorta 1998; Schorta 2000; Desrosiers 2004.
13 For the silks of Sens and Auxerre see Marielle Martiniani-Reber in *Byzance* 1992, cat nos 104, 285 (154, 377).
14 H.A. Klein in Bagnoli *et al.* 2010, cat. no. 67 (128).
15 Schorta 2005.
16 Hahnloser 1971, cat. no. 252 (217), Tav. CCVII. The relic was given back to the Archdioceses of Zara.
17 For the early 13th-century reliquary of the hand of Attala, see Anton Legner in *Ornamenta Ecclesiae, Kunst und Künstler der Romanik* 1985, cat. no. H 53 (147).
18 About medieval funerary rituals see: Boase 1972; Binski 1996; DuBruck and Gusick 1999.
19 On the representation of death in Books of Hours see Wieck 1999.
20 Thiofridus Epternacensis (Thiofrid of Echternach) 1996, 2.3. 84–92.
21 The Padua inventory is quoted in Bock 1970, vol. 2, 157. The Durham napkins are mentioned in the 1383 inventory of St Cuthbert's shrine redacted by Richard of Segbruk, the *feretrarius* of the cathedral, which was published in Raine 1828, 122. On St Cuthbert's shrine see Battiscombe 1956.
22 *Egeria's Travels* 2002, 155–6.
23 Anonymous, *The Canonization*, in *The Book of St Gilbert* 1987, 185–95.
24 Jocelin of Brakelond 2008, 98–102.
25 Ibid.
26 Jocelin of Brakelond 1907 (also available online: http://www.fordham.edu/halsall/basis/jocelin.asp). Italics used by current author for emphasis and not in original text.
27 'Life of St Theodora of Thessalonike', trans. by A.-M. Talbot in Talbot 1996), 223–4. I wish to thank the author for this reference.
28 Adam of Eynsham. *Magna Vita Sancti Hugonis.* From 'Bishop Hugh of Lincoln's Devotion to Relics (1186–1200)' in Shinners 2007, 181–3.
29 Karsten Wantik has demonstrated the ceremonial use of Neolithic axes and the importance of wrapping in Neolithic culture see Wantik 2006, 91. James L. Fitzsimmons has investigated the wrapping of the bodies of deceased Mayan kings as an attempt to localize their ritual power in a finite space (Fitzsimmons 2009, 81). The importance of wrapping in contemporary culture has been discussed by Hedry 1993.
30 Valerio Valeri has described this in regards to the ancient culture of Hawaii (Valeri 1985, 301).
31 Published online at: http://www.fordham.edu/halsall/source/perpetua.asp.
32 *Lives of the Brethren of the Order of the Preachers 1206–1259* 1955 (also available online at: http://www.domcentral.org/trad/brethren/bretho6.htm).

33 That is how this passage was commonly explained. Schiller and Schreiner 1990, vol. 5.1, 197–9.

34 For the St Servais shrine see Kroos 1985.

35 Durandus 2007, 154.

36 Ibid.

37 Ibid.

38 *Sicardi Cremonensi Episcopi Mitralis de Officiis* 2008), 95–6.

39 Sabatino 1945; Muthesius 1997; Delogu 1998; Martiniani-Reber 1999; Jacoby 2004.

40 This is for example the case in the 13th-century bestiary at the Bodleian Library (MS. Bodley 764). On this see Barber 1992, 199.

41 'Adam de paradyso statim post culpam Deus eiecit. Non distulit; sed statim separauit a deliciis, ut ageret penitenciam; statim tunica uestiuit eum pellicea, non serica.' *Decretum Gratiani, Decreti Pars Secunda, Causa XXXIII. Quaestio III* (now available online on the site of the Bayerische Staatsbibliothek (http://geschichte. digitale-sammlungen.de/decretum-gratiani/online/angebot). The online version follows Emil Friedberg's standard edition of 1879.

42 Richter 1968.

43 Guibert of Nogent 2000.

44 I wish to thank Julia Smith for this reference. Galland 2004, cat. no. 50 (111). The inscription on the parchment reads 'Socini Luplireni'. If the stain in the middle is indeed blood, it is possible that *socini* is a transformation of *sanguinis*.

45 Thiodfrid, *Flores*.

46 On this relic see Balfour 1944, 287; Astell 2006, 102.

47 On the Dioscurides fragment see Marielle Mariniani-Reber, 'Les Dioscures', in *Byzance* 1992, 155. On the subject of textile relics see: Martiniani-Reber 1992; Schorta 1998; Böse 2006.

48 Stauffer 1991, 19, 47–51.

49 Shinners 2006, 182.

50 It is unclear whether the relics of the Three Magi were ever in Milan as the legend attests. On this, see Geary 1988). The textile found in the shrine of the Magi in Cologne in 1864 was the subject of a detailed study by Irmgard Timmerann (Timmerann 1982). On the fragments in Ribeauvillé, see Martiniani-Reber 1987; *Byzance* 1992, 151.

51 This is, for example, the case with some textiles associated with the relics of St Ambrose in Milan. See Martiniani Reber 1987, 198.

52 Chaganti 2008, 15.

53 See for example the *Bamberg Relic-Book*, printed by Hans Mair in 1493. On this, see Gabriella K. Szalay in Bagnoli *et al.* 2010, cat. no. 126 (225).

54 Westermann-Angerhausen 2011.

55 Cox Miller 2011; Smith 2011.

56 For the icon of St Demetrios, see Kathryn B. Gerry in Bagnoli *et al.* 2010, cat. no. 115 (201).

Bibliography

Astell, A.W. 2006. *Eating Beauty. The Eucharist and the Spiritual Acts of the Middle Ages*, London and Ithaca.

Athanasius of Alexandria 1892. *Select Works and Letters, Nicene and Post-Nicene Fathers*, vol. IV, Series II, ed. P. Schaff and H. Wace, New York.

Bagnoli, M. 2010. 'The stuff of heaven: material and craftsmanship in medieval reliquaries' in Bagnoli *et al.* 2010, 137–47.

Bagnoli, M., Klein, H.A., Mann, C.G. and Robinson, J. (eds) 2010. *Treasures of Heaven: Saints, Relics and Devotion in Medieval Europe*, Baltimore and London.

Balfour, R. 1944. *The Seraphic Keepsake*, London.

Barber, R. 1992. *Bestiary: MS Bodley 764*, Woodbridge.

Battiscombe, C.F. 1956. *The Relics of Saint Cuthbert: Studies by Various Authors Collected and Edited with an Historical Introduction*, Oxford.

Bertelli, C. 1967. 'The image of Pity in Santa Croce in Gerusalemme', in *Essays Dedicated to Rudolf Wittkover On his Sixty-Fifth Birthday*, London, 40–55.

Binski, P. 1996. *Medieval Death, Ritual and Representation*, London.

Boase, T.S.R. 1972. *Death in the Middle Ages: Mortality, Judgment and Remembrance*, New York.

Bock, F. 1970 (repr.). *Geschichte der liturgische Gewänder des Mittelalters*, Graz.

The Book of St Gilbert 1987. Edited by R. Foreville and G. Keir, Oxford Medieval Texts, Oxford, 185–95.

Böse, K. 2006. 'Spürbar und unvergänglich: Zur Visualität, Ikonologie und Medialität von Textilen und textilen Reliquiaren im Mittelalterlichen Reliquienkult' in *Marburger Jahrbuch für Kunstwissenschaft* 33, 7–27.

Bynum, C.W. 2011. *Christian Materiality: An Essay on the Late Medieval Religion*, New York.

Byzance. L'art byzantin dans les collections publiques françaises 1992, Paris.

Chaganti, S. 2008. *The Medieval Poetics of the Reliquary: Enshrinement, Inscription, Performance*, New York.

Cox Miller, P. 2011. 'Figuring relics: a poetic of enshrinement", paper delivered at the conference *Saints and Sacred Matter. The Cult of Relics in Byzantium and Beyond*, Dumbarton Oaks Spring Symposium with the Walters Art Museum, Friday 29 April–Sunday 1 May 2011.

Dado of Rouen 1902. *Vita S. Eligius*, in *Monumenta Germaniae Historica SS Rer. Merov.* 4, ed. B. Krusch, Munich.

Delogu, P. 1998. 'L'importazione di tessuti preziosi e il sistema economico romano nel IX secolo' in *Roma Medievale. Aggiornamenti*, Florence, 123–41.

Desrosiers, S. 2004. *Soieries et autres textiles de l'antiquité au XVI siècle*, Paris.

DuBruck, E.E. and Gusick, B.I. (eds) 1999. *Death and Dying in the Middle Ages*, New York.

Durandus, G. 2007. *The Rationale Divinorum Officiorum: The Foundational Symbolism of the Early Church, its Structure, Decoration, Sacraments, and Vestments*, Louisville.

Egeria's Travels 2002. Trans. and ed. John Wilkinson (3rd edn), Warminster.

Fitzsimmons, J. L. 2009. *Death and the Classic Maya Kings*, Austin.

Galland, B. 2004. *Les Authentique de reliques du sancta Sanctorum*, Vatican City.

Geary, P. 1988. 'I Magi a Milano', in *Millennio Ambrosiano. La città del vescovo dai carolingi a Barbarossa*, ed. Carlo Bertelli, Milan, 274–97.

Guibert of Nogent, 2000. 'On saints and their relics', trans. T. Head, in *Medieval Hagiography: An Anthology*, ed. T. Head, New York and London, 406–22.

Hahnloser, H.R. (ed.) 1971. *Il tesoro di San Marco, Tesoro e Museo*, Florence.

Hedry, J. 1993. *Wrapping Culture. Politeness, Presentation and Power in Japan and Other Cultures*, Oxford.

Jacoby, D. 2004. 'Silk economics and cross-cultural artistic interaction: Byzantium, the Muslim world and the Christian West", in *Dumbarton Oaks Papers* 58, 197–240.

Jocelin of Brakelond 1907. *The Chronicle of Jocelin of Brakelond Monk of St Edmundsbury: A Picture of Monastic and Social Life on the XIIth Century*, trans. and ed. L.C. Jane, with an introduction by Abbot Gasquet, London.

Jocelin of Brakelond 2008. *Chronicle of the Abbey of Bury St Edmunds*, trans. D. Greenway and J. Seyers, Oxford.

Kroos, R. 1985. *Der Schrein des Heiligen Servatius in Maastricht und die vier zugehörigen Reliquiare in Brüssel*, Munich.

Lives of the Brethren of the Order of the Preachers 1206–1259, 1955. Ed. and trans. P. Conway O.P., London.

Martiniani-Reber, M. 1987. 'Stoffe tardoantiche e medioevali nel tesoro di Sant'Ambrogio', in *Millennio Ambrosiano, Milano una Capitale da Ambrogio ai Carolingi*, ed. C. Bertelli, Milan, 178–201.

Martiniani-Reber, M. 1992. 'Le rôle des étoffes dans le cultes des reliques au Moyen Age', *Bulletin du CIETA* 70, 53–8.

Martiniani-Reber, M. 1999. 'Teintures et Textiles des Eglises Romaine au Haut Moyen Âge d'Après Le Liber Pontificalis', in *MEFRM* 111, 289–305.

Muthesius, A. 1997. *Byzantine Silk Weaving: AD 400 to AD 1200*, ed. E. Kislinger and J. Koder, Vienna.

Ornamenta Ecclesiae, Kunst und Künstler der Romanik 1985, Cologne.

Raine, J. 1828. *Saint Cuthbert. With an Account of the State in Which his Relics Were Found*, Durham.

Richter, D. 1968. 'Die Allegorie der Pergamentbearbeitung: Beziehungen zwischen handwerlichen Vorgängen und der geistlichen Bildersprache des Mittelalters" in *Fachliteratur des Mittelalters: Festschrift für Gerhard Eis*, ed. G. Keil, R. Rudolf, W. Schmitt and H. J. Vermer, Stuttgart, 83–92.

Sabatino Lopez, R. 1945. 'Silk industry in the Byzantine Empire', in *Speculum* 20, 1–42.

Schiller, G. and Schreiner, R. 1990. *Ikonographie Der Christlichen Kunst*, Gütersloh.

Schmedding, B. 1978. *Mittealterliche Textilien in Kirchen und Klöstern der Schweiz*, Bern.

Schorta, R. 1998. 'Reliquienhüllen und textile Reliquien im Welfenschatz' in *Der Welfenschatz und sein Umkreis*, Mainz, 139–76.

Schorta, R. 2000. 'The textiles found in the shrine of the patron saint of Hildesheim Cathedral', *Bulletin du CIETA* 77, 45–56.

Schorta, R. 2005. 'La presentation des reliques', in *La Grande Chasse De Sion, Chef d'Oeuvre d'Orfevrerie du XI siècle'*, Paris, 211–15.

Shinners, J. (ed.) 2007. *Medieval Popular Religion, 1000–1500: A Reader* (2nd edn), Peterborough and Plymouth.

Sicardi Cremonensi Episcopi Mitralis de Officiis 2008. Ed. G. Sarbak and L. Weinrich, CCCM, 228, Turnhout.

Smith, J.M.H. 2011. 'Relics: the making of a tradition in Latin Christianity', paper delivered at the conference *Saints and Sacred Matter. The Cult of Relics in Byzantium and Beyond*, Dumbarton Oaks Spring Symposium with the Walters Art Museum, Friday 29 April–Sunday 1 May 2011.

Stauffer, A. 1991. *Die mittelalterlichen Textilien von St. Servatius in Maastricht*, Riggisberg.

Talbot, A.-M (ed.) 1996. *Holy Women of Byzantium*, Washington, DC.

Thiofridus Epternacensis (Thiofrid of Echternach), 1996. *Flores Epytaphii Sanctorum*, ed. M.C. Ferrari, CCCM 133, Turnhout.

Timmerann, I. 1982. 'Seide, Purpur und Gold-Untersuchungen zu den Gewebfragmenten aus dem Schrein der heiligen Drei Könige im Dom zu Köln', in *Die Drei Könige: Darstellung und Verehrung*, 115–25.

Valeri, V. 1985. *Kingship and Sacrifice: Ritual Society in Ancient Hawaii*, Chicago.

Wantik, K. 2006. *Ceci n'est pas une Hache: Neolithic Deposition in the Northern Netherlands*, Leiden.

Westermann-Angerhausen, H. 'The memory of objects: spolia in reliquaries', paper delivered at the conference *Saints and Sacred Matter. The Cult of Relics in Byzantium and Beyond*, Dumbarton Oaks Spring Symposium with the Walters Art Museum, Friday 29 April–Sunday 1 May 2011.

Wieck, R.S. 1999. 'Death desired: Books of Hours and the medieval funeral', in DuBruck and Gusick 1999, 431–76.

Chapter 14
Common Ground
Reliquaries and the Lower Classes in Late Medieval Europe

Sarah Blick

It is hard to believe that two wildly divergent reliquaries on display in the treasury of the cathedral of Notre Dame, Tournai, Belgium, are in fact, essentially, the same kind of object. One is a large, magnificent, glittering reliquary dedicated to the Virgin Mary dated to 1200–5, made by Nicholas of Verdun and composed of silver and copper-gilt and adorned with enamels and gems (**Pl. 1**), while the other is a small, rough-hewn, wooden box from the late 14th or early 15th century, made by an anonymous and not particularly skilled artisan (**Pl. 2**).[1] Instead of golden relief sculpture, crudely cast pilgrim badges are nailed to its side in a haphazard fashion and a quartz bead is wired onto its lid in lieu of rock-crystal adornment. Yet both reflect the same wish: to contain a sacred relic as a repository of healing and spiritual strength. Where they differ is in their media, the skill or lack thereof in their construction and, most importantly, in whether it was the rich or poor who were allowed to access and handle them.

While much attention has been paid to the glorious, golden, bejewelled reliquaries made by the finest artisans, often only the upper classes had direct access to this sort of splendour. Members of the lower classes were rarely allowed to touch or examine such opulent objects closely; usually, they would have seen them as the reliquaries were paraded past in procession or were perched on top of lofty shrine bases, fenced off by iron gates and guarded by clerics, at times from watching chambers.[2] Pilgrims could nestle into the niches of shrine bases or duck under the reliquaries when they were being carried on a litter in procession, but being able to actually handle the reliquary, much less the relic itself, was mostly reserved for members of the upper class and the clergy.[3]

However, because crowds bolstered claims of sacred power, clerics at pilgrimage sites hoped to attract people of all classes and to that end purchased indulgences, created spectacular artwork and spread the word of their saint through poems and songs.[4] The importance of the presence of the poor is found in the common visual trope of crippled peasants writhing below (but not touching) a reliquary in

Plate 1 Nicholas of Verdun, reliquary of the Virgin Mary, 13th century, Mosan, (95 x 115 x 50.5cm). Cathedral of Notre Dame, Tournai (photo: author)

Plate 2 Handmade reliquary, late 14th century, presumably Mosan, wood with pewter badges and quartz, (8 x c. 24.5 x 9.3cm). Tournai Cathedral (photo: Genevra Kornbluth)

Plate 3a–b a) Canterbury ampulla in shape of chasse reliquary, 13th century, tin. Collection of Brian North Lee (photo by permission of owner); b) Pilgrim ampulla with nail hole, 14th–15th century, lead, found in West Lindsey, Lincolnshire (photo courtesy of the Portable Antiquities Scheme, PAS SWYOR-469121)

hopes of a miraculous cure.[5] The lower classes as crowds were welcome, but as individuals they were held at bay for fear of thieving and general disorderly conduct. Still, the desire for contact with such power inspired some to fashion their own reliquaries. These crude pieces were considered efficacious in helping to transform humble domestic spaces by sanctifying them and their inhabitants regardless of class.

These objects are the reverse of how one usually envisions reliquaries: sumptuous creations, traditionally the province of the rich and powerful, encasing hard-won, expensive relics. Heroic tales of relic acquisition and reliquary adornments given by heads of state enhanced the aura of a typical reliquary. Yet, what is a reliquary but a container for the sacred? It demarcates what is sacred, and protects and sometimes celebrates what is contained within, such as in the 6th-century reliquary box with stones from the Holy Land in the Vatican Museums.[6] For the less dexterous, other kinds of pilgrim reliquaries such as ampullae, which were mass-produced and of low-quality pewter (or tin/lead variants), were easily purchased (**Pl. 3a–b**).

Reliquaries such as ampullae were usually filled with some kind of secondary relic, such as holy water (or sometimes water used to wash the official reliquary). Even a stone plucked from the ground of a church which housed a powerful relic could become a relic in its own right through, as Ronald C. Finucane put it, 'holy radioactivity,' which was perhaps not as powerful as the original, but functional nonetheless.[7] The poor, as one 13th-century cleric criticized, found their own relics in 'stones, wood, trees, or fountains on account of anyone's dream or deception'.[8] Yet, as relics (for example pieces of bone, small stones or strips of cloth) look the same once denuded of their covers, all such finds were theoretically effective. Devotees without access to even these humble offerings could still obtain the amuletic power of the saints by consuming water, butter, apples, cheese or moulded bread onto which saints' names were written.[9] Stones, sticks, leaves, pottery sherds, wooden boards and small metal sheets could all mark the space in which they were placed as sacred.[10] The independent, flexible and changeable nature of these sacred objects troubled some church officials because they were barely distinguishable from magical practices. Nonetheless, these objections were little heeded as the ubiquity of such practices indicates.

While the affluent preferred devotional objects made of precious metals and gems, a number of medieval commentators made no distinction regarding media in relation to the effectiveness of a devotional object.[11] (Indeed clerics were buried with lead chalices and patens so that they could administer the sacrament to the risen on Judgement Day.)[12] Devotional paraphernalia could be of any media and of any size, for use in private or public.[13] Without the heavenly craftsmanship or intrinsically potent materials, poorly made objects composed of media such as bread dough, pipe clay and papier mâché were considered equally serviceable.[14]

Reliquaries, whether gold or lead, were part of the same devotional culture. Although most people could not access the most coveted relics or their rich containers, their determination to share in the banquet of devotional opportunities is reflected in the widespread ownership of their own reliquaries and sacred images. These unpretentious reliquaries, which survive in abundance, provide an insight into the devotional world of the lower classes, something usually only seen through the filter of opinions of people from a different class. They also illustrate how rich objects were received by the poor and how they understood their iconography, shape and function. What was common, was common throughout all classes; many reliquaries were cheap and easily accessible.

Other objects make it quite apparent that the line between the exclusive and the common was porous in the later Middle Ages. For example, from the 12th to the 16th century, bells, fonts and morses (metal pins to hold copes together) were adorned with pilgrim badges, enhancing their already considerable power.[15] Some elegant 14th and 15th-century manuscripts also featured tawdry badges sewn into or replicated in paint in their margins,[16] and groups of 15th-century nuns filled reliquaries with cheap sculptures, pilgrim badges and special plants picked up on their pilgrimages.[17] These kinds of reliquaries make an even

Plate 4 Detail of Pieter Brueghel the Younger, *Battle of Carnival and Lent*, last quarter of 16th century, Flemish, oil on wood. Musées Royaux des Beaux-Arts, Brussels

in mind the tenuous line between public and private. While people enjoyed public interaction with the sacred, they also sought to take some of the sanctity home. They brought their own tokens to churches for blessing, placing them on altars[21] and purchased wax votives on site. These activities are depicted in a detail of a painting by Pieter Brueghel the Younger, who shows devotees outside a church door buying wax votives while others inside the church are placing tokens at the base of the crucifix near the column (**Pl. 4**). These pieces, once graced by being near relics within the church, were brought home and venerated in private.

Privacy allowed time for more deeply felt communication with the holy. From the early Middle Ages onwards, priests recommended the daily worship of images to increase emotions in the devotee, but examples of private objects in the West are sparse. Documentation of widespread personal ownership of private devotional objects by the upper classes appear by the 12th century in miracle accounts, but it would not be until the 13th century when there is evidence for similar ownership among the lower classes.[22] Two factors made this possible: the growing affluence of the lower classes and the use of mass production to create these works.[23]

Sophisticated or crude, any image was '[an] archetype, containing levels of meaning within their histories and emblems that reified their powers of healing and salvation'.[24] Private images and reliquaries had the same powers as their public renditions, but as they were no longer held aloof from the worshipper, the divinity could interact personally with the beholder. Such pieces could be worshiped, as Bishop Peacock stated in the 15th century, 'before a bare wall in a church, or in a corner … [of a] house or … field'.[25] Nailed to a wall or placed on a table, they invoked a domestic altar.[26]

Creating the sacred outside of church required individuals to construct where, when and how they prayed, looked for heavenly signs and utilized personal rituals (often influenced by the magical practices seen at church through the Eucharist, for example).[27] Private conjurations helped people cope with daily life, sickness, fear of crime, evil, concerns surrounding a good crop, sick animals and so forth.[28] Such practices allowed people to 'invoke sacred power to create order in the daily life of an agrarian and pastoral society. They differ[ed] from the sacraments in being immediately accessible, relying only on individual memory and [the] desire to put them into practice.'[29]

stronger case for how flimsy the distinction (in practice) was between rich and poor.

How, why and where reliquaries for the lower classes were used

With the survival of so many examples, why has there been such little investigation of reliquaries made for the lower classes? Not being graced with beauty or distinguished craftsmanship, most are discovered by metal detectorists in humble circumstances (on river foreshores or in fields) often without significant archaeological context and almost no documentation. What we have left are the pieces themselves and some clues as to how they were used and viewed.

As a personal rather than group relic and reliquary, such a piece could be actively and intimately used. Although the relic came first – miracle stories tell and images show the ingestion or daubing of holy water or oil to cure all manner of ailments[18] – often the reliquary container became a focus of devotion. Pilgrim ampullae, for instance, by virtue of once containing the sacred, retained the power to console. (Similarly, tombs where saints were once laid such as that of St Thomas Becket at Canterbury and St Swithun at Winchester[19] continued to attract devotees, even when vacant.) Once emptied, pilgrim ampullae could be nailed to a wall in a home or stable (**Pl. 3b**).[20]

What is perhaps most intriguing is the idea of private devotion that these kinds of objects made possible, if we keep

Plate 5 Carpow reliquary, 15th century, copper alloy. Perth Museum and Art Gallery (photo: after Hall 2007, fig. 7.1)

Plate 6 (left) Folding reliquary with image of standing saint, 14th century. Museum of Decorative Arts, Prague, Bureau Monumenten en Archeologie (photo: after Bruna 2006, fig. 114)

Plate 7 (right) Charlemagne kneeling before the Virgin and Child, 14th century, pewter, Aachen, Germany. Collection of B. de Bree (photo: after Van Beuningen 1993, 89, ill. 33)

Popular reliquaries

Many pilgrim ampullae which acted like reliquaries (carrying holy water, oil or dust from sacred tombs) echoed the shapes and general iconography of more expensive reliquaries,[30] such as a 13th-century ampulla made for the Thomas Becket cult at Canterbury (**Pl. 3a**). It features a seated Becket and the crucified Christ on the narrow ends, while scenes of Becket's martyrdom and rows of figures of kings and clerics adorn the longer sides.[31] Other examples include 14th and 15th-century pilgrims' badges which present miniature replicas of head and arm reliquaries as well as larger shrines.[32]

Small, amuletic reliquaries in the form of ampullae or *phylacteria* (amulets or charms) were worn around the neck and over the heart, which was sometimes considered the gateway to the soul and needed protection against the devil.[33] The amulets of the wealthy featured gems and gold, while the poor found protection in metal, shell and parchment.[34]

Amulets could also acquire power not only through relics and powerful media, but through images and texts (such as the inscriptions found on many 13th-century Canterbury ampullae, intoning 'Thomas is the best doctor of the worthy sick').[35] While clerics often criticized amulets (as a preservative against affliction), they were primarily concerned with their misuse rather than with their effectiveness.[36] Many clerics denounced amulets as punishable superstition (such as in the 13th-century *Summa Confessorum* from Salisbury and by John Mirk in the early 15th century who condemned them because they placed people in the grip of the devil).

As the desire for ever greater personal interaction with the divine grew, so did the demand for sacred, amuletic jewellery, including complex hinged containers, lockets and chains.[37] Most common are brooches and necklaces whose cavities were filled with relics. These personal and portable reliquaries could be made of precious metals and gems or of lead or copper alloy, such as the Carpow reliquary. Riveted at all four corners and rather crudely made, it contained a sliver of the True Cross (**Pl. 5**).[38] Lockets could also contain

items that were picked up such as special plants or small stones, and religious figures (as objects of power) were also dangled on chains for pleasure or used for ligature charms.[39]

Beyond this, a newly developed sophistication in casting and piecing together made complicated pieces easier to produce and allowed for some customization. Tiny, base-metal folding triptychs and oratories with elaborate iconographic programmes allowed more people to own pieces such as those owned by wealthy devotees, which were created with ivory or precious metals.[40] Folding was integral to the do-it-yourself reliquary. Two almost complete examples have been discovered thus far, but many fragments from similar vessels have been found.[41]

Cast in openwork designs, they lay flat until the purchaser pulled the soft metal apart and folded the object into shape, firmly fastening it with the built-in clips. On the top left of the example illustrated here, the long sides feature

Plate 8 Pilgrim badge with frame for mirror, 15th century, Aachen, Germany. Collection of H.J.E. Van Beuningen, Cothen, Netherlands (photo: after Van Beuningen 1993, 211, no. 2323)

gabled and cusped Gothic arches with a four-part quatrefoil roof line (**Pl. 6**). At its gable end under a cross is a bishop saint with a pilgrim kneeling in devotion. Unfortunately, the opposite end does not survive. The hollow cage allowed one to see and rattle the object placed within (probably a pebble or another physical souvenir taken from the site). While other reliquary shaped pieces, ampullae in particular, were often purchased already filled with holy water and such like, folding reliquaries allowed the devotee to place their own relic inside. Their cage-like structure also mimicked the later medieval tendency of some reliquaries to reveal the relics within.[42]

The new techniques also made it possible for the poorer devotee to set up a personal shrine on a mantle or table. With their own architectural structure, objects such as the 14th-century altar with Charlemagne kneeling before the Virgin and Child created the space for an entire scene. This included a three-dimensional space that not only framed this view, but also melded a crib-like structure with that of the skeleton of a chasse reliquary (**Pl. 7**).[43] Note the quatrefoil top and the square legs that recall more luxurious examples. There are also examples of tiny reliquaries with their own processional staves.[44] Presumably, they could evoke a similar devotional experience as that of seeing the larger version processed before the devotee's eyes. Such objects might also reflect Franciscan recommendations that children should play with and decorate toy altars.[45]

Certain humble pieces were created to capture more ephemeral relic power. For example, at Aachen Cathedral, when the main relics went on display every seven years, an extraordinary number of pilgrims flooded in, inspiring the clerics to exhibit the relics outside the tower gallery.[46] Unable to come close to the relics or reliquaries, pilgrims purchased badges with mirrors. Widespread belief held that mirrors reflecting a sacred image could assimilate and fix some of the sanctity expressed and could later be dispensed by pointing the mirror towards a loaf of bread to be eaten or towards one's own eyes. The idea of seeing or beholding is clearly highlighted, as the mirror is centred in each badge with an image of the relic (here the Virgin's cloak) immediately above or below it (**Pl. 8**).

As proof that a reliquary's humble media and poor quality did not inhibit its perceived value, the poor quality late 14th-century oak box which inspired this article was discovered in 1856 inside the sumptuous Reliquary of the Virgin at Tournai Cathedral![47] This explains why such a modest (and flammable) piece survived for so many centuries, but it does not explain why the bones found within the smaller reliquary were not removed and placed in a more becoming container before being placed in the shrine. The scruffy box itself must have been considered of some value or it would have been discarded long ago.

When examined overall, what is evident is that the devotional objects regularly accessed and owned by the poor spoke the same visual language as those produced for wealthier, better educated patrons. Much work remains to be done regarding these objects. What were their actual costs, and geographically where were certain forms more popular and why? A more accurate definition of the poorer classes is necessary as well. However, what this short paper illustrates is that the poor understood and accessed the same ideas and the same devotional forms as the wealthier and better educated. Ultimately, as human beings, their desires and actions were identical.

Notes

1. *Polistoire*, British Library Harleian MS 636 f. 201b, col. 2, 1-15-f. 202b; Mason 1920, 71–3; Stanley n.d., 306–8.
2. Blick 2009; Ghrádaigh 2009; Belghaus 2011; Nilson 1998, 117–18.
3. Erasmus 1849, 56–7; Erasmus 1967.
4. Swanson 2006; Henry of Avranches 1935; Golden 2009; Gelfand 2005.
5. *Book of Additions (Liber additamentorum)*, British Library, London, Cotton MS Nero D I.
6. Pantanella 2010; Beebe 2006; Bagnoli *et al.* 2010, cat. no. 13.
7. Finucane 1977, 26; Skemer 2006, 68; Beebe 2006, 106.
8. Skemer 2006, 89. Golding 2001, 145.
9. Skemer 2006, 110, 127–8.
10. Skemer 2006, 128; Wogan-Browne 1994.
11. Skemer 2006, 5–6.
12. Stroud and Kemp 1993, 156–7; Tweddle 1986, 208–9.
13. Marks 2004, 18.
14. Rudy 2009; Marks 2004, 229; Baggs 1968.
15. Köster 1984.
16. Van Asperen 2009; Foster-Campbell 2011.
17. Kruip 2006; Rudy 2011, ch. 1.
18. Boertjes 2007; Spencer 1971; Spencer 1998, 38–9.
19. Nilson 1998, 54–7.
20. Köster 1984.
21. Scribner 1987, 36; Franz 1902, 87–92, 96–7, 107–13.
22. Ringbom 1965, 14.
23. Horsfield 1989, 208.
24. Roffey 2006, 27.
25. Pecock 1860, vol. 1, 169.
26. Ringbom 1965, 38; Heyne 1899, 271, fig. 70; Schultz 1892, 106.
27. Scribner 1987, 7.
28. Ibid., 8, n. 32.
29. Ibid., 8.
30. Spencer 1998, 65–71, 144.
31. Ibid., fig. 20k.
32. Ibid. 1998, 98–117, 144; Bruna 2000, 73–9.
33. Skemer 2006, 12–13; Scribner 1987, 7; Richmond 1984, 198.
34. Horrox 1994, 198; Hinton 2005, 243–5.
35. Spencer 1998, 45.
36. Skemer 2006, 5–6.
37. Hinton 2005, 245; Van Beuningen 2001, 360, no. 1516.
38. Cherry 1994; Hall 2007, 75–91.
39. Jones 2007, 92–107.
40. Campbell 1998, 72, XXVIIc.
41. Bruna 2006, fig. 114; Pieters 1997–8, 6, no. 43. Prague 1985, 25, no. 186.
42. Belting 1990, 82; Bagnoli 2010, 141–3.
43. Van Beuningen 1993, 89, ill. 33; Koldeweij 1989, 124–6, pl. 10; Van Heeringen 1988, 37, fig. 19.
44. Bruna 2006, fig. 115.
45. Webb 1990, 159; Trexler 1980, 377; Klapisch-Zuber 1985, 115, 320–2.
46. Köster 1973; Spencer 1998, 259.
47. Gay 1887, 403.

Bibliography

Baggs, A.P. 1968. 'Sixteenth-century terracotta tombs in East Anglia', *Archaeological Journal* 125, 296–301.

Bagnoli, M. 2010. 'The stuff of heaven: materials and craftsmanship in medieval reliquaries', in Bagnoli *et al.* 2010, 136–47.

Bagnoli, M., Klein, H.A., Mann, C.G. and Robinson, J. (eds) 2010. *Treasures of Heaven: Saints, Relics and Devotion in Medieval Europe*, Baltimore and London.

Beebe, K. 2006. 'Knights, cooks, monks and tourists: elite and popular experience of the late-medieval Jerusalem pilgrimage', in *Elite and Popular Religion: Papers Read at the 2004 Summer Meeting and the 2005 Winter Meeting of the Ecclesiastical History Society*, ed. K. Cooper and J. Gregory, Woodbridge, 99–109.

Belghaus, V. 2011. 'Everybody's darling: transformation of value and transformation of meaning in the veneration of St. Elizabeth of Thuringia', in Blick and Gelfand 2011, vol. 2, 179–230.

Belting, H. 1990. *The Image and its Public in the Middle Ages: Form and Function of Early Paintings of the Passion*, trans. M. Bartusis and R. Meyer, New Rochelle, NY.

Blick, S. (ed.) 2007. *Beyond Pilgrim Souvenirs and Secular Badges: Essays in Honour of Brian Spencer*, Oxford.

Blick, S. 2009. 'Watching chambers', in Taylor *et al.* 2009, 817.

Blick, S. and Gelfand, L. (eds) 2011. *Push Me, Pull You: Physical and Spatial Interaction in Late Medieval and Renaissance Art*, 2 vols, Leiden.

Boertjes, K. 2007. 'Pilgrim ampullae of York Minster and the healing oil from the shrine of St William', in Blick 2007, 48–63.

Bruna, D. 2000. 'Quelques images de chefs-reliquaires B travers les enseignes de pèlerinage', in *Gevonden Voorwerpen, Lost and Found: Essays on Medieval Archaeology for H.J.E. van Beuningen*, ed. D. Kicken, A.M. Koldeweij and J.R. ter Molen, Rotterdam, 73–9.

Bruna, D. 2006. *Enseignes de plomb et autres menues chosettes du Moyen Âge*, Paris.

Campbell, M. 1998. 'Medieval metalworking and Bury St Edmunds', in *Bury St Edmunds. Medieval Art, Architecture, Archaeology and Economy*, ed. A. Gransden, British Archaeological Association Conference Transactions, 69–80.

Cherry, J. 1994. *The Middleham Jewel and Ring*, York.

Erasmus, D. 1849. *Pilgrimages to Saint Mary of Walsingham and Saint Thomas of Canterbury*, trans. J.G. Nichols, Westminster.

Erasmus, D. 1967. 'A pilgrimage for religion's sake', *The Colloquies of Erasmus*, Chicago.

Finucane, R.C. 1977. *Miracles and Pilgrims: Popular Beliefs in Medieval England*, New York.

Foster-Campbell, M. H. 2011. 'Pilgrimage through the pages: pilgrims' badges in late medieval devotional manuscripts', in Blick and Gelfand 2011, vol. 1, 227–74.

Franz, A. 1902. *Die Messe im deutschen Mittelalter*, Freiburg.

Gay, V. 1887. *Glossaire archéologique du Moyen Age et de la Renaissance*, vol. I, Paris.

Gelfand, L. 2005. '"Y me tarde": the Valois, pilgrimage, and the Chartreuse de Champmol', in *Art and Architecture of Late Medieval Pilgrimage in Northern Europe and the British Isles*, ed. S. Blick and R. Tekippe, Leiden, 567–86.

Ghrádaigh, J.N. 2009. 'Iron grilles in churches', in Taylor *et al.* 2009, 297–9.

Golden, R.M. 2009, 'Music and pilgrimage', in Taylor *et al.* 2009, 463–8.

Golding, B. 2001. 'The Church and Christian life', in *The Twelfth and Thirteenth Centuries: Short Oxford History of the British Isles*, ed. B. Harvey, Oxford, ch. 4.

Hall, M.A. 2007. 'Crossing the pilgrimage landscape: some thoughts on a Holy Rood reliquary from the River Tay at Carpow, Perth and Kinross, Scotland', in Blick 2007, 75–91.

Henry of Avranches 1935. *The Shorter Latin Poems of Master Henry of Avranches Relating to England*, ed. J.C. Russell and J.P. Hieronimus, Cambridge, MA.

Heyne, M. 1899. *Fünf Bücher deutscher Hausaltertümter, I, Das deutsche Wohnungswesen von den ältesten geschichtlichen Zeiten bis zum 16. Jahrhundert*, Leipzig, 1899.

Hinton, D.A. 2005. *Gold and Gilt, Pots and Pins: Possessions and People in Medieval Britain*, Oxford.

Horrox, R. (ed.) 1994. *Fifteenth-Century Attitudes*, Cambridge.

Horsfield, Rev. R.A. 1989. 'The pomander of prayer: aspects of late medieval English Carthusian spirituality and its lay audience', in *De Cella in Seculum: Religious and Secular Life and Devotion in Late Medieval England*, ed. M.G. Sargent, Cambridge, 205–23.

Jones, P.M. 2007. 'Amulets: prescriptions and surviving objects from late medieval England', in Blick 2007, 92–107.

Klapisch-Zuber, C. 1985. *Women, Family and Ritual in Renaissance Florence*, Chicago.

Koldeweij, A.M. 1989. 'Karel de Grote-souvenirs uit Aken', in *Annus Quadriga Mundi. Opstellen over middeleeuwse aan Prof. Dr. Anne C. Esmeijer*, Zutphen, 116–28.

Köster, K. 1973. *Gutenberg in Strassburg*, Eltville-on Rhine.

Köster, K. 1984. 'Mittelalterliche pilgerzeichen', in *Wallfahrt kennt keine Grenzen*, ed. L. Kriss-Rettenbeck and G. Möhler, Munich, 203–23.

Kruip, M. 2006. 'Le jardin clos: un pèlerinage spirituel', in *Foi et Bonne Fortune: Parure et Dévotion en Flandre Médiévale*, ed. J. Koldeweij, Bruges, 231–4.

Marks, R. 2004. *Image and Devotion in Late Medieval England*, Stroud.

Mason, A. 1920. *What Became of the Bones of St Thomas?*, Cambridge.

Nilson, B. 1998. *Cathedral Shrines of Medieval England*, Woodbridge.

Pantanella, C. 2010. 'Reliquary box with stones from the Holy Land', in Bagnoli *et al.* 2010, 36–7.

Pecock, R. 1860. *The Repressor of Over Much Blaming of the Clergy*, ed. C. Babington, vol. 1, London.

Pieters, M., Cools, E., Koldeweij, J. and Mortier, A. 1997–8. 'Middeleeuwse en latere insignes en devotionalia uit Raversijde (gemeente Middelkerke en stad Oostende, prov. West-Vlaanderen)', *Archeologie in Vlaanderen* 6.

Prague 1985. *Katalog sbirky stredovekého umleckého remesla muzeum v praze*, Museum Catalogue of Praha, Museum of Decorative Arts, Prague.

Richmond, C. 1984. 'Religion and the fifteenth-century English gentleman', in *The Church, Politics and Patronage in the Fifteenth Century*, ed. B. Dobson, New York, 193–208.

Ringbom, S. 1965. *Icon to Narrative: The Rise of the Dramatic Close-up in Fifteenth-Century Devotional Painting*, Abo.

Roffey, S. 2006. 'Devotional objects and cultural context: the medieval parish church', in *Catholic Collecting, Catholic Reflection 1538–1850*, ed. V.C. Raguin, Worcester, MA, 21–30.

Rudy, K.M. 2009. 'Terracotta sculptures' in Taylor *et al.* 2009, 739–40.

Rudy, K.M. 2011. *Virtual Pilgrimage in the Convent: Imagining Jerusalem in the Late Middle Ages*, Turnhout.

Schultz, A. 1892. *Deutsches Leben im XIV. und XV. Jahrhundert*, Vienna.

Scribner, R.W. 1987. *Popular Culture and Popular Movements in Reformation Germany*, London.

Simon, R. 2006. 'Devotional objects and cultural context: the medieval parish church', in *Catholic Collecting: Catholic Reflection 1538–1850, Objects as a Measure of Reflection on a Catholic Past and the Construction of Recusant Identity in England and America*, ed. V. Raguin, Worcester, MA, 21–30.

Skemer, D.C. 2006. *Binding Words: Textual Amulets in the Middle Ages*, University Park, PA.

Spencer, B. 1971. 'A scallop-shell ampulla from Caistor and comparable pilgrim souvenirs', *Lincolnshire History of Archaeology* 1/6, 59–66.

Spencer, B. 1998. *Pilgrim Souvenirs and Secular Badges: Medieval Finds from Excavations in London*, London.

Stanley, A. n.d.. *Historical Memorials of Canterbury*, New York.

Stroud, G. and Kemp, R.L. 1993. *Cemeteries of the Church and Priory of St Andrew, Fishergate*. York.

Swanson, R.N. (ed.) 2006. *Promissary Notes on the Treasury of Merits: Indulgences in Late Medieval Europe*, Leiden.

Taylor, L.J. *et al.* (eds) 2009. *Encyclopedia of Medieval Pilgrimage*, Leiden.

Trexler, R. 1980. *Public Life in Renaissance Florence*, New York.

Tweddle, D. 1986. *The Archaeology of York: Vol. 17, The Small Finds. Finds from Parliament Street and Other Sites in the City Centre*, York.

Van Asperen, H. 2009. *Pelgrimstekens op Perkament. Originele en nageschilderde bedevaartssouvenirs in religieuze boeken (ca. 1450–ca. 1530)*, Nijmegen.

Van Beuningen, H.J.E. and Koldeweij, J. 1993. *Heilig en Profaan 1, 1000 laat-middeleeuwse insignes uit de Collectie H.J.E. Van Beuningen*, Cothen.

Van Beuningen, H.J.E., Koldeweij, J. and Kicken, D. 2001. *Heilig en Profaan 2, 1200 laat-middeleeuwse insignes uit openbare en particuliere collecties*, Cothen.

Van Heeringen, R.M., Koldeweij, A.M. and Gaalman, A.A.G. 1988. *Heiligen uit de Modder in Zeeland Gevonden Pelgrimstekens*, Utrecht.

Webb, D.M. 1990. 'Woman and home: the domestic setting of late medieval spirituality', in *Women in the Church*, ed. W.J. Sheils and D. Wood, Oxford, 159–74.

Wogan-Browne, J. 1994. 'The apple's message: some post-Conquest hagiographic accounts of textual transmission', in *Late-Medieval Religious Texts and Their Transmission: Essays in Honour of A.I. Doyle*, ed. A.J. Minnis, Cambridge, 39–53.

Chapter 15
A Shrine Reunited?
The Collaborative, Scientific Study of Two Reliquary Panels from the Walters Art Museum and the British Museum

Glenn Gates, Susan La Niece and Terry Drayman-Weisser

A scientific study was conducted collaboratively between the owning institutions of two medieval Mosan reliquaries: the Walters Art Museum gabled reliquary panel of St Oda, previously known as the reliquary panel of Triumphant Christ (57.519), and the British Museum gabled reliquary panel of St Oda (1978,0502.7). The non-invasive methods used for this exercise were energy dispersive X-ray fluorescence (XRF), X-radiography, stereomicroscopy and Raman spectroscopy. The objectives of this study were to distinguish medieval materials from post-medieval materials and to determine what technical evidence may exist that would link these two reliquaries to each other and to the 12th-century shrine of St Oda of Amay, a town in current day Belgium near Huy. The study was able to distinguish some modern materials from the majority which are likely to be medieval. Scientific analyses of the two reliquaries revealed marked similarities in dimensions, construction and elemental compositions of the enamels and alloys, confirming close links between the two objects. No evidence was found to disprove their supposed link to the shrine of St Oda of Amay.

Introduction

For the *Treasures of Heaven* exhibition (2010–11), the Walters Art Museum's gabled reliquary panel of St Oda (**Pl. 1**) was displayed adjacent to the British Museum's gabled reliquary panel of St Oda (**Pl. 2**).[1] These two medieval Mosan reliquary panels were last recorded together in the late 19th century before one went to Baltimore after it was purchased by Henry Walters around 1900 from Jacques Seligmann. The other arrived at the British Museum in 1978 from the Wernher Collection of Luton Hoo. The oldest documentation of the panels together is a photograph of the two objects in the Colworth Collection from 1862.[2] They were described in detail by Neil Stratford.[3] These two works are strikingly similar in dimensions, materials and design. The overall height of both panels is *c.* 585mm, the width is *c.* 370mm and the length of each gable side is *c.* 280mm. In both reliquary panels, a chamfered oak panel supports a central silver repoussé panel framed by decorative metal, champlevé enamel plaques, rock crystal and translucent horn windows over small cavities containing relics.[4] The chamfering on the front of the panels mirrors that on the reverse. The chamfering on the reverse may have accommodated the construction of a well-sealed box with mitred corners, rather than one with butt joins. Chamfering on the front may have been done to give more depth to the silver panel images, making them appear as if they are set back in a niche. Additionally, the British Museum reliquary includes vernis brun (gilded copper with a brown varnish) plaques;[5] the Walters Art Museum reliquary does not. The design relationships between these two reliquaries are based on an interesting symmetry of opposites that suggests that the designs were created with an awareness of each other. For example, on the Walters Art Museum reliquary, the single enamelled plaque above the trefoil arch is decorated with a central hemispherical crystal flanked by two ridged hemiellipsoid crystals, but the same design element on the British Museum reliquary is decorated with vernis brun instead of enamel, and a central ridged

Plate 1 The Walters Art Museum gabled reliquary panel of St Oda (57.519), late 11th/12th and 13th century, Mosan (Belgium), 58.5 x 38 x 5.6cm. From the bottom left, progressing clockwise, the eight compartments are identified by a single hand, written in red ink on vellum as containing relics of St Bernard of Clairvaux, St Benedict, St Augustine, St Gregory, St Silvester, St Mengoldus, the Holy Innocents and St Denis (Stratford 1993)

Plate 2 The British Museum gabled reliquary panel of St Oda (1978,0502.7), 12th and 13th century, 58.3 x 38 x 6.5cm. From the bottom left, progressing clockwise, the first five compartments are identified by writing in the same hand as containing relics from one of the 11,000 Virgins [of Köln], with the remaining relics from St Elizabeth of Thuringia, the milk of the Blessed Virgin Mary and St Agnes (Stratford 1993)

hemiellipsoid crystal is flanked by two hemispherical crystals. The symmetry of opposites is discussed extensively elsewhere.[6] On the backs of both oak panels (**Pls 3–4**) are holes and broken wooden dowels. The similar construction method and placement of holes and dowels is consistent with the panels being part of one larger wooden structure. There are also fixings for the suspension of the British Museum panel as a stand-alone reliquary and a scar and two holes for nails from a similar fixing on the Walters Art Museum panel.

According to Stratford, the Walters Art Museum central silver plaque pre-dates the rest of the work and was probably created in the 11th or early 12th century.[7] Stratford considers that its reuse was probably contemporary with the creation of the two gable-shaped reliquary panels under discussion. The central silver plaque on the British Museum gabled panel depicts St Oda herself, adding weight to its attribution to the 12th-century gabled reliquary chasse for St Oda of Amay. In the 13th century, this chasse was disassembled and the two decorated gabled pieces are said to have had the relics inserted to become individual reliquaries when a new shrine for St Oda of Amay was created.[8] The suggestion on stylistic grounds of reuse of the Walters Art Museum silver relief plaque from another construction is supported by the fact that the edges of the plaque do not fit the trefoil arch (**Pl. 5**), while the British Museum plaque fits neatly within its arch. The current shrine of St Oda, still at Amay, is dated to

around 1240–50, giving an approximate date as to when the earlier shrine was disassembled and these two gabled pieces became individual reliquaries.

However, an alternative possibility was considered for this study. With historicism increasingly fashionable during the 19th century, medieval objects were particularly popular with collectors at that time. Objects were made to satisfy these demands, either by creating whole new objects in the medieval style or by creating new objects with medieval parts. These scenarios were considered when the St Oda reliquary panels were examined as the oldest known documentation for both objects dates only to 1862.

The reuniting of the two reliquaries for the *Treasures of Heaven* exhibition provided the opportunity to compare and contrast their materials scientifically. Specifically, an approach was applied that employed exclusively non-destructive analytical techniques to elucidate their materials and the structural or design changes that occurred throughout their histories. These analyses included X-ray fluorescence (XRF), X-radiography and stereomicroscopy on both, Raman spectroscopy on the British Museum reliquary and computed tomography (CT) on the Walters Art Museum reliquary. Material analysis had never before been applied to the Walters Art Museum reliquary, but some material analysis had been conducted previously on the British Museum reliquary as part of a study on Mosan and related medieval artefacts in the British Museum.[9]

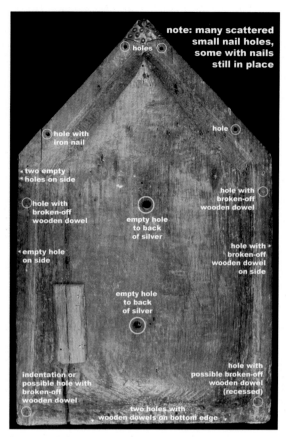

note: many scattered small nail holes, some with nails still in place

holes

hole with iron nail

hole

two empty holes on side

hole with broken-off wooden dowel

hole with broken-off wooden dowel

empty hole to back of silver

empty hole on side

hole with broken-off wooden dowel on side

empty hole to back of silver

indentation or possible hole with broken-off wooden dowel

hole with possible broken-off wooden dowel (recessed)

two holes with wooden dowels on bottom edge

Plate 3 The back of the Walters Art Museum reliquary panel of St Oda, with annotations in white summarizing observations

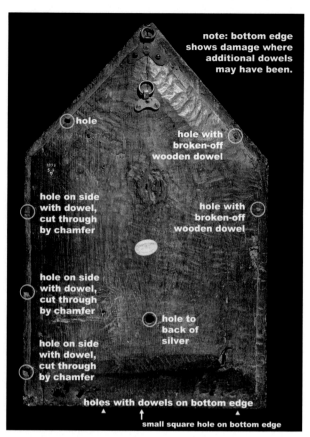

note: bottom edge shows damage where additional dowels may have been.

hole

hole with broken-off wooden dowel

hole on side with dowel, cut through by chamfer

hole with broken-off wooden dowel

hole on side with dowel, cut through by chamfer

hole to back of silver

hole on side with dowel, cut through by chamfer

holes with dowels on bottom edge

small square hole on bottom edge

Plate 4 The back of the British Museum reliquary panel of St Oda, with annotations in white summarizing observations

The primary reason for this examination was to test scientifically the attribution of these two reliquaries as medieval and from the same 12th-century shrine of St Oda. This study aimed to analyse the construction and materials of the Walters Art Museum and British Museum reliquaries, producing qualitative data distinguishing technology and compositions of medieval production from elements produced at a later date and to determine similarities and differences between the materials used in assembling the two reliquaries.

Medieval shrines

Finding elements from different periods on a predominantly medieval object is not unusual; the changing and recycling of parts on shrines was common practice in medieval times and later. For example, at least 33 changes were documented for the shrines of St Domitianus and St Mengoldus, which are

Plate 5 In this detail of the Walters Art Museum reliquary, it is clear that the straight, angled edges of the central silver panel do not fit the trefoil arches of the frame; Christ's nimbus and cross have also been cut down

still in use at the Collegiate Church of Notre Dame in Huy, Belgium, and are from the same time period and geographical region as the St Oda reliquaries. The reasons for these changes or repairs include: general maintenance and cleaning, processions, fire, theft, translation of relics, relocation, iconoclasm, donations for embellishment, exchanging of parts on the same shrine or with other shrines, upgrading (with the old copper and gold sold to goldsmiths for recycling, perhaps for use on other objects) and changes to church architecture requiring alterations in the dimensions of the shrines.[10] Since the Walters Art Museum and British

Plate 6 The shrine of St Amandus, Walters Art Museum (53.9), is pictured on the right inside a computed tomographic (CT) scanner. On the left is the computed tomography (CT) image of the reliquary, with tree rings clearly resolved for dendrochronology

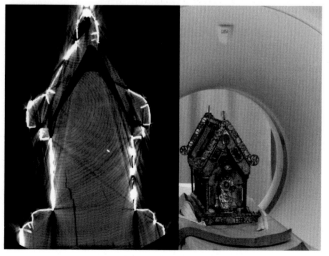

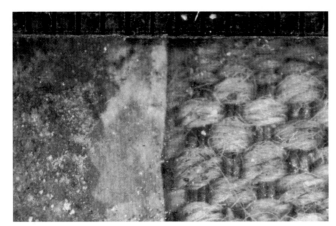

Plate 7 Photomicrograph of textile with metal-wrapped threads in the relic cavity for St Benedict on the Walters Art Museum panel with a 1mm increment ruler at the top of image

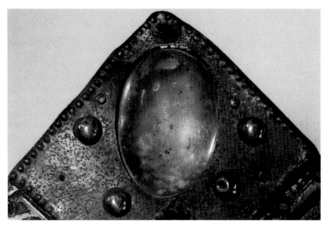

Plate 8 Photomicrograph of the apex of the British Museum reliquary, showing red material behind rock-crystal gem

Museum reliquaries have presumed histories as cultural objects, it would not be surprising for them both to show medieval parts and alterations from later periods.

Confirming that these objects are truly medieval can therefore be problematic. Decorative parts may be medieval or later, but a critical question is whether or not the core or the support for the decorative parts and relics is medieval. For example, in a previous study of the Walter Art Museum's shrine of St Amandus, XRF analysis distinguished probable medieval parts from modern parts that included post 18th-century, high zinc brass columns and post 19th-century enamel plaques containing uranium (**Pl. 6**).[11] The question about the date of the original object was answered when a computed tomography (CT) scan of the entire shrine revealed tree rings in the wooden core that subsequent dendrochronology confirmed as indeed medieval.[12] Based on this success, CT scanning was conducted on the Walters Art Museum's St Oda reliquary panel.

Analytical methods

The analytical tools used for this investigation were all non-destructive and no sampling of materials was conducted. Stereomicroscopy was used to examine both reliquaries in detail. X-radiography was used to examine the construction of the reliquaries, as was computed tomography or CT scanning. Raman spectroscopy was used to examine the gems on the British Museum reliquary. Air-path X-ray fluorescence (XRF) was used to analyse the metals and the enamels on both reliquaries. All experimental conditions are described at the end of this article.

Results and discussion

Stereomicroscopy

The features of the Walters Art Museum and British Museum panels were described in detail by Stratford.[13] A primary focus of visual examination for this current study was to determine the contents of the reliquary cavities behind the horn windows and to determine if any materials were placed beneath the rock-crystal settings. Unlike the Walters Art Museum panel, the British Museum shrine has not been disassembled to examine or restore it. On the panels, it is possible to see only diffuse images through the

translucent horn windows covering the reliquary compartments. All relic cavities in the panels contain tituli or script written with red ink on parchment dated independently to the 13th century, as discussed elsewhere;[14] these describe the contents of the cavities and the respective saints. Specifically, Stratford reports for the British Museum reliquary: 'The relics beneath the horn mounts are identified on vellum by tituli written in red ink by a single hand of the thirteenth century. The tituli read: (clockwise, from bottom left, only the English translation is reported here) (1)-(2)-(3) of the skull of one of the thousand Virgins [of Koln]; as (1)-(3); (5) of one of the eleven thousand Virgins; (6) of St Elizabeth widow, that is St Elizabeth of Thuringia; (7) of the milk of the Blessed Virgin Mary; (8) St Agnes, virgin.' For the Walters reliquary, Stratford reports: 'The tituli read: (clockwise, from bottom left) (1) of the winding-sheet of St Bernard of Clairvaux; (2) a bone of St Benedict; (3) of St Augustine; (4) of the throne of St Gregory; (5) of the head of St Silvester; (6) of St Mengoldus of Huy; (7) of the Holy Innocents; (8) of the staff of St Denis.'

On the Walters Art Museum panel, the cavities for St Benedict, St Silvester and a relic of the Holy Innocents contain a pale beige textile, coarsely woven, with silver coloured metal-wrapped threads in one direction and undecorated yarn perpendicular to the silver coloured threads (**Pl. 7**). The undecorated yarns appear to be two-ply with a Z twist, but the metal wrap appears to be an S twist. The observed structure of the textile is plain weave 2/2. An additional fabric without metal-wrapped threads was present in the cavity for St Augustine. Although the Walters Art Museum textile appears to be coloured beige, it is difficult to know its original colour given the yellowed perspective of viewing through the horn. Possibly, the fabric was once more brightly coloured, but has faded over time. While fabric was sometimes used as a relic in the medieval period, there is no evidence to support or deny that the fabric on the Walters Art Museum panel was intended as a relic. The cavities for St Denis and St Augustine contain a dark brown resinous material with tiny flakes of gold, possibly intermixed. No textile fragments were observed in the relic cavities in the British Museum panel. No bone or other relics are visible in the compartments of the Walters Art Museum reliquary; parts of the British Museum relics

Plate 9 X-radiograph of the Walters Art Museum reliquary

Plate 10 X-radiograph of the British Museum reliquary

are faintly visible through the horn windows and X-radiography had to be used to identify them (see below).

The rock-crystal gems in both panels may have been set in the frame for purely decorative purposes, but during this period such crystals were sometimes used as covers for relics. Examination through the rock-crystal gems was difficult due to distortions from refraction, inclusions and faults in the mineral. Therefore, no definitive conclusions could be drawn; however, some new observations were made. The 'gem' at the bottom of the Walters Art Museum panel is thin and flat, not cabochon shaped like the others, and contains many random bubbles, suggesting the material is glass; it is likely a replacement and covers what appears to be a well-preserved, possibly modern, vivid blue textile. Progressing in a clockwise direction, the lower gemstone on the left side of the frame covers parchment with a red inscription. Visible through the other two on the left side are a coarse weave fabric with traces of red, likely indicating the original colour. It was very difficult to see anything through the rock crystal at the apex of the Walters Art Museum panel, except a pink hue around the edges, perhaps indicating a faded red colourant behind the crystal. It cannot be determined whether the colourant is in contact with the back of the crystal. Only parchment was seen through the next and the last gems on the right. Through the crystal between these two, a flat metallic looking material was observed in the upper half. It may be a relic, but it could also

be a piece of metal foil, at least partly copper based since there appears to be green corrosion on it. Several of the British Museum stones appear to have metal foils behind them, in particular the crystal at the apex, which seems to have a foil with a red coating behind the lower part of the stone (**Pl. 8**), but no evidence of relics of any sort.

The rock crystals in the trefoil arch of the Walters Art Museum panel were also examined. Through the large central crystal it was possible to see parchment with dark blue-black lines more prominent to the left of centre, as well as a small splinter of wood in the 8 o'clock position. Under the smaller crystals flanking the central one is parchment. The one to the left was reddish, while that to the right was white. No such details were observed on the British Museum trefoil-headed arch.

X-radiography

The X-radiograph of both panels provided technical evidence substantiating many of the visual observations reported elsewhere.[15] The central silver plaques on both were made from hammered sheet, confirmed by the presence of rounded, darker areas in the X-radiograph that correspond to thinner metal from individual hammer blows during forming. The relief image was raised with the repoussé technique from the reverse; the details were then chased from the front surface. On the Walters Art Museum reliquary, damages to the silver sheet were visible as bright

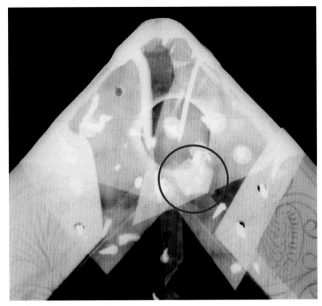

Plate 11 The more dense pentagonal shape just below and to the right of the rock crystal at the top of the frame of the Walters Art Museum panel

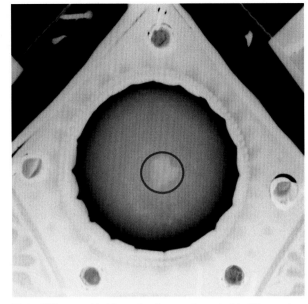

Plate 12 The roughly triangular denser shape behind the centre of the rock crystal directly over Christ's head on the Walters Art Museum panel

white areas on the X-radiograph (**Pl. 9**), a result of denser lead containing solder repairs. The metal strips behind the silver relief that were used to fill out to the edges of the frame were clearly visible at the upper angled edges, but may not be in their intended positions. Many nails were revealed by X- radiography in the wood of both panels, some rounded modern and some handmade rectilinear nails. The suspension loops on the back of the British Museum panel are prominent in the radiographic image (**Pl. 10**).

Some of the sheet metal framing elements on the Walters Art Museum reliquary exhibited different grey values in the X-radiographs, indicating varying densities or thicknesses of the pieces of metal, and suggesting they did not all come from one source. Possibly some parts were made for this frame, but others were likely to have been reused from other objects, as noted by Stratford.[16] There are differences in the layout and style of the vine interlace and animal pattern engravings on the outermost strips, especially in the use of

dots for shading on animals, the size of the arches of the vine loops and the amount of background space left undecorated. The least dense strips appear to have similar engraving styles and are therefore likely to be associated, but there are a variety of engraving patterns in the denser strips, making it difficult to associate them with each other.

The gem mounts and silver 'balls' representing pearls are hollow hemispheres made with a doming block (by forcing silver sheet from the reverse into a hollow form). They were cut out of a larger sheet, trimmed and pushed through holes in the metal frame element from behind; in the radiographic images of both panels their untidily cut edges are visible behind the frames.

In the British Museum X-radiograph presented in **Plate 10**, the outlines of the central figures appear stark white since they were executed in very high relief repoussé. The central panel was made from a single silver sheet, with the head of St Oda almost, but not quite, freestanding. St Oda's

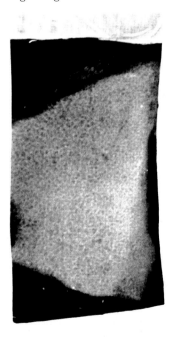

Plate 13 X-radiograph of the British Museum reliquary showing the centre left relic compartment with vellum inscription 'de capite/xi:m:vgi' ('of the skull of one of the eleven thousand Virgins [of Köln]') which does appear to contain bone

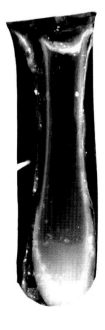

Plate 14 X-radiograph of the British Museum reliquary showing the bottom right relic compartment with vellum inscription 'de lacte bte marie vgis' ('of the milk of the Blessed Virgin Mary'). The contents of the vial appear white in the image suggesting a dense material like lead white pigment

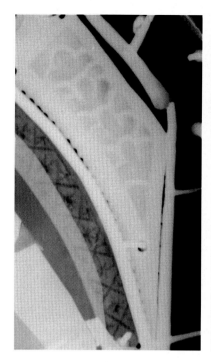
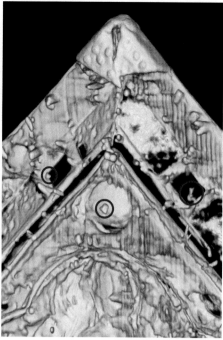

Plate 15 (left) A detail of the lower right-hand region of the enamelled plaque above the trefoil arch on the Walters Art Museum panel, showing traditional medieval preparation for enamelwork

Plate 16 (right) A detail of the apex of the Walters Art Museum panel CT image, from the perspective of looking through the back of the reliquary panel. From left to right, the red circles indicate radio-opaque material inside the relic cavity for St Silvester (head fragment), radio-opaque material underneath the rock crystal above Christ's head (noted in Pl. 12) and radio-opaque material inside the relic cavity for St Gregory (throne fragment)

halo was added and it slips in around the back of the head creating the inverted V-shape in the X-radiograph. The British Museum piece has a number of vernis brun pieces that are attached by wire ties. The vernis brun was applied as a decorative border to the hem and belt of St Oda and to the halos of all three figures. No pieces attached with wire ties were observed on the silver panel of the Walters Art Museum reliquary.

There are some unexplained shapes of different densities in the X-radiographs. For example, there was a more dense pentagonal shape just below and to the right of the rock crystal at the top of the frame of the Walters Art Museum panel (**Pl. 11**). Possibly, this was metal foil that was originally behind the rock crystal to create a brighter reflection. There was also a roughly triangular denser shape in the centre of the rock crystal directly over Christ's head (**Pl. 12**). Since there appeared to be a raised area in the parchment beneath the rock crystal, perhaps a relic is hidden below. These observations require further study.

It is significant that the X-radiographic study revealed items which appear to be bone in the cavities of the British Museum panel (**Pl. 13**) and a vial containing a dense material in the compartment bearing the text 'de lacte bte marie vgis' (of the milk of the Blessed Virgin Mary) (**Pl. 14**). It seems likely from this description that the vial would have contained a white liquid. It is suggested that this may prove to be a liquid coloured by lead white pigment, which would appear dense in a radiographic image, unlike real milk. No relics are discernable in the X-radiograph of the Walters Art Museum panel.

Finally, there was evidence that the copper plaques for the champlevé enamelwork were prepared in the traditional medieval technique. Deep troughs were created around the periphery of the cells to be filled with enamel. These appear in the X-radiograph as dark outlines at the edges of the cells since the metal was made thinner there (**Pl. 15**). The interior surface of the cell was then cut away, but less deeply, so these areas appear paler than the gouged edges.

Computed tomography

Computed tomography (CT) was attempted on the Walters Art Museum panel in order to image the tree rings for dendrochronology, as was successfully achieved previously on the St Amandus reliquary, and to image the interior of the relic compartments. Unfortunately, it was not possible to obtain acceptable images of tree rings on the Walters Art Museum reliquary because the metal caused flaring or distortions of the CT images. The CT images of the Walters Art Museum reliquary confirmed some of the observations that resulted from examining the X-radiograph, as noted in **Plate 16**, and revealed radio-opaque material in the relic cavities for St Silvester, St Gregory and St Denis which were not observed in the X-radiograph.

X-ray fluorescence elemental analysis (XRF)

Analysis of the red ink used for the tituli with 13th-century style script was performed through the horn windows. It revealed the presence of mercury on both the British Museum and Walters Art Museum reliquaries, suggesting the use of a mercuric sulphide or cinnabar/vermilion coloured ink. In addition, a black ink on a fibrous or perhaps a woven material was observed in the relic compartment of St Mengoldus of Huy on the Walters Art Museum panel. XRF analysis of that ink revealed a high iron content, suggesting the use of iron gall ink, the most widely used ink in the medieval period. These results were entirely consistent with materials used in the medieval period or later.

The metal wrapping around the threads present in the Walters Art Museum panel was confirmed as silver using XRF analysis through the horn windows. XRF analysis of the central silver plaque on the Walters Art Museum and the British Museum reliquary indicated primarily silver with the small quantities of copper and lead that would be expected for medieval production prior to electrolytic refining.[17] Gold and mercury were also detected within gilt areas on the silver panels, indicating amalgam gilding.

Plate 17 The Walters Art Museum reliquary with colour coding for different copper alloy compositions: blue shading indicates copper, green shading indicates brass and yellow and pink shading indicate industrial age brass (schematic diagrams created by Tony Venne)

Plate 18 The British Museum reliquary with colour coding for different copper alloy compositions: blue shading indicates copper, green and orange shading indicate brass and pink shading indicates industrial age brass. The metal of the enamelled plaques was not accessible for analysis, but it would be expected to be copper (Oddy et al. 1986) (schematic diagrams created by Tony Venne)

The analyses of the copper-based metal components in the two reliquaries were distinguished by five different qualitative compositions, as indicated by the colours of shading in **Plates 17–18**. The most prevalent metal composition, indicated in blue shading, was copper containing minor impurities of lead and antimony; mercury and gold, indicating amalgam gilding, were also detected on both panels on the copper components marked in blue. Mercury gilding and copper sheet with impurities of lead are consistent with medieval technology.[18] The blue shading indicates where analyses were performed.

XRF analyses of all the relic window frames and the gem-set panel at the top of the Walters Art Museum gable indicated brass had been used for these components: copper and zinc with a minor response for lead, tin, iron and a trace of silver; most analyses also contained a trace of nickel. This brass composition (indicated with green shading) is consistent with pre-19th-century technology. No mercury or gold was detected, suggesting these elements were never gilded, contrary to a previous report;[19] the golden colour is provided by the brass alloy. On the British Museum reliquary, a similar brass alloy was used for the bottom left gem mount, perhaps containing slightly less zinc, and this is indicated with orange shading. The relic window frames on the British Museum gable are also ungilded brass with a similar range of zinc content, but with

a significant arsenic content and with tin detectable in most of the frames, so these are shaded in darker green in **Plate 18**. This might suggest that the relic frames on the two gables were not contemporary, or at least not made in the same workshop.

The XRF data for several of the metal elements on the panels suggest that they are post-medieval additions. Those that are shaded in pink indicate that high zinc leaded brass was used with minor amounts of tin; sometimes arsenic was detected. The zinc content of these areas was very high, suggesting a post mid-18th century production date. The yellow shading indicates a brass alloy that is gilded, but no mercury was detected. This suggests an electroplated metal that was a product of 19th-century technology.

Stratford noted that the enamels have identical colour palettes on both panels. The red, white, blue, light blue, yellow and green opaque enamels on both the Walters Art Musuem and the British Museum reliquaries were analysed using XRF with a helium purge, as mentioned above. This technique has limitations in the analysis of enamels because it cannot detect sodium or the small concentrations of magnesium, aluminium, phosphorous, sulphur and chlorine expected in these enamels. However, potassium and heavier elements in the enamels on the two reliquaries were looked for. Significantly, tin was not detected in the enamels analysed, suggesting the enamel was applied before the 13th century when the expected opacifier would generally be tin oxide in western European enamelwork.[20]

The elemental compositions of the red enamels on both the Walters Art Museum and British Museum reliquaries were certainly distinct when compared to all the other coloured enamels. The red enamels all had a high potassium content, which was about 15 times the potassium content of all the other coloured enamels. Also detected in the red enamel was significant calcium, with small amounts of copper, iron, lead, manganese and a trace of antimony; the copper is the probable colourant. This is consistent with previously reported analysis of Romanesque Mosan enamelwork.[21]

In the other colours, significant antimony was detected. This suggests the enamel opacifier is calcium antimonate for enamel that is not coloured red. No evidence of the use of a tin oxide opacifier was detected. Cobalt was detected in the deep blue coloured enamel, whereas copper appeared to be the colourant for the light blue and green enamel. Lead was detected in all the enamels, but more lead was detected in those coloured yellow and green, probably attributable to a lead antimonate yellow colourant. All of these characteristics are consistent with previously reported analysis of Romanesque Mosan enamelwork.[22]

Conclusion

Scientific analyses of the two reliquaries revealed marked similarities in dimensions, construction and elemental compositions of the enamels and alloys, confirming close links between the two objects. With certainty, these two reliquaries must have been created with knowledge of each other, given the complementary design, arranged as a symmetry of opposites. Elemental analysis has confirmed the composition of the enamels on both as being typical of Mosan enamelwork. The materials of most of the other components of both reliquaries are consistent with a medieval date, with some changes made over time, as is typical of medieval objects. There are only a few components which are attributable to the 19th century and unsurprisingly the more modern metal components identified by analysis are mainly at the corners, which are particularly vulnerable to damage, and consistent with what might be expected if these panels had been in use for centuries. This scientific study has not been able to directly associate the panels with the original 12th-century shrine of St Oda at Amay, but has found no evidence that they could not have been part of that shrine. Certainly the scientific evidence could support Stratford's conclusion that the vernis brun, the stamped gilt-copper border palmettes that were analysed and the enamelled and gem-set border plaques of both reliquaries were made in a Mosan workshop in the later 12th century. The current limits of non-destructive examination of these panels can take this no further, but any future study of these gable ends might benefit from direct dendrochronological matching of the panels of oak wood.

Instrumentation and conditions

Air-path, energy dispersive X-ray fluorescence (XRF) analysis was conducted at the Walters Art Museum using a Bruker ARTAX 800 instrument. For metal analysis on the Walters Art Museum reliquary, a rhodium X-ray tube was used, collimated to 1.5mm diameter, and powered at 50kV and 200μA for 120 seconds. At the British Museum the XRF of the metal components of the reliquary was undertaken using an air-path Bruker ARTAX instrument fitted with a molybdenum X-ray tube producing a beam collimated to 0.65mm in diameter, and operated at 50kV and 500μA for 100 seconds. It was not possible to remove any potentially unrepresentative surface material prior to carrying out the analyses, thus only qualitative results could be obtained.

For enamel analysis of the Walters Art Museum and British Museum reliquaries, a rhodium X-ray tube was used at the Walters Art Museum, equipped with a polycapillary lens to produce an 80mm diameter spot size, and powered at 50kV and 600μA for 120 seconds. The 80mm diameter spot size was necessary to analyse the small areas of enamel *in situ*. No filters were used during the XRF analysis; however, a helium purge was used to optimize detection of light elements. The qualitative data was compared to a glass standard of known composition, known as 'Brill B' or Corning USNM#117218.001, which is a soda lime glass approximating the elemental composition of medieval glass.[23]

Digital X-radiography was conducted at the Walters Art Museum using a Polaris (Kimtron Inc.) control system and a Varian X-ray tube powered to 80kV and 2.2mA for 60 seconds. Images were captured using GE Imaging Technologies equipment, including a phosphor imaging plate, a Pegasus Scanner CR50P, Rhythm Acquire software ver 4.0 and Rhythm 2.2 Review software. The radiography of the British Museum reliquary was undertaken using a Siefert DS1 X-ray tube. Exposure conditions were 75kV and 10mA for 4 minutes. Images were collected on Agfa Sructurix film, then scanned using an Agfa RadView digitiser with a 50 micron pixel size and 12 bit resolution.

Stereomicroscopy was conducted at the Walters Art Museum using a Wild M3Z stereomicroscope at 40x to 250x magnification, and at the British Museum using a Leica MZ-Apo stereomicroscope.

At the British Museum, the rock-crystal gems were identified by Raman spectroscopy using a Dilor Infinity Raman spectroscope with a green (532nm) laser at a maximum power of 4mW at the surface with a spot size of a few microns. Analyses were carried out *in situ* on the unprepared surfaces of the gems. Spectra were collected for total times of between 2 and 10 minutes (including multiple repeats to avoid the effect of cosmic rays). Spectra produced were identified by comparison with reference spectra for quartz.

Computed tomography (CT) was conducted on the Walters Art Museum reliquary panel by Barry Daly at the University of Maryland Medical Center, with assistance from Alec Brown and hospital staff. CT exposure conditions were 140kV and 335mA every 0.65mm using a helical scan mode.

Acknowledgements

The authors would like to thank: Martina Bagnoli, Walters Art Museum curator, for her support throughout this investigation; Barbara Fegley, Walters Art Museum

Registrar, for arranging time for analysis at the Walters Art Museum of the British Museum reliquary during a hectic installation schedule; James Robinson, former British Museum curator, for his unfailing support of the scientific study; Janet Ambers, British Museum scientist, for conducting the Raman spectroscopic analysis; Caroline Cartwright, British Museum organic materials scientist, for the wood and horn identification; Meredith Davey for assistance with the figures; and finally, Barry Daly and Alec Brown for their help with the CT imaging.

Notes

1 Bagnoli *et al.* 2010, 176–7.
2 Verdier 1981.
3 Stratford 1993.
4 Identification of the wood as oak and the relic compartment windows as horn was provided by Caroline Cartwright (British Museum) using optical microscopy; identification of the stones as rock crystal was provided by Janet Ambers (British Museum) using Raman spectroscopy.
5 Lemeunier 2006.
6 Stratford 1993; Verdier 1981.
7 Stratford 1993, 93.
8 Ibid.
9 By Susan La Niece, British Museum analysis reference number PR04164.
10 Lemeunier 2005.
11 Walters Art Museum conservation staff participating in the research include Jennifer Giaccai, Terry Drayman-Weisser, Julie Lauffenburger, Meg Craft, Angela Elliott and Colleen Snyder.
12 See http://thewalters.org/pachydermpubs/medieval-reliquary/; see also 'X-ray fluorescence of a medieval Mosan reliquary of Saint Amandus', 57th Annual Denver X-ray Conference, Denver CO, USA, 4–8 August 2008.
13 Stratford 1993.
14 Ibid.
15 Ibid.
16 Ibid.
17 Mass and Matsen 2012.
18 Oddy 2000.
19 Stratford 1993.
20 Biron, Dandridge and Wypyski 1996.
21 Freestone 1993.
22 Ibid.
23 Vicenzi *et al.* 2002.

Bibliography

Bagnoli, M., Klein, H.A., Mann, C.G. and Robinson, J. (eds) 2010. *Treasures of Heaven: Saints, Relics and Devotion in Medieval Europe*, Baltimore and London.

Biron, I., Dandridge, P. and Wypyski, M. 1996. 'Techniques and materials in Limoges enamels', in *Enamels of Limoges 1100–1350*, ed. J.P. O'Neil, New York, 48–62.

Freestone, I. 1993. 'Compositions and origins of glasses from Romanesque champlevé enamels', in Stratford 1993, 37–45.

Lemeunier, A. 2005. 'The eventful lives of two Mosan chasses', in *Art and Architecture of Late Medieval Pilgrimage in Northern Europe and the British Isles*, ed. S. Blick and R. Tekippe, Leiden, 99–119.

Lemeunier, A. 2006. 'Le vernis brun dans la decoration des chasses rhéno-mosanes (XIe–XIIIe siècle)', in *Medieval Reliquary Shrines and Precious Metalwork*, ed. K. Anheuser and C. Werner, London, 47–53.

Mass, J. and Matsen, C. 2012. 'Quantitative non-destructive analysis of historic silver alloys', in *Studies in Archaeological Sciences: Handheld XRF for Art and Archaeology*, ed. A. Shugar and J. Mass, Leuven, 215–47.

Oddy, W.A. 2000. 'A history of gilding with particular reference to statuary', in *Gilded Metals: History Technology and Conservation*, ed. T. Drayman-Weisser, London, 1–19.

Oddy, W.A., La Niece, S. and Stratford, N. 1986. *Romanesque Metalwork: Copper Alloys and their Decoration*, London.

Stratford, N. 1993. *Catalogue of Medieval Enamels in the British Museum, Volume II: Northern Romanesque Enamel*, London, 90–7.

Verdier, P.V. 1981. 'The twelfth-century chasse of St Ode of Amay', *Wallraf-Richartz-Jahrbuch* 152, Cologne, 7–94.

Vicenzi, E., Eggins, S., Logan, A. and Wysoczanski, R. 2002. 'Microbeam characterization of Corning archaeological reference glasses: new additions to the Smithsonian Microbeam Standard Collection', *Journal of Research of the National Institute of Standards and Technology* 107, 719–27.

Chapter 16
The Construction and Conservation History of the Hildesheim Portable Altar

Maickel van Bellegem and
Lloyd de Beer

Introduction

The Hildesheim portable altar (**Pl. 1**) was acquired by the British Museum in 1902. It has been on permanent display in the medieval galleries since acquisition and it was included more recently in the international touring exhibition *Treasures of Heaven*.[1] Portable altars, such as this example from Hildesheim, Germany, were devices which could connect those living on earth with the eternal power of the saints through the relics they held within them; the altar in question contains the relics of 40 such individuals and their names are listed on the reverse. Utilized in holy ceremony, altars such as this were constructed from materials of great monetary value and perhaps more importantly were directly connected to liturgical ritual, with transubstantiation becoming part of Church doctrine after the Fourth Lateran Council of 1215. Materials employed in their construction often included ivory and precious metals, rare gems, manuscript illuminations and exotic stones. However, the most precious part of the object – the fragments of the saintly bodies – was, in the case of the portable altar, almost always hidden from view.

An enamelled plaque (**Pl. 2**) at the British Museum depicts Bishop Henry of Blois holding a crozier and a large rectangular object, which has been arguably identified as a portable altar.[2] This plaque serves as an introduction to the following investigation into the history, the mechanics of construction and the conservation of the Hildesheim portable altar. The body of Bishop Henry is rendered kneeling, contained within a semicircle and surrounded by a legend which gives evidence for his proposed intellect, virtue and piety. Henry's head is placed directly against the central stone of the altar he cradles. At the bottom right of this plaque, the words 'HENRICUS EPISCOP' are engraved. These words which announce Henry's role as bishop are separated by the objects which he carries – altar and crozier – both of which are religiously symbolic and political investitures of his episcopal role. Henry's mind, body and role as bishop are all irrevocably tied to the objects he holds. Further text on the plaque announces Henry's role as patron of the object: '+ ARS AVRO GEMMISQ(UE) PRIOR, PRIOR OMNIBVS AVTOR. DONA DAT HENRICVS VIVVS IN ERE DEO'.[3] This inscription suggests that his choice of including a portable altar in a representation of himself was key to his image, his patronage and the agency of his authority.

The Henry of Blois plaque helps us to understand the way in which portable altars were viewed in the late 12th century. This link between object, patronage and ecclesiastical hierarchy is reiterated in the Hildesheim altar through the inscription 'ThIDERICVS:ABBAS:III:DEDIT', which is engraved under the feet of the Virgin and places the name of the donor – in this case Theodoric, Abbot of St Godehard – in the mind of those who will use the altar both during his life and after his death. Both Henry and Theodoric are depicted in the position of a pious servant. In Henry's case, he kneels, offering crozier and altar up to God, while Theodoric is literally positioned at the foot of the Virgin and infant Christ. These acts of declaration connect patronage to the power of the altar and link the donors' memory to the reliquary itself. Theodoric's text is part of the complex matrix of material, iconography and physical space which defines the altar and its use.

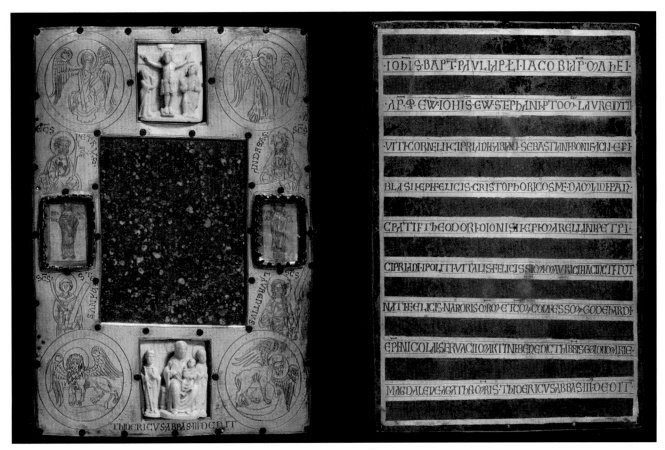

Plate 1 Front and reverse of the Hildesheim portable altar, 1190–1200, copper gilt over a wood core, limestone, painted vellum, rock crystal and ivory, 35.4 x 25.1cm. British Museum, London (1902,0625.1)

A combination of materials has been used in the construction of the altar. Principally it has a wooden core covered with copper gilt sheets which have been fastened using either silver or copper alloy nails. Set into the front there is a central red stone with a piece of painted vellum mounted behind crystal on either side. The painting on the left shows St Bernard of Hildesheim and on the right St Godehard, to whom the abbey of Godehardiklosters at Hildesheim was dedicated. Above and below the central stone there are ivory carvings; the upper depicts the Crucifixion, the lower shows the Virgin and Child. The front copper gilt sheet is, at each corner, engraved with symbols of the four evangelists and figures of St Peter, St Andrew, St Laurence and St Stephen in between. On the reverse there are alternating bands of vernis brun and gilding engraved with the names of 40 saints to whom the altar is dedicated (**Table 1**). Beneath the central red stone 34 relic bundles have been found, each consisting of various relic materials such as bone fragments, stones, wood shavings and hair wrapped in pieces of textile and tied with threads with tituli attached. These are vellum labels inscribed with the name of the saint or saints to aid identification of the relics and are associated with the saints whose names are listed on the back.

Although the shrine was previously opened in 1980, and again in 2008 for conservation, it was the reactions that followed the opening of the new medieval gallery at the British Museum in March 2009 that renewed interest in the relics themselves. This subsequently led to the altar being opened once more in 2010 in preparation of the *Treasures of*

Heaven exhibition, for which a selection of relics was displayed at the various venues of the exhibition. This article includes previously unpublished information from reports kept in the archival records of the British Museum.[4] Those reports are the work of others than the authors of this article, and although due reference is given throughout the text to the specific reports, we would like to acknowledge their names here: R. White (National Gallery, London), P. Palmer (Natural History Museum, London), M. Brandt (Hildesheim Diozesan Museum, Hildesheim), D. Klemm and W. Grimm (Institut fur Allgemeine und Angewandte Geologie, Munchen), F. Muller (Deutsches Naturstein-Archiv, Wunsiedel) and M. Hockey, M. Hughes, S. La Niece, M. McCord, I. McIntyre, A. Middleton, A. Oddy and N.

Plate 2 Detail of enamelled plaque depicting Bishop Henry of Blois holding a crozier and a large rectangular object, 1150–71, gold, enamel and copper alloy, w. 182mm. British Museum, London (1852,0327.1)

Plate 3 Illustration dating to 1858 showing the front of the
Hildesheim portable altar by G. Jeune in Viollet-le-duc 1858

Stratford (British Museum). This paper will present
documentary evidence for the collecting history of the altar
followed by an overview and discussion of conservation
interventions, the different materials and methods of
construction of the altar, supported by scientific analysis
dating to the 1980s and 2008/2010, with final conclusions
presented at the end of the chapter.

The collecting history of the altar
The Hildesheim portable altar was acquired by the British
Museum in 1902 through a sale at Christies of the
Carmichael collection.[5] In the catalogue the altar is
described in 32 lines, including the list of saints names
engraved on the back, and is illustrated with a photograph.
Notably it mentions: 'these enclose panels of rock-crystal,
behind which are miniature paintings of Saints upon a gold
ground; no doubt these miniatures, which are of late 13th
Century date, replace the relics that must have formerly
been behind the crystal faces'. Further it describes:

> From the Collection of M. Renesse-Breidbach, in the
> Catalogue of whose Collection it states that this altar came
> from the ancient abbey of Sayna, near Coblentz; but, however,
> from researches made more recently, it was probably a gift
> made in the middle of the 13th Century to the abbey Scheida.
> From the Debruge Dumenil Collection.

Prior to its sale in 1902 its provenance can be traced
through the collections of Sellières, Prince Soltykoff,
Debruge Dumenil and Count De Renesse-Breidbach.[6] It was
sold respectively in 1890, 1861, 1847 and 1835. The catalogue
for the Soltykoff sale in 1861 mentions: 'l'interieur, divise en

compartiments, contient de nombreuses reliques' ('The
inside, divided into compartiments, contains many relics').
Similarly the relics are mentioned in the *Dictionnaire Raisonne
Mobilier Francais de l'Epoque Carlovingienne a la Renaissance* by M.
Viollet-le-Duc in 1858. It specifically mentions: 'Sous la table
de marbre sont renfermees un grand nombre de reliques dans
un morceau de toile de coton' ('Under the marble slab are
contained many relics in a piece of cotton cloth'). The overall
description spans over four pages including two illustrations,
of which one is reproduced in **Plate 3**. Some minor
differences between the illustration (**Pl. 3**) and the altar
(**Pl. 1**) can be noted, such as the bald head/hair of Sts Peter
and Stephanus and the number of rosettes around the central
stone and at the bottom. Additionally, the damaged repair
and loss of the border on the right setting of the crystal and
the small hinge and loop along the sides are not represented
in the illustration. The nature of these differences suggests
the likelihood that they are small mistakes or idealizations by
the illustrator rather than representations of features present
on the object at the time.

The description from the catalogue of the sale from the
Debruge Dumenil collection in 1847 also spans four pages.
Remarkably it mentions on page 737: 'Ces peintures, du
XIII ciecle, ont peut-etre remplace des reliques qui, dans
l'origine, se trouvaient sous le cristal' ('These 13th-century
paintings perhaps have replaced relics that in the beginning
were underneath the crystal'). It also gives the full
inscription of the names of the saints on the back.

The earliest known reference to the altar is in the sale
catalogue for the collection of De Renesse-Breidbach in
1835. This has a seven-line description and relates how:
'provient de l'ancienne abbaye de Sayne pres de Coblence;
elle est d'une superbe conservation' ('comes from the ancient
Abbey Sayne near Koblenz; it is beautifully preserved'). The
attribution of the altar to Hildesheim has been discussed by
Steinberg and has been generally accepted since 1938.
Steinberg also provided a suggestion for how the altar may
have come from Hildesheim into the collection of Count De
Renesse-Breidbach.[7]

Restoration intervention and analysis dating to the 1980s
The Department of Conservation and Scientific Research
holds documentation dating to 1979/80 that relates to the
work done on the portable altar.[8] This includes a report of its
examination and treatment, results from x-ray diffraction
(XRD), infrared spectroscopy, gas chromatography and
x-ray fluorescence (XRF) analyses and a report on the
unwrapping of the relics. It also includes a series of
photographs. Although on the record envelope 'Restoration'
has been ticked as a requirement, there is no specific
indication of the reasons for initiating the examination and
restoration work other than in the report on the contents,
which mentions a request from the Department of Medieval
and Later Antiquities (M & LA) to remove and supervise the
photography of the vellum tituli. This request came from Mr
Neil Stratford, Keeper of M & LA at that time, but could
only have been made after the re-discovery of the relic
bundles after its opening up in 1980.

The three-page 'Report of examination of portable altar
1902,0625.1' is structured by material and location on the

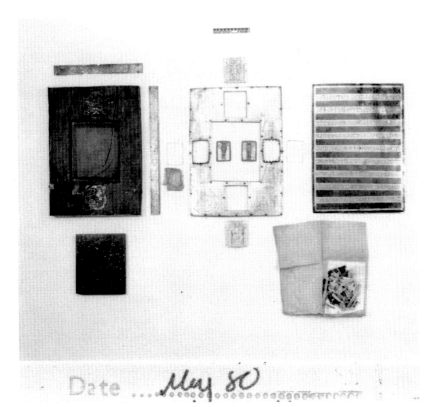

Date ... May 80

Plate 4 Photograph of the dismantled portable altar, May 1980

altar. Regarding the wood, it mentions a severe crack (**Pl. 4**) in addition to one woodworm hole and one dead beetle found underneath the relics. To prevent the crack from spreading a small hole was drilled where it started and two brass screws were inserted in the top section to take the strain of any movement in the wood, although it was noted that the crack should not be completely closed as this would cause strain elsewhere in the wood and put the nail holes out of line. It was suggested that the nail holes in the top surface of the wood lined up at one time with the rosettes (described as copper with black fill) on the top sheet, but because of shrinkage in the wood they no longer matched. Later on it describes how the right side panel was put over an oak strip, which was added to make up the difference between the shrinkage of the oak and the size of the metal panels (see **Pl. 5** where the front panel projects beyond the panel on the side). It also mentions that parts of brass hinges (of which only one set remains) are set back into the wood and the side panels are cut to receive these and a loop and swivel hook. It was suggested that this was done at the same time as the cutting and riveting of the rosettes.[9] For the metal panels it describes how some were removed, lightly cleaned and flattened out a little to improve their appearance. For the right side panel four new nails made from brass wire were inserted in the four corners. Some corners on other panels did not receive new nails because there was no wood underneath them (due to mentioned shrinkage). The nails on the top side panel are described as being of silver, about 12mm long and tapered along their whole length. The crystals and paintings on vellum were removed and cleaned. It mentions a difference in the crystals, with the right hand one being well finished and the left hand one being unfinished. The ivories were removed and lightly cleaned, and the observation is made that the head on the left hand side of the lower panel is a replacement using elephant ivory,

whereas the panels are said to be walrus. It records that the head was removed and repositioned using nitrocellulose adhesive, as were the panels themselves.

The textiles and relic bundles are described in the 'Report on the contents of a twelfth century portable altar', written by M. McCord in 1980.[10] As mentioned previously, the work done was in response to the request to detach the vellum tituli to allow photography. Since this necessitated untying each relic bundle it was decided to compile a descriptive list of the textiles, part of which is reproduced in **Table 1**. It states that during the course of the project some conservation work was essential and two pieces of textile were treated. The textiles were visually examined and was limited to thread counts, spin and weave notation and fibre identification. Overall condition of all the textiles was described as good if slightly dry, and only the wrappings of St Tonatus and St Ciprian were said to be 'dangerously embrittled and these were of sufficient interest to warrant

Plate 5 Front and reverse of the portable altar presumably taken for the exhibition *The Year 1200* at the Metropolitan Museum of Art, New York in 1970

their full conservation; both to prolong their existence and to ease examination'. Conservation treatment for these two textiles was described, including an extensive account relating to the choice of textile support, which was governed by two factors: the fragility of the pieces was such that they could not be sewn and that they were to be returned to such a limited space. Therefore they were mounted on silk crepeline using a thermoplastic adhesive.[11]

The report suggests that identification of the geographical and temporal origins of the textiles (linen, cotton and silk, patterned and plain) may be possible and that the four figured compound weaves could be identified iconographically by comparison to pieces with a known provenance in other museums and ecclesiastical treasuries.[12] The report indicates that there are at least three periods to which the textiles could belong. The oldest fibres are likely to be woven fragments from the two relic bundles of Sts Cyriacus and Martin and St Christopher. They are suggested to be contemporary with the first collection of these two relic bundles. The second oldest group of fabrics include the majority of the tabby-weave silks and linens and figured silks, dating approximately to the 9th–10th century, and represent the wrappings of the relics at the time of enclosure in the altar between 1185 and 1203. The cottons are more likely to post-date these by about 400 years and may even be 19th century. Cotton cannot have been grown in Europe, although the fabric could have been woven and finished in Britain or Holland, two of the first countries to develop a cotton industry in the 17th century. Linen was grown and used throughout the Middle Ages in much of northern Europe so it was assumed that the linens were woven in or close to the abbey. For the silks an origin was suggested as probably from the eastern Mediterranean, although Italy has also been mentioned as a possibility.

The report contains results from XRD analyses on the large transparent stone, the black material in the heads of the rosettes and the brown layer on the copper. The results suggest the transparent stone to be quartz, i.e. rock crystal. The black material, which was thought to be niello, was shown to be amorphous indicating that it is not niello, which would be crystalline. No further investigations were carried out however. The brown layer on the copper was similarly shown to be amorphous by XRD. Additionally a sample was analysed using infrared spectroscopy and compared with experimentally reproduced vernis brun following the instructions of Theophilus.[13] Both spectra are said to be virtually identical, strongly suggesting that the dark brown layer is vernis brun. Further support for this conclusion was derived from gas chromatographic analysis of another sample carried out in the Scientific Department of the National Gallery. The results of this suggest 'the use of a simple linseed oil which may have undergone heating or boiling'.

In 1982 a request was made by the then curator Leslie Webster for five relic bundles to be taken out of the altar for a temporary display. No further documentation relating to this event is present in the archives. In 1984 the altar was opened, presumably to facilitate XRF analysis.[14] The front and back panel were reported to be respectively 99 and 99.2% copper. The report states that analysis was done on a

small area abraded on the reverse of each panel and that the side panels were not removed, as I. McIntyre (Senior Conservator) feared damage to original (silver) nails. It also mentions that mercury was present in the gilding and that no tin or zinc was detected.

Further analysis was made in 1995 when the central red stone, previously described as being porphyry, was suggested to be a fossiliferous limestone, resembling the Purbeck marble of Dorset.[15] Based on comparison with material in the collection of the Natural History Museum, a likely source was suggested to be 'a band of brown shelly limestone of the Upper Purbeck (Upper Jurassic), which outcrops at Peveril Point, Swanage, above the Broken Shell limestone. This material has been quarried and used as a decorative material in churches.' Various explanations for the rock's presence in the altar have been considered, including it being a replacement that was inserted after the object came to England; a venerable relic of the early Anglo-Saxon missions to Lower Saxony; and it being original, which implies late 12th-century contacts between England and Hildesheim.

Conservation interventions in 2008 and 2010

During preparations for the refurbishment of the medieval gallery in 2007 it was found that both the front and rear panels were coming away from the wood where the nails were no longer holding these in position due to previous removal and insertion of nails and crushing of fibres (**Pl. 6**). One of the crystals appeared to be loose in its setting and additionally the front panel had an old protective coating showing early signs of deterioration such as brush marks and some tarnishing of the metal. It was decided to take off the front panel to assist the removal of the protective coating and allow further assessment of the risk to the vellum behind the crystals. Ethical issues regarding opening the altar were considered based on the wider approach to the conservation of religious heritage.[16] However, for example, breaking a seal which is considered to be a legal transaction according to church law was in this instance not considered applicable. No physical seal was present when the altar was opened in 1980. The British Museum's 2006 policy for handling and examining human remains was adhered to.[17] A multidisciplinary team of four conservators with the appropriate expertise related to the components of the altar worked on the treatment (**Pl. 7**).[18] It was decided to fill the nail holes in the wooden core using thin poplar (Populus tremula) wood wedges, cut to shape and glued with cold setting fish glue to provide a better purchase for the brass nails that would be inserted later. Poplar provides a firm grip, yet is softer than the original oak so that if the panel is placed under stress the modern parts will fail rather than the original oak during any shrinkage or expansion. The ivory plaques were cleaned using cotton swabs lightly moistened with a solvent of deionized water and industrial methylated spirit. Possible traces of black and blue pigment and gilding were observed under magnification on both plaques, although no scientific analyses have been conducted to confirm this. The painted vellum was assessed and despite some wrinkling of the vellum, the pigment layers were found to be stable with no

Table 1 List of relic bundles with associated saint's names. The weave and spin notations, bundle contents etc. are based on the report by McCord 1980 in RL4336

Registration number	Object title	Name on tituli	Name on altar	Specified area	Threads per cm warp	Threads per cm weft	Spin warp	Spin weft	Yarn	Construction and colour	Size (cm)	Tie-threads	Notes	Contents apart from dust and grit
1902,0625.1.a 1902,0625.1.b	St Agatha St Benedict	Agathe v y m. S. Benedicti Abbis.	AGATHE MARTIRIS BENEDICTI ABBATIS,	face	30 29	24 59	Z Z	Z ?	Linen Silk	Tabby Compound weave multicoloured	5 diameter 6 by 4.5	2 S ply linen 2 present, A. 2 S ply linen, b. Spun linen	See appendix C, RL4336 1980	1 tie thread, Z spun linen/ tow
1902,0625.1.c	St Blaise	Blasii. Epi & mris.	BLASII EPISCOPI	back	44 44	50 33	Z	?	Silk	Tabby yellow	6 by 4.5 8 by 4.5	2 present, a. 2S ply linen, b. z spun silk. orange	Needle holes around 3 sides.	Bone
1902,0625.1.d	St Boniface	Bonifacy, evoy?	BONIFACII EPISCOPI		36	31	Z	Z	Silk	Tabby, rose-pink	8 by 4.5	Z spun tow	Selvedge present with warps in 3s. piece dyed	Bone.
1902,0625.1.e	St Christopher	de humero S. Christophori Mrt	CRISTOPHORI	outer inner contents	80 38 ?	44 36 ?	? Z Z	? Z Z	Silk Schappe silk Cellulose linen	Tabby, bright red Tabby, rusty-pink Tabby	6 by 7 by 2 6 by 7 by 5.5 1.5 by 2mm	2 S ply linen	Almost triangle Fold caught with 2S ply linen stitch	Bone, amber coloured stone/ carnelian? Small, very degraded fragments Z spun tabby-weave cellulose fibre, linen
1902,0625.1.f	St Cyprian	Cipriani mr	CIPRIANI	face back	34 15	27 27	s	?	Silk	Compound weave multicoloured	6 by 4.5	2 S ply linen	See appendix C, RL4336 1980	Bone
1902,0625.1.g	St Denis	Dionisii epi y mr.	DIONISII	face back	32 22	22 22	Z	?	Silk	Compound weave multicoloured	7.5 by 2	Z spun linen	See appendix C, RL4336 1980	Bone
1902,0625.1.h 1902,0625.1.i 1902,0625.1.j	St Egidius Giles St Felice St Felicissimus	Egidij cofs. felicis pp y mr. felicissimi	EGIDII FELICIS FELICISSIMI		44 48 48	38 36 26	Z Z Z	Z ? Z	Linen Silk Silk	Tabby Tabby, blue Tabby warp: sand, weft: dark green	7.5 by 7 5 by 4 11 by 3	Z spun tow Z spun tow loose Z spun tow	Hem present Selvedge present	Bone
1902,0625.1.k	St Godehard	S. Godehardi epi y cf.?	GODEHARDI EPISCOPI		40	36	Z	?	Silk	Tabby, grey-violet	8.5 by 7.5	2 S ply silk, cream		Bone
1902,0625.1.l 1902,0625.1.m 1902,0625.1.n	St Hippolitus St Jacintus St Jacob	S Hippoliti Mr. Jacinti .m. Jacobi apti.	IPOLITI IACINTI IACOBI APOSTOLI		38 36 34	32 42 33	Z Z Z	Z ? Z	Cotton Silk Linen	Tabby white Tabby, pink Tabby	10 by 8 6 by 5.5 4 by 3	2 S ply linen 2 S ply tow 2 present, both Z spun singles linen	Irregular shape Selvedge present	Bone Bone
1902,0625.1.o 1902,0625.1.p	St John the Baptist St John the Evangelist	Sci Johannis bapti De crinib; iohis evg.	IOHANNIS BATISTE IOHANNIS EWANGELISTE	outer inner outer	32 34 40	16 30 30	Z Z Z	s Z z	Silk Linen Silk	Tabby, terracotta Tabby Tabby, red	4 by 6.5 5.25 by 8.5 2 by 15	2 S ply blue linen 4 S ply tow	Hem present sewn with 2 S ply silk piece dyed	Hair, unspun white fibre with blue dye offset. Open knot of Z spun brittle dark brown wool
1902,0625.1.q	St Laurence	laurenty m.	LAURENTII	inner	36 34	34 30	z ?	z ?	Silk Silk	Tabby, blue Tabby, rose-pink	4.5 by 4.5 4.5 by 3.5	2 present, a. 5S ply linen, b. 2S ply silk	Bias cut	Bone
1902,0625.1.r	St Mary Magdalene	Marie magdalene	MARIE MAGDALENE	outer inner	22 44	20 30	Z s	Z ?	Linen Silk	Tabby Tabby, blue	7 by 4.5 9 by 4	Z spun tow, ? Silk tassel, 3 strands Z spun yellow		Bone, wood shaving, yellow silk (tie-thread?) looped into weave of blue silk wrapper at one long side.
1902,0625.1.s	St Matthew	Mathei aptizev.?	MATHEI APOSTOLI ET EWANGELISTE		34	34	Z	Z	Linen	Tabby	4.5 by 3	2 present both Z spun singles linen		
1902,0625.1.t	St Maurice, Companions of	de ossib? socim? Sci mauricy.	MAURICII		36	28	Z	Z	Linen	Tabby	9 diameter	2 S ply linen	Hem present.	Bone
1902,0625.1.u	St Nicolas	Nicolai epi.	NICOLAI		32	32	Z	Z	Linen	Tabby	3.5 by 3	Z spun linen		

Registration number	Object title	Name on tituli	Name on altar	Specified area	Threads per cm warp	weft	Spin warp	weft	Yarn	Construction and colour	Size (cm)	Tie-threads	Notes	Contents apart from dust and grit
1902,0625.1.v	St Pancras	2 Tituli: Pancacii? mart; S. Pancraty mart.	PANCRATII		38	30	Z	Z	Cotton	Tabby, white	6 by 4.5	2 S ply tow		Bone ?toe
1902,0625.1.w	Sts Cornelius and Cyprian	Cornelij y Cypani m?.	CORNELII CIPRIANI		28	28	Z	Z	Linen	Tabby	4 by 2.5	2 S ply linen		
1902,0625.1.x	Sts Cosma and Damian	SS Cosma et Damiani Mart	COSME DAMIANI		40	32	Z	Z	Cotton	Tabby, white	6 diameter	2 singles Z spun tow used together	Almost a circle	Bone
1902,0625.1.y	Sts Cyriacus and Martin	2 Tituli:Ciriaci martini; SS Cijriaci et Martini	MARTINI	outer	37	34	Z	Z	Cotton	Tabby, white	8.5 by 6	2 present, a. 2S ply tow, b. S spun tow	French seam present	Textile: 1. Inner wrapper, 2. Red fibres adhering to
				inner	5	38	Z	Z	Linen	Tabby	6 by 4 by 3.5			lump of mud, 3. Three small fragments of very fragile tabby weave cellulose fibre, Z spun, 4. Bundle of blond, friable Z spun silk.
				contents	?	?	Z	Z	Cellulose	Tabby	1 by 2 mm		three small fragments	
1902,0625.1.z	St Servatius	2 Tituli: Servatij epiy cf?; S Servatij Epi conf	SERVACII		34	32	Z	Z	Linen	Tabby	7 by 3.5	2 S ply linen, burnt sienna	2 hems present	Green stained bone. Very brittle brown and white silk fibres.
1902,0625.1.aa	Sts Fabriani and Sebastiani	1 of 2 tituli: Fabiani y Sebastiani; 2 of 2 tituli: SS Fabiani et Sebastiani	FABIANI SEBASTIANI		37	34	Z	Z	Cotton	Tabby white	7 by 6	2 S ply tow		
1902,0625.1.ab	Sts Felice and Naboris	SS Felicis et Naboris	FELICIS NARORIS, MARTIRUM ET CONFESSORUM		38	32	Z	Z	Cotton	Tabby, white	8 by 6	Z spun linen	Selvedge present	Bone fragments, some burnt. Red-wool fibres
1902,0625.1.ac	Sts Peter and Marcellinus	1 of 2 tituli: Marcellini y Pet? 2 of 2 tituli: SS Marcellini et Petri	PETRI MARCELLINI		48	32	Z	?	Silk	Tabby, blue	4.5 4.5	Z spun tow		Bone
1902,0625.1.ad	St Stephen	Stephani, pthomr.	STEPHANI PROTOMARTIRIS		31	28	Z	Z	Linen	Tabby	4.5 by 3.5	2 S ply linen		Bone
1902,0625.1.ae	St Theodore	Theodori mr.	THEODORI	face	46	32	Z	?	Silk	Tabby, blue	5 by 3.5	2 S ply linen	See appendix C, RL4336 1980	Bone
1902,0625.1.af	St Tonatus	S Totnati Mart	TOTINAT	back	44	46	Z	?	Silk	Compound weave blues	9 by 5	Z spun tow		
					38	39								
1902,0625.1.ag	St Vitalis	vitalis . m.	VITALIS	outer	30	28	Z	Z	Linen	Tabby	5.5 by 4.5	5 ply	Selvedge present.	? Stone conglomerate. Bone, burnt.
				inner	48	50	?	?	Silk	Tabby, lime-green	2 by 2.5			
1902,0625.1.ah	St Vitus	S Viti Mart	VITI	napkin	36	28	Z	Z	Silk	Tabby yellow	8 by 6	2 S ply linen	3 hems present, one possibly also a selvedge	Bone
					30	32	Z	Z	Linen	Tabby	62 by 30			
				1 fragment from behind St Bernhard	24	24	Z	Z	Linen	Tabby	10 by 2.5			
				2 fragment from behind St Bernhard	25	22	Z	Z	Linen	Tabby	29 by 4.5			
			PAVLI APOSTOLI										unaccounted for	

Ply is single in all weaving yarns.

Name on tituli: '?' indicates unreadable or questionable

Spin notation: lower case indicates slight spin, '?' indicates undiscernable.

Warp count is given as the greater number unless presence of selvedge or spin indicated otherwise.

Plate 6 Gap in the metal sheets, 2007

Plate 7 Conservators Judith Rayner, Philip Kevin and Jane Hamill working on the altar in 2008

sign of recent losses, cracking or flaking. The gilded copper front and sides were cleaned and the deteriorated protective coating was removed using acetone. Finally, to reassemble the front, three missing brass nails were replaced with new brass nails that were manufactured from 15mm solid brass panel pins by hammering the tops flat. A fixing was manufactured from brass wire to hold the back panel in position; this passes along the oak strip on the side (added in 1980) and then around the brass nail going through the side panel. The wire was manipulated into position with a perspex tool. The misaligned piece of crystal was repositioned and the pieces of vellum were supported with inserts of several layers of MicroChamber® paper (containing a combination of molecular sieves and alkaline buffers to trap and neutralize the byproducts of deterioration and airborne pollutants), cut and folded to size so they would not be visible (**Pl. 8**). These hold the painted vellum pieces securely in place while cushioning them from the pressure of the original metal swivels. A small piece of folded, unbleached linen was also inserted behind the paper to help support the loose crystal. This corresponds to the arrangement under the other crystal, where the existing piece of textile (two fragments from behind St Bernhard in **Table 1**) was still present.

The wood has previously been described as oak, although no actual supporting observations were mentioned. The possibility for dendrochronology was considered to establish the age and origin of the tree, but the requirement for a clear edge over a substantial number of tree rings was not met.[19]

In preparation for the *Treasures of Heaven* exhibition it was requested that the altar be re-opened to document and examine the relic bundles more fully. Consequently, in 2010 the altar was re-opened and a selection of six bundles were unwrapped by a textile conservator with the procedure filmed as part of a BBC documentary. The selection of bundles to be opened was decided upon based both on their condition and by curatorial interests to display relic bundles at all three venues. Each exhibition venue was allocated different relics for display, thereby minimizing possible fading of the still bright and colourful textile dyes. Some of the bundles were considered too fragile for overseas transport and these were kept back for display at the British Museum only. This was because either their ties were split or too fragile to hold the bundle securely; the fabric wrappings had holes through which bone fragments could be seen and possibly lost; or the wrappings were loose and did not hold the contents firmly enough in place, risking

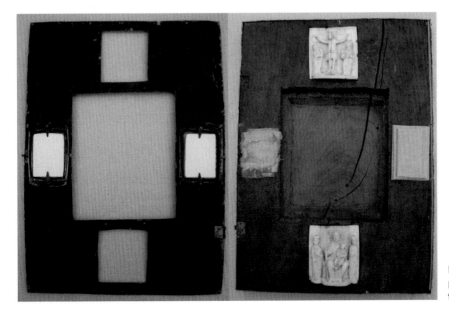

Plate 8 Photographs showing the additions of paper and linen positioned to provide support to the painted vellum, 2008

Plate 9 Sequence showing the unwrapping by Nicole Rode of the textile of the relic bundle of St Mary Magdalene (1902,0526.1r)

the contents shifting and abrading one another during transport.

Before and during the unwrapping an attempt was made to document the exact tying and wrapping method in order to re-tie each bundle as accurately as possible (**Pl. 9**). Similarly the re-wrapping of the 1980s reflected the tying manner evidenced at the time. The relics were photographed from many angles and notes were made about the path of the tying string, i.e. fold lines and the order in which to re-fold fabrics. The main feature noted was the number of times the string had been wrapped around the bundle, and the length of each thread left after the knot or twist was made. Fourteen small samples of textiles from nine bundles were taken to be used for dye analyses, which are in progress and will be published elsewhere in due course. In relation to the examination of the contents of the bundles, it was decided that no destructive analyses should be undertaken. Thus so far the contents were only examined visually.

The central stone has been described as 'marbre lumachelle',[20] then Imperial porphyry and more recently Purbeck marble. Lumachelli marble, as described by Phillips, is of 'irridescent colours, found in veins in Bleyberg in Corinthia. Its colours are attributed to the shells of a variety of nautilus';[21] the 'Bleiberg' referred to is in the province of Corinthe in Austria. This material, which was apparently mined during the medieval period, has a composition that would give the same analytical results as limestone. Comparison of photographs of this type of stone – provided by M. Heinrich from the Geologische Bundesanstalt in Vienna – suggest similarities (mostly in the red matrix), but appear not to show the same stone as in the portable altar, which does not have the iridescent colours of shell fragments. Red Purbeck marble was used in churches in England at the time suggested for the manufacture of the altar,[22] but to the authors' knowledge, there has been no discussion of the likelihood of this stone, as used in the portable altar, as being original or a later replacement. In addition to the possibilities considered in 1995 there may be similar outcrops existing on the continental side of the Channel in France. Therefore, the

suggestion that the stone originates from Peverill Point seems plausible but cannot be proven.

Conclusions

The available documentation relating to the collection history of the portable altar indicates that the altar was opened during the 19th century while it was in the Soltykoff collection and that the presence of the relics underneath the central stone was known at that time. By 1902, when acquired by the British Museum, this knowledge appears to have been lost and the belief that the relics would originally have been present underneath the crystal windows seems to have been prevalent. This idea that they would have been beneath the crystal is noteworthy considering it has more recently been suggested that the visibility of relics became a novelty in the 13th century.[23] The alterations such as the brass hinges and hook or the black rosettes may be added features from when the portable altar was opened during the 19th century. The black inlay of the rosettes is organic in nature rather than the expected niello, and their copper surfaces are not gilded, which might also be expected. The size of the hinge seems relatively small and it seems likely that it failed after a short period, when the altar was closed permanently again using additional brass nails.

The works undertaken both in 1980 and in 2008/10 are typical of the restoration and conservation practices in a museum at this time. The work in 1980 was slightly more interventive, for example the drilling of a hole in the wood to slow down splitting due to dimensional changes and natural movement in the wood, and the addition of a wooden section to compensate for the shrinkage of the wood and subsequent gap between substrate (wood) and copper sheets. Currently, such issues are more likely to be accepted as being part of the ageing process of the object and the risk of deterioration in the future would be reduced by using preventive measures to create a stable environment for storage and display. Another difference between the 1980 and 2008/10 interventions is the extent and form of documentation. The documentation of the 2008/10 interventions includes a record of the decision-making process and also benefited from the wider dissemination offered by the production of a BBC documentary to accompany the exhibition and inclusion as a story line on the Museum's Facebook page.

The analyses conducted over the years have thrown light on the various materials that have been used in the construction of the altar. In particular, the presence and identification of what appears to be vernis brun has to the knowledge of the authors not previously been published elsewhere. On the majority of objects from the medieval period the vernis brun design can merely be recognized by the contrast between the copper and gilt surface, since invariably the varnish itself has been physically lost.

Interestingly, two years after the altar was opened in 1980, it was re-opened to display some of the relics in 1982. Similarly, two years after the altar having been opened in 2008, it was re-opened in 2010 to display the relics once again. It would seem that the attention created by opening the altar generates even more interest and the will to open the altar to see the relics again. The continuing, conflicting demands of public interest and display and those related to the long-term preservation and safety of the object itself will need continued due consideration in the future and measures will have to be devised to manage these.

Acknowledgements

In addition to the acknowledgements made in the introduction to this chapter to those who worked on the previous examination of the altar and its documentation in the 1980s, the authors would like to thank the following people for their contribution and support in the most recent examination: M. Heinrich from the Geologische Bundesanstalt in Vienna, and Janet Ambers, Daniel Antoine, Caroline Cartwright, Pippa Cruickshank, Thibaut Deviese, Jane Hamill, Anna Harnden, Catherine Higgitt, Marilyn Hockey, Philip Kevin, Denise Ling, Judith Rayner, James Robinson, Nicole Rode and David Saunders of the British Museum.

Notes

1 See also Bagnoli *et al.* 2010.
2 See Stratford 1993, 56.
3 'Art comes before gold and gems, the creator before everything. Henry, alive in bronze, gives gifts to God.' Stratford 1993, 54.
4 BM archive, see RL4336 1980, RL6685 1995 and PE1902,0625.1.
5 See London 1902.
6 See Anvers 1935; Labarte 1847; Viollet-le-Duc 1858; Paris 1861 (all accessible in the National Art Library, London).
7 Steinberg 1938, 71.
8 These unpublished documents are archived as RL4336 1980 and RL6685 1995, but have been made available recently via the Museum's online documentation system. The record envelope was a documentation system traditionally used in the Research Laboratory for examination and analyses. The Conservation Department was formed in 1975 and was still developing its own documentation systems for which the requisition card used in this case is an example. The agreed treatment states: 'Remove top to enable examination of the inside. Then contact N.S.' The actual work undertaken would have been discussed with Neil Stratford once the altar was opened.
9 The location of rosettes, riveted over on the reverse of the panel, matches approximately the nail holes in the wood. It is possible that the pins of the rosettes were cut off and riveted over at the time when the hinges were added. Certainly the front could not have been held by nails when it was hinged.

10 Additionally, Margaret McCord presented her findings to the AGM of the Centre International d'etude des Textils Anciens in Prato, October 1981. Submission for publication in *Textile History* or as part of a British Museum Occasional Paper appears to have been contemplated, but for reasons unknown this did not take place, see PE 1902,0625.1.
11 A 1/10 dilution of Vinamul 6515 in water was brushed onto suitably dyed silk crepeline. After drying the textiles were laid over the appropriate adhesive areas and attached using an iron set at 80°C through silicon release paper.
12 In the report M. McCord acknowledges the contributions of Ms Mary Clarke, Mr Donald King, Ms Anna Musthesias and Dr Brigitte Schmedding for their assistance with the identification and dating of the patterned textile fragments. It goes beyond the scope of this article to investigate if their findings still stand given advances in the understanding of textile history.
13 See RL4336 1980 for a letter from Raymond White to Andrew Oddy, 17 July 1980. See Wolters 2010 for further reading on the technique of vernis brun.
14 See RL4336 1980 and also Oddy *et al.* 1986.
15 See PE1902,0625.1 for a letter dated 28 November 1994 from T. Haysom to N. Stratford, and a letter dated 30 October 1995 from Dr O Williams-Thorpe to Dr John Cherry, and RL6685 1995.
16 See Os 2000, 189. For the opening of the St Godehard shrine in Hildesheim Cathedral in 2010 which was partially documented on film, see Hildesheimer Dom 2010. For further reading about the conservation of living religious heritage and reliquary shrines see also Stovel *et al.* 2005 and Anheuser and Werner 2006.
17 See British Museum Policy on Human Remains 2006.
18 For a fuller description of the condition and treatment see also the British Museum's Collections Online, the link for which is given in the reference for RL4336 1980.
19 The wood was described as oak in RL4336 although no supporting observations were mentioned. Wood identification would be done by microscopy or/and with the aid of SEM. Requirements for dendrochronology which would date and geographically provenance the wood as raw material were discussed with Janet Ambers.
20 Labarte 1847; Viollet-le-Duc 1858; and Christies 1902.
21 Phillips 1818.
22 See Blair 2001.
23 See Os 2000, 138.

Bibliography

Anheuser, K. and Werner, C. (eds) 2006. *Medieval Reliquary Shrines and Precious Metalwork, Proceedings of a Conference at the Musee d'art et d'histoire, Geneva, 12–15 September 2001*, London.

Anvers 1835. *Catalogue d'une belle collection de porcelains et antiquites chinoises et des indes, ainsi que de vieilles armes et armures. Faisant partie du magnifique cabinet delaisse par fue M. le comte Clemens Wenceslas de Renesse-Breidbach, Dont la vente aura lieu a Anvers, au Salon-d'Exposition, rue de Venus, par le Greffier Ter Bruggen, le 1er Octobre 1835 et jours suivans. De l'imprimerie de J.-E. Rysheuvels, a Anvers.*

Bagnoli, M., Klein, H.A., Mann, C.G. and Robinson, J. (eds) 2010. *Treasures of Heaven: Saints, Relics and Devotion in Medieval Europe*, Baltimore and London.

Blair, J. 2001. 'Purbeck marble', in *English Medieval Industries: Craftsmen, Techniques, Products*, ed. J. Blair and N. Ramsey, London, 42–56.

British Museum Policy on Human Remains 2006. http://www.britishmuseum.org/about_us/management/museum_governance.aspx (accessed 3 May 2012).

Hildesheimer Dom 2010. 'Opening and conservation of St Godehard shrine', http://www.domsanierung.de/en/shrine_godehard (accessed 29 November 2013).

Labarte, J. 1847. *Description des objets d'art qui composent la collection Debruge Dumenil precede d'une introduction historique*, Paris, 737–40.

London 1902. *Catalogue of the Well-known Collection of Works of Art of the Classic, Mediaeval and Renaissance Times, Formed by Sir Thomas Gibson Carmichael, Bart. Of Castle Craig, N.B.*, Monday 12 May 1902, Lot 37, London.

Oddy, W. A., La Niece, S. and Stratford, N. 1986. *Romanesque Metalwork: Copper Alloys and their Decoration*, London.

Os, H. van 2000. *The Way to Heaven, Relic Veneration in the Middle Ages*, Amsterdam.

Paris 1861. *Catalogue des objets d'Art et de haute curiosite composant la celebre collection du Prince Soltykoff don't la vente aura lieu Hotel Drouot, Salle 7 Les Lundi 8 Avril et jours suivants*, Lot 23, Paris.

PE1902,0625.1: unpublished documentation envelope held in the Prehistory and Europe Department of the British Museum.

Phillips, W. and Latham Mitchill, S. 1818. *An Elementary Introduction to the Knowledge of Mineralogy*, New York.

RL4336 1980: unpublished Research Laboratory envelope, Portable altar of ?13th C. of Thidericus (Theoderic), Received 18.7.79, Completed 11-08-80, accessible via http://www.britishmuseum.org/research/search_the_collection_database/search_object_details.aspx?objectid=51032&partid=1&IdNum=1902%2c0625.1&orig=%2fresearch%2fsearch_the_collection_database%2fmuseum_number_search.aspx (accessed 5 January 2012).

RL6685 1995: unpublished Research Laboratory envelope, Examination of portable altar from Hildesheim, Received 20-1-95, completed 9.5.95, accessible via http://www.britishmuseum.org/research/search_the_collection_database/search_object_details.aspx?objectid=51032&partid=1&IdNum=1902%2c0625.1&orig=%2fresearch%2fsearch_the_collection_database%2fmuseum_number_search.aspx (accessed 05 January 2012).

Steinberg, S.H. 1938. 'A portable altar in the British Museum', in *Journal of the Warburg Institute*, vol. 2, no. 1 (July), 71–2.

Stovel, H., Stanley-Price, N. and Killick, R. (eds) 2005. *Conservation of Living Religious Heritage, Papers from the ICCROM 2003 Forum on Living Religious Heritage: Conserving the Sacred*, ICCROM Conservation Studies 3, Rome.

Stratford, N. 1993. *Catalogue of Medieval Enamels in the British Museum, Vol. 2, Northern Romanesque Enamel*, London.

Viollet-le-Duc, M. 1858. *Dictionnaire raisonne du Mobilier Francais de l'Epoque Carlovingienne a la renaissance*, Paris, 19–22.

Wolters, J., 2010. 'Techniken und Historishe Merkmale des Braunfirnisses – eine Richtigstellung. Mit einem Gesamtkatalog Historischer Braunfirnisarbeiten', in *Sonderdruck aus dem Jahrbuch des Römisch-Germanischen Zentralmuseums Mainz*, vol. 57, Mainz, 390–504.

Chapter 17
New Discoveries Related to the Portable Altar of Countess Gertrude

Shelley Reisman Paine, David B. Saja and Linda B. Spurlock

Summary

The portable altar of Countess Gertrude is a beautiful medieval reliquary dating to around 1045. A container of relics constructed from fine materials, it remained part of the Guelph Treasure for over 900 years. The altar was opened in 2009, only the second time since it was purchased in 1931, to remove the relics in preparation for display in the exhibition *Treasures of Heaven: Saints, Relics and Devotion in Medieval Europe* at the Cleveland Museum of Art. A team including a mineralogist, biological anthropologist and conservator took this rare opportunity to study the gemstones and 13 relics. This most recent study produced new information, highlighting previous repairs, showing reuse of stone and gemstones and confirming that the majority of the bones were human. It also created as many questions as answers, which are included as areas for further study at the end of this chapter.

History

The portable altar (**Pl. 1**) was made *circa* 1045 in Lower Saxony at the request of Countess Gertrude of Brunswick, and was part of a group of religious objects she commissioned after the death of her husband, Count Liudolf of the Brunon family, in 1038.[1] These liturgical objects became part of the acclaimed Guelph Treasure. The collection was assembled and owned by descendants of the Brunon and Guelph families, and in a 1482 inventory numbered 140 individual pieces.[2]

The Guelph Treasure remained in the family for a remarkable nine centuries until after the First World War when the German aristocratic house of Braunschweig-Lüneburg began to sell portions of the Treasure. A syndicate of German dealers, Julius R. Goldschmidt, Z.M. Hackenbroch and Saemy Rosenberg, purchased the Treasure in 1930. Although the treasure was of national historical significance, the German government could not raise the funds for its purchase. The Treasure, at this point reduced from 140 to 85 objects over the centuries due to loss and attrition, was prepared for sale. In 1931 the dealers began to sell the remaining 85 objects to multiple individuals and institutions during an exhibition and tour in Germany and the United States. In 1931 William Milliken, first as a curator of paintings and decorative arts and then as the second director of the Cleveland Museum of Art, purchased nine of those religious objects. The portable altar of the Countess Gertrude, an extraordinary object from the Guelph Treasure, thus became part of the Cleveland Museum of Art's collection.

The portable altar is a fully functional altar, a medieval symbol of Christ. It has the same liturgical function and use in religious ceremonies as a large altar, namely to focus the Mass and consecrate the Eucharistic bread and wine. The portable altar was therefore used by Gertrude's chaplain during travel as well as in the Church of St Blaise, the final resting place of the count and countess located within their castle compound.

The words 'GERDRVDIS XPO FELIX VT / VIVAT IN IPSO / OBTVLIT HVNC LAPIDEM GEMMIS / AVROQ NITENTEM' (In order to live happily in him Gertrude presented to Christ this stone glistening with gold

Plate 1 Oblique view of the portable altar of Countess Gertrude, *c.* 1045, German (Lower Saxony), gold over wood, enamel, red porphyry, gems, pearls and niello, 10.5 x 27.5 x 21cm. Cleveland Museum of Art, gift of the John Huntington Art and Polytechnic Trust (CMA 1931.462)

Plate 2 Top of the portable altar showing porphyry stone and niello inscription

and precious stones)[3] surround a piece of royal porphyry centred on the top of the portable altar (**Pl. 2**) and express the religious hopes of the Countess Gertrude. In fact, the portable altar is a poignant reflection of the Countess' religious aspirations and worldliness. It is clad primarily in gold and adorned with gemstones and other materials and is decorated with iconography of important religious and historic figures. The portable altar was in compliance with the Seventh Ecumenical Council of Nicea in 787, which stipulated that all consecrated altars were to contain sacred relics.

Description and condition

The portable altar is a composite object (h: 10.5cm, w: 27.5cm, d: 21.0cm) consisting of a porphyry altar stone supported by an oak box clad on the exterior with gold, silver and gilded silver panels secured with nails, and embellished with bezel-set precious, semi-precious and glass gemstones, shell and other materials. Artistic embellishments of the altar include repoussé, filigree of beaded wire and sinusoidal ribbon, niello and enamelled elements. Each side has a single decorative central gold panel with repoussé images of religious or historic figures posed under separate arches. All of the four panels depict a unique set of figures and arches made in a distinctive decorative technique. The underside is clad with a single sheet of silver secured with nails. In the centre of the bottom is a door used to access the relics.

Wooden box

Decoration and embellishments cover the box obscuring construction methods. Wood grain is noted in 39 empty bezels. The wood is longitudinal grained in the empty bezels on the front and back of the altar and cross grained on the left and right sides (**Pl. 3**). A limited interior view through the trap door in the underside of the altar appeared to reveal a single piece of wood under the altar stone. An x-radiograph did not reveal how the wood box was fabricated, but did clearly illustrate two simple hinges and a locking mechanism in the trap door.

Altar stone

The altar stone (**Pl. 2**) that covers most of the top is a single polished slab of porphyry with near perfectly shaped visibly large crystals of feldspar. The groundmass is aphonitic with no visible grains other than the feldspar phenocrysts. The phenocrysts are on average 2.4mm in length, with a 2:1 length to width ratio and no distinct twinning. The long axes of the phenocrysts are aligned subparallel to each other, forming a geologic fabric trending left to right across the altar stone. There are three apparent colour bands that transect the polished surface of the altar stone. Each band is distinguished by the absence of light coloured phenocrysts. Two are parallel to each other and are aligned subparallel to the phenocryst fabric. The third is at almost 90 degrees to the other two, orientated diagonally along the proper left side of the altar

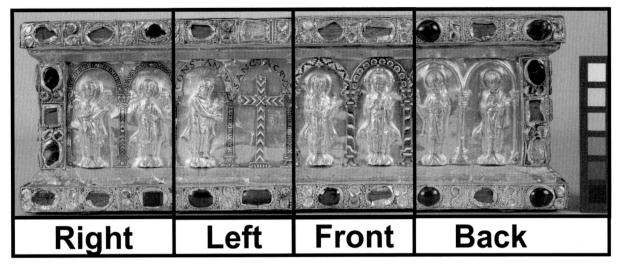

Plate 3 Composite image combining all four sides of the altar

stone. These bands are a geologic feature known as a 'shear band' or 'strain localization'; they are a 'thin zone of very high shear strain' indicating deformation during or after crystallization of the rock.[4] Also at the proper front left corner of the altar stone, at the terminus of one of these bands, is an irregular blotch of light coloured minerals. This colouration is an area of mineral alteration most likely associated with the deformation. Just to the right of this is a recent 2.5cm long fracture in the altar stone, which was not part of the original rock.

Gold panels, repairs and decorative metalwork

There is a three-tiered decorative band that surrounds the porphyry on the top of the altar. An x-radiograph revealed that each of the three bands is separate and secured to the box with nails. The outer and inner bands are mitred strips of gold and display a similar repetitive curvilinear floral design overall. There is only one apparent exception located above and below the space between 'VIVAT' and 'IN IPSO' where a heart-shaped design element is noted. Both of these design motifs are made with only beaded wire. The middle gilded silver band is butt joined and includes the niello inscription quoted above.

Repairs have been made to all of the mitred joints with the exception of the proper front left corner. The repairs include the addition of inserts of unadorned gold and gilded silver or inserts with a repoussé motif, each secured with nails. In the proper left back corner of the top (**Pl. 2**), the repoussé motif repair is possibly reused from another object since it is of a different pattern than the beaded wire motif. Two types of repairs to the silver cladding include the addition of three silver overlays secured with nails, and nails used to secure either side of two separations in the metal to the wood support. There is a thin, even, coherent and adherent layer of medium grey corrosion, presumed to be silver sulphide, on the cladding and overlays.

Each side of the altar is composed of three primary decorative components. They include a central gold panel depicting figures in repoussé posed under arches; an undecorated strip of gold above and below the central panel; and the ornate bezel strip at the perimeter edges of the object. The central gold panel on the back of the altar is

secured directly to the wood support with gold nails. The remaining gold panels are secured to the wood support with gold nails that also hold in place the architectural elements. The undecorated horizontal strips are formed over the contour of the wood support and are laterally continuous around the altar with overlapping joins that are nailed at the corners of the altar.

The ornate bezel strips have two basic designs, those used horizontally above and below the central panel and those used vertically to the left and right of the central panel. Each design can be divided into a rectangular grid defined by filigree. The horizontal grid is a repeat motif composed of a large rectangle adjacent to a small rectangle at 90 degrees. One large bezel (~16 x 12mm) is centred in the large rectangle and two small circular bezels (~6 x 6mm) each occupy half of the small rectangle. Two types of filigree elements have been used: a beaded wire and a sinusoidal ribbon. Beaded wire outlines the large and small rectangles. Where space permitted, large bezels are ringed first by a beaded wire, then the sinusoidal ribbon, followed by an outer beaded wire. The small circular bezels and nail holes are ringed by only one beaded wire. Sinusoidal ribbon is used to bracket the two small circular bezels in the top and bottom bezel strips and produce breaks between large bezels in the side bezel strips. The vertical bezel strips along the left and right edges have the same repeat grid format but with less filigree. The strips are secured to the wood support with nails located in the four corners of each large rectangle with some additional nails added out of pattern. Currently many of these are empty nail holes.

The front of the altar contains 28 bezels: 11 along both the horizontal top and bottom ornate strips and 3 along the vertical left and right edges. In contrast the back has 24: 9 along both the top and bottom and 3 on both the left and right edges. There are 20 on both the left and right sides: 7 along both the top and bottom and 3 on the left and right edges.

While each repoussé figure on the central gold panels is similar in style, none appear to be identical. Eight have been identified at this time. The front panel portrays a central figure of Christ and six saints. St Peter is to the proper right of Christ and is identified by his keys. Each figure stands under a cloisonné arch. There are four matching arch,

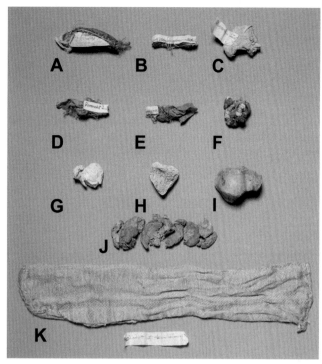

Plate 4 Contents of the altar

column, capital and base sets each with a different red, green, white and blue opaque floral and geometrically applied cloisonné designs. They are arranged to be bilaterally symmetrical – the right mirroring the left – on either side of Christ. The arch above Christ includes a cross in the design (**Pl. 3**).

The back panel does not have applied enamel arches. The Virgin Mary is the central figure and stands among six saints, each under a repoussé arch and framed within columns with only minor variations in the leaf-like designs of the capital. The designs of the sets are arranged to be bilaterally symmetrical on either side of Mary.

The proper left side of the altar depicts St Michael standing upon the slain dragon in the middle of four angels. Each figure is under an applied matching arch, column, capital and base set delineated in geometric niello designs. The designs are arranged to be bilaterally symmetrical on either side of St Michael.

The proper right side of the altar depicts four historic figures, under simple applied repoussé arch, capital, column and base sets delineated in niello. Four sets are used for the figures and a fifth for a central white, turquoise and blue cloisonné cross. The sets are decorated with simple geometric niello designs that include the name of the figure in the arch: 'SANCTA CRVX' is inscribed in niello above the cross; to the proper right of the cross, 'SIGISMVNDVS' above King Sigismund and 'CONSTANTI[N]VS' above Emperor Constantine; and to the proper left of the cross, 'S[AN]C[T]A ELENA' above Helena, and 'S[AN]C[T]A ADALHEIT' above Empress Adelheid, wife of Otto I.[5]

Bezel material

The small round bezels hold two types of material, nacre (pearl or shell) and silver. Only 40 silver, 1 pearl and 4 shell forms remain in the 240 small bezels. Several of these forms are broken; with only fragments caught in the bezel they

reveal a dome shape. In the centre of these broken silver forms is either a white wax or black resin material possibly used as a support during fabrication.

Only 46 precious, semi-precious and translucent glass gemstones remain in the 92 large bezels: 35 glass, 10 mineral and 1 mineraloid. The glass gemstones are of three colours: 9 red, 8 green and 18 blue. The colours of the minerals include 2 purple amethyst, 4 red garnet, 1 red carnelian, 1 purple fluorite and 2 blue sapphire. The mineraloid is an organic carbon known as black jet. Two stones, a blue sapphire and a garnet (identity uncertain), have crude holes drilled parallel to their longest dimension.

The gemstones were identified on the basis of their inclusions and thermal conductivity readings using a Presidium Duo Tester. Glass gemstones were identified by their ubiquitous air bubbles, and the fluorite specimen was verified by a cleavage feather displaying Newton's colours and deep abrasion on the crest of the cabochon dome which indicates softness (hardness of <5 on the 1–10 Mohs hardness scale). A sapphire, located on the proper right side of the altar, has a star asterism.

The perimeter of the gemstones is dominantly in the shape of an oval cabochon. There are 35 oval, 8 rectangular, 2 triangular and 1 lozenge-shaped gemstones. Of these, there are 26 cabochon stones and 20 stones with one table facet. Curvatures of the cabochon profile vary from low (nearly flat) to high (nearly pointed) domes. Their perimeter shapes vary from oblate circles to elongate ovals.

The gemstones are placed bilaterally symmetrical around each face of the altar and arranged in the same way as the filigree and enamel. They are placed in matching pairs by colour, perimeter shape (oval, rectangle or triangle) and cut (cabochon or table faceted). Pairing is not by gemstone type; precious stones are paired with glass of the same or similar colour. Two blue glass stones on the front of the altar have a triangle or elongated trillion shape. They are set, with their acute points orientated towards each other, symmetrically about the centre line of the altar.

Gemstones show abrasion, conchoidal loss and complete fracture separating the gemstone into two or more pieces. Several gemstones, especially those near corners, show heavy abrasion. The apex of the soft fluorite cabochon, on the corner of the proper right side, has a 5mm diameter area that is abraded nearly flat. Ten gemstones show complete fractures and nine gemstones reveal conchoidal loss. The majority of these are glass. Particularly noteworthy is a gemstone of durable garnet on the front of the altar, which is fractured into two pieces. On the proper left side of the altar there are three gemstones adjacent to each other; all are glass and all have at least one complete fracture. One of these gemstones is fractured into five pieces and another into three pieces still locked in their bezel setting. Also on the proper left side is one bezel with a little less than half of the original gemstone remaining in its bezel.

Empty bezels expose either cloth or wood grain. The cloth is an open coarsely woven fabric with a thread count of 40 per cm. It is typically taupe in colour, except in one bezel on the proper right side of the altar where the fabric weave includes red and blue bands.

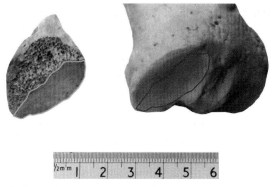

Plate 5 Reliquary fragment on left, modern tibia on right, positioned in the same orientation

Plate 6 Reliquary talus on left, modern talus on right

Contents of the altar

Ten relics were removed from the reliquary for examination: seven originally wrapped in fabric, two bones without any wrapping and one desiccated, non-osseous tissue stored in a Spanish Mudéjar silk bag (**Pl. 4K**). External morphology and x-radiographs of the relics were compared to human and non-human skeletal elements from the Hamann-Todd Osteological and the Vertebrate Zoological Collections at the Cleveland Museum of Natural History.

The two bones not wrapped in cloth were available for detailed examination (**Pl. 4H–I**). **Plates 4H** and **5** show a small fragment of a human tibia, a portion from the knee joint. The smooth surface, where the femur glides against the tibia, is outlined in green on the reliquary fragment (**Pl. 5** left) and corresponds to the same area outlined in red on the modern bone (**Pl. 5**, right). The fragment is attributed to St Gregory.[6]

Plates 4I and **6** show a nearly complete human talus, a bone from the ankle. The red line in **Plate 6** delimits the portion missing from the reliquary talus. This bone was mistakenly described as 'an unidentified hip bone' by de Winter.[7] This bone is attributed to St Januarius.

Three bones were wrapped in cloth and not available for detailed examination. By density and internal anatomy, bone can be distinguished in the x-radiograph as shown in these wrapped specimens (**Pl. 7**). In **Plate 7A** a fragment of a long bone shaft can be seen, but cannot be identified as human or non-human since no diagnostic features are present. This bone is attributed to St Hermetis. The bone in **Plate 7B** is possibly a metatarsal, a bone in the sole of the foot. It is broken, but the distal end is intact. The anatomy of the intact portion does not closely resemble any human metatarsal because it is grooved, and the shaft is more curved than what is typically seen in a human. However, it does not resemble the metatarsal of a bear, wolf, lion, pig or seal, mammals large enough to resemble humans that are commonly found in Europe. This bone is attributed to St Adelaide. **Plates 7C** and **8** show a portion of a human occipital bone that includes the rim of the foramen magnum

at the base of the skull. The red line in **Plate 8** is a tracing of the reliquary fragment superimposed onto the modern skull indicating to which portion of the skull it corresponds. It is attributed to St Vincent.

The remaining contents are non-osseous materials and a rock wrapped in cloth. The wrappings around the remaining relics could not be removed and the contents were examined using the x-radiograph. The items 'D', 'E' and 'F' in **Plate 4** are small quantities of unknown tissue. 'D' is attributed to St Gertrude and 'E' to St Marcian. 'F' is a bundle of ten tiny packets and according to the 1482 inventory includes the remains of Sts Stephen, Sophie, Perpetua, Paul, Barnaba(s), Philip, Simon, Thaddeus, John the Apostle and James. **Plate 4G** is reported to be a 'chip of unpolished marble . . . identified in 1482 as a fragment of the block used to support the Holy Cross on Mount Golgotha'.[8]

A cloth sack with desiccated tissue (**Pl. 4J**) was also inside the altar. This tissue was mistakenly identified as 'an arm bone' by de Winter.[9] The tissue has the appearance and texture of leather. An x-radiograph shows that a small metal nail is present. It is attributed to St Bartholomew. One version of St Bartholomew's death details how he was flayed, and in some artworks he is depicted holding his own skin (for example, in Michelangelo's *Last Supper*). For this reason it seems appropriate that his relic consists of flesh. In total, the non-osseous contents of the altar are attributed to 7 of the original 12 disciples: in **Plate 4F** are Paul, Philip, Simon, Thaddeus, John the Apostle and James and in **Plate 4J** is Bartholomew.[10]

Discussion and scientific analysis

We believe the altar stone is Imperial Porphyry from Mons Porphyrites in the Eastern Desert near Hurghada, Egypt.[11] It is very similar in its bulk colour and phenocryst size, shape and abundance. The Imperial Porphyry is an andesite by composition, not a rhyolite – a typical pink porphyritic rock.

Some materials used to make this altar were reused from other older objects. If the altar stone is Imperial Porphyry, it

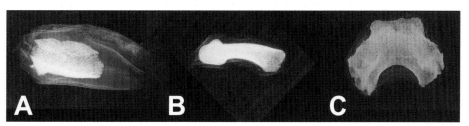

Plate 7 X-radiograph of wrapped bone fragments A, B and C

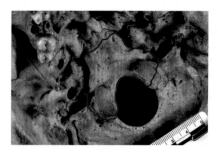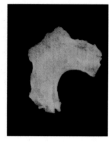

Plate 8 Reliquary fragment in x-radiograph on right, base of modern skull on left

would have been reused, as was common in the Middle Ages, since the quarries were lost to history in the 4th century and only rediscovered in 1823.[12] Reuse of porphyry is well known.[13] In describing the portable altar, de Winter references the Egyptian quarries but does not mention the stone by name.[14] More evidence of the reuse of materials in the altar are two gemstones set into the large bezels that have crudely drilled holes through their long axes indicating that originally they were beads reused from an object such as a necklace. Similar drill holes can also be seen in a gemstone in the Ceremonial Cross of Countess Gertrude (Cleveland Museum of Art, 1931.55), the three great altar crosses of Essen and other works from around the same time period. Furthermore, Lasko believes that small enamels on the altar cross of Abbess Theophanu of Essen were also made for another object and reused in the making of the cross of Essen.[15]

Missing gemstones are likely to be the result of handling. Of the 46 remaining gemstones, 12 show damage beyond normal abrasion, such as conchoidal loss and through fracturing. Ten are broken into two or more pieces still held in place by the bezel, and 5 have significant fragments missing. Of the broken stones 11 are glass and 1 is a garnet. Glass is highly elastic and withstands significant impact, but garnet is even more resilient. Garnet is the main mineral of emery. The damage to it would indicate that the altar has seen some rough handling over the centuries, possibly connected to the number of times that the Guelph Treasure had been handled, packed and transported over the past 900 years.

One bone may not be human. This is interesting, but not surprising. Surely there are not enough genuine saints' bones to be included in every Christian reliquary. Some must be non-human animal bones chosen, intentionally or unintentionally, for their superficial resemblance to human bones.

Future investigations

DNA work on a tiny portion of the tissue in **Plate 4J** could determine if it is human and if so, whether it is male. If male, analysis can show to which Y-DNA haplogroup he belonged, which indicates the geographic region from where his paternal ancestors came. For either male or female, the haplogroup of maternal ancestors can be determined from the mitochondrial DNA, a type of DNA only inherited from the mother.

The composition of several materials used in the altar's construction still need to be verified. The wood is believed to be oak, but its identification needs to be verified by an

expert. Various metals other than gold are used for nails, small bezel forms and the bottom of the altar. X-ray fluorescence spectroscopy would easily determine their composition. Fourier transform infrared spectroscopy (FTIR) was used to examine the wax and resin materials and did not get reliable results. In the future mass spectrometry should be used.

Each figure imaged in relief around the sides of the altar show distinctly different characteristics and iconography. An in-depth examination of objects and clothing on the figures depicted may lead to the identification of the remaining saints.

Acknowledgements

We would like to thank Lyman M. Jellema and Roberta Muehlheim from the Cleveland Museum of Natural History for help with photography and access to comparative, non-human bone specimens; from the Cleveland Museum of Art, Chris Edmonson, for her tireless literature searches and support, Joan Neubecker for photographing the altar and Marcia Steele, for her support and encouragement throughout the project. We would like to especially thank Stephen N. Fliegel, Curator of Medieval Art at Cleveland Museum of Art, for his love of medieval artwork and his enthusiastic support of this project.

Notes

1 Klein 2007.
2 Milliken 1931.
3 Ibid., 24.
4 Neuendorf *et al.* 2005, 593.
5 De Winter 1985, 39.
6 According to de Winter 1985, 37 of the relics are attributed to specific saints in the 1482 inventory of St Blaise Cathedral Treasury kept at the Niedersachsisches Staatsarchiv in Wolfenbüttel (Register VII B Hs 166).
7 Ibid.
8 Ibid., 37.
9 Ibid., 37.
10 Ibid.
11 Maxfield and Peacock 2001.
12 Werner 1998.
13 Werner 1998; Maxfield and Peacock 2001; Peacock and Maxfield 2007.
14 De Winter 1985, 37.
15 Lasko 1994, 138.

Bibliography

De Winter, P. 1985. 'The sacral treasure of the Guelphs', *The Bulletin of the Cleveland Museum of Art* 72(1), 1–160.
Klein, H.A. 2007. 'Portable altar of Countess Gertrude', in *Sacred Gifts and Worldly Treasures: Medieval Masterworks from the Cleveland Museum of Art*, ed. H.A. Klein, with contributions by S.N. Fliegel and V. Brilliant, New York, 116–18.
Lasko, P. 1994. *Ars Sacra 800–1200*, 2nd edn, New Haven.
Maxfield, V. and Peacock, D. 2001. *The Roman Imperial Quarries: Survey and Excavation at Mons Porphyites 1994–1998*, vol. 1: *Topography and quarries*, London (Excavation Memoir 67).
Milliken, W.M. 1931. 'The Gertrudis altar and two crosses', *The Bulletin of the Cleveland Museum of Art* 18(2), 23–6, 31–4.
Neuendorf, Klaus K.E., Mehl J.P., Jr., and Jackson, J.A. (eds) 2005. *Glossary of Geology*, 5th edn, Alexandria, Virginia.
Peacock, D. and Maxfield, V. 2007. *The Roman Imperial Quarries: Survey and Excavation at Mons Porphyrites 1994–1998*, vol. 2: *The Excavations*, London.
Werner, L. 1998. *Via porphyrites*, Saudi Aramco World, Houston, Texas.

Chapter 18
Relics of Gender Identity
Interpreting a Reliquary of a Follower of St Ursula[1]

Samantha Riches

A wooden reliquary bust of an unknown female saint (**Pl. 1**) was selected by the British Museum as the face of its marketing campaign for the 2011 exhibition *Treasures of Heaven: Saints, Relics and Devotion in Medieval Europe*.[2] This piece is identified as 'probably a companion of St Ursula', and her elaborate hairstyle, flushed cheeks and half-smile were seen repeatedly by everyone who attended the show, as well as many people who did not for her image appeared on publicity material in various locations, including railway stations, for several months. These viewers possibly identified her as an ideal of female virtue and piety, and some may have noted her long straight nose, which is strongly associated with high social status in late medieval understanding and accords with her dress, jewellery and richly plaited hair. Just before the exhibition opened a metal detectorist in Lancashire made a timely find: a pilgrim souvenir or dress fitting (**Pl. 2**) that is very similar to the reliquary bust. This was identified as a rare piece of evidence for a later medieval cult of St Ursula in England; it may well have belonged to a pilgrim who had been to Cologne, where her cult was centred. The emphasis on beauty and nobility is again clear, but we should be wary of assuming that the meanings encoded in the symbolism of these images extend no further. A late medieval devotee of St Ursula and her followers did not necessarily read the same set of assumptions into visual imagery as the 21st-century viewer.[3]

One of the most significant advances in the practice of history in the modern era has been the development of the understanding that gender is, and always has been, a fluid, mutable concept. It may be tempting to assume that it is only recently that some men and women have chosen to perform gender roles which are at odds with the biological sex of their bodies, but it is increasingly becoming apparent that gender has always been a complicated topic even if its

Plate 1 Reliquary bust of an unknown female saint, probably a companion of St Ursula, *c.* 1520–30, painted and gilded oak, height 42.4cm. The Metropolitan Museum of Art, The Cloisters Collection, 1959 (59.70) (image © The Metropolitan Museum of Art)

Plate 2 Pilgrim souvenir or dress fitting, probably a follower of St Ursula, c. 1500–30, silver, length 45mm. Museum of Lancashire, Preston (photo courtesy of the Portable Antiquities Scheme, LANCUM-61F133)

complexity has not always been overtly recognized. It has long been accepted that an individual's life experience is shaped by many factors, such as their social class, personal economic power and level of literacy. This concept has been refined further by an increasing recognition of the significance of gender – at a most basic level, this relates to biological sex and the cultural values attached to it – as well as the ways in which gender interacts with other factors in life experience. It is only relatively recently that historians have begun to view gender roles with a fuller awareness of the concept that 'man' and 'woman', 'male' and 'female', 'masculine' and 'feminine' are not discrete conceits which can be used to label particular human bodies and behaviours, but are derived from context-specific norms. Furthermore, bodies, both real and fictional, can be identified as exhibiting signs of 'gender slippage', a term which implies the adoption of the dress or the performance of a pattern of behaviour which is conventionally associated with a body of a different biological sex.[4] These understandings have wide implications for historians of all periods and specialisms, not only researchers who consciously label themselves as 'gender historians'. This paper examines the application of gender theory to the cult of an overtly 'female' saint, and suggests that the process of viewing various types of evidence, here chiefly hagiographical and art historical, through the lens of gendered readings uncovers a number of intriguing insights into late medieval conceptions of the gender of saints and consequently the gender of men and women too.[5]

The cult of the pseudo-historical St Ursula is centred on Cologne, where she is said to have been martyred with her followers in the late 4th or early 5th century. This cult is worthy of study for many reasons,[6] but our starting point here is that this medieval legend seems anomalous on several levels to the historian of gender. Most obviously, Ursula is identified as a virgin martyr who consented to marriage,[7]

blurring the boundaries between chastity and unchastity in a most effective way, but her credentials as a cross-gendered figure extend well beyond this. For example, Ursula is described in written sources as a royal leader whose followers included her own fiancé and a pope (also pseudo-historical), as well as many thousands of others; a group which was often understood to contain men as well as women.[8] This concept of a female leader with hordes of followers is extremely rare in medieval hagiography, and she is also one of a small number of female saints whose narratives employ travel as a significant motif. As I argue below, this trope is generally identified strongly as a male attribute; above all, she and her virginal female followers are explicitly described with the language appropriate to soldiers,[9] a body of people who are almost exclusively identified as masculine.[10]

These apparent examples of gender slippage reflect aspects both of medieval hagiography and the contemporaneous medieval perception of human gender. We need to be aware of the extent to which saints are constructed: all hagiography, whether written, visual or oral, inevitably privileges some factors within the narrative of an individual's life in order to emphasize their worth as an exemplar, for instance, or perhaps their power as an intercessor. Therefore, the proponents of the cult of St Ursula may have found it expedient to be able to highlight, or even simply invent, aspects of her story which would encourage others to venerate her, or to meet their own personal needs, and some of these emphases seem to have involved portraying her as an authoritative, masculinized figure.[11] Meanwhile, from the viewpoint of gender history, the fact that slippages occur in the understandings of this saint reminds us of the extent to which an insistence on binary gender is overly limiting: St Ursula's ambivalent positioning within a nexus of gender identities indicates very clearly that it is possible for an individual to be neither simply 'male' nor 'female', but demonstrably playing a role which transcends such blunt distinctions. Bringing these two ideas together – the construction of saints and the complexities of gender – it appears that saints' gender roles are particularly prone to this kind of ambivalence, for it allows a demonstration of transcendence above earthly, bodily concerns whilst at the same time permitting the saint to reflect some of the intricacies of real human existence within a socially sanctioned religious milieu.

The complex tale of the princess and martyr Ursula and her 11,000 virgins occurs in a number of varied, and sometimes conflicting, medieval narratives. The legend seems to derive from a 4th or 5th-century epigraph on a stone in the choir of the Church of St Ursula at Cologne,[12] which claims that a ruined basilica was rebuilt in honour of virgins who had been martyred in that place. The developed narrative is focused on St Ursula herself, even though she was a relatively late entrant into the legend of the 11,000 virgins.[13] She is identified as the daughter of a Christian king who is often said to be the ruler of England, Wales or Cornwall.[14] He and his wife were pious but childless, and entreated God to send them an heir. They were duly rewarded with a daughter whom they named Ursula.[15] Her virtue and beauty were universally praised, and this led a powerful pagan king to seek her as the bride for his son and heir, Etherius.[16] Ursula's father was greatly troubled by the request as, while he had no wish to marry his Christian daughter to a worshipper of idols, he was afraid that refusal might offend the king and result in dire consequences for the people of his realm. Ursula then took matters into her own hands: acting on God's inspiration she told her father that she would accept the match, but only on certain conditions. She wished that the wedding should be postponed for three years, during which time she would go on pilgrimage to Rome. She was to be provided with an escort of ten virgins, and each of these as well as Ursula herself were to be given another thousand virgins as companions. Eleven ships were to be built to take them to the continent, and while they were on their travels her future bridegroom was to be instructed in the Christian faith. Terms were agreed, Etherius was baptized, the virgins were assembled and the company set off.[17]

They landed initially at the German port of Tiel, then travelled on to Cologne. Here an angel appeared to Ursula and predicted that all the virgins would return to the city, where they would be martyred. Following the angel's instructions they sailed on to Basel and over the Alps on foot to Rome. There they received the blessing of Pope Cyriacus,[18] who was himself a Briton. That same night the pope was accorded a vision that he would be martyred with the 11,000 virgins; he baptized many of the virgins who had not yet received the sacrament, then renounced his office and ordained his successor.

Meanwhile, Etherius had succeeded to his father's throne. He too received an angelic revelation that instructed him to join Ursula and her companions in order to receive the crown of martyrdom with them at Cologne. As the company approached the city they were attacked by a band of Huns. The entire party was slaughtered, although their chief, dazzled by Ursula's beauty, offered to spare her life if she would marry him. She scorned his offer and was killed by an arrow.

This attenuated version gives some sense of the developed late medieval narrative, but in many ways the most interesting aspects of the story rest in the details of the various retellings, both literary and visual. Most significantly for our purposes, the *Golden Legend* version of the story discusses St Ursula and her virginal colleagues as soldiers, and it is worth examining this part of the story:

> In accordance with the compact, the virgins were assembled and the well-stocked triremes made ready. Now the queen (*suis regina*) [i.e. Ursula] disclosed the secret to those who had become, as it were, her fellow soldiers (*cōmilitonibus*), and all took the oath of this new knighthood (*in novam militiam omnes coniurant*). They engaged in the customary preludes of war. They ran hither and they ran yon. At times, simulating the conditions of war, they pretended to flee the field of battle. They took part in all sorts of contests, trying whatever came to their minds and leaving nothing neglected. Sometimes they came in at midday, sometimes barely before dark. Princes and primates came to witness this unusual spectacle, and all were filled with admiration and joy. Ursula in time converted all the virgins to the faith.[19]

This brief extract provides many interesting comments on the gender roles assigned to Ursula and the 11,000 virgins.

Initially we should note that Ursula is described as a queen: she is not literally a queen within the narrative, for her father is never said to have died, and the term is perhaps used to indicate that she is a female leader in her own right rather than using the reflected agency given to her by a royal husband.[20] It is incontestable that Ursula acted as a figure of authority: she set the conditions for her marriage; she amassed a large body of followers around her, both men and women; she ordered a fleet of boats to be built; she led her virgins in a regimen of training and initiated them into a new knighthood. The conversion of the 11,000 to Christianity can also be interpreted as an act of authority. Furthermore, the overt military references strongly label St Ursula, and indeed her female followers, as masculinized figures: it is hard to interpret the reference to 'this new knighthood' as anything other than a chivalric order, a concept which is strongly masculinized.[21]

The description of the preparations for the journey made by Ursula and the virgins is rather imprecise in the *Golden Legend* version, but at least one artist interpreted this episode to mean training in order to manoeuvre the fleet of boats, which again is a masculinized activity. An extensive cycle of the legend of St Ursula, comprising 30 subjects, commissioned and signed by the brothers Jürgen and Johann van Scheyven and dated 1456, is augmented by inscriptions from a 15th-century verse life of St Ursula. The stanza relating to the image depicting the women engaged in nautical exercises (**Pl. 3**) reads as follows:

> Sy voere spleen off und neder
> Her ind der voirt ind weder
> Dat weerde lange ind manichen dag
> Dad id dye woerlt woll besach.[22]

> They practised steering, moving away and returning, going from here to there, coming and going. They continued this for a long time, for many days, much to the interest of bystanders.

The *Golden Legend* describes St Ursula and her followers as 'fellow soldiers' and members of a 'new knighthood': these naval manoeuvres contribute to a fascinating combination of overtly masculine ideas being applied to a group of women. Furthermore, they are concepts related to a high social status: whilst soldiers and sailors are not necessarily associated with elevated class, the use of the term 'knighthood' does seem to carry this connotation, as does the ability to act as a naval commander.[23] Medieval invocation of the biblical concept of the soldier of Christ armed with the breastplate of righteousness, the shield of faith and the sword of the spirit[24] is well established in association with Christian martyrs generally and soldier-saints such as St George in particular.[25] However, here it is being applied to a group of ostensibly female figures, and clearly extended into a commentary of social position: these are officer-class women, not mere foot soldiers. The ideas being applied to Ursula and her female followers are not just about a 'default' masculinity, but a developed, privileged masculinity which is invariably the hallmark of the supreme gender role. The *Golden Legend* reference to 'princes and primates' watching the women highlights the gender role they are adopting: these men represent this privileged form of masculinity, and they choose to watch, with admiration, a

Plate 3 Panel of nautical manoeuvres, from a cycle of the legend of St Ursula, dated 1456, polychromed wooden panel. St Ursula Basilica, Cologne (photo: Rheinisches Bildarchiv Köln, rba_ d031522_01)

group of women adopting their own gender position. An alternative, or perhaps even simultaneous, interpretation plays on the Charivaresque aspect of the scene as the men's roles are effectively usurped by the women: the world is turned upside down by these 'mere females' taking over the privileged roles of their male audience, something which could provide considerable amusement to the actual spectators of this visual cycle.[26]

This reading of St Ursula and her followers may seem to be undermined to some extent by the description of the women 'simulating the conditions of war ... pretend[ing] to flee the field of battle'. This could indicate a lack of true masculine valour, but another interpretation is that the women were practising making a tactical retreat, perhaps even a feigned retreat where the real intention is to take the enemy by surprise. The Van Scheyven cycle and its accompanying verses indicate that the 'field of battle' is actually the sea. Hence the women are described as 'coming and going': they are practising manoeuvring their boats for different sea and weather conditions and perhaps also to prepare for the eventuality of being attacked by enemies. We should also note that there is no mention of cowardice on the part of the women when they were approaching Cologne for the second time, even though all knew that they were going to be martyred. The one exception was a virgin named Cordula who hid on one of the ships to avoid the massacre.[27] However, her courage rallied the following morning, and she surrendered so that she too could receive the crown of martyrdom: this underlines the bravery of all her companions.

The narrative of St Ursula gives us valuable information about the medieval perception of gender roles, but this information is not always easy to interpret. Although the idea of the medieval woman as a permanent and inevitable second-class citizen with no autonomy has frequently been

exposed as a modern misconception,[28] it is still possible to misread nuances of meaning within specific texts. Here we have a woman behaving with considerable authority, but does this necessarily mean she was viewed by her devotees as some kind of quasi-male? Could they have thought that her authority resided in her role as a royal heiress, her (un)married status or perhaps her virginity? Or was the crucial factor her sanctity? These gender slippages could be interpreted as no more than a *post hoc* invention by (male) hagiographers, with no relation at all to the lives of real medieval men and women. This may be a tempting conclusion to draw, but it seems very unlikely that hagiographers, who were attempting to foster the cult of their favoured saint, would choose to present an image of sanctity which had no relevance to the lives of ordinary people, and it is significant that people would choose to venerate a saint who displayed such obvious forms of gender slippage. However, St Ursula is by no means the only saint whose legend displays this kind of mutability,[29] and it can be argued that it is the very specialness and separateness of sanctity that is marked by the blurring of gender roles, indicating that the saint is transcending normal earthly conventions.

A particularly important comparative figure is St Sunniva,[30] a pseudo-historical Irish princess who succeeded to a kingdom on the death of her father. Like Ursula, she cannot be confidently located to a specific chronology, but her relics were discovered on the Norwegian island of Selja in 996 and a Latin homily, the primary source of her narrative, was written to mark the translation of her relics to Bergen in 1170. Sunniva is said to have refused the marital advances of a pagan tyrant, and in an attempt to evade his wrath she undertook a voyage with many followers, trusting God to bring them to a safe haven. Like St Ursula, St Sunniva is one of a very small number of voyaging female saints: St Mary Magdalene is the best-known example,[31] and it is arguable that this trope is used to masculinize the saints in question. Certainly the motif of travel is commonly associated with male saints, most obviously the apostles,[32] St Brendan and St Columba, and the inclusion of this motif in the hagiography of a few select women – authoritative women at that – tends to underline the fact that these particular saints stand outside conventional models of saintly femininity.

When we turn to the means of St Ursula's martyrdom we find another possible site of gender slippage. I have argued elsewhere that the conventional late medieval narrative, both literary and visual, of female virgin martyrs involves a sequence of different tortures, often involving some degree of sexualization such as a focus on naked flesh.[33] These features are notably absent from St Ursula's narrative: she is killed by a single arrow strike and never seems to be described or depicted in any state of undress. Whilst it would be overly simplistic to claim that an absence of motifs of torture and nudity are sufficient in themselves to challenge a female gender role, they do seem to be indicative of a regendering of St Ursula when they are considered alongside the other 'masculinizing' tropes such as leadership, travel and the use of military and naval imagery. That said, the gendering implications of the motif of the arrow are considerably more complex than a simple masculine/feminine binary: the trope of penetration clearly deserves special attention in the cult of any saint.

St Sebastian, a pseudo-historical soldier first recorded in a martyrology of 354, is the most obvious saint whose hagiographic representation employs the motif of penetration in the form of arrows; another example is St Edmund (c. 840–69), the king of the East Angles who was killed by Danish invaders in a hail of arrows according to several sources. However, in both cases the emphasis on penetration with arrows is part of their construction: as the *Golden Legend* account makes clear,[34] St Sebastian was actually beaten to death at a later point in the narrative, a motif which never seems to be depicted, whilst some accounts of the death of St Edmund omit any reference to arrows.[35] This tends to imply that the trope of the near-naked male body penetrated by arrows that forms the standard iconography of St Sebastian, and also occurs within the cult of St Edmund,[36] is not an inevitable part of the narrative. It is, rather, the product of a deliberate decision which through repetition may at some time have developed into an issue of tradition.

Lances and swords are other obvious ways of penetrating the body, as are the nails of crucifixion. Significantly, penetration of a male body is demonstrably present in some versions of St Ursula's narrative: the death of her fiancé Etherius, pierced by a sword and dying in the arms of his beloved, is recounted in an anonymous text published in 1183,[37] and this episode formed the largest and most significant image (**Pl. 4**) of a 15th-century German cycle of St Ursula featuring at least 19 subjects.[38] In effect, Etherius is given the 'feminized' death that Ursula avoids. We cannot escape the fact that the female body is culturally positioned as inherently penetrable, and is defined as a legitimate site of penetration in a way that the male body rarely has been; the thwarted sexual ambitions of the leader of the Huns are sublimated into the arrow which dispatches the woman who spurns him. The descriptive phrase used by Guy de Tervarent in his redaction of the narrative of St Ursula's death is particularly telling in this context. The leader of the Huns promises to spare the 11,000 if Ursula will agree to marry him: 'Leur chef lui-même, pénétré soudain d'un passion scélérate, jura de par ses dieux…' (Their chief, penetrated by a cunning passion, swore by his gods…).[39] This author, consciously or not, uses sexualized imagery to discuss the motivations of this man, and contrasts his unholy wish to penetrate the virgin with his own penetrability as well as the woman's ultimate submission to a penetration which takes her life, but not her virgin status.

The crux of the issue is that penetration requires two participants (willing or unwilling) – the penetrator and the penetrated. The act of penetration says as much about the active party as the passive. A sexualized reading of the motif – whether homoerotic or heteroerotic – is not inherent but is mapped onto the body of the saint, whether by an artist, writer, reader or spectator. In consequence it is inevitable that the sexualized motif is also mapped onto the action of their assailant. According to this understanding the torturers of Sebastian and the executors of Edmund and Ursula are implicated – and indeed stigmatized – by their

Plate 4 Detail of *The Martyrdom of St Ursula and the 11,000 Virgins* showing the death of Etherius, with St Ursula supporting him, c. 1492, oil on canvas, 163.3 x 232.4cm. Victoria and Albert Museum, London (5938-1857) (© Victoria and Albert Museum, London)

penetrative acts. The sexual role being constructed is only in part concerned with the passive bodies of the martyrs; the actions of their assailants are also strongly negatively sexualized, though necessarily through sublimated forms of sexual activity in order both to preserve the chastity of the martyrs and also to indicate their ultimate victory over the flesh.

All saints, particularly martyrs, are constructed to reflect the life and passion of Christ. He is a site of penetration by nails and a lance,[40] and it is perhaps surprising that so few saints are strongly connected to clearly penetrative imagery. However, if we cast our net a little wider, it swiftly becomes apparent that any form of torture which breaches the boundaries of the body – flagellation, flaying, assault with hooks, combs or knives and indeed the beheading which is the culmination of most martyrdom stories – can be seen to compromise the gender role of both the passive victim and the active perpetrator. This is not a simple feminine/masculine dichotomy, nor even one which relies upon exclusively homoerotic or heteroerotic readings, but a complex understanding where corporeal aggression, most easily coded by a phallic intrusion into the body, is represented in contrast to spiritual resistance and transcendence over the fragility of human flesh.

The beautiful St Ursula and her followers, as represented in the reliquary shown in **Plate 1**, combine aspects of several different gender roles, some of which they share with ostensibly male saints whose masculinity was by no means a simple matter. The gendering of these figures, through the appearance and activities ascribed to them, tends to have little to do with any historical reality which these saints may have experienced. However, it certainly offers an alternate reading of the formula of 'saints as exemplars' – following the example offered by these saints may have been easier said than done for readers, listeners and viewers destined to live in the real world. It is impossible to be definitive about the perceptions of the contemporary audiences of these late medieval texts and images: these gender slippages and other deviations from convention may have been intended to indicate to 15th-century devotees that saints were simply above such earthly concerns.

Notes

1   Grateful thanks are due to Maria Craciun, who invited me to speak at the conference 'The Cult of Saints in Eastern and Central Europe (1400–1800)' in September 2003; Maria subsequently encouraged me to develop my thinking on St Ursula on the basis of my conference paper, 'The performance of gender through saints' cults: virgins, cross-dressers and societal norms'. I would also like to thank Robert Mills and Sarah Salih for their perceptive comments on drafts of this text, and Johanna Gummlich-Wagner of the Rheinisches Bildarchiv for her assistance in procuring **Plate 4** and clarifying the authorship of this image.

2   The exhibition *Treasures of Heaven: Saints, Relics and Devotion in Medieval Europe* was held at the British Museum from 23 June–9 October 2011.

3   This is not to say that medieval people did not read piety and virtue into these images. Scott Montgomery notes that the Dominican friar Giovanni Dominici encouraged the placement of images of the 11,000 virgins in the home where little girls could see them, and observes that they were 'exemplary figures of feminine virtue': Montgomery 2010, 43. It is arguable that Montgomery may be understating the true significance to Dominici and his contemporaries of the utility of such images in engendering particular attitudes and behaviours in young girls.

4   Cross dressing – adopting clothing which is usually associated with the 'opposite' sex – is one of the most obvious sites of gender slippage, but there are many other potential loci; context is deeply significant. Thus some activities, such as women preaching or men looking after small children, *may* be constructed as counter to the biological sex of the body performing the act – this will depend on the time and place where the action is carried out.

5   A good starting point for further information on theorizing medieval gender roles is Partner 1993.

6   The most recent scholarly discussion of the cult of St Ursula is Montgomery 2010. See also Zehnder 1985: this work provides a useful bibliography.

7   St Ursula is not the only identifiable virgin saint who agreed to marriage, but this is a rare phenomenon. St Cecilia, another pseudo-historical virgin martyr, is perhaps the most obvious comparative example. Her legend displays other aspects of gender slippage too, including masculinized behaviour, such as conversion, and the description of her husband and brother-in-law's deaths: their souls '[went] forth like virgins from the bridal chamber'. For the narrative of St Cecilia see: de Voragine 1993, vol. II, 318–23; the quotation is at p. 322. Latin quotations given in the text of this paper are derived from a version of the *Legenda Aurea* (1504) held at the National Library of Scotland, clxviii–clxix.

8   The gendering of large crowds is a fascinating topic that cannot be explored here due to limitation of space. However, it is worth bearing in mind that biblical crowds, such as the 5,000 fed with the five loaves and two fish, are almost always explicitly male, with women and children not counted amongst the number. The fact of the numbering (and naming) of the virgins can in itself be seen as a masculinizing trope. Grateful thanks to Bob Mills for setting me on this track.

9   Military language is employed in the *Golden Legend* narrative (c. 1260) of St Ursula: de Voragine 1993, vol. II, 256–60, at p. 257. This is not an isolated case: Sabine Baring-Gould notes that the Chronicle of Sigebert of Gemblours (d. 1112) speaks of 'the most famous of wars...waged by the white-robed army of the eleven thousand holy virgins, under their leader, the virgin Ursula': Baring-Gould 1914, vol. 12, 539.

10 There are a few examples of female saints who are described as physically fighting, such as St Perpetua (d. 203) who took part in a gladiatorial contest, and the legend of the Amazonians was well known in late medieval Europe, but imagery or discussion of female soldiers who are explicitly Christian is extremely rare in in that period. St Joan of Arc (d. 1431) was an actual medieval female Christian soldier, of course, but it is important to remember that she was strongly masculinized by her dress and actions. For example, her refusal to wear women's clothing was repeatedly discussed during her trial for witchcraft and heresy: Schibanoff 1996.

11 For a comparative example of what seems to be a conscious masculinization of images of a female saint, see Winstead 2003.

12 For the early history of the cult of St Ursula, see Kristin Hoefner's chapter in this book.

13 The development of the cult of the 11,000 virgins, and the eventual identification of Ursula as the leader, is described very clearly in Montgomery 2010.

14 The near-total absence of any cult of St Ursula in pre-Reformation Britain suggests that any connection to this country is purely speculative. Indeed, even Geoffrey of Monmouth's narrative of the 11,000 virgins in his *History of the Kings of Britain*, c. 1136, which claims them as English, is likely to reflect a Germanic tradition, perhaps passed on via a colony of merchants from Cologne which is recorded in London from the 10th century. Harben 1918, 598; Geoffrey of Monmouth 1966, 141–2.

15 The *Golden Legend* does not provide a gloss of the name of this saint, perhaps because this account is entitled 'The Eleven Thousand Virgins', in keeping with the earliest forms of the narrative. At least one version of the narrative, the *Regnante Domino*, indicates that the name Ursula was chosen because it was believed that the new baby would one day strangle the Devil, as King David had once wrestled with a bear – Ursula is a form of the Latin for 'little bear'. For the *Regnante Domino* see *Acta Sanctorum* 1869, 157.

16 The 12th-century 'discovery' of a tombstone of a man named Etherius in the necropolis at Cologne led to this name being given to Ursula's previously anonymous fiancé. The carved inscription seems to be contemporary with its finding, and this tends to suggest that it was produced to meet the needs of the growing cult. De Tervarent 1931, 23ff, 26.

17 Jacobus makes it clear that the virgins were accompanied by men from the outset of their journey, including a number of bishops, as well as at least one matron with her children: De Voragine 1993, vol. II, 257. This accords with the need to account for the presence of the bones of men and children amongst the Cologne relics.

18 The absence of papal records of Cyriacus is explained by the outrage of the Roman cardinals at his decision to abdicate his office in favour of the pursuit of a group of virgins – they excised his name from their lists when he went off 'with a lot of silly women': De Voragine 1993, vol. II, 258.

19 De Voragine 1993, vol. II, 257.

20 St Katherine of Alexandria provides a parallel identification as a ruler in her own right. She is also strongly defined as a figure of authority, defeating 50 philosophers in debate amongst other achievements. On St Katherine see Lewis 2000; Jenkins and Lewis 2003.

21 It seems to have been very rare for women to have been admitted into medieval chivalric orders. The Order of the Garter (founded 1347–8) did admit women, but they do not seem to have been granted full membership status. See Riches 2000, 108.

22 De Tervarent 1931, 73.

23 Despite the use of military language in the *Golden Legend* it is clear from the narrative of voyaging that the virgins are actually sailors rather than soldiers. The (mis)use of the concept of knighthood in relation to sailors probably reflects the author's wish to demonstrate the privileged status of the women: there seems to be no naval equivalent for the concept of a chivalric order. The elision between military and naval terminology also results from the bluntness of language as a semantic tool, in the same way as the complexities of gender roles are so difficult to express linguistically.

24 This formulation is based on Ephesians 6, 13–17.

25 Riches 2000, 22. See also Lewis 1995, 276.

26 The concept of Charivari originally relates to the mocking serenade given to newly married couples in parts of medieval Europe, especially to show disapproval of an unequal match or the too-hasty remarriage of a widow. By extension, it can be used to indicate humorous discussion of gender roles. I am indebted to Catherine Lawless for this observation.

27 De Voragine 1993, vol. II, 259.

28 To cite but one example, in 1448 the Englishwoman Margaret Paston wrote to her husband John asking him to send to her not only almonds and sugar, but also crossbows, bolts, poleaxes and protective clothing. These items were needed because Margaret was leading a number of servants in the protection of the Paston property from the threats of an aggrieved and powerful neighbour, Lord Moleyns, during her husband's absence in London on business. British Library, London, Add. MS 34888, f. 29; published in Davies 1971.

29 Pressure of space does not allow a full enumeration of examples, but interested readers are invited to consider St Katherine of Alexandria and St George as examples of saints whose legends and iconography clearly display gender slippage. See nn. 11, 20 and 33 for indicative reading.

30 St Sunniva is strikingly similar to St Ursula in several respects, not least in that her cult is primarily associated with the place where she died whilst she is largely ignored in the place where she is supposed to have originated from. Hence, Sunniva is an Irish princess venerated in Norway, whilst Ursula is an English (or Welsh or Cornish) princess whose veneration is centred on Cologne and is mainly attested in Central and Eastern Europe. Likewise, both saints' legends seem to have been invented as a result of a need to give an identity to relics: the remains of Sunniva and her followers were found on the island of Selja whilst Ursula and the 11,000 virgins were discovered at Cologne. Another point of comparison is with the version of the legend of the 11,000 virgins used by Geoffrey of Monmouth (see above, n. 14): Geoffrey's rationale for the women's journey is markedly different to that conventionally presented in the legend associated with St Ursula, for he writes of a band of 11,000 English noblewomen (plus 60,000 from the lower orders) destined to be married to the army of Britons who had conquered Armorica (an archaic name for Brittany), whilst the more popular form maintains that only St Ursula herself was to be married. There is no mention in Geoffrey's account of a three-year voyage culminating at Cologne: the massacre is located on islands where the women are driven by a storm. St Sunniva and her followers were also overcome by a storm and suffered shipwreck followed by death; the company died when a cave collapsed onto them, which is interpreted as an act of deliverance by God to protect them from a worse fate at the hands of Hakon, jarl of Hladir (a reference which locates the story to 995–1000). Geoffrey's tale does not indicate that the 11,000 virgins died in quite this way, but it is notable that both stories involve shipwreck on offshore islands and an untraditional martyrdom. On St Sunniva see: O'Hara 2004 and Baring-Gould 1914, 543; On Geoffrey of Monmouth's version see Geoffrey of Monmouth 1966, 141–2 and Tatlock 1950, 236–41.

31 St Mary Magdalene is another example of a female saint who was in part constructed to stand outside the conventions of feminine behaviour, although unfortunately this aspect of her cult is largely overlooked in much recent scholarship on this saint, such as Haskins 1993.

32 The Middle English term 'apostylesse' was used, apparently exclusively, in relation to St Mary Magdalene. This feminization highlights the understanding that apostolicism, a highly public, visible act which tends to include authoritative activity such as preaching and travel, is an inherently masculine activity. See Salih 2002, 127.

33 I have used this model as a means of discussing the emasculinization of St George, whose martyrdom narrative accords far more closely to those of female virgin martyrs, such as Sts Catherine, and Barbara, than those of other male saints. See Riches 2002, 65–85.

34 De Voragine 1993, vol. I, 100.

35 Sources which describe St Edmund's death are divided over the manner of his demise. John Lydgate is an example of a writer who compares the body of the saint to 'an yrchoun fulfillid with spynys thikke' (a hedgehog covered with spines), whilst Symeon of Durham is one of a number of authors who make no reference to arrows, noting simply that the Danes 'killed the most holy king Edmund, on whom had been inflicted various tortures (*diuersis penis laceratum*)'. These differences of approach tend to reinforce the contention that different conceptions of martyrdom could be equally applicable to the same saint, and that the invocation of a specific motif of torture may have resulted from a conscious decision on the part of a hagiographer who wished to highlight a particular meaning encoded within some aspect of the saint's life or death. St Edmund's virginity may well be the issue which the arrow motif was intended to emphasize: Lydgate calls him 'Blyssyd Edmu[n]d / kyng martir and vyrgyne'. See Horstmann 1881, 376, 410; Symeon of Durham 2000, text p. 98, translation p. 99.

36 For example, the 14th-century wall painting of the martyrdom of St Edmund at Stoke Dry (Northamptonshire) depicts him bound to a tree wearing only a skirt-like garment and his crown, his naked torso filled with arrows.

37 Two records of anonymous revelations followed on from those of St Elizabeth of Schönau (d. 1165), which were tremendously significant in 'authenticating' the large number of relics found in Cologne. The individuals most associated with these anonymous revelations are the Blessed Hermann Joseph (d. 1241) and Richard of Whitchurch. Both men were Premonstratensian canons, at Steinfeld and Arnsberg respectively, although Richard was actually an Englishman. Their affiliation may be connected to the fact that St Norbert, founder of the Premonstratensian order, was strongly associated with the cult of St Ursula and the 11,000 virgins, and is known to have collected some of the 'relics' during a visit to Cologne in 1123: Baring-Gould 1914, 549.

38 This image, painted on canvas and now in the Victoria and Albert Museum, London, is the primary focus of Kauffmann 1964.

39 De Tervarent 1931, 6.

40 However, we should be wary of assuming that any act of penetration necessarily stigmatizes the perpetrator. An interesting variation on the theme of the sexual aggressor penetrating a passive body is to be found in the Rothschild Canticles (*c.* 1320), fols 18v–19r: in this image a woman holds a lance aligned with the wound in Christ's side. This image is known as 'The *sponsa* penetrates Christ's side', although the act of penetration is perhaps implied rather than explicit. Its significance has been discussed by a number of authors; most recently Robert Mills proposed it as an example of the potential for elision and mobility in the gender roles of both the depicted – the penetrating woman and Christ – and the spectator. In this context, however, it is worth noting that it is by no means a *negative* image: Christ is presented as an active participant, welcoming his 'wife' into his body, and this reinforces the impression that the reading of gender roles, and the significance of tropes of penetration, is a complex business. See Mills 2002, 160–2.

Bibliography

Acta Sanctorum 1869. October, vol. IX, Paris and Rome, 157–63.

Baring-Gould, S. 1914. *The Lives of the Saints*, Edinburgh.

Davies, N. (ed.) 1971. *Paston Letters and Papers of the Fifteenth Century*, Oxford.

De Tervarent, G. 1931. *La Légende de Sainte Ursule dans la littérature et l'art du moyen age*, Paris.

De Voragine, J. 1504. *Legenda Aurea*, Lyon.

De Voragine, J. 1993. *The Golden Legend*, ed. and trans. W. Granger Ryan, Princeton.

Geoffrey of Monmouth 1966. *The History of the Kings of Britain*, ed. and trans. L. Thorpe, Harmondsworth.

Harben, H.A. 1918. *A Dictionary of London*, London.

Haskins, S. 1993. *Mary Magdalen: Myth and Metaphor*.

Horstmann, C. 1881. *Altenglische Legenden Neue Folge*, Heilbronn.

Jenkins, J. and Lewis, K.J. (eds) 2003, *St Katherine of Alexandria. Texts and Contexts in Western Medieval Europe*, Turnhout.

Kauffmann, C.M. 1964. *The Legend of St Ursula*, London.

Lewis, K.J. 2000. *The Cult of St Katherine of Alexandria in Late Medieval England*, Woodbridge.

Lewis, S. 1995. *Reading Images. Narrative Discourse and Reception in the Thirteenth-Century Illuminated Apocalypse*, Cambridge.

Mills, R. 2002. 'Ecce Homo', in Riches and Salih 2002, 152–73.

Montgomery, S.B. 2010. *St Ursula and the Eleven Thousand Virgins of Cologne. Relics, Reliquaries and the Visual Culture of Group Sanctity in Late Medieval Europe*, Oxford.

O'Hara, A.J. 2004. 'Papar, princesses and Cistercians. The construction of an Irish saint in twelfth-century Norway', unpublished MA dissertation, University of St Andrews.

Partner, N.F. (ed.) 1993. *Studying Medieval Women: Sex, Gender, Feminism*, Cambridge, MA.

Riches, S. 2000. *St George. Hero, Martyr and Myth*, Stroud.

Riches, S. 2002. 'St George as a male virgin martyr', in Riches and Salih 2002, 65–85.

Riches, S.J.E. and Salih, S. (eds) 2002. *Gender and Holiness. Men, Women and Saints in Late Medieval Europe*, London.

Salih, S. 2002. 'Staging conversion. The Digby saint plays and *The Book of Margery Kempe*', in Riches and Salih 2002, 121–34.

Schibanoff, S. 1996. 'True lies: transvestism and idolatry in the trial of Joan of Arc', in *Fresh Verdicts on Joan of Arc*, ed. B. Wheeler and C.T. Wood, New York, 31–60.

Symeon of Durham 2000. *Libellus de exordio atque procursu istius, hoc est Dunhelmensis, ecclesie: Tract on the Origins and Progress of this the Church of Durham*, ed. and trans. D. Rollason, Oxford.

Tatlock, J.S.P. 1950. *The Legendary History of Britain. Geoffrey of Monmouth's Historia Regum Britanniae and its Early Vernacular Versions*, Berkeley.

Winstead, K.A. 2003. 'St Katherine's Hair', in *St Katherine of Alexandria. Texts and Contexts in Western Medieval Europe*, ed. J. Jenkins and K.J. Lewis, Turnhout, 171–200.

Zehnder, F.G. 1985. *Sankt Ursula. Legende – Verehrung – Bilderwelt*, Cologne.

Chapter 19
Embodying the Saint
Mystical Visions, *Maria Lactans* and the Miracle of Mary's Milk[1]

Vibeke Olson

Make the fountain of life flow into my mouth: whence the living waters take their rise and flow forth. All ye who thirst, come to her: she will willingly give you to drink from her fountain. He who drinketh from her, will spring forth into life everlasting: and he will never thirst . . .

St Bonaventure, Psalm 81, Psalter of the Blessed Virgin Mary[2]

In his *Ave Maria* motet of *circa* 1484, Josquin des Prez (*c.* 1450–1521) added a new concluding sentiment to the close of the traditional angelic salutation: 'Et benedicta sint beata ubera tua, quae lactaverunt regem regum et Dominum noster' ('and blessed be your holy breasts which nursed the king of kings, our lord God').[3] Josquin's modification of the popular hymn to address Mary's breasts and her nursing of the infant Christ is but one example of the veritable obsession the Middle Ages had with Mary's breasts and the milk they produced. From the abundance of images of Mary suckling the infant Christ, mystical visions of nursing or being nursed, accounts of miracles attributed to her milk, miracles as a form of *imitatio*, prayers and poems celebrating Mary's breasts and milk to reliquaries containing the precious substance, one could say the period was quite literally awash in Marian milk.[4]

While devotion to the cult of the Virgin was a spiritual staple throughout the Middle Ages it was not without its challenges, the most problematic of which, from a devotional standpoint, was the lack of her corporeal remains. Like her son, she was assumed bodily into heaven leaving no physical remains behind to be seen or touched. Thus she was venerated *in absentia*, and as a result tremendous significance was placed on her images, on visions of her or on items in some way associated with her life here on earth – her girdle, her hair, her shift and of course her milk.[5] Of these remains, her milk was by far the substance most frequently invoked in prayers, referred to in images and experienced in visions because, as I aim to show, it had the capacity to evoke a tangible encounter involving the senses of sight, touch and taste.[6] In this paper, I will consider the various strategies employed by those who sought the Virgin's physical presence through the study of how relics intersect with image, text and vision. In doing so, it will become clear that Mary's milk was not only the unifying feature of these devotional strategies, but also the catalyst for a dynamic, sensory and interactive devotional experience. In particular, I will focus on milk as the reward for piety, the ingestion of milk for healing purposes, as well as the miraculous production of milk.

Milk relics

In order to appreciate the extent of the cult of the Virgin and her milk, one must begin by considering the sheer number of milk relics themselves. John Calvin (1509–64), in his *Treatise on Relics* (1543), mocked those relics purporting to be the Virgin's milk stating, 'With regard to the milk, there is perhaps not a town, convent, or nunnery where it is not shown in large or small quantities. Indeed, had the Virgin been a wet-nurse her whole life, or a dairy, she could not have produced more than is shown as hers in various parts.'[7] While Calvin's statement was intended as a criticism on the cult of relics in the medieval Catholic church, it does in fact draw attention to the number of milk relics that existed in the Middle Ages. For instance, several churches in Rome claimed possession of drops of Mary's milk,[8] among them a crystal phial containing her milk at Santa Maria Maggiore,[9] and a vessel of milk 'of wonderful whiteness' among the treasures of the Sancta Sanctorum.[10] Other milk relics were said to be in the collections of St Mark's in Venice, the Church of the Celestines in Avignon and St Anthony's in Padua,[11] as well as the cathedrals of Chartres and Toulon.[12] Mary's milk could also be found among the relics contained in the Arca Santa in Oviedo,[13] in the collection of the treasury of Saint-Denis in Paris,[14] and as part of the small collection on the gable-end of the reliquary shrine of St Oda now housed in the British Museum.[15] In his *De pignoribus Sanctorum*, a treatise on the veneration of relics, Guibert of Nogent (*c.* 1055–1124) mentions that some of Mary's milk was kept in a dove made of crystal at Laon Cathedral,[16] and according to Erasmus (1466–1536), a relic of Mary's milk was also kept at Walsingham, where it was placed on the high altar.[17] A relic of the Virgin's milk was processed every August on the feast of the Assumption at Cluny[18] and according to Robert du Mont, her milk was carried by bishops in a pyx at the head of the army during the Battle of Ascalon in 1124.[19] Louis IX received a milk relic from the imperial treasury at Constantinople on behalf of Baldwin II around 1240 and Pope Adrian was credited with sending a milk relic to Reims.[20] Also in France, Harduin, a 7th-century bishop of Le Mans, was said to have received some milk of the Virgin from a pilgrim who had returned from the Holy Land.[21]

Plate 1 Gerard David, *Madonna with Child*, c. 1490, oil on oak, 42 x 35.5 cm. Gemäldegalerie, Berlin (Inv. No. 537A) (photo © bpk, Berlin/Gemäldegalerie, Staatliche Museen, Berlin, Germany/Jörg P. Anders/Art Resource, NY)

Milk relics were common souvenirs brought back from visits to the Holy Land and the source of most of these relics was likely the *Crypta Lactea* (Milk Grotto) in Bethlehem. According to legend, Mary spilled some of her milk on the floor of the grotto while nursing the infant Jesus.[22] Earth, scraped from the walls and floor of the grotto and then pulverized, was referred to as the milk of the Virgin and one source tells us that cakes made from this powder were distributed throughout the Holy Land and sold to pilgrims as souvenirs.[23] This no doubt accounts, at least in part, for the incredible volume of milk relics claimed by medieval treasuries.

Why milk?

While the quantity of Marian milk attests to its popularity as a relic, it does not begin to address the reason for the obsession with her milk more so than say her hair or any other physical object she may have left behind. To be sure, it is a reference to her singular role as the mother of Christ; after all it was her milk that first nourished him in his incarnate form. As such, it has a direct connection to the physical being of Christ himself.[24] From the perspective of medieval medical understanding, a mother's blood nourished and formed the foetus in the womb and was transformed after birth into milk via a lacteal duct, which connected womb to breast.[25] Thus, as Barbara Lane has shown, Mary's milk could be understood in a Eucharistic sense, as a symbolic referent to Christ's blood.[26] Without a doubt, these direct connections to Christ's physical person aided in the wide dissemination of milk relics and the popularity of the cult of the Virgin's milk. However, I believe yet another factor needs to be taken into consideration and that is the very nature of milk itself as a consumable and exudative substance, a subject Caroline Walker Bynum has studied in her work.[27] In several of the images, visions and miracles I consider in this essay, milk is presented with the intent that it should be consumed. This I argue is a key factor in evoking an absent saint. Christ's body, which like Mary's was absent, could be physically evoked through the miracle of the transubstantiation of wine and host in the celebration of the Mass. For Mary, however, no such ritual existed. Nevertheless, I would assert that Mary's milk, like Christ's sacrificial blood, was something that could be partaken of, or even in some cases miraculously produced, even if only in an imagined or visionary experience. For that reason, it was not only a powerful devotional object that could be seen and touched, but also and perhaps more importantly it was a concrete manifestation of her physical being by means of its ingestibility and miraculous appearances, and the idea that devotees could quite literally embody the saint within themselves.

Milk of the mother

What then were some of the strategies used by devotees who sought to invoke the Virgin's physical presence through her milk? On par with the plethora of milk relics are the numerous images of the *Maria lactans*, particularly those in which we see supplicants receiving her milk or Mary offering her breast and milk to the spectator (**Pl. 1**). In his work on visionaries and images, Jeffrey Hamburger has

Plate 2 Master IAM von Zwoll, *The Lactation of St Bernard*, c. 1480–5, engraving, 320 x 241mm. Amsterdam, Rijksmuseum, Rijksprentenkabinet (inv. no. RP-P-OB-1093) (photo by permission of the Rijksmuseum, Amsterdam)

Plate 3 *Virgin Mary and Christ Child*, Book of Hours, Rouen, France, c. 1500. Pierpont Morgan Library (MS M.151, fol. 78v) (photo by permission of The Pierpont Morgan Library, NY)

highlighted the important role that images played as aids to personal devotion.[28] Images were a highly effective means not only for focusing one's prayers, but also for prompting visions and miracles. Just as relics were sources of direct and personal contact with a saint, images were a means to miraculous and visionary experiences through the contemplation of a likeness of the saint, and in our case also through a signifier for the relic itself, Mary's breast. The connection becomes quite clear when we consider images such as those representing the miraculous lactation of St Bernard of Clairvaux (1090–1153). Legend informs us that once, while reciting the *Ave Maris Stella* prayer before a statue of the Virgin and Child, Bernard spoke the words: 'Monstra te esse matrem' ('show yourself to be a mother') at which point the statue promptly came to life and sprinkled three drops of her milk into the mouth of the saint (**Pl. 2**).[29] In return for his devotion, Bernard was rewarded not only with the living manifestation of the Virgin and Child, but also an interactive experience, complete with the opportunity to see, feel and taste. Devotion before the image of the nursing Virgin produced a vision and a tangible, imbibable encounter with that popular item of Marian veneration, her milk.

Milk of salvation

One principle aim of relic veneration was salvation, and many scholars have argued that references to the lactating Virgin are expressions of her mercy and her role as a *mediatrix* in humanity's quest for deliverance.[30] Beth Williamson, for instance, in her study of the *lactans* motif has

clearly associated it with the Virgin's intercession. According to Williamson, it was Mary's motherhood above all that made her intercession especially effective.[31] I would also add that the offering of her milk, the very substance of her efficacy, is further potent and tangible proof of her mercy and mediation.

Accordingly, pursuit of the Virgin's mercy through her physical appearance and the receipt of her milk is a commonly found devotional strategy, particularly in conjunction with prayers to the Virgin. An interesting conflation of the representation of Mary as heavenly intercessor with a visionary experience of praying before her image and receiving her milk can be seen in a miniature from a late 15th-century French Book of Hours that prefaces the *Fifteen Joys of the Virgin* (**Pl. 3**). The prayer begins as follows: 'Sweet lady of mercy, mother of pity, fountain of all that is good, who carried Jesus Christ nine months in your precious womb and who nursed him with your sweet breasts.'[32] The miniature depicts the owner of the book, kneeling in supplication before the Virgin and Child, illustrating the line in the prayer, which reads: 'and I kneel 15 times in front of your blessed image'. The child in her arms does not suckle; instead the Virgin expresses a stream of milk directly towards the kneeling supplicant in a manner reminiscent of Bernard's vision and likely alluding to that event. Once again, an image is venerated, it comes to life and the devotee is rewarded not only with the Virgin's mercy, but moreover with a tangible sensory experience through the consumption of her milk. Similarly, in an

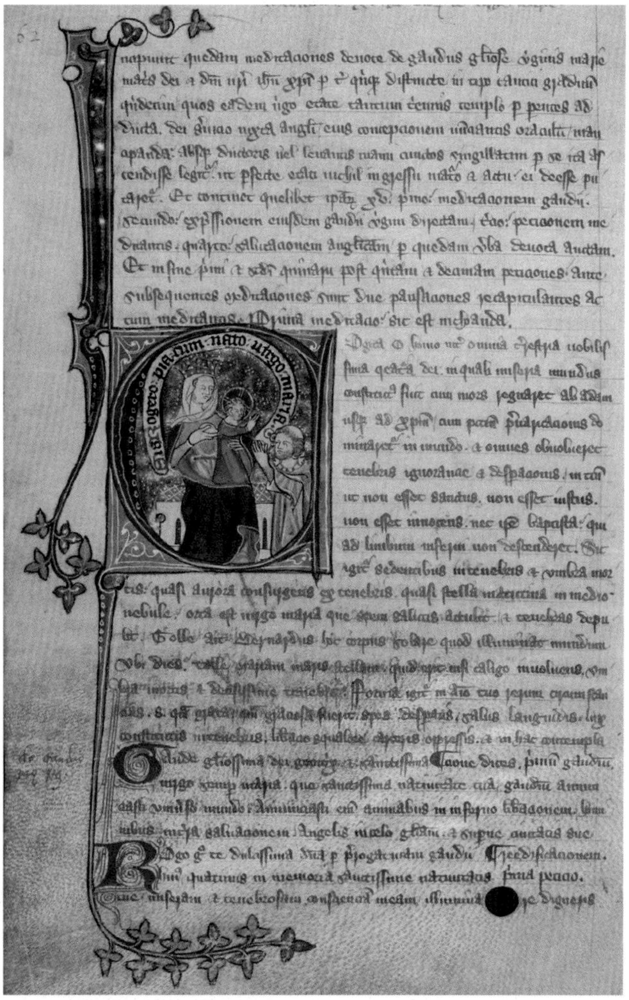

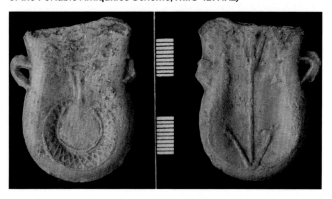

Plate 4 Roger of Waltham before the Virgin and Child in an historiated initial accompanying Stephen of Salley's *Meditations on the XV Joys of the Blessed Virgin Mary Devotional and Philosophical Miscellany*, produced between 1299 and 1399. Glasgow University Library (MS Hunter 231, p. 62)

historiated initial accompanying Stephen of Salley's (d. 1252) *Meditations on the Fifteen Joys of the Blessed Virgin Mary*, we find an image once again of the book's owner, Roger of Waltham (d. 1336), kneeling before the Virgin and Child (**Pl. 4**). The Virgin proffers her breast not to the infant, but instead to Roger, offering him a taste of her milk. A line from the sixth meditation reads: 'But, more fortunate still is the Virgin, chosen not only to contain in her womb God, the Container of all things, but also to fondle him at her bosom, to hold

Plate 5 Lead ampulla from Walsingham depicting the phial containing the relic of the Holy Milk, late 14th–early 16th century (photo courtesy of the Portable Antiquities Scheme, NMS-1BA4A2)

him in sweet embrace, to kiss his holy lips and to comfort him with her breasts filled from heaven.'[33] In this case, however, it is Roger not the infant who will shortly be comforted by a taste of the heavenly contents of Mary's breasts as a reward for his piety.

Medicinal milk

While the gift of Mary's milk might be an acknowledgement of her willingness to intercede on a penitent's behalf, another, perhaps more immediate motivation for the veneration of Mary's milk was for healing the sick.[34] For instance, Rachel Fulton has noted that Marian miracle stories show Marian devotion as largely functional and primarily focused on rescue and healing.[35] In our case, the rescue and healing incurred were the direct result of contact with Mary's milk, particularly through ingestion. The medicinal properties of the Virgin's milk are clearly elucidated by John Lydgate (*c.* 1370–*c.* 1451) in his *Life of Our Lady* (1416–22): 'For in that licour was full remedye, Holy refute, and pleynly medycyne',[36] as well as by Petrarch who made reference to 'the flask of the Virgin's milk [in the Sancta Sanctorum] by which so many had been restored to health'.[37] Further, Susan Signe Morrison has shown that women who made the pilgrimage to Walsingham could purchase ampullae (**Pl. 5**) filled with water and drops of the Virgin's milk to be ingested for healing purposes, as too were the scrapings obtained from the Milk Grotto.[38] However, not all of the cures provided by Mary's milk were the result of ingesting the contents of a pilgrim's ampulla; in some instances Mary's milk was received directly through physical interaction with her in a vision. In one account, a sick nun from Töss nursed at the breast of the Virgin and was cured,[39] and in another the ailing Lukardis of Oberweimar (d. 1309) had a vision of the Virgin nursing the Child and asked to be suckled by her.[40] But it was not just women who were cured through the ingestion of Mary's milk, men also benefitted. In fact, most of the miracle accounts indicate that men were the primary recipients of her healing milk. For example, Vincent of Beauvais (*c.* 1190–1264?), in his *Speculum historiale*, tells of a sick cleric who was nursed by the Virgin.[41] Further, in a group of eight 13th-century collections of Marian legends, the miracles effected on men by the Virgin's milk are the most numerous.[42] In an historiated initial from the *Hornby Hours* (**Pl. 6**), we see an image of just such a miracle: an ailing monk is miraculously cured by the appearance of the Virgin who expresses her milk directly onto him. A similar story, as recorded by Gautier de Coincy in 1223, states: 'With much sweetness and delight, from her sweet bosom she drew forth her breast, that is so sweet, so soft, so beautiful, and placed it in his mouth, [and] gently touched him all about and sprinkled him with her sweet milk.'[43] Among the more common of these miracle stories were the healing of a monk with an ulcerated face, the healing of a delusional monk, the healing of a leprous hermit and the healing of Fulbert (*c.* 960–1028), bishop of Chartres (1006–28).[44] According to the legend, Fulbert was particularly dedicated to the Virgin and would invoke her as *protectrix* during his prayers, specifically asking her to care for various parts of his body, for example his veins, teeth, throat, jaw, chest and so forth.[45]

Plate 6 Miracle of the Virgin's Milk being given to a monk from a Book of Hours, *Use of Sarum* (The 'Neville of Hornby Hours'), 2nd quarter of the 14th century, possibly the 4th decade, illuminated manuscript. The British Library, London (MS Egerton 2781, fol. 24v.) (photo © British Library Board)

Plate 7 Crib of the Infant Jesus, 15th century, wood, polychromy, lead, silver-gilt, painted parchment, silk embroidery with seed pearls, gold thread and translucent enamels, 35.4 x 28.9 x 18.4cm. Metropolitan Museum of Art, New York (photo © The Metropolitan Museum of Art /Art Resource, NY)

So dedicated was he in fact, that when he fell gravely ill, in return for his devotion the Virgin appeared and gave to him her milk whereupon he was miraculously healed.[46] Subsequently, he collected three drops of milk that were left behind and placed them in a splendid reliquary.[47] By doing so, one might imagine that he hoped others could receive the same miraculous healing by means of the Virgin's milk as he had done.

Like Fulbert, others prayed to the Virgin to invoke her curative abilities. One such prayer was written by Anselm of Lucca (d. 1086) for countess Matilda of Tuscany (1046–1115): 'Deign, most merciful lady, to apply your health-giving hands to my pains and the remedy of your purifying to my wounds . . ..'[48] One could easily imagine such prayers recited by a supplicant before either a relic of Mary's milk or an image of *Maria lactans* with the hope of incurring his or her very own lactation miracle.

Visionary milk

Such an assumption is not so far fetched as we have evidence that mystical visions involving milk and lactation were brought about through interaction with images as we have already encountered with Bernard. In another such example, Blessed Paula of Florence (d. 1368) also followed

Bernard's example when she experienced a vision while contemplating an image of the Virgin suckling the Christ Child. In her vision, the nursing Virgin appeared to her and the child allowed a few drops of his mother's milk to fall onto Paula's lips.[49] Others, however, had much more dynamic interactions which reflect a kind of Marian *imitatio* whereby the visionary, placing herself in the role of Mary, suckles and delivers the milk.[50] For example, the mystic Margaretha Ebner (1291–1351) tells of her experience interacting with a cradle (perhaps one similar to **Pl. 7**), and a small figure of the Christ Child: 'I have an image of the Child, our Lord, in a cradle. I was so powerfully compelled by my Lord with great sweetness, longing and desire and also by his request because it was said to me by my Lord, "if you don't give me to suckle, then I will take myself away at the moment you love me most". So I took the image out of the cradle and laid it on my bare breast with great longing and sweetness and felt the strangest possible grace in the presence of the Lord . . . my longing and my desire is to nurse the Christ Child . . . .'[51] In her vision, Margaretha casts herself as Mary fully embodying her presence through the act of nursing.

In many cases, such visions and imitations were stimulated not only by images but also by texts, particularly devotional manuals such as the *Meditations on the Life of Christ*, which encouraged readers to imagine themselves as participants in the events about which they were reading: 'Kiss the beautiful little feet of the infant in your arms and delight in him. You may freely do this . . . [he] will patiently let himself be touched by you as you wish . . . Then return him to the mother and watch her attentively as she cares for him . . . nursing him . . . and remain to help her if you can.'[52] This connection can be seen with the 14th-century visionary Adelheid Langmann (1306–75). Her *Revelations* recount how 'our Lady, the sweet queen Maria, came one night as she lay in her bed and carried the Child on her arms and gave her the child while she was in bed. And it was so beautiful that it was unspeakable and he suckled her breast and stayed with her until they sounded matins and she had such great joy . . ..'[53] In her vision, Adelheid herself acted as a kind of proxy for Mary. Further, the Beguine mystic Gertrude van Oosten (d. 1358) had such a visceral response when contemplating the Nativity that, like Mary, her own breasts would fill with milk.[54]

Other women went to such extremes in their imitation of Mary that they performed miracles of their own by providing others, or sometimes even themselves, with their own miraculous milk as a kind of simulacrum for Mary's. According to the *Life of Lidwina of Schiedam* (1380–1433), on the night of the Nativity, Lidwina had a vision of a heavenly company of lactating women, among them the Virgin Mary. The next morning Lidwina rubbed her own breast, producing milk with which she suckled her maid.[55] Similarly, St Cilina imitated the healing power of Mary by restoring vision to the blind St Montanus through the application of milk from her breast.[56] Christina the Astonishing (*c.* 1150–1224) on the other hand, saved herself with milk miraculously produced from her own breasts while hiding in the woods for nine weeks. In the words of her biographer Thomas Cantimpré: 'This is an astonishing thing, unheard of since the incomparable and unparalleled Virgin, Christ's mother.'[57] In the course of their Marian imitations, these six women recalled the physical presence of the Virgin each through the performance of her own miraculous *lactatio*.

Conclusion

Whether a reward for piety, a miraculous medication or the product of an interactive *imitatio*, Mary's milk was the common thread in many devotional strategies. The substance of Mary's milk was a legitimate referent to her physical being, as evidenced by the numerous relics. Although the object of a non-corporeal devotional cult, Mary could be embodied by those seeking her through images and visions of her milk, as well as through the partaking of or producing that very same substance. Hans Belting has observed that viewers were expected to contribute with their own imaginations what the image, and in our case relic, lacked in terms of reality or illusion.[58] Thus, through their desires, imitations and visions emphatically focused on milk, supplicants could make tangible the absent object of their devotion, the Virgin Mary. Her milk was the vehicle for these interactive devotions, a material token of her corporeal self that fully engaged the senses of sight, touch and taste. Through the ingestion or production of miraculous milk, those who sought the Virgin Mary could physically embody the absent saint within themselves.

Notes

1 I would like to express my gratitude to James Robinson and Anna Harnden for organizing the Matter of Faith conference and subsequent publication and for inviting me to contribute to the volume.
2 Cumming 1852.
3 For more on the *lactans* motif in Josquin's work see Kirkendale 1984. See also Brown 1990, 794–5, who notes Josquin's concluding sentiment in this motet as the musical equivalent of a Maria *lactans* painting.

4 There is no lack of scholarship on the topic of Maria *lactans*. On the *lactans* image see, for example: Williamson 1998; Williamson 2009a; Williamson 2009b; Corrington 1989; Miles 1986; Lane 1984, esp. 1–39; Mundy 1981–2; Lasareff 1938; and Meiss 1936, to name a few.
5 On the absence of Mary and the significance of her image and relics, see Maniura 2009. See further Ward 1987, 133: 'The absence of her body was partially mitigated by minor relics of clothing or hair; by miraculous relics like her milk; by statues and icons, often miracle working; or simply by the dedication of churches to her.'
6 Ellington 2001, 132, has noted that Mary's milk was the only Marian relic to appear with any frequency in miracle stories. See also Ahsmann 1930, 142 and Bétérous 1983–4, 403–11.
7 Krasinski 1854, 185.
8 These included Santa Maria del Popolo, Santa Maria in Campitelli, San Nicholas in Carcere and St Alexis. See further Waller 1853, 560.
9 Nichols 1889, 134.
10 As noted by Flavio Biondo, *Roma instaurata* in *Opere omnia*, 272, cited in Stinger 1998, 41.
11 Calvin, *Treatise*, translator's note in Krasinski 1854, 249.
12 Waller 1853, 560.
13 On the contents of the Arca Santa see Harris 1995, 86. See also Beltran 1993.
14 Félibien 1973, pl. 1.
15 Bagnoli *et al.* 2010, 116–17 and pl. 82.
16 D'Archery, who later published the works of Guibert in 1651, noted that other relics of Mary's milk were venerated in France and elsewhere (Waterton 1879, 200).
17 Erasmus, *Colloquies*, 633, 635–6, 638 cited in Marshall 2003, 48, Dickinson 1956, 91 and Waterton 1897, 195. See further the discussion of relic forgeries including the Virgin's milk in Marshall 2003, 39–73.
18 Fulton 2002, 271.
19 Waterton 1879, 199.
20 According to the *Metropolis Remensis Historia*, published in 1679 cited in Waterton 1879, 200, n. 125.
21 Waterton 1897, 205.
22 Further on the grotto, see Sered 1986.
23 Waterton 1879, 204. He notes further that according to Mislin, demand was so great for the substance that the once small grotto had become 'greatly enlarged'.
24 For instance, Williamson 2009b, 385 noted, 'The *lactans* motif stresses the physicality of the maternal relationship, showing that the Christ Child was really born of a woman and that that woman really nourished him with her milk.'
25 For milk in relation to medieval medical theories, see Seymour and Trevisa 1975, 5 and 34.
26 Lane 1984, esp. 1–39. See also Bullough 1973.
27 Bynum 1985 and 1988.
28 Hamburger 1989.
29 Dewez and van Iterson 1956.
30 See n. 4 above.
31 Williamson 2009a, 165.
32 'Doulce dame de miséricorde, mère de pitié, fontaine de tous biens, qui portastes Ihésucrist .ix. mois en vos précieux flans et l'alaitastes de vos doulces mamelles.' For the complete prayer see Leroquais 1927, vol. 2, 310–11.
33 O'Sullivan 1984, 37–9.
34 Bonser 1962, 235.
35 Fulton 2002, 201–2. See also Ward 1987, 152 regarding the 1145 *Miracles of the Virgin* at Saint-Pierre-sur-Dives in which most of the miracles in the collection were cures. Sumption 1975, 75, also commented on the role of the Virgin as a healer of the sick, citing in particular Hughes Farsit who wrote on the outbreak of ergotism in 1128, and noted that sufferers sought the healing powers of the Virgin when no other remedy could be found.
36 Lauritis *et al.* 1961, 3:58, 550.
37 Petrarch, *Epistolae familiares*, 9:13, cited in Sumption 1975.
38 Morrison 2000, 5. The pulverized scrapings mixed with water were said to cure various ailments, particularly those associated with fertility, childbearing and lactation (Waterton 1879, 203).
39 F. Vetter (ed.) 1906, *Das Leben der Schwestern zu Töss beschrieben von*

Elsbet Stagel (Deutsche Texte des Mittelalters 6), 53–4, cited in Bynum 1988, 131.

40 Life of Lukardis, chap. 6, *Analecta Bollandiana* 18, 318–19, cited in Bynum 1988, 131–2.

41 Vincent of Beauvais 1494, *Speculum historiale* 7:84, fol. 80r, cited in Bynum 1988, 328.

42 Bétérous 1975, 404–5.

43 Gautier de Coincy, *Miracles de la Nostre Dame*: 'Moult doucement et par grant delit / De son douz sain trait mamele / Qui tan test douce, sade et bele, / Et li boute dedenz la bouche, / Moult doucement partout li touché, / Et arouse de son douz lait', translated in Warner 1983, 198–9.

44 Bétérous 1983–4, 148–9. For the story of the healing of the monk with ulcerations see also Neuhaus 1886, no. 6, 29 and no. 13, 70.

45 'Through the triumph of his holy cross and through your glorious intercession, holy mother of God, perpetual virgin Mary, may the Lord guard against my veins, teeth, jaw, mouth, from all pain and infirmity.' The prayer continues with invocations for his throat, chest, heart, stomach, all his members, interior and exterior, especially his hands, and also his feet. 'Pia uirgo Maria, caeli regina, mater Domini', in Barré 1963, 155–8, translated in Fulton 2002, 220.

46 For accounts of the healing of Fulbert, see William of Malmsbury, *Gesta Regum Anglorum*, who wrote: 'quem Domini mater Maria olim aegrotum lacte mamilliarum suarum visa fuerat sanare' (and Albéric des Trois-Fontaines), *Chronicon*, year 1022 on Fulbert in which he recounts the miracle: 'Florebat Fulbertus . . . que etiam ab eadem Dei genetricis in infermitate sua visitatus, esse dicitur, et de ejus lacte sanctissimo recreatus. Hic enim multo amore et felicissimo in honorem B.M.V. Dei genetricis exarsit', cited in Gripkey 1938, 19.

47 Bétérous 1975, 409.

48 Anselm of Lucca, *Oratio venerabilis Anselmi episcopi ad sanctam Mariam. Cum superni Regis potenciam considero*, cited in Fulton 2002, 225–6.

49 Cited in Meiss 1936, 461, n. 91. According to Sered 1986, 10 and Warner 1983, 199, this event reportedly took place in Florence in 1368. Others had experiences similar to Bernard. For one, the German mystic Henry Suso (1300–66) also had a vision in which Mary appeared to him and allowed him to taste the 'heavenly drink' (Suso, H. 1876–80, *Deutsche Schriften*, 1, 74, cited in Hirn 1959, 365). Further, the theologian Alanus de Rupe (1428–75) received the gift of Mary's milk in a vision in which he wed the Virgin and she 'opened to him her paps and poured great plenty of her own milk into his mouth' (cited in Waller 2010, 114).

50 Hale 1990, 199–200. While women are primarily the ones performing most Marian *imitatia*, there are references to men nursing Christ. One such example is Friederich Sunder of Engelthal (*c.* 1254–1328) whose visionary experiences included Christ suckling at the breasts of Sunder's soul. See Siegfried Ringler 1980, *Viten- und Offenbarungsliteratur in Frauenklöstern des Mittelalters: Quellen und Studien* (Münchener Texte und Untersuchungen zur deutschen Literatur des Mittelalters 72) Munich, 415, cited in Hamburger 1989, 177–8.

51 Philipp Strauch (ed.) 1882, *Die Offenbarungen der Margaretha Ebner*, in *Margaretha Ebner und Heinrich von Nördlingen. Ein Beitrag zur Geschichte der deutschen Mystik*, Freiburg i.Br. and Tübingen, 87, translated in Hale 1990, 196. Cradles like the one used by Margaretha were also common among the Beguines; see Ziegler 1993.

52 Ragusa and Green 1961, 39–40. Note in particular illustration 42 of the stay at the manger with Mary suckling the child (Ragusa and Green 1961, 53).

53 Philipp Strauch (ed.) 1878, *Die Offenbarungen der Adelheide Langmann, klosterfrau zu Engelthal* Strassburg, 66–7, translated in Hale 1990, 196. See also Rubin 2009, 264.

54 *The Life of Gertrude van Oosten*, 3:14, in J. Bollandus and G. Henschenius, *Acta sanctorum*, ed. J. Carandet *et al.* (hereafter AASS) January, vol. 1 (Paris, 1863), 350, cited in Bynum 1988, 123.

55 *Vita prior*, 6:58–60, AASS April, vol. 2 (Paris, 1865), 282; John Brugman, *Vita posterior*, pt. 3, 4:193–4, AASS April, vol. 2 (Paris, 1865) 341–2; and Thomas à Kempis, *Life of Lidwina*, pt 2, chap. 4, in Thomas à Kempis, *Opere omnia*, ed H. Sommalius, vol. 3 (1600–1: new ed. Cologne 1759), 135–6, all cited in Bynum 1988, 126.

56 Ward 1987, 138.

57 Thomas Cantimpré, *The Life of Christina the Astonishing*, 1:9 in Newman 2008, 132–3; and also translated in Spearing 2002, 77 and Petroff 1986, 185.

58 Belting 1990, 62.

Bibliography

Ahsmann, H.P.J.M. 1930. *Le Culte de la Sainte Vierge et la littérature française profane du moyen âge*, Utrecht and Nijmegen.

Bagnoli, M., Klein, H.A., Mann, C.G. and Robinson, J. 2010. *Treasures of Heaven: Saints, Relics and Devotion in Medieval Europe*, Baltimore and London.

Barré, H. 1963. *Prières anciennes de l'occident à la mère du Sauveur: Des origines à saint Ansélme*, Paris.

Belting, H. 1990. *The Image and its Public in the Middle Ages: Form and Function of Early Paintings of the Passion*, trans M. Bartusis and R. Meyer, New Rochelle, NY.

Beltran, S.S. 1993. 'Las origines y la expansion del culto a las reliquias de San Salvador de Oviedo', in *Las peregrinaciones a Santiago de Compostela y San Salvador de Oviedo en la Edad Media*, ed. J.I. Ruiz de la Peña Solar, Oviedo, 33–55.

Bétérous, P.V. 1975. 'A propos d'une des légendes mariales les plus répandues: Le lait de la Vierge', *Bulletin de l'association Guillaume Bude* 4, 403–11.

Bétérous, P.V. 1983–4. *Les collections de miracles de la Vierge en gallo et ibéro-roman au XIIe siècle: étude comparés: themes et structures* (Marian Library Studies, new series, 15–16), Dayton, OH.

Bonser, W. 1962. 'The cult of relics in the Middle Ages', *Folklore* 73(4), 234–56.

Brown, H.M. 1990. 'The mirror of man's salvation: music in devotional life about 1500', *Renaissance Quarterly* 43(4), 744–73.

Bullough, V.L. 1973. 'Medieval medical and scientific attitudes towards women', *Viator* 4, 485–501.

Bynum, C.W. 1985. 'Feast, fast, and flesh: the religious significance of food to medieval women', *Representations* 11, 1–25.

Bynum, C.W. 1988. *Holy Feast and Holy Fast: The Religious Significance of Food to Medieval Women*, Berkeley and Los Angeles.

Corrington, G.P. 1989. 'The milk of salvation: redemption by the mother in late antiquity and early Christianity', *The Harvard Theological Review* 82(4), 393–420.

Cumming, J. (trans.) 1852. *Saint Bonaventure, The Psalter of the Blessed Virgin Mary*, London.

Dewez, L. and van Iterson, A. 1956. 'La lactation de saint Bernard: Légende et iconographie', *Cîteaux in de Nederlanden* 7, 165–89.

Dickinson, J.C. 1956. *The Shrine of Our Lady of Walsingham*, Cambridge.

Ellington, D.S. 2001. *From Sacred Body to Angelic Soul: Understanding Mary in Late Medieval and Early Modern Europe*, Washington, DC.

Félibien, M. 1706 (repr. 1973). *Histoire de L'Abbaye Royale de Saint-Denys en France*, Paris.

Fulton, R. 2002. *From Judgment to Passion: Devotion to Christ and the Virgin Mary, 800–1200*, New York.

Gripkey, M.V. 1938. *The Blessed Virgin Mary as Mediatrix in the Latin and Old French Legend Prior to the Fourteenth Century*, Washington, DC.

Hale, R. 1990. '*Imitatio Mariae*: motherhood motifs in devotional memoirs', *Mystics Quarterly* 16(4), 193–203.

Hamburger, J. 1989. 'The visual and the visionary: the image in late medieval monastic devotion', *Viator* 20, 161–204.

Harris, J.A. 1995. 'Redating the Arca Santa of Oviedo', *The Art Bulletin* 77(1), 82–93.

Hirn, Y. 1959. *The Sacred Shrine: A Study of the Poetry and Art of the Catholic Church*, Boston.

Kirkendale, W. 1984. '*Circulatio*-tradition, *Maria lactans*, and Josquin as musical orator', *Acta Musicologica* 56(1), 69–92.

Krasinski, V. (trans.) 1854. *John Calvin, A Treatise on Relics, 1543*, Edinburgh.

Lane, B.G. 1984. *The Altar and the Altarpiece: Sacramental Themes in Early Netherlandish Painting*, New York.

Lasareff, V. 1938. 'Studies in the iconography of the Virgin', *The Art Bulletin*, 20(1), 26–65.

Lauritis, J.A., Klinefelter, R.A. and Gallagher, V.F. (eds) 1961. *A Critical Edition of John Lydgte's 'Life of Our Lady'*, Pittsburgh.

Leroquais, V. 1927. *Les livres d'heures manuscrits de la Bibliothèque nationale*, 3 vols, Paris.

Maniura, R. 2009. 'Persuading the absent saint: image and performance in Marian devotion', *Critical Enquiry* 35(3), 629–54.

Marshall, P. 2003. 'Forgery and miracles in the reign of Henry VIII', *Past and Present* 178, 39–73.

Meiss, M. 1936. 'The Madonna of humility', *The Art Bulletin* 18(4), 435–65.

Miles, M.R. 1986. 'The Virgin's one bare breast: female nudity and religious meaning in Tuscan early Renaissance culture', in *The Female Body in Western Culture: Contemporary Perspectives*, ed. S.R. Suleiman, Cambridge, 193–208.

Morrison, S.S. 2000. *Women Pilgrims in Late Medieval England*, London.

Mundy, E.J. 1981–2. 'Gerard David's *Rest on the Flight into Egypt*: further additions to grape symbolism', *Simiolus* 12(4), 211–22.

Neuhaus, C.L. (ed.) 1886. *Adgar's Marienlegenden nach der Londoner handschrift, Egerton 612* (Altfranzösische bibliothek, 9), Heilbronn.

Newman, B. (ed.) 2008. *Thomas of Cantimpré: The Collected Saints' Lives*, Turnhout.

Nichols, F.M. (trans.) 1889. *The Marvels of Rome or A Picture of the Golden City: An English Version of the Medieval Guide-Book*, London.

O'Sullivan, J.F. (trans. and ed.) 1984. *Stephen of Sawley, Treatises*, Kalamazoo, MI.

Petroff, E.A. (ed.) 1986. *Medieval Women's Visionary Literature*, Oxford.

Ragusa, I. and Green, R.B. (eds) 1961. *Meditations on the Life of Christ: An Illustrated Manuscript of the Fourteenth Century*, Princeton, NJ.

Rubin, M. 2009. *Mother of God: A History of the Virgin Mary*, New Haven.

Sered, S.S. 1986. 'Rachel's tomb and the Milk Grotto of the Virgin: two women's shrines in Bethlehem', *Journal of Feminist Studies in Religion* 2(2), 193–203.

Seymour, N.C. and Trevisa, J. (eds) 1975. *On the Properties of Things. John Trevisa's Translation of Bartolomaeus Angelicus' De Properitabus Rerum: A Critical Text*, 2 vols, Oxford.

Spearing, E. (ed.) 2002. *Medieval Writings on Female Spirituality*, New York.

Stinger, C.L. 1998. *The Renaissance in Rome*, Bloomington, IN.

Sumption, J. 1975. *Pilgrimage: An Image of Mediaeval Religion*, Totowa, NJ.

Waller, J.G. 1853. 'Some accounts of relics', in *The Living Age*, 39, ed. E. Littell and R.S. Littell, Boston.

Waller, G. 2010. 'The Virgin's "pryvytes": Walsingham and the late medieval sexualization of the Virgin', in *Walsingham in Literature and Culture from the Middle Ages to Modernity*, ed. D. Janes and G. Waller, Farnham, 113–29.

Ward, B. 1987. *Miracles and the Medieval Mind: Theory, Record and Event, 1000–1215*, Philadelphia.

Warner, M. 1983. *Alone of All her Sex: The Myth and Cult of the Virgin Mary*, New York.

Waterton, E. 1879. *Pietas Mariana Brittanica: A History of English Devotion to the Most Blessed Virgin Marye, Mother of God*, London.

Williamson, B. 1998. 'The Virgin *lactans* as second Eve: Images of the *salvatrix*', *Studies in Iconography*, 19, 105–38.

Williamson, B. 2009a. *The Madonna of Humility: Development, Dissemination and Reception c. 1340–1400*, Woodbridge.

Williamson, B. 2009b. 'Altarpieces, liturgy, and devotion', *Speculum* 79(2), 341–406.

Ziegler, J.E. 1993. 'Reality as imitation: The role of religious imagery among the Beguines of the Low Countries', in *Maps of Flesh and Light: The Religious Experience of Medieval Women Mystics*, ed. U. Weithaus, Syracuse, NY, 112–26.

Chapter 20
Art as Evidence in Medieval Relic Disputes
Three Cases from Fifteenth-century France

Erik Inglis

While reliquaries declare the identity and the power of their relics, these proclamations were not made in a void, nor to universal acceptance. We can gauge the response to reliquaries by examining inquiries into the authenticity of relics, which occurred when different institutions claimed the same relic. Such disputes were so common as to be proverbial, as we see from a manuscript in the Walters Art Museum, Baltimore. Dating to around 1490, it features illustrated proverbs popular in late medieval France. These include some that we are still familiar with, such as 'don't look a gift horse in the mouth' or 'in the land of the blind the one-eyed man is king'. Other proverbs in the book are now less familiar, such as a picture of a priest displaying relics to a crowd of faithful, which illustrates the proverb 'every priest praises his own relics' (**Pl. 1**).[1] If this is so, its converse is also true – many priests will disparage their rival's relics! This paper addresses three such disputes: at St Omer in northern France, at Avallon, in Burgundy, and at Paris. Reliquaries played an important evidentiary role in all three.

In St Omer there was a centuries-long dispute over who possessed the relics of St Omer himself: on one side was the collegiate church of St Omer, on the other side the monastery of St Bertin. The dispute over the saint's body began in the 11th century; each side produced works of art to establish its claims. The collegiate church produced multiple manuscripts of the *Life of St Omer*, of which an illuminated copy still survives in the Bibliothèque municipale in St Omer. Both sides also produced reliquaries, now lost.[2]

Because art history as a discipline is usually preoccupied with origins, most art historians dealing with objects like these investigate their genesis, asking how they respond to the circumstances that spurred their production. More recently, medieval art historians have studied the reception of works by later viewers.[3] The relic trials are useful here, demonstrating that the objects realized their designers' hopes by continuing to make their arguments for centuries and that later viewers still attended to the objects' argument.

The dispute between St Bertin and the collegiate church had entered one of its hot phases in the 1460s, prompting the canons of St Omer to appeal to the Parisian *Parlement*, which served a judicial role in the kingdom.[4] *Parlement* dispatched Jean Haberge, a royal counsellor and future bishop of Evreux, to look into the matter. On the ground in St Omer, Haberge transcribed charters that had been produced in a dispute between the two sides a century earlier, in 1324.[5] He also collated the lives of the saint kept in each institution; thus, the 11th-century *Life of St Omer* found a very interested viewer 400 years after it was made. St Omer owned at least two manuscripts containing the saint's *Vita*, a now lost copy, which had but one picture, and the slightly later illustrated version that still survives. It is unclear how many copies Haberge inspected, and what survives of his report says nothing of their age or images.[6]

His report is more revealing about the reliquaries, which he inspected at each church before a crowd of interested onlookers. At St Omer, his account reports: 'we

Plate 1 'Every priest praises his own relics', *Proverbes en rimes,* **1490. Walters Art Museum, Baltimore, W.313, p. 63**

inspected the chasse on both sides and on top, and found it sound and whole'; opening it, he found inside 'enclosed certain authenticating letters' including one sealed by the Abbot of St Bertin.[7] Such *authentiques*, inscribed slips of parchment that name the relics held by a reliquary, remain a common feature of extant medieval reliquaries.

From St Omer Haberge went to the monastery of St Bertin, where the monks showed him their chasse. Haberge reports that inscriptions on the reliquary identified its many contents, which included pieces of Christ's tomb, Peter's beard and unspecified relics of St Maurice. Additionally, the chasse also had an image labelled as St Omer on its corner. In their attempt to dismiss the monks' case, the canons of St Omer argued that the image and its label were no more than 50 years old, and claimed that they had been produced and added to a pre-existing reliquary in the wake of an earlier dispute. The monks of St Bertin dismissed this charge, 'saying and affirming that these had been written and portrayed on the corner of the chasse for ages [*de toute ancienneté*]'.[8]

Thus the age of the object was recognized as important, and subject to dispute and disagreement. There is no indication, however, of any standards or criteria by which the age of the plaque might have been assessed. Haberge here is simply a reporter; in his account we have no sense of how he evaluated the evidence.[9] Nor do we know how *Parlement*, which rendered judgement slowly, weighed the varied evidence. This phase of the dispute was not settled for a quarter century; in 1495 an *arret* of *Parlement* found in favour of St Omer's canons, dismissing the 'certain very old letters and writings' that the monastery used to justify their claim to have part of the saint in their reliquary. *Parlement* ordered the monks to remove the image and label of St Omer from their reliquary. St Bertin's abbot removed the image, and destroyed it along with its inscriptions – and then joined the canons in a communal procession to advertise their new found amity.[10]

A similar inquiry arose in the 1470s about who held the skull of Lazarus.[11] King Louis XI, who was very devoted to relics, sparked this inquiry in 1479 when he visited the Burgundian town of Avallon, where a head reliquary, now lost, showed Lazarus with a bishop's mitre. Grateful for the privilege to kiss a skull identified as that of Lazarus, Louis sent two goldsmiths to measure the skull for a new reliquary. However, before they could complete their work, Louis heard that the church of St Lazarus in Autun also claimed to have the skull of St Lazarus; determined not to donate a reliquary to the wrong skull, he ordered an inquest.

As at St Omer, the inquisitors interrogated the locals, and examined the church's books, reliquary and artwork. The local informants testified that people frequently came to venerate the relics; these visitors ranged from dignitaries like Louis XI and a visiting bishop to local women with premature babies. The locals also recognized the existing dispute with Autun. A 60-year old informant was asked 'whether there were any letters, charters or old documents or other official proofs that the head was St Lazarus's, or of how it arrived there. He replied that he had not seen any, except the old martyrology of the church, and he also said that in the choir stalls of the church there was sculpted the story of how the head of Lazarus was brought to the church as can be seen.'[12]

The two types of evidence mentioned by this informant – images and books – were both taken seriously by the inquisitors. They noted that the church has several depictions of Lazarus and that they are done in an 'ancient style' and were 'very old'. Describing the cupboard where the reliquary was stored, they recorded that it 'had on both sides two large images made in an old construction, representing the sisters of the blessed Lazarus … and about it was represented the resurrection of the blessed Lazarus in an old style, on one part, and on the other part appeared a picture depicting certain miracles done by the blessed Lazarus, which picture is very old'.[13] A related inquiry at Autun in 1482 also described some images on the north portal of St Lazarus's as executed in 'the old style [*ymagines modo antiquo formate*]'.[14] As at St Omer, this is loose terminology – and it is notable that while the inquisitors at Avallon qualify some of the church's decoration in this way, they say nothing about the style of the reliquary itself. But Avallon also believed that it had precise chronological evidence in the church's martyrology, a list of saints' feast days that could also serve as a repository for the history of the church. The martyrology recorded that the skull had been given to them by Henry of Burgundy, an 11th-century aristocrat, and that Blanche de Dreux de Bretagne had presented the reliquary in 1322. Thus, they used their documents the same way an art historian would today, and the documents allowed them to date the object to the year it was made.

The inquisitors, however, raised questions about this evidence; while they described the martyrology as being written on parchment in very old letters – 'in pergameno et littera bene antiqua scripto' – they also noted that the inscription concerning Henry's gift of the relic seemed to be written over an erasure, suggesting it was of more recent vintage, and expressed a similar degree of skepticism about the record of Blanche's donation.[15] However, when they opened the actual reliquary, they found an 'authentic' record of Henry's donation of Lazarus's skull. They wrote that it was 'in antique letters, containing these words: "This is the head of St Lazarus which was given to Avalon by Henry of Burgundy"'.[16]

The inquests at St Omer and Avallon show two mindsets working together. One of these is the mindset accustomed to identifying relics. Thus the evidence deemed worth considering includes both textual evidence and the oral tradition conveyed by local informants, especially those who are both venerable and alert.[17] The other is a mindset arising from the document-based culture of the *Parlement*, many of whose officers were notaries and secretaries. As such, they were trained to assess the age, format and authenticity of documents by using criteria such as seals, spelling and handwriting. The development of such criteria for documents prepared the inquisitors to recognize that an object's age mattered – but they did not yet have equivalent criteria to determine it. They had all the right questions, but none of the tools.

The same combination of excellent questions and inadequate tools is displayed in the most completely documented and interesting dispute known to me, which set the monastery of St Denis against the cathedral of Notre Dame in Paris.[18] In what follows, I rely on Ingeborg Bähr's excellent account of this debate.[19] The disagreement was over the possession of relics of St Denis. As with the dispute at St Omer, this debate was long standing. It began in the late 12th and early 13th century, when Notre Dame claimed to have received a gift from Philip Augustus of several relics, including the top of the head of St Denis.[20] This angered the monks of St Denis, who had always claimed to possess the entire body of their patron. The dispute flared up in the early 15th century, and, as with the case at St Omer, was put before *Parlement*. Remarkably, while we do not know how the case was resolved, we have the briefs of each side, allowing us to see the evidence they presented and how they responded to their opponent's evidence. Each side turned not just to written histories, but also treated images as equally vital and trustworthy sources. The monks pointed to images showing St Denis carrying his entire head, while the canons pointed to those that showed Denis lacking the top of his head.

To support their cause, the monks or their advocate did picture research in Paris. They were especially pleased to point to images at Notre Dame itself, where, after scouring the building for images that favoured their argument, the monks found three (none of which survive). The first, dating probably to the mid-13th century, was a sculpture on the

Plate 2 'The Martyrdom of St Denis', *Vie de St Denis*, c. 1250. Bibliothèque nationale de France, Paris, Ms. n. a. fr. 1098, fol. 44

south transept portal that showed a saint carrying his head. The canons replied that because this figure lacked episcopal vestments, it was not St Denis, but St Lucain.[21] The second was a stained glass window; although this was labelled with a different saint's name, the monks said that it had previously been labelled as Denis, and accused the canons of having recently relabelled it to save their case.[22] St Denis's advocate pointed most triumphantly to two scenes on the cathedral's choir screen, one showing Denis being martyred through the neck, the other showing him carrying his head – and both of them labelled. The monks would seem to have conclusive evidence here, with clearly labelled monumental images supporting their claims in their enemy's own building. But the canons countered: those are new images! They pointed to documents in their archives which showed the images on the choir screen has been made only forty years earlier, and attributed the iconography thus not to time honoured tradition, but to the willful innovations of the independent artisan who carved them.[23]

Against this innovative image, the canons pointed to images which used their preferred iconography and which they claimed were much older. These included the cathedral's principal chasse, which held its relic of St Denis. The canons claimed that this reliquary was quite old (*moult ancienne*).[24] Here the canons almost certainly knew that they were playing fast and loose with chronology, for Delaborde points out that the chasse, whose creation was amply documented in the chapter's archives, had been made in the

1370s. Thus, it was about the same age as the choir screen that they had dismissed as new.[25] The canons insisted similarly if more plausibly on the age of other depictions of Denis which supported their case: 'Item in the stalls of the choir of the church which are not new. Item in several old windows which it is easy to see (*bon à veoir*) are not in the new fashion (*la nouvelle façon*) like that cited by the monks.'[26] They also relied on the jamb sculptures from two of the cathedral's portals. They claimed that the Virgin Portal on the west facade (damaged during the French Revolution and now filled by 19th-century statues) had a statue of St Denis in their preferred iconography, together with a standing king that the canons identified as Philip Augustus, 'demonstrating who gave the said head [relic] to the church'. A similar depiction of St Denis appeared on the south transept portal. Their advocate specified that 'these doors are very notable and ancient and it is easy to see that they were not newly made and also that they were not made without great and mature deliberation'.[27]

As this indicates, the canons claimed that old images were more trustworthy because they 'were ancient, made in the time of the martyrdom or shortly afterward, when the manner of the martyrdom was fresher and better known than it is now'.[28] This emphasis on age is essential; it also led the canons to dismiss a document used by St Denis as a recent work that had been artificially aged to make it appear more trustworthy.[29]

The canons were not able to use these grounds to dismiss another image the monks produced which came from the well-known and still extant life of St Denis illuminated in the mid-13th century, which was about 150 years old at the time it was introduced as evidence (**Pl. 2**). The canons acknowledged the age of this image. To enlist it in support of their position, they focused not on its date but its iconography: the old image showed St Denis being decapitated with an axe; now an axe, the canons said, was notoriously clumsy (*mal tranchans*), and it was more than likely that in using an axe to behead Denis, his executioner had failed to strike a clean blow, and had dislodged that part of his head claimed by Notre Dame.[30] Here the image is accepted as old and thus was valuable evidence of the event, and the only question is how to interpret that evidence.

The dispute between St Denis and Notre Dame demonstrates that images and written records were equally regarded as potentially valid sources of information. This striking embrace of images makes sense in a world that had at least since Gregory the Great accorded quasi-scriptural weight to pictures of biblical narratives. The canons even paraphrased Gregory's famous equation of word and image when they invoked 'old paintings, which are the books of simple folk and laypersons'.[31] However, the dispute also demonstrates that its partisans were able to discriminate about which images were most useful. In her summary of the debate, Bähr notes that they used several criteria to assess whether an image was historically trustworthy. Age was uppermost: old images were better than new ones, and traditional images more trustworthy than iconographic novelties. Monumental public works were more trustworthy than private works; and works produced by non-partisans were better than works produced by one of the parties.[32]

This is not the incurious, ahistorical approach to earlier art that we might expect from a period lacking the blessings of an academic art history. Instead, the partisans on each side use fairly sophisticated criteria that remain familiar to art historians today. Thus, when we consider how these objects spoke to their medieval viewers, we need to take their age and history into account. To clarify, let's return to the priest keen to praise his own relics (**Pl. 1**). Many of the essays in the *Treasures of Heaven* catalogue discussed how viewers were prepared to assess reliquaries and how reliquaries relied on that preparation in addressing viewers. Cynthia Hahn explained how a reliquary's appearance appealed to its viewer's aesthetic sensibilities; the reliquary's beauty made an argument that would be useful to the priest.[33] Martina Bagnoli noted that medieval books on stones – called lapidaries – offered interpretations of specific types of stones which could contribute to the meaning of reliquaries.[34] Writing about the Talisman of Charlemagne, James Robinson remarked how 'sapphires [like the one in the Talisman] were prized for their celestial connotations, [and] also because they cooled the body and chastened the spirit'.[35]

The disputes discussed in this chapter demonstrate how 15th-century viewers also recognized age as an important component of these objects, and that we as art historians must think about this historical awareness. For a priest looking to praise his relics, the age of the reliquary and other art works in the church could help by demonstrating the antiquity of the claim and the prestige of the donor.

Notes

1   MS W.313, p. 63. Randall *et al.* 1989–97, vol. II, part 2, 366–74.
2   For the manuscripts and their original context, see Argent Svoboda 1983; Abou-El-Haj 1994; Ugé 1996, 887–903; Deremble 2000, 39–48; Hahn 2001.
3   Caviness 2006, 65–85; a notable early example is Cahn 1992, 44–60, 194–6.
4   In what follows I draw on Bled 1914–20 and De Bonnaire 1754.
5   De Bonnaire 1754, 407–8.
6   De Bonnaire published extracts from Haberge's collation of the manuscripts, ibid., 393–406.
7   'visitasmes lad. châsse aux deux côtez & dessus, & icelles trouvasmes saine & entiere … & entre les ligatures & ledit petit coffret estoents encloses & enclavées certaines lettres antentiques' ibid., 415.
8   'estre fait depuis cinquante ans en çà lesdits de S. Bertin disant & affirmant ce que dessus avoir esté escript et pourtrait au coing de ladite châsse de toute ancienneté', ibid., 416, Bled 1914–20, 60–1.
9   A year later, Haberge was the intermediary who delivered a relic of St Omer to St Hilaire in Poitiers; Rédet 1852.
10 De Bonnaire 1754, 414, 416; Bled 1914–20, 69–74.
11 De Charmasse 1865. This inquiry is cited in Montgomery 1997, 51; Cornelison 2002, 450, n. 73, 451, n. 76. Werckmeister 1972, 1, quoting Grivot and Zarnecki 1961, 146, n. 2; portions of this account are published in *Le tombeau de Saint Lazare et la sculpture romane à Autun après Gislebertus* 1985.
12 'Interrogatus an vider aliquas litteras, cartas vel antiqua munimenta seu alias approbationes prelatorum per quas appareat ipsum caput esse caput beati Lazari vel quomodo fuit apportatum in dicta ecclesia: dicit quot nichil unquam vidit, excepto martirologio ipsius ecclesie ad quod se reffert, et etiam dicit quod in sedibus chori ipsius ecclesie Avalonis istoria est sculpta quomodo caput beati Lazari fuit apportatum in ipsa ecclesia, quod oculo poterit perpendi', de Charmasse 1865, 49.
13 The 'armarium … habens a duobus lateribus suis duas magnas ymagines ex antiqua constructione factas, representantes, per

eorum inspectionem duas sorores beati Lazari, … et desuper dicto armario est depicta resuscitatio beati Lazari more antiquo, ex una parte, et ex alia parte apparet quedam pictura que videtur designare certa miracula per beatum Lazarum facta, quequidem pictura est bene antiqua', de Charmasse 1865, 70–1.

14 Werckmeister 1972, 1, quoting Grivot and Zarnecki 1961, 146, n. 2; portions of this account are published in *Le tombeau de Saint Lazare et la sculpture romane à Autun après Gislebertus* 1985.

15 De Charmasse 1865, 62–6.

16 'Reperimus unum parvum breve antiquum in pergameno descriptum littera antiqua … continens verba sequentia: HOC EST CAPUT BEATI LAZARI QUOD ATTULIT AVALONEM HENRICUS CUI BURGUNDIA OBEDIEBAT', de Charmasse 1865, 69–70.

17 For the memory of witnesses, see Guenée 1976–7.

18 Delaborde 1884.

19 Bähr 1984. The trial is also discussed in Camille 1996, 118–19.

20 There is a good account of this confusing history in Hinkle 1966, 1–13.

21 Delaborde 1884, 367; Bähr 1984, 52.

22 Delaborde 1884, 359, 361–2, 400.

23 Ibid., 360, 400; Bähr 1984, 44–7.

24 Delaborde 1884, 368, 400.

25 Ibid., 368.

26 'Item ès chaires du cuer de ladite église qui ne sont pas nouvelles. Item en plusieurs anciennes verrières, quie est bon à veoir qui ne sont pas de la nouvelle façon comme celle de laquelle arguent lesdiz religieux', ibid., 400.

27 'Lesqueulx portaulx sont mout notables et anciens et est bon à veoir qu'ilz ne sont pas fais de nouvel et aussy qui'ilz ne furent mie fais sans grant et meure délibéracion et advis'. Ibid., 363–4, 400; Bähr 1984, 53.

28 'Figures et paintures anciennes faites du temps dudit martire ou tentost après, que pour lors la manière d'icelui martire estoit plus nouvelle et plus sceue qu'elle ne pouroit maintenant estre', Delaborde 1884, 399; Bähr 1984, 44.

29 Delaborde 1884, 386; Bähr 1984, 54.

30 Delaborde 1884, 358, n. 2; Bähr 1984, 43.

31 'Painctures enciennes, lesquelles sont les livres des simples gens et personnes laycz', Delaborde 1884, 325; Bähr 1984, 44, 49.

32 Bähr 1984, 55.

33 Hahn 2010.

34 Bagnoli 2010, 138–9.

35 Robinson 2010, 113.

Bibliography

Abou-El-Haj, B. 1994. *The Medieval Cult of the Saints: Formations and Transformations*, Cambridge.

Argent Svoboda, R. 1983. 'The illustrations of the *Life of St Omer* (Saint-Omer, Bibliothèque municipale, Ms. 698)', unpublished PhD dissertation, University of Minnesota.

Bagnoli, M. 2010. 'The stuff of heaven: materials and craftsmanship in medieval reliquaries', in Bagnoli *et al.* 2010, 137–47.

Bagnoli, M., Klein, H.A., Mann, C.G. and Robinson, J. (eds) 2010. *Treasures of Heaven: Saints, Relics and Devotion in Medieval Europe*, Baltimore and London.

Bähr, I. 1984. 'Aussagen zur Funktion und zum Stellenwert von Kunstwerken in einem Pariser Reliquienprozess des Jahres 1410', *Wallraf-Richartz-Jahrbuch* 45, 41–57.

Bled, O. 1914–20. 'Les reliques de Saint Omer et le les reliques de Saint Bertin', *Mémoires de la société des antiquaires de la Morinie*, vol. 32, 5–110.

Cahn, W. 1992. 'Romanesque sculpture and the spectator', in *The Romanesque Frieze and its Spectator: The Lincoln Symposium Papers*, ed. D. Kahn, London and New York, 44–60.

Camille, M. 1996. *Master of Death: The Lifeless Art of Pierre Remiet, Illuminator*, New Haven and London.

Caviness, M.H. 2006. 'Reception of images by medieval viewers', in *A Companion to Medieval Art: Romanesque and Gothic in Northern Europe*, ed. Conrad Rudolph, Malden, MA, 65–85.

Cornelison, S. 2002. 'A French king and a *Magic Ring*: The Girolami and a relic of St Zenobius in Renaissance Florence', *Renaissance Quarterly* 55, 434–69.

De Bonnaire, L. 1754. *La Vérité de l'histoire de l'église de S. Omer, et son antériorité sur l'abbaye de S. Bertin*, Paris.

De Charmasse, A. 1865. 'Enquete faite en 1482 touchant le chef de Saint Lazare conservé à Avallon', *Bulletin de la Société d'études d'Avallon*, vol. 7, 1–87.

Delaborde, H.F. 1884. 'Le procès du chef de Saint Denis en 1410', *Mémoires de la Société de l'histoire de Paris et de l'Ile-de-France* 11, 297–409.

Deremble, C. 2000. 'L'illustration romane de la Vie de Saint Omer, manuscrit 698 de la Bibliothèque de Saint-Omer', in *La cathédrale de Saint-Omer 800 ans de mémoire vive*, ed. N. Delanne-Logié and Y.-M. Hilaire, Paris, 39–48.

Grivot, D. and Zarnecki, G. 1961. *Gislebertus, Sculptor of Autun*, London.

Guenée, B. 1976–7. 'Temps de l'histoire et temps de la mémoire au Moyen Âge', *Annuaire-Bulletin de la Société de l'histoire de France*, 25–35, reprinted in Guenée, *Politique et histoire au Moyen Age*, Paris, 1981, 253–63.

Hahn, C. 2001. *Portrayed on the Heart: Narrative Effect in Pictorial Lives of Saints from the Tenth through the Thirteenth Century*, Berkeley, CA.

Hahn, C. 2010. 'The spectacle of the charismatic body patrons, artists and body-part reliquaries', in Bagnoli *et al.* 2010, 163–72.

Hinkle, W. 1966. 'The King and Pope on the Virgin portal of Notre-Dame', *Art Bulletin*, XLVIII, 1–13.

Le tombeau de Saint Lazare et la sculpture romane à Autun après Gislebertus 1985. Musée Rolin, Autun.

Montgomery, S. 1997. '*Mittite capud meum … ad matrem meam ut osculetur eum*: the form and meaning of the reliquary bust of Saint Just', *Gesta* 36, 48–64.

Randall, L.M.C. *et al.*, 1989–97. *Medieval and Renaissance Manuscripts in the Walters Art Gallery*, 3 vols, Baltimore.

Rédet, L.-F.-X. 1852. 'Documents pour l'histoire de l'église de St-Hilaire de Poitiers', in *Mémoires de la Société des antiquaires de l'Ouest*, vol. 15, 159–62.

Robinson, J. 2010. "From altar to amulet: relics, portability and devotion', in Bagnoli *et al.* 2010, 111–16.

Ugé, K. 1996. 'Creating a useable past in the 10th century: Folcuin's Gesta and the Crises at Saint-Bertin', *Studi medievali* 37, 887–903.

Werckmeister, O.K. 1972. 'The Lintel fragment representing Eve from Saint-Lazare, Autun', *Journal of the Warburg and Courtauld Institutes* 35, 1–30.

Chapter 21
Contested Relics
Winefride and the Saints of the Atlantic Churches[1]

Madeleine Gray

The magnificence of the reliquaries brought together for the *Treasures of Heaven* exhibition should not blind us to the fact that the excavation and dismemberment of the bodies of the holy dead was not universally accepted in medieval Europe. If, as Patrick Geary (and others) have said, relics are the repositories of constructed cultural and social meaning, that meaning will not be the same in all societies. In some cultures, attitudes to relics will be influenced by scepticism, in others by distaste and the fear of pollution; but in many parts of early western Christendom, reverence for the remains of the holy dead went side by side with the attitude that the saints had chosen their resting places and should not be disturbed. When cultures with divergent attitudes on these matters of faith came into conflict, the clash of cultural values could be played out over the bones of the saints.

The account by Robert Pennant, prior of Shrewsbury, of the translation of the relics of the Welsh saint Gwenfrewi (his *vita* of the saint uses the Latin version of her name, Wenefreda: this is usually anglicized as Winefride, which I will use in this article to avoid confusion) from north Wales to Shrewsbury in 1138 reads at first like Geary's template for monastic *furta sacra* (holy theft).[2] Underlying the monks' desperation for a relic is the competitive spiritual environment which Geary describes as a frequent precondition for relic theft: Shrewsbury was a new Norman foundation in a region which already had several important Anglo-Saxon abbeys.[3] Initially the monks' prayers for a relic were unproductive. One of the brothers fell seriously ill. The sub-prior had a vision of a previously unknown saint, Winefride, who instructed the brothers to go to her holy well and celebrate Mass. Encouraged by the monks of Chester, they did so, and their colleague was healed. The monks were then determined to acquire 'even a small part of her most holy body'. They met with some local opposition, but eventually the body was exhumed and brought to Shrewsbury. The saint manifested her approval by working miracles on the journey and in her new home.[4]

On more careful reading, however, it becomes apparent that Prior Robert was anxious to dispel accusations of relic theft. He described a lengthy process of negotiation, which began before the death of Henry I in 1135, derailed by the dispute between Stephen and Matilda and completed in 1138. He claimed to have secured the support of the bishop of Bangor (although Winefride's burial place at Gwytherin was actually in the diocese of St Asaph, there is no evidence for a bishop of St Asaph at that date,[5] and the bishop of Bangor was known to be sympathetic to relic translation[6]) and the 'prince of that land' (by 1138 this would have been Owain Gwynedd: he succeeded his father in 1137, but had been the effective ruler of Gwynedd for some years previously). Owain is quoted as saying:

> Perhaps, seeing that the respect owed her is not rendered by her own people, she desires to be taken elsewhere so that she might receive from strangers the honour which either her own people disdain to give her or neglect to give.[7]

Nor was the journey to Winefride's burial place at Gwytherin secret: the monks from Gwytherin were accompanied by the prior of Chester and a priest from north Wales as well as several others. Robert of Shrewsbury's account also downplays the extent of local resistance. The prior was warned both by Owain Gwynedd and a man he met on the way to Gwytherin that he would encounter opposition. However, the parish priest was won over by a vision, the chief local opponent was bought off (showing himself to be venal) and the saint was exhumed and taken away without resistance.

There are still, however, features of the story which suggest a different attitude to relics in Wales from that of the Norman monks of Shrewsbury. Robert describes how he was divinely guided to the saint's burial place, which was ' … separate from another cemetery where the bodies of those who die now are buried, and it is filled with the bodies of many other saints'.[8] In his account of Winefride's life, he had already mentioned the numerous saints buried at Gwytherin, including Cybi and Sannan, although Cybi was also claimed by his foundation at Holyhead (Anglesey). Robert of Shrewsbury's description of the monastic graveyard has led Tristan Gray Hulse to suggest that it may have been revered as 'another Rome', in the same way as Bardsey was.[9] Gerald of Wales described a similar cemetery of saints at Ynys Seiriol (Puffin Island, Anglesey), where 'many bodies of saints are deposited'.[10]

The significant detail, though, is that all these saints are said to be buried in a graveyard, not even in the small cemetery chapel. The implication of Robert's account is that Winefride's grave was not marked out, though the priest's dream mentions the 'lapidem' and 'laminam … quae sacro corpora superposita fuerat' ('the stone placed over her body').[11] Gwytherin has several early inscribed stones, but none of these quite fit Robert's description. Four are now placed upright in the north part of the churchyard. One is inscribed 'VINNEMAGLI FILI SENEMAGLI' and dates from the 5th or early 6th century. The others are plain and Nash-Williams describes them as '?menhirs'.[12] Two of the stones were recorded in a visitation of 1711, but the others could feasibly have been moved; it is possible though unlikely that the second one from the east could originally have been a grave cover.[13] Inside the church are two later incised cross slabs.[14] One is clearly from the early 14th century and has the inscription '+ H[I]C: IACET:LLEWARCH:CAPELL'. The other is an expanded arm cross with faint traces of carving on the left side. Colin Gresham dated the north Wales cross slabs of this type to the late 13th century, but Lawrence Butler, Peter Ryder and Alexsandra McClain have all suggested dates as

early as 1100 for similar slabs in northern and central England.[15] Gresham identified and drew the carving on the sinister side of the Gwytherin slab as a sword, which would generally be understood as indicating the burial of an elite male. It is possible that it might be the sword with which Winefride is frequently depicted as the instrument of her near martyrdom, but it is much more likely that we are looking at the burial *ad sanctos* of a local landowner.

We cannot therefore identify the 'lapis' or 'lamina' over Winefride's burial place. It seems, however, that it may have been like the 'special graves' mentioned by Nancy Edwards in her study of the early medieval archaeology of Celtic saints' cults as focal points for other burials,[16] although it was clearly a flat stone rather than the Irish gabled and corner-post shrines.[17] Nancy Edwards and John Blair have both suggested that the stones placed over the burial places of the saints may have become venerated as contact relics, although their examples of the carved tomb covers of Sts Iestyn and Pabo are rather later in date than the account of Winefride's translation.[18]

This was in fact the typical practice of early medieval Wales. The Welsh churches of the early medieval period had a distinctive attitude to relics. The bodies of the saints were usually kept whole and undisturbed in their original burial places.[19] There could be gruesome prohibitions on moving or even touching them. Lifris's life of St Cadoc concludes with a disturbing story of how the saint built a monastery in Scotland. Three of his disciples were buried in the church porch and he forbade the local people to see the tombs. One peasant managed to look into the sarcophagus; his eye split open and the optic nerve hung down his face.[20]

The whole landscape in which the saints worked and in which they were buried thus becomes sacred, in the form of a massive contact relic. There is a clear focus in the Welsh *vitae* on God appointing the place for the saints' activities. Rhigyfarch's life of St David, for example, depicts God moving St Patrick on from Rosina Vallis in order to leave the place for David to settle.[21] Not that this topos is exclusive to Wales: John Blair has pointed to the emphasis on place in the lives of many of the Anglo-Saxon saints.[22] The ivory pyx depicting St Menas in the *Treasures of Heaven* exhibition makes reference to the story that the camel carrying his body stopped to indicate the place appointed for his burial.[23] However, it seems we are looking at a spectrum of responses, with the Welsh association of saint and landscape at one end

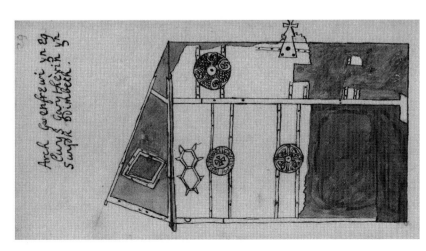

Plate 1 St Winefride's reliquary at Gwytherin: sketch by Edward Lhuyd or one of his associates, *c.* 1700, entitled *Arch Gwenfrewi yn Eglwys Gwytherin yn Swydh Ddimbech.* Bodleian Library, MS Rawl. B. 464, fol. 29r (by permission of The Bodleian Libraries, The University of Oxford)

Plate 2 The remnants of St Winefride's reliquary in St Winefride's Well Museum at Holywell (photo: M. Gray)

and the continental European belief in the mobility of holiness at the other.

This is not of course to say that relics were not venerated in Wales. The number of Welsh place names with the element *Merthyr* (from the Latin *martyrium*, in this context understood as the burial place of a saint or the location of relics) embeds relic cults into the landscape.[24] The resistance to the removal of Winefride's relics, however much Robert of Shrewsbury's account downplays it, testifies to the reverence in which they were held. His own description of the saints' graveyard, 'frequented by great crowds of people' in search of healing, but forbidden to animals, is further evidence. Churches might be built over graves:[25] this, rather than burial in an existing church, probably explains the grave of St Eleri, which Robert says was 'in basilica sui nominis' ('in the church which bore his name'). The 'lignea ecclesiola', the small wooden church which Robert describes in the cemetery, is a common enough feature in early Welsh archaeology. Called the *cell y bedd*, the cell of the grave, and often rebuilt in stone from the 12th century onwards, these could be separate structures or part of the parish church, often built over a special burial place. At Pennant Melangell (Montgomeryshire), the present church seems to have incorporated an earlier *cell y bedd* from which Melangell's relics were translated to a magnificent stone sarcophagus in the 12th century. At Basaleg, the cell known as Capel Gwladus was an entirely separate structure.[26] But even the most revered of saints could be buried outside: St David, for example, was said rather vaguely to have been buried somewhere in the grounds of his monastery, 'in sua sepelitur civitate'.[27]

The *vitae* of the saints also exhibit a concern to locate their relics or to explain their absence. According to Lifris, St Cadoc was miraculously transported to Italy and buried in Beneventum with Elli and seven other disciples. Lifris gives him a deathbed speech anticipating the possible dispersal of his relics. The *vita* goes on to describe the construction of a basilica over his tomb which no Briton can

enter so that they cannot steal the relics or the 'sacrum humum' ('the sacred soil').[28] There is a similar reference to soil as a relic in the Gwytherin priest's dream: the angel who speaks to him says 'si pulverem istum hinc ejicere voluerit, similiter patere' ('if he wants to take away the very dust from here, likewise yield').[29]

Strangely, however, Lifris's *vita* of St Cadoc goes on to describe his monks moving around with 'the shrine of the saint and other relics' and the miraculous protection of the shrine from the marauding Danes and English. In the Welsh tradition, much more weight was placed on 'secondary' relics, the possessions of the saints – bells, books, staves, liturgical vestments.[30] It is possible that the relics which are described in the *Liber Landavensis* as being deposed from altars as part of the rituals of cursing and excommunication from the 8th century onwards may have been secondary relics.[31] However, Lester Little has suggested that it is more likely that these passages are interpolations as there are no other references to similar cursing rituals in pre-conquest Wales, while they were standard usage in Normandy.[32]

In this reluctance to disturb the bodies of the saints, Wales was in line with the early Christian tradition. Successive popes had declared the exhumation and translation of relics to be sacrilege, and it was not until the 8th century that they allowed relics to be taken from the catacombs and sent to churches in northern Europe.[33] However, Wales was unusual (or perhaps unusually extreme) even on the Atlantic fringe in the persistence of prohibition on the removal of relics. There was a similar reluctance to disturb the holy dead in Brittany.[34] David Rollason has pointed to the transfer of Breton relics to the court of King Athelstan in the early 10th century, but this was clearly a response to Norman depredations.[35] In Ireland, however, there is early evidence for fragmentary relics from abroad and even for the moving of bodies of Irish saints, although in most cases they were transferred to special graves in cemeteries, less frequently to high altars.[36] Alan Thacker suggests that there was in fact less reluctance to move bodies in Ireland than in early mainland Europe and for that reason it was never treated as a major episode in saintly *vitae*.[37] Scotland seems to have been broadly similar to Ireland,[38] and it may be significant that the bishop of Bangor who gave his support to the translation of Winefride's relics was known as David 'the Scot'. In England the situation was more complex, with what has been described as a two-tier system. The bodies of royal and regionally significant saints were translated to shrines inside churches and sometimes (though rarely) divided. There was, however, a significant subsidiary layer of purely local saints whose bodies were largely left undisturbed; their 'shrines' above ground were in fact empty constructions over their graves.[39]

The Welsh tradition was forcibly disrupted by the Norman conquest of Wales. The same bishop who gave his support for the removal of Winefride's relics had already allowed the Norman bishop of Llandaff to take the supposed relics of St Dyfrig from Bardsey Island to construct a history of legitimacy for his cathedral and diocese. They were received at Llandaff with great ceremony and installed in a tomb before the altar of St Mary.[40] This was a clear break with tradition and may provide a context for the cursing rituals described by Little.[41] Geary suggests that relic theft was often said to have taken place at times of invasion, disruption or 'cultural discontinuity'.[42] He has also pointed to the underlying chauvinism of some stories of relic theft. Accounts of theft from other cultures relate primarily to those of the relics of martyrs from Rome, but also from areas outside orthodoxy: Spain, North Africa and the Near East were all seen as legitimate targets. In these there was the lure of the exotic and danger. However, theft across the English Channel, both by and from Anglo-Saxon communities, was also common.[43]

Working mainly on Frankish sources, Geary suggests implicitly that relic theft took place within a cultural world in which it was seen as acceptable and even praiseworthy in principle.[44] It was not always so: the removal of the relics of Dyfrig and Winefride could rather be seen as cultural aggression and expropriation. While not exactly relic theft, it could certainly be described as forcible translation in spite of the superficial appearance of consent. We could perhaps compare the political pressures on Bishop David with those on successive popes which resulted in their giving reluctant approval for the removal of relics from the Roman catacombs and their eventual dispersal through northern Europe.[45] Descriptions of the early removal of relics from Rome include scenes of hostile crowds and the jostling of those carrying the relics away.[46] Like Rome, Wales was well endowed with saints, and Robert of Shrewsbury actually states that his monks were specifically looking for the relics of a Welsh saint because they had heard they were plentiful. This is reminiscent of Geary's discussion of the mechanisms for circulating relics to areas of shortage – mechanisms which included theft and expropriation as well as gift and sale.[47] There is an increasing body of literature on relics as the focus for political power and the ways in which relic translation could be used as an aspect of oppression and control.[48] Edmund of England sent the relics of numerous northern saints including Hild of Whitby, Ceolfrith of Monkwearmouth and Aidan of Lindisfarne to Glastonbury as booty from his military campaigns in the north.[49] Like the removal of Winefride's relics, this was not strictly speaking theft but they were certainly removed by force.

There are a few other examples of relic translation, removal and even fragmentation in Welsh contexts. By the 13th century the monks of Glastonbury were claiming that a relic of St David had reached their monastery in 962, but the evidence for this is uncertain.[50] The monks of Shrewsbury went back to Gwytherin and removed the relics of St Eleri, who was according to Robert Pennant the founder of the religious community in which Winefride ended her days.[51] The bodies of several saints were moved from their burial places into churches dedicated to them: Melangell and David are probably the best known of these. However, most of the saints of Bardsey remained there: St Deiniol, for example, was venerated at his cathedral in Bangor but his relics remained at Bardsey.[52] Paradoxically, the story of the miraculous multiplication of the body of St Teilo, so that his three foundations of Penally, Llandeilo Fawr and Llandaf could each have one, confirms the value that the Welsh placed on the undivided body of the saint.[53]

Plate 3 Capitular seal of St Asaph Cathedral in the cathedral treasury, mid-15th century (photograph by permission of the National Museum of Wales and the Dean and Chapter of St Asaph)

It is possible that the relics of St David (uniquely for Wales) had been translated to a shrine by the end of the 11th century and reading between the lines of the *Annales Cambriae* it seems more than likely that they were stolen during a Viking raid.[54] However, in addition to Glastonbury's claim, Leominster claimed a relic of his arm and the priory at Ewenny (Glamorgan) claimed to have discovered his body outside the south door of the church. Somehow those remains were acquired by the cathedral at St Davids, but they were subsequently plundered by Edward I and others.

Although her body had been moved, the church at Gwytherin still claimed a relic of Winefride and a reliquary. This is known from a sketch made by Edward Lhuyd or one

Plate 4 St Winefride in the 15th-century stained glass at Llandyrnog, Denbighshire (photo: M. Gray)

of his associates (**Pl. 1**), and two fragments of it survive at her other shrine at Holywell (**Pl. 2**).[55] On the capitular seal of St Asaph (**Pl. 3**), Winefride may be holding this reliquary, although it is also possible that the rectangular object in her hands is a book or a book bag.[56] Whether the reliquary was 8th- or 9th-century English work (as claimed by James Graham-Campbell), manufactured in Wales under Irish influence and possibly at a slightly later date (as suggested by Butler) or was a 12th-century Irish work (as argued more recently by Cormac Bourke),[57] it cannot be connected with Winefride's bodily remains, which Robert Pennant clearly stated were interred in the monastic graveyard. To judge from the surviving fragments, the reliquary measured 260mm x 208mm x *c.* 350mm, too small to contain more than a few bones. Iconographic evidence suggests the casket may have contained one of the 'secondary' relics of the earlier Welsh tradition, possibly a book. Winefride is traditionally depicted as a learned saint, holding a book, as in stained glass at Llandyrnog (Denbighshire) (**Pl. 4**) and in the Beauchamp chapel at Warwick. Winefride's surviving relics (including the fragments of the Gwytherin reliquary and some very fragmentary corporeal relics sent to St Omer and subsequently to Rome, returned to Shrewsbury and shared with Holywell) have also played an important part in the construction of an identity for the post-Reformation Catholic community in Wales.[58] Both of the fragments of the reliquary are now in St Winefride's Well Museum at Holywell; a fragment of Winefride's bones is still venerated daily in the well chapel.

A parallel process of adaptation has taken place with the traditional life story of the saint. In Robert Pennant's account she is an innocent girl who seeks out and accepts male leadership. She finally makes her way to Gwytherin where she enters a community founded by St Eleri. However, there is a slightly earlier version which survives in Latin but has probable Welsh origins.[59] In this she is a forthright and determined young woman who becomes a religious leader and reformer. Like St Ursula, she travels – in this case to Rome. She introduces Benedictine coenobitic monasticism to Britain and founds her own religious house: there is no mention of Eleri. This anonymous *vita* cannot be earlier than the 1120s, but must pre-date that of Robert Pennant as it describes her as being buried in Gwytherin.[60]

At its simplest, the anonymous *Vita Prima* is *What Winefride Did*; Robert Pennant's *vita* is *What Happened to Winefride*. And what happened – the removal and disruption of her corporeal relics – is emblematic of a cultural conflict and shift as immense as the transformation in cultural attitudes represented by the reworking of her life story.

Notes

1   I am grateful to Tristan Gray Hulse for sharing his research on the life and cult of St Winefride and for reading this paper in draft form and making several valuable comments.
2   Robert of Shrewsbury's *Vita et translatio S. Wenefredae* survives in three MSS: Oxford Bodleian Laud Misc. 114 (12th century, 'possibly the original' according to Baring-Gould and Fisher 1911, vol 3, 186), Cambridge Trinity College O.4.42 (13th century) and Brussels, Bibliothèque Royale 8072 (17th century). The Latin text was edited in *Acta Sanctorum* (hereafter *AASS*) Nov. T. I, 708–31, and translated in Pepin and Feiss 2000. References to the Latin are to *AASS* and translations are from Pepin and Feiss 2000.
3   Geary 1990, 58–86.
4   Pepin and Feiss, 77–93.
5   See, for example, Thomas 1908–13, vol. 3, 214; Fryde *et al.* 1986, 295.
6   See p. 166.
7   Pepin and Feiss 2000, 81.
8   Ibid., 86.
9   Pers. comm.
10 Thorpe 1978, 190.
11 *AASS* 729. The word 'laminam' is apparently unclear in the original manuscript. Pepin and Feiss translate it as 'layer of marble' but this seems unlikely. No marble tomb slabs survive from medieval north Wales, and there only a few from the south (Badham and Norris 1999, 21); the 'blew marble' effigies which Browne Willis (1719) saw at Llandaff were in fact blue lias.
12 Nash-Williams 1950, 120–1.
13 http://www.cpat.demon.co.uk/projects/longer/churches/ conwy/16790.htm (consulted 18 November 2011); for photographs see http://cistercian-way.newport.ac.uk/image. asp?imageName=gwytherin_vinnemaglus_L, http://cistercian-way.newport.ac.uk/image.asp?imageName=gwytherin_ stones_L, http://cistercian-way.newport.ac.uk/image. asp?imageName=gwytherin1_L (consulted 18 November 2011).
14 Gresham 1968, 101–2, 107–8.
15 Butler 1964; Ryder 1985, 9; McClain 2007.
16 Edwards 2002, 228–34.
17 Marshall and Walsh 2005, 58–66; Picard 1999; Sheehan 2009.
18 Edwards 2002, 236; Blair 2002, 494.
19 Edwards 2002, 237–8.
20 Wade-Evans 1944, 100–1.
21 James 1967, 2, 30.
22 Blair 2002.
23 Bagnoli *et al.* 2010, cat. no. 20, 42.
24 *University of Wales Dictionary*, vol. 3, 2436; Thomas 1971, 89.
25 Edwards 2002, 236 for examples.
26 Ibid., 231–8; Petts and Turner 2009; Pritchard 2009.
27 James 1967, 27, 48.
28 Wade-Evans 1944, 107–11.
29 Pepin and Feiss 2000, 85.
30 Edwards 2002, 252–65; Redknap 2009; Glenn 2009.
31 Evans and Rhys 1893, 167–8, 189–90, 212–14, 214–15, 222–3, 267–8.
32 Little 1991; for a discussion of this problematic text see W. Davies 1978 and J.R. Davies 2003.
33 McCulloh 1980; Thacker 2000; Smith 2000.
34 Smith 1990.
35 Rollason 1986, 94.
36 Edwards 2002, 239–42.
37 Thacker 2002, 37.
38 Thomas 1971, 141–59.
39 Thacker 2002, 39–40; Blair 2002, 490–4.
40 Evans and Rhys 1893, 81–3, 329–31.
41 See above, n. 32.
42 Geary 1990, 7.
43 Ibid., 131–3.
44 Geary 1990, xii. Cf Geary 1994, 177–93 and esp. 190–3 for the suggestion that some aspects of the trade in relics may have been specific to the Carolingian context.
45 McCulloh 1980.
46 Smith 2000.
47 Geary 1994, 208–13.
48 For an overview see Walsham 2010, 24–7, Meijns 2010, and references therein; more specifically Lifshitz 1995, Bozóky 2006.
49 Rollason 1986, 95.
50 Thomas 1974, 171–2, referencing 13th-century interpolations to William of Malmesbury's *De Antiquitate Glastoniensis Ecclesiae*.
51 Falconer 1635, 172–3; Thomas 1908–13, vol. 2, 313. I am grateful to Tristan Gray Hulse for these references and additional information from his own notes. Andrew Breeze has, however, recently challenged the identification of Eleri with Gwytherin, raising the intriguing possibility that the monks may have been cheated (Breeze 2012).
52 Thorpe 1978, 184.
53 Davies 2003, 118.

54 This paragraph is derived from Cowley 2007, 274–9.

55 Butler and Graham-Campbell 1990; Edwards and Gray Hulse 1992; Edwards and Gray Hulse 1997.

56 I am grateful to Pamela Thompson of the St Asaph diocesan office for producing the seal matrix for me, and to Evan Campbell and Rebekah Pressler for their help with the examination of the National Museum of Wales's modern impression of the seal.

57 Bourke 2009.

58 On the sometimes confused history of these relics see *AASS* Nov. T. I, 698; Swift 1910, 70; Holt 1971, 102. I am grateful to Tristan Gray Hulse for these references. See also the chapter by Andrea de Meo, this volume.

59 British Library Cotton Claudius A v, edited in *AASS* Nov. t. I, 691–708, ed. and trans. Wade-Evans 1944, 288–309, also trans. Pepin and Feiss 2000, 97–113. For a discussion see Winward 1999.

60 For discussion of this see Gregory 2012; Gray forthcoming.

Bibliography

Badham, S. and Norris, M. 1999. *Early Incised Slabs and Brasses from the London Marblers*, London.

Bagnoli, M., Klein, H.A., Mann, C.G. and Robinson, J. (eds) 2010. *Treasures of Heaven: Saints, Relics and Devotion in Medieval Europe*, Baltimore and London.

Baring-Gould, S. and Fisher, J. 1911. *The Lives of the British Saints…* 3 vols, London.

Blair, J. 2002. 'A saint for every minster? Local cults in Anglo-Saxon England' in Thacker and Sharpe 2002, 456–94.

Bourke, C. 2009. 'The shrine of St Gwenfrewi from Gwytherin, Denbighshire: an alternative interpretation' in Edwards 2009, 375–88.

Bozóky, E. 2006. *La Politique des Reliques de Constantin à Saint Louis: Protection Collective et Légitimation du Pouvoir*, Paris.

Bozóky, E. and Helvétius, A.-M. (eds) 1999. *Les reliques. Objets, cultes, symboles*, Turnhout.

Breeze, A. 2012. 'St Eleri of Gwytherin', *Transactions of the Denbighshire Historical Society* 20, 9–18.

Butler, L.A.S. 1964. 'Minor medieval monumental sculpture in the East Midlands', *Archaeological Journal* 121, 111–53.

Butler, L.A.S. and Graham-Campbell, J. 1990. 'A lost reliquary casket from Gwytherin, North Wales', *Antiquaries Journal* 70, 40–8.

Cowley, F. 2007. 'The relics of St David' in *St David of Wales: Cult, Church and Nation*, ed. J. Wyn Evans and J.M. Wooding, Woodbridge.

Davies, J.R. 2003. *The Book of Llandaf and the Norman Church in Wales*, Woodbridge and Rochester, NY.

Davies, W. 1978. *An Early Welsh Microcosm: Studies in the Llandaff Charters*, London.

Edwards, N. 2002. 'Celtic saints and early medieval archaeology' in Thacker and Sharpe 2002, 225–66.

Edwards, N. (ed.) 2009. *The Archaeology of the Early Medieval Celtic Churches*, Society for Church Archaeology Monograph 1, Leeds.

Edwards, N. and Gray Hulse, T. 1992. 'A fragment of a reliquary casket from Gwytherin, North Wales', *Antiquaries Journal* 72, 91–100.

Edwards, N. and Gray Hulse, T. 1997. 'Gwytherin', *Archaeology in Wales* 37, 87–8.

Evans, J.G., and Rhys, J. (eds) 1893. *Text of the Book of Llan Dâv: Reproduced from the Gwysaney Manuscript*, Oxford.

Falconer, John (ed.) 1635. *The Admirable Life of Saint VVenefride Virgin, Martyr, Abbesse. Written in Latin aboue 500. Yeares Ago, by Robert, Monke and Priour of Shrewsbury …*, Saint-Omer.

Fryde, E.B., Greenway, D.E., Porter, S. and Roy, I. 1986. *A Handbook of British Chronology*, 3rd edn, London.

Geary, P.J. 1990. *Furta Sacra: Thefts of Relics in the Central Middle Ages*, Princeton, NJ.

Geary, P.J. 1994. *Living with the Dead in the Middle Ages*, Ithaca and London.

Glenn, V. 2009. 'St Fillan's crozier – its cult and its reliquaries, AD 1000–2000', in Edwards 2009, 389–404.

Gray, M. forthcoming. 'Saints on the edge: the reconfiguring of sanctity in the Welsh march', in *Rewriting Holiness*, ed. M. Gray, London.

Gregory, J. R. 2012. 'A Welsh saint in England: translation, orality, and national identity in the cult of St. Gwenfrewy, 1138–1512', unpublished PhD dissertation, University of Georgia, Athens.

Gresham, C. 1968. *Medieval Stone Carving in North Wales*, Cardiff.

Holt, G. (ed.) 1971. *The Letter Book of Lewis Saban, S.J. (Rector of St Omer College)…*, Catholic Record Society.

James, J.W. (ed.) 1967. *Rhigyfarch's Life of St David*, Cardiff.

Lifshitz, F. 1995. 'The migration of Neustrian relics in the Viking age: the myth of voluntary exodus, the reality of coercion', *Early Medieval Europe* 4(2), 175–92.

Little, L.K. 1991. 'Spiritual sanctions in Wales', in *Images of Sainthood in Medieval Europe*, ed. R. Blumenfeld-Kosinski and T. Szell, Ithaca and London.

Marshall, J.W. and Walsh, C. 2005. *Illaunloughan Island: An Early Medieval Monastery in County Kerry*, Bray.

McClain, A. 2007. 'Medieval cross slabs in the North Riding of Yorkshire: chronology, distribution and social implications', *Yorkshire Archaeological Journal* 79, 155–93.

McCulloh, J.M. 1980. 'From Antiquity to the Middle Ages: continuity and change in Papal relic policy from the sixth to the eighth century', in *Pietas: Festschrift für Bernhard Kötting*, ed. E. Dassmann and K.S. Frank. Munster, 313–24.

Meijns, B. 2010. 'The policy on relic translations of Baldwin II of Flanders (879–918), Edward of Wessex (899–924) and Æthelflaed of Mercia (d. 924): a key to Anglo-Flemish relations?' in *England and the Continent in the Tenth Century: Studies in Honour of Wilhelm Levison (1876–1947)*, ed. D. Rollason, C. Leyser and H. Wiliams, Turnhout.

Nash-Williams, V. E. 1950. *The Early Christian Monuments of Wales*, Cardiff.

Pepin, R. and Feiss, H. (eds), 2000. *Two Mediaeval Lives of Saint Winefride*, Toronto.

Petts, D. and Turner, S. 2009. 'Early medieval church groups in Wales and western England', in Edwards 2009, 281–300.

Picard, J.-M. 1999. 'Le culte des reliques en Irlande (VIIe–IXe siècle)', in Bozóky and Helvétius, 39–56.

Pritchard, A. 2009. 'The origins of ecclesiastical stone architecture in Wales', in Edwards 2009, 245–64.

Redknap, M. 2009. 'Early medieval metalwork and Christianity: a Welsh perspective', in Edwards 2009, 351–74.

Rollason, D. 1986. 'Anglo-Saxon relic cults as an instrument of royal policy, c. 900–1050', *Anglo-Saxon England* 15, 91–103.

Ryder, P. 1985. *The Medieval Cross Slab Grave Cover in County Durham*. Durham: Architectural and Archaeological Society of Durham and Northumberland Research Report no. 1.

Sheehan, J. 2009. 'A peacock's tale: excavations at Caherlehillan, Iveragh, Ireland', in Edwards 2009, 191–206.

Smith, J.M.H. 1990. 'Oral and written: saints, miracles and relics in Brittany, c. 850–1250', *Speculum* 65 (2), 309–43.

Smith, J.M.H. 2000. 'Old saints, new cults: Roman relics in Carolingian Francia', in *Early Medieval Rome and the Christian West*, ed. J.M.H. Smith, Leiden, 317–40.

Swift, T., S.J. 1910. *The Life of Saint Wenefride*, Holywell.

Thacker, A. 2000. 'In search of saints: the English church and the cult of Roman apostles and martyrs in the seventh and eighth centuries', in *Early Medieval Rome and the Christian West*, ed. J.M.H. Smith, Leiden, 247–78.

Thacker, A. 2002. '*Loca sanctorum*: the significance of place in the study of the saints', in Thacker and Sharpe 2002, 1–43.

Thacker, A. and Sharpe, R. (eds) 2002. *Local Saints and Local Churches in the Early Medieval West*, Oxford.

Thomas, C. 1971. *The Early Christian Archaeology of North Britain*, Oxford.

Thomas, D.R. 1908–13. *Esgobaeth Llanelwy. A History of the Diocese of St. Asaph*, 3 vols, Oswestry.

Thomas, I.G. 1974. 'The cult of saints' relics in Anglo-Saxon England', unpublished PhD thesis, University of London, 1974.

Thorpe, L. ed. and trans. 1978. *Gerald of Wales: The Journey through Wales and The Description of Wales*, Harmondsworth.

Wade-Evans, A.W. 1944. *Vitae Sanctorum Britanniae et Genealogiae*, Cardiff.

Walsham, A. 2010. 'Introduction', in *Relics and Remains*, ed. A. Walsham, Past and Present Supplement 5, Oxford.

Willis, B. 1719. *A Survey of the Cathedral-church of Landaff*, London.

Winward, F. 1999. 'The lives of St Wenefred', *Analecta Bollandiana* 117, 89–132.

Chapter 22
The Horn of St Hubert in the Wallace Collection

Jeremy Warren

Most people would probably think that the Wallace Collection, that temple to the decidedly pagan arts of 18th-century France, would be the last place to find objects of Christian devotion. However, whilst honouring his father, the 4th Marquess of Hertford's appreciation for the 18th century, Sir Richard Wallace (1818–90) ensured that his own contribution to the Wallace Collection reflected his genuine personal passion for the Middle Ages and the Renaissance. Wallace created at Hertford House a world-class collection of European arms and armour, together with a smaller but significant collection of medieval and Renaissance paintings, sculptures and decorative arts.

Within this part of the collection there are a surprising number of objects designed to hold relics or fragments from reliquaries, and even one or two relics themselves. As well as the 'Horn of St Hubert' (the subject of this paper), these include a phylactery with a rectangular compartment for the relic set within four lobes (**Pl. 1**),[1] not dissimilar in form to the phylactery with scenes from the discovery of the True Cross by St Helena displayed in the *Treasures of Heaven* exhibition.[2] In its present state the relic compartment of the Wallace Collection phylactery (which has in its lower side a horn window which would once have been transparent, allowing the contents to be viewed) contains four relics labelled in a 17th-century hand as relics of the 6th-century St Lupentius. However, the inscription on the cover of the relic compartment reads: 'Jesus of Nazareth, King of the Jews', implying that it was originally made to contain a relic of Christ. The Wallace Collection reliquary might well originally have been made to house a fragment of the Crown of Thorns, with the spiky engraved trees and foliage surrounding the relic compartment being intensely thorn-like. Evidence for some royal connection seems to lie in the large *fleur-de-lis* in vernis brun on the reverse, accompanied

Plate 1 Reliquary, now containing relics attributed to St Lupentius, but possibly originally a reliquary of the Holy Thorn. Northern France or Meuse region, 14th century, gilt-bronze, champlevé enamel, cabochon gemstones and vernis brun. The Wallace Collection, London (© By kind permission of the Trustees of the Wallace Collection)

Plate 2 The Horn of St Hubert, Southern Netherlands, early 15th century, with later 15th-century embellishments, cow horn, ambergris, silver, enamel, gold-wire and silk, length 49.6cm, diameter (at mouth) 5.8cm. The Wallace Collection, London (© By kind permission of the Trustees of the Wallace Collection)

by a plethora of tiny *fleurs-de-lis* stamped into the silver sides of the reliquary.

Perhaps the best-known relic in the Wallace Collection is an Irish bell shrine associated with another 6th-century saint, Mura, who lived in Donegal, where the bell shrine remained for many centuries until its sale in the 1840s.[3] After passing through a number of collections, including that of Lord Londesborough, the 'Bell of St Mura' was acquired by Sir Richard Wallace in 1879, the same year that he bought the Horn of St Hubert. The Wallace Collection, like the British Museum with its Holy Thorn Reliquary, owns a reliquary formerly in the Geistliche Schatzkammer in Vienna, but stolen during the 1860s by the duplicitous Viennese art dealer, Salomon Weininger. It is a rock-crystal casket made around 1560 in Milan, with low relief carvings depicting the four seasons and the symbols of the Zodiac.[4]

With this iconography, it was perhaps a rather incongruous object to have served, as it once did, as a container for a number of severed toes, said to have come off the feet of victims of the Massacre of the Innocents. These still reside in the Geistliche Schatzkammer, housed within the imitation casket substituted by Weininger.[5]

However, the most historically significant relic in the Wallace Collection is unquestionably the so-called 'Horn of St Hubert', patron saint of hunters, mathematicians, opticians and metalworkers (**Pls 2–4**).[6] In its current state, battered and by no means spectacular, the Horn certainly deserves to be better known as a relic, since its story is a fascinating one in which legend needs to be carefully separated from the facts such as they are, a recurring issue with relics.

Described in the 1920 catalogue of the Wallace Collection as a 'curious relic',[7] the Horn of St Hubert consists

Plate 3 and 4 Details of Plate 2, showing (left) a band of plain ambergris and one of the enamelled rings and (right) architectural decoration

Plate 5 Detail of serving knife with the arms of Philip the Good, Duke of Burgundy, France or Burgundy, c. 1430–40, iron, steel, rosewood, gold, silver, enamel and copper, enamelled, length of handle 13.4cm, length of blade 27.7cm. The Wallace Collection, London (© By kind permission of the Trustees of the Wallace Collection)

Plate 6 *The Vision of St Hubert*, German, c. 1450–1500, hand-coloured woodcut, 18.9cm x 12.9cm. British Museum, London (1856,0815.92)

of a cow horn which has been extensively decorated. The most significant surviving decoration is a series of applied sections of moulded decoration, depicting scrolling floral designs and, in the largest sections, architectural details of an ecclesiastical building. Near the mouthpiece of the horn there are some thinner, smoothly applied layers. The moulded decoration is now severely damaged, but what remains is enough to show that it was of the highest quality. Close to the mouth of the horn there is a band of gold or silver-gilt thread formed by fine wire having been wound over a silk core and, above this, there are the remains of a further band of red silk around the mouth of the horn. Further down the horn, and set amidst the applied decoration, are two silver bands decorated with inlaid enamelled foliage. Despite the loss of most of the enamel, the decoration of these rings is of high quality and may be compared with the better preserved enamelling on other contemporary objects. Such examples are the serving knife of Philip the Good, Duke of Burgundy (1396–1467), of c. 1430–40 (**Pl. 5**);[8] a knife, also in the Wallace Collection, perhaps made before 1429 and bearing the arms of Philip the Good's chancellor, Nicolas Rolin (1376–1462) (or of his son Guillaume);[9] or a 15th-century travelling spoon in the British Museum.[10] Although it is clear that the decoration was once much more extensive, some areas of the surface of the horn do appear to have always been left bare, for

example in the middle. It would no doubt have been regarded as important to leave some part of the precious relic physically tangible, as well as recognizable for what it actually originally was.

Hubert was born around 656 and died in 727.[11] He spent most of his life in the area of the Ardennes, the forested area covering parts of the southern Netherlands, Luxembourg and France. In around 712 he became bishop of Liège, where he founded the collegiate church of Saint-Pierre. The earliest near contemporary accounts of his life focus on his activity as a churchman and a converter of pagan souls. After his death in 727, St Hubert was buried in the crypt of Saint-Pierre, from where in 743 his body was exhumed, smelling sweetly and showing no evidence of decay. Some 80 years later, in 825, the body (still uncorrupted) was again exhumed and transferred in its sarcophagus to the abbey church in the small town of Andange, later re-named Saint-Hubert. It was in fact only *after* the saint's arrival in Saint-Hubert, which nestles in the heart of the Ardennes forest, that stories relating to St Hubert with forest and hunting elements in them started to multiply. From the 11th century Hubert began to be invoked for the protection from and cure for rabies, whilst it seems that it was as late as the early 15th century that the story of the vision of Christ to the early Christian martyr Placidus, subsequently St Eustace, was transferred almost verbatim to Hubert.[12]

Plates 7–8 The chapel of St Hubert, Chauvirey-le-Châtel, completed 1484 (Pl. 7 © Monuments historiques, Pl. 8 Ministère de la Culture (France) – Médiathèque de l'architecture et du patrimoine – diffusion RMN)

In this well-known story, Hubert was portrayed as having begun his life as a wealthy young aristocrat, given to worldly pleasures, including hunting. After the death of his wife and son he retreated into the Ardennes, giving himself up entirely to the chase, even on holy days. One Good Friday he was in the forest when he realized that the stag at which he was taking aim carried the figure of the crucified Christ between its antlers, while a voice sounded out: 'Hubert, unless you turn to the Lord and lead a holy life, you shall quickly go down into hell.' In this version of the hagiography, this admonishment motivated Hubert to give away all his wealth and worldly goods, enter the Church and begin his life of good works. Numerous works of art from the 15th century depict St Hubert's vision of the stag, for example a print dated 1450–1500 (**Pl. 6**), or the panel from the workshop of the Cologne painter known as the Master of the Life of the Virgin, of *c.* 1485–90, in the National Gallery, London. In both images Hubert's hunting horn is in a prominent position, hung from his belt.[13]

The horn now in the Wallace Collection is therefore most unlikely to date from earlier than the 15th century when it was first documented, although it has never been the subject of technical examination to help determine its origins. It is also one of at least four relics of this type to have survived, all of which date from the 15th or 16th centuries. The others are horns in the abbey church of Saint-Hubert, a further example in the museum in Puy-en-Velay[14] and yet another in the church of Tervuren, near Brussels. From the 16th century comes a horn sheathed in copper painted in enamel in Limoges in 1538 by Léonard Limousin, now in a private collection in London.[15] The Wallace Collection horn is first recorded in the late 15th century, when the small chapel built

for it within the curtilage of the castle of Chauvirey in the Haute-Saône region of France was constructed (**Pls 7–8**). It remained there until 1869 and was mentioned as still present in the chapel in Bouvot de Chauvirey's *La Terre de Chauvirey*, published in 1865.[16] Exactly how it got to Chauvirey is not entirely certain and the story of its history from 1484 (the date of the chapel's completion) depends on a resumé of documents, the whereabouts of which are unknown and may no longer exist.

In April 1879, Sir Richard Wallace bought the horn from the comte de Scey, a sugar magnate who had already sold what remained of the castle together with its surviving chapel ten years earlier. With the horn came a cache of documents which, it appears, Richard Wallace left with the French critic and writer Charles Yriarte (1832–98), who seems to have acted as a go-between for this transaction. Lady Wallace's bequest to the nation did not include the archives associated with the collection, which instead passed to her residuary legatee, Sir John Murray Scott. In 1942, the Trustees of the Wallace Collection were able to acquire a series of eight letters from Yriarte and the comte de Scey to Wallace, which document the purchase.[17]

The letters from the comte include little of significance, but document his complaint that the price agreed was rather low, Wallace's immediate addition of another 1,000 francs and Scey's subsequent grovelling letter of thanks. In his letter of 27 March 1879, the comte also added a letter of 28 May 1876 from the priest of Chauvirey-le-Châtel confirming that the chapel remained at the time of writing an active centre for the worship of St Hubert. Yriarte wrote to Wallace that the horn had also arrived accompanied by a bag containing a 'voluminous archive of documents', which told

Plate 9 The altar from the chapel of St Hubert in its pre-1998 state (Ministère de la Culture (France) – Médiathèque de l'architecture et du patrimoine - diffusion RMN)

Plate 10 The iron case, in the form of a hunting horn, constructed to hold the Horn of St Hubert, France, 17th or 18th century. The Wallace Collection, London (© By kind permission of the Trustees of the Wallace Collection)

its entire history. He was evidently asked by Richard Wallace to go through these documents and in 1882 wrote to Wallace with a summary of their contents.[18] It is not clear however that Yriarte ever passed the original documents on to Sir Richard Wallace and certainly there has been no further sign of them since. Consequently, we have to depend for what we know of the horn's history upon Yriarte's summary of the documents' contents. However, there seems no reason to doubt that Yriarte's account, made to his good friend and patron Richard Wallace, was accurate.

According to Yriarte, the history of the horn as told in the documents he summarized began in 1468 when Charles the Bold, Duke of Burgundy (1433–77), marched a second time on the city of Liège, this time to rescue his relative Louis de Bourbon, Prince-Bishop of Liège, who had been besieged in his palace there by the rebellious populace. Charles the Bold, Duke of Burgundy from 1467 until his gruesome death in the battle of Nancy in 1477, and known to his enemies as 'Charles the Terrible', was one of the pivotal figures in 15th-century history, the last of the Valois Dukes of Burgundy and an ally of England through his third marriage to Margaret of York.[19] The fiercely independent city of Liège had been a thorn in the side of the Burgundian dukes for some time and was one of the main barriers to their ambition to unite their northern and southern territories. Charles the Bold had already taken Liège once in the previous year, 1467, but had agreed on that occasion to spare the city from pillage.[20] On finding himself forced to subdue Liège again, this time with the help of the French king Louis XI, he set out to teach the city a lesson its citizens would not forget by razing it to the ground.[21] Charles's orders for the destruction of the entire city, with the exception of churches and religious houses, led to several days of systematic looting. Although Philippe de Commynes suggested that only around 200 inhabitants were killed and that the great majority appeared to have escaped before the pillaging began,[22] other accounts imply that the death toll was much higher. Certainly, any citizens found remaining were thrown into the River Meuse or put to the sword. Amidst the slaughter and pillage, the Duke's main concern seems to have been for the protection of relics.

Olivier de la Marche, a member of the Burgundian force, reported how 'the Duke of Burgundy hurled himself into the church to save the relics and finding there several archers who were engaged in pillage, slew two or three of them with his own hand'.[23] Philippe de Commynes likewise reported that Charles prevented his own troops from entering the church of St Lambert, killing one of the soldiers engaged in pillage.[24] However, although the major churches may have been spared, others were evidently thoroughly ransacked. The horn may or may not have been taken from a church before or during the looting.

According to the documents from which he was working, Yriarte stated that before the start of the troubles in 1468, the oliphant had been deposited for protection with the Prince-Bishop Louis de Bourbon who, on his rescue, presented it to his cousin Duke Charles as a token of his gratitude. This may be correct since, after the destruction of Liège, Charles the Bold seems to have concerned himself with the return of stolen relics, issuing two orders demanding the restitution of stolen objects to the churches, partly in response to Pope Paul II's furious edicts to the same effect: 'and for a long time thereafter the Pope pronounced heavy edicts against all those who had in their possession any object whatever belonging to the churches of the said city, unless they returned them, and the said Duke sent commissioners throughout his territories to carry out the orders of the Pope.'[25] Charles also, of course, made in 1471 his great if somewhat vainglorious gift to the city of Liège, the celebrated reliquary depicting St George presenting Charles the Bold, kneeling and holding a tiny reliquary containing the presumed finger of St Lambertus. Charles had in fact already commissioned the reliquary in 1467.[26]

Yriarte then wrote to Wallace that Charles the Bold built a chapel to St Hubert within his castle at Chauvirey. Charles was certainly devoted to Hubert – indeed, after he had subdued Liège in 1467, he had made a special pilgrimage of thanksgiving to the abbey of Saint-Hubert.[27] However, Chauvirey and its castle was at that time at the very edge of the Burgundian domains, and in fact formed part of the lands of a local lord, Pierre de Haraucourt,[28] whose main

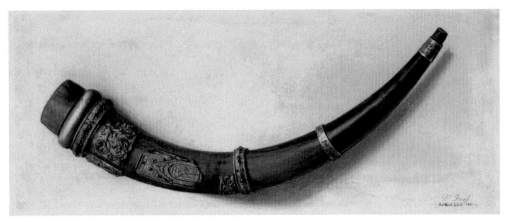

Plate 11 Blaise Desgoffe, *The Horn of Saint Hubert*, 1881. Musée Condé, Chantilly (© RMN-Grand Palais (domaine de Chantilly) / Franck Raux / René-Gabriel Ojéda)

power base was within the Duchy of Lorraine, the other great geographical barrier to Charles's territorial ambitions. It seems more conceivable that the horn was given to Pierre de Haraucourt as a means of gaining his goodwill and support for Burgundian ambitions. Pierre's family was deeply devoted to the cult of St Hubert, and was related to the La Marck family who even claimed to be descended from Hubert.[29] Charles seems to have gone further still, since the intensely Burgundian architectural style of the chapel is of an order of grandeur and sophistication quite unlike anything else in the region.[30] Therefore, perhaps as part of his attempt to gain the favour of the Haraucourt family, Charles also sent one of his architects to Chauvirey.

We also understand from Yriarte that it was around this time that Charles the Bold had the decoration applied to the horn, supplementing the three silver rings, which is stated to have formed its only earlier decoration. This decoration was said, according to Yriarte, to have been made from ambergris, a substance formed from a material found in the stomach of the sperm whale (*physeter macrocephalus*) and prized since ancient times for its extraordinary scented properties. The material has not been subjected to scientific analysis, but visual examination would suggest that it is not gesso, so it may well indeed be an exceptionally rare form of black ambergris, the most sought-after variety of this material. Yriarte's statement that the architectural decoration on the horn was a faithful reproduction of the architecture of the chapel seems to be borne out by comparison between the window forms in the applied decoration and the surviving chapel windows. Finally, evidence for Yriarte's statement that the horn was kept suspended from a pillar of the chapel is to be found in the hole made near the mouth of the horn, clearly for some form of suspension cord.

The date 1484 has been inscribed twice internally in the chapel, presumably the date of its completion. Although its nave has been demolished, it has otherwise survived over the centuries, including most recently in the 1930s when it was nearly transported stone-by-stone to the Cloisters Museum in New York.[31] Today it stands, without its castle, in what is now the tiny village of Chauvirey-le-Châtel. The chapel was also, according to Yriarte, furnished at Charles the Bold's expense with the fine 15th-century stone altar depicting St Hubert's vision, sadly stolen in 1998, although the key central section has since been recovered (**Pl. 9**). The horn itself was handsomely endowed with funds which even

allowed the appointment, until 1790, of its own personal chaplain. The chapel became a very popular place of pilgrimage, with pilgrims praying before the horn, in particular for protection from and cure for rabies.[32] The horn appears to have remained untouched during the French Revolution. In fact the only disturbance it suffered came rather earlier, in 1636 and the following years, when French troops under Cardinal Richelieu invaded the Franche-Comté, besieging and later taking and destroying the castle of Chauvirey.[33] The horn was moved at this time for safe-keeping with the Ursuline nuns in the nearby town of Gray who, with the return of peace ten years later, refused to give it back, until they were forced to do so by a decree from the local Parliament.[34] The nuns are said to have held on to one of the horn's three silver rings,[35] but far worse damage seems to have been caused around this time with, no doubt, the best of intentions. A crude iron case in the form of a hunting horn was made for the relic, perhaps to protect it on its journey back from Gray. However, as Yriarte suggested to Richard Wallace, it is this case (also in the Wallace Collection)[36] which seems to have caused most of the severe damage to the delicate ambergris decoration (**Pl. 10**).

The presence of the Horn of St Hubert in the chapel in Chauvirey-le-Châtel can therefore be convincingly, if indirectly, documented from the late 15th century to the middle of the 19th century. One question which should be addressed is why Sir Richard Wallace, who could have afforded to buy the most glamorous and splendid objects (the British Museum's Holy Thorn Reliquary, for example, was itself on the art market in the early 1870s), was content instead to acquire this damaged, somewhat unostentatious object. It would seem that the extraordinary historical associations of the relic were a significant motive for him. One of the very few comments we have which tell us anything about Sir Richard Wallace's tastes as a collector refers directly to the Horn of St Hubert. In their diary for 27 August 1880, the French art critics Edmond and Jules Goncourt wrote of how 'somebody was telling me about the taste in art of Richard Wallace, buying the hunting horn of St Hubert, not for the object's inherent artistic interest, but for the history which it brings with it, and which he looked forward to recounting to the Prince of Wales, on the first occasion he showed it to him'.[37] Hence Wallace's commission to his friend Yriarte to sift through and report back on the bag of documents.

The Goncourts' statement is extremely important for our understanding of Sir Richard Wallace, emphasizing as it does the importance of history to him. Wallace was evidently an extremely well-read and intelligent man, who was acutely aware of history, which informed much of the collecting he undertook on his own account after, in 1870, he inherited the fortune of his father, the 4th Marquess of Hertford, although not his title. Wallace acquired in fact a number of objects with claims of association to great historical figures, often on grounds no more or less firm than those supporting the provenance of many Christian relics. Thus, the Wallace Collection today owns objects acquired by Wallace and which have a secure historical provenance, for example a parrying dagger given to King Henri IV of France by the city of Paris on the occasion of his marriage to Marie de'Médicis in 1600,[38] as well as other objects for which the historical evidence is less secure, such as a set of 17th-century tobacco pipes, reputed to have belonged to Sir Walter Raleigh.[39] Richard Wallace would certainly have been attracted to the Horn of St Hubert because of its impeccable provenance, as well as, in the words of the Goncourts, 'the history which it brings with it'. When Sir Richard Wallace's friend and collecting rival, the duc d'Aumale, heard about his fabulous new acquisition and asked him for an image of it, Wallace commissioned a painting of the horn from the artist Blaise Desgoffe (**Pl. 11**), writing to the Duke that 'I think that a photograph or a drawing would give you neither its character, nor its colour.'[40] Desgoffe's painting can be admired in the duc d'Aumale's temple to French history at the Musée Condé in Chantilly[41] while the real horn, divorced from its original context and not a relic St Hubert himself would have recognized, but nevertheless still pregnant with history and intensely moving as an object, may be admired and studied in London, in the galleries of the Wallace Collection.

Notes

1 Wallace Collection, Inv. W16.
2 Bagnoli *et al.* 2010, 180, no. 88.
3 Wallace Collection, Inv. W2.
4 Wallace Collection, Inv. W65. Rainer 2009, 83–5, Abb. 33.
5 Ibid., Abb. 32. For Weininger and his activities in the forgery of works of art, see also Hayward 1974 and more recently Truman 2012, 99–100.
6 Wallace Collection, Inv. W31. For the horn, see Mann 1951 and Hardwick 1981, 46–8.
7 Wallace Collection 1920, 76.
8 Wallace Collection, Inv. A881. Mann 1962, vol. II, 26–7, pl. 146.
9 Wallace Collection, Inv. A880. Ibid., 426, pl. 146.
10 British Museum, PE 1899,1209.3. Robinson 2008, 234.
11 For St Hubert, see the *Biographie Nationale de Belgique* 1886–7, vol. 9, Brussels, 593–602; Dierkens 2010.
12 Dierkens 2010, 8.
13 National Gallery, London, inv. NG252. From the Werden altarpiece.
14 Gaidoz 1887, 66, n. 3.
15 Hackenbroch 1954; Wilson 2009.
16 Bouvot de Chauvirey 2011, 4–5.
17 Acquired from Dr Macbeth-Elliott, physician to Miss Mary Scott, the last surviving sister of Sir John Murray Scott. The letters are kept on the object file for the horn.
18 Letter of 1 July 1879.
19 For Charles the Bold, see for example Kirk 1863–8; Vaughan 2002; Dubois 2004; Marti *et al.* 2008.
20 Kirk 1863–8, vol. I, 444–50; Dubois 2004, 178–80.

21 Kirk 1863–8, vol. I, 528–46; Dubois 2004, 208–12.
22 Commynes 1924–5, vol. I, 161–2.
23 '… et le duc de Bourgoingne se bouta en l'eglise pour saulver les reliques, et trouva aucungs archiers qui faisoient le pillaige et en tua deux ou trois de sa main' (de la Marche, vol. III, 86–7).
24 Commynes 1924–5, vol. I, 162.
25 '… et aussy long temps après le pape prononça grans censures contre tous ceulx qui avoient aucune chose appartenant aux eglises de ladicte cite, s'ilz ne le rendoient, et ledit duc deputa commissaires pour aller par tout son pays faire executer le mandement du pape')(Commynes 1924–5, vol. I, 162–3).
26 For the reliquary of St Lambert, see Campbell 1980 and also Kupper and George 2007, 48–51 and 58–61.
27 On 9 December 1467; de la Marche, vol. III, 68, n. 1.
28 Bouvot de Chauvirey 2011, 30–1.
29 Roser 1994, 29, 36, n. 12, where it is suggested that the Haraucourt and La Marck families were responsible for introducing and developing the cult of St Hubert in Burgundy in the 15th century.
30 Roser 1994, 33–4.
31 See Engerand 1936.
32 For the cult of St Hubert as a protection against rabies, see Gaidoz 1887.
33 For an account of the taking of Chauvirey in 1642, see d'Arbigny 1908.
34 A copy of the Act of the Parliament in Dole requiring the nuns to restore the horn to the chapel was, according to Yriarte, among the papers in the dossier acquired with the horn. See also Bouvot de Chauvirey 2011, 5.
35 Bouvot de Chauvirey 2011, 5, 8, n. 27, where it is stated that when the Ursuline nuns were driven from their convent during the French Revolution, the ring was passed for safe-keeping to the last Mother Superior of the convent, Madame d'Hurerourt, and then passed to her descendants.
36 Wallace Collection, Inv. A1335. Mann 1962, 622–3.
37 'Quelqu'un m'entretenait du goût d'art de Richard Wallace, achetant le cor de chasse de saint Hubert, non pour l'intérêt de l'objet, mais pour l'histoire qui s'y rapporte, et qu'il pourra raconteur au prince de Galles, la première fois qu'il le lui montrera.' Goncourt and Goncourt 1887–96, vol. 6, 90.
38 Wallace Collection, Inv. A790. Mann 1962, 397–8, pl. 140; Capwell 2011, 178–9.
39 Wallace Collection, Inv. W116. Oswald 1970, 232, 242, pl. 207.
40 Letter of 17 July 1881, '…Je crois qu'une photographie ou un dessin n'en donnerait ni le caractère, ni la couleur, et ayant M. Desgoffe sous la main, je lui ai demandé d'en faire une etude à l'huile de grandeur exacte..' Cited in Garnier-Pelle 1997, 136.
41 Musée Condé, Inv. 542. Garnier-Pelle 1997, 136–8, no. 87.

Bibliography

Bagnoli, M., Klein, H.A., Mann, C.G. and Robinson, J. (eds) 2010. *Treasures of Heaven: Saints, Relics and Devotion in Medieval Europe*, Baltimore and London.

Bouvot de Chauvirey, M.A.-A. 2011. *La Terre de Chauvirey*, Memphis 2011 (reprint of 1865 edn).

Campbell, M. 1980. *The Gold Reliquary of Charles the Bold*, London.

Capwell, T. 2011. *Masterpieces of European Arms and Armour in the Wallace Collection*, London.

Commynes, P. de, 1924–5. *Mémoires*, ed. J. Calmette, 3 vols, Paris.

D'Arbigny, F. 1908. 'Prise du château de Chauvirey en 1642', *Bulletin de la Société Historique et Archéologique de Langres* 5, 13–18.

de la Marche, O. 1883–8. *Mémoires d'Olivier de La Marche*, ed. H. Beaune and J. d'Arbaumont, 4 vols, Paris.

Dierkens, A. 2010. 'Saint Hubert, Patron des Chasseurs et Guérisseur de la Rage', *Bloc-Notes (Bulletin périodique du Trésor de la Cathédrale de Liège)* 23, 3–10.

Dubois, H. 2004. *Charles le Téméraire*, Paris.

Engerand, R. 1936. 'Une Tempête autour d'une Chapelle. Chauvirey-le-Chatel', *L'Illustration*, 29 August 1936.

Gaidoz, H. 1887. *La Rage et Saint Hubert*, Paris.

Garnier-Pelle, N. 1997. *Chantilly, Musée Condé: peintures des XIXe et XXe siècles*, Paris.

Goncourt, E. and Goncourt, J. 1887–96. *Journal. Mémoires de la Vie Littéraire*, 9 vols, Paris.

Hackenbroch, Y. 1954. 'A Limoges enamel hunting horn', *The Connoisseur* 133, 249–51.

Hayward, J. 1974. 'Salomon Weininger, Master Faker', *The Connoisseur* 169, 170–9.

Kirk, J.F. 1863–8. *History of Charles the Bold, Duke of Burgundy*, 3 vols, London.

Kupper, J.-L. and George, P. 2007. *Charles le Téméraire. De la violence et du sacré*, Liège.

Mann, J. 1950. 'The Horn of Saint Hubert', *The Burlington Magazine* 92, 161–5.

Mann, J. 1962. *Wallace Collection Catalogues. European Arms and Armour*, 2 vols, London.

Marti, S., Borchert, T.-H. and Keck, G. (eds) 2008. *Karl der Kühne. Kunst, Krieg und Hofkultur*, Stuttgart.

Oswald, A. 1970. 'The clay tobacco pipe. Its place in English ceramics', *Transactions of the English Ceramic Circle* 7, pt 3, 222–45.

Rainer, P. 2009. '"Es ist immer dieselbe Melange". Der Antiquitätenhändler Salomon Weininger und das Wiener Kunstfälscherwesen im Zeitalter des Historismus', *Jahrbuch des Kunsthistorischen Museums Wien* 10, 28–95.

Robinson, J. 2008. *Masterpieces of Medieval Art*, London.

Roser, S. 1994. 'La chapelle Saint-Hubert à Chauvirey-Le-Châtel', *Histoire de l'Art* 28, 27–36.

Truman, C. 2012. 'Jewelry and precious objects', in *Decorative Arts in the Robert Lehman Collection*, ed. W. Koeppe *et al.*, New York, 95–101.

Vaughan, R. 2002. *Charles the Bold, the Last Valois Duke of Burgundy*, rev. edition, Woodbridge.

Wallace Collection 1920. *Illustrated Catalogue of the Furniture, Marbles, Bronzes, Clocks, Candelabra, Majolica, Porcelain, Glass, Jewellery, Goldsmith's and Silversmith's Work, Ivories, Medals, Illuminations, Miniatures and Objects of Art Generally in the Wallace Collection*, London.

Wilson, T. 2009. 'The Limoges enamel horn' in *Horace Walpole's Strawberry Hill*, ed. Michael Snodin, New Haven and London, 202–3, 289, no. 65.

Chapter 23
Preserved Miraculously
Relics in the Old Catholic St Gertrude's Cathedral in Utrecht, Netherlands

Anique de Kruijf

The Reformation brought an abrupt end to the medieval practice of public relic devotion in the Netherlands. Relics from countless towns, such as Utrecht, in the Northern Netherlands were gathered and transported to safe Catholic locations such as Cologne and Louvain. Around 1650, the threat to the relics slowly diminished and Catholics began to bring them back to the Netherlands.[1]

Introduction
On 1 March 1597, Mother Superior Geertruijdt of the convent of St Agnes in Arnhem in the east of the Netherlands wrote a letter to Sasbout Vosmeer. Her convent was under increasing threat from reformers and the building had suffered repeated attacks. Geertruijdt told Vosmeer that she and the other sisters had done everything in their power to protect the convent's valuables and that God himself had given her additional strength to rescue the holy possessions of the convent. She concludes her report by stating that it was God who had 'miraculously preserved his holy things'.[2] Geertruijdt had reported this to Sasbout Vosmeer on account of his position as apostolic vicar, a type of deputy bishop whom the pope had appointed to the Northern Netherlands, which was now a mission area. The episcopal hierarchy of the Catholic religion no longer existed. The dishonoured Catholic Church had been committed to the care of the apostolic vicar and it was therefore Vosmeer's responsibility to protect the Catholic religion from the threats of the Reformation.[3]

The rise of Calvinism threatened not only the Catholic religion, but Catholic heritage as well. Protestants confiscated church buildings and they removed or demolished Catholic valuables including liturgical possessions, statues, paintings and perhaps most significantly of all, relics. Protestants believed that relics were the ultimate example of devotional excess in the Catholic Church. In one church in Arnhem the reformers crushed the relics with their feet, while in another they made

Plate 1 Reliquary bust of St Frederic made by Elyas Scerpswert, 1362, gilded silver, h. 45cm. Rijksmuseum, Amsterdam

Plate 2 Glass cylinder containing a piece of St Willibrord's rib, glass, bone and brocade, main altar in St Gertrude's Cathedral, Utrecht

fun of the relics by walking around with the holy remains attached to their hats.[4] Catholics did their utmost to try and save the relics, as unlike gold and silver they were irreplaceable. Many relics and their containers were successfully saved and can now be found in the collection of relics in St Gertrude's Cathedral in Utrecht. This treasure house reveals some spectacular stories about these Catholic rescue operations.

The Reformation in Utrecht

The medieval churches of Utrecht contained a variety of relic types and although it appears that Utrecht was never a major centre for pilgrimage, the relics were extremely valuable to the clergy and religious laymen of Utrecht. This is evident from the many reliquaries that were donated to and acquired by Utrecht churches, which were displayed and used in public rituals organized for their promotion such as processions.[5]

In 1578 the reformers or Calvinists claimed the buildings of the Catholic Church for their own meetings throughout the Netherlands. Before these buildings could be functional for their religious use, the reformers felt that the buildings needed to be cleansed. This meant that everything that reminded them of the former Catholic use of the buildings had to be removed or demolished. Gold and silver objects were melted down. Many relics had been mounted in reliquaries made of precious metals, which were destroyed by the reformers who viewed this material as idolatrous.

However, the contents of the reliquaries were of much greater value to the Catholics than the containers. During this period of religious tension many reliquaries were emptied and then handed over to the Protestants who proceeded to melt them down. Of the many reliquaries that were made and used in late medieval Utrecht, only two have survived. Firstly, there is a gilded silver bust of St Frederic, a bishop of Utrecht in the 9th century (**Pl. 1**). The underside of the bust contains an inscription that details how the bust was made by Elyas Scerpswert in 1362. The second reliquary to have survived is an ivory casket with gilded silver strips and is discussed below (**Pl. 3**). Despite the survival of these two reliquaries, it is generally believed that the Reformation left most surviving relics without their mountings. It was during this period that many relics were temporarily wrapped in pieces of textile or paper.

The Reformation in Utrecht displaced those who still held onto their Catholic beliefs. The parishioners of the medieval church of St Gertrude were forced to abandon their church building in 1580. Not much is known about the activities of this parish immediately after the expulsion, but it is possible that Mass may have been celebrated in the private home of one of the parishioners.[6] This hidden church became a safe haven, not only for religious celebration but also for relics from towns all across the Northern Netherlands. Today, over 1,700 relics are kept in the successor of the hidden church: the Old Catholic St Gertrude's Cathedral in Utrecht. Amongst these 1,700 holy remains are five spectacular relics of St Willibrord.

The relics of St Willibrord

In 1301 the canons of the chapter of St Salvator in Utrecht received a magnificent gift from the abbey of Echternach in Luxembourg, consisting of five small relics of St Willibrord. The arrival of the relics would have been met with great celebration by the people of Utrecht as Willibrord was the first bishop of the city. Although bishop of Utrecht, Willibrord had decided upon burial in Echternach and the result of this was that for almost 600 years Utrecht lacked remains – both corporeal and ephemeral – of its founder bishop.[7] With the transfer of these relics, Utrecht became the proud owner of a piece of Willibrord's pallium, a part of his shroud, a fragment of his chasuble, a portion of his leather sandal and a part of Willibrord's rib, now wrapped in a extraordinary brocade pouch that was made around AD 800 (**Pl. 2**). The relics of Willibrord are exceptional not only because Willibrord is so important to Utrecht, but because the dispersal of these relics can be reconstructed. In other words, the movements of these relics can be traced through history.

In around 1400 the canons of the chapter of St Salvator placed the relics in the ivory casket mentioned above (**Pl. 3**). They remained in this casket for over 150 years, but they later had to be moved due to the forces of the Reformation. The canons of St Salvator took the ivory casket along with other valuables to Emmerich in Germany where the tensions created by the Reformation had not yet been felt. A safe haven for the objects was found through a former inhabitant of Utrecht and a confidant of the Utrecht chapter, Jan van den Eynde. In 1609 Utrecht canons made an inventory of their belongings in Emmerich.[8] They decided to bring the valuables back to Utrecht and hide them in the house of Pompeius van Montzima who was the treasurer of St Salvator chapter and therefore a logical choice.

Plate 3 (above) Reliquary casket, *c.* 1400, France, ivory with gilded silver strips, h. 12cm. Rijksmuseum, Amsterdam

Plate 4 (right) *Ostensoria,* 1600–10, glass and silver, h. 41cm. Museum Catharijneconvent, Utrecht

By 1637, however, Van Montzima was dying and sent for canon Gerrit van den Steen, a man who was known in Utrecht as the 'last catholic clergyman'. Among other things, Van den Steen took the ivory casket with the relics of St Willibrord from Van Montzima.[9] In the same year, the chapter of St Salvator, which by now consisted mostly of Protestant members, lay claim on its possessions. Canon Gerrit proved his worth by preserving the precious relics contained in the reliquaries. He returned the casket to the chapter, but not before he had emptied it of its precious contents. Although it is impossible to be certain, it appears that the chapter did not notice that the relics were missing, or if so, they did not care. Canon Gerrit kept the relics personally for another 30 years. In 1666 he gave the valuables to his friend Abraham van Brienen. At this time Van Brienen was pastor of St Gertrude's parish which celebrated Mass in the hidden church. As the relics and

Plate 5 Alb of St Odulphus, linen, *c.* 800. Museum Catharijneconvent, Utrecht

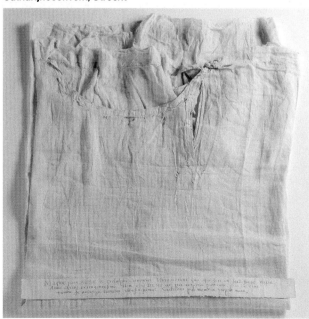

reliquary had now become separated, Van Brienen placed the remains of St Willibrord in two *ostensoria* (reliquaries made of glass) owned by his parish (**Pl. 4**). Although these were not originally made for the relics of St Willibrord – the trigonal bases show images of Sts Barbara, Dorothea and John the Evangelist – this was not important. The silver reliquaries provided a safe and glorious mounting for the relics, something that seems to have been the utmost priority for Van Brienen.[10] From this point onwards, the parish of St Gertrude took good care of St Willibrord. In the early 20th century when the cathedral was built as the successor to the hidden church, the relics were transferred and became part of the cathedral treasury.

The alb of St Odulphus

Another successful survival story relating to the relics of Utrecht concerns the alb of St Odulphus (**Pl. 5**). This beautiful linen alb, probably made around AD 800, is part of the cathedral treasure, but kept at the Museum Catharijneconvent in Utrecht for conservation reasons. Odulphus was a canon and assistant to Bishop Frederic of Utrecht in the early 9th century and he was buried in St Salvator's church in Utrecht. In 1580 the safety of this church was threatened by reformers who intended to demolish the entire building. The grave of St Odulphus was therefore opened and the apostolic vicar Sasbout Vosmeer dug up the alb with his own hands.

Vosmeer sent the alb and countless other relics he had saved from all across the Northern Netherlands to Cologne where his brother Tilman Vosmeer lived. The Reformation had not yet reached Cologne, so Tilman offered the perfect hiding place for the holy remains. As he was his brother's secretary, he registered the valuables he received. His relic lists are extremely informative in that they detail Sasbout and Tilman's rescue of approximately 600 relics. The journey of the alb of St Odulphus is therefore the same as that of many relics. In 1615, a year after Sasbout died,

Tilman arranged for the relics to be transferred to the Collegium Alticollense in Cologne. This was a college founded by Sasbout himself that offered clerical education to young men from the Netherlands where schooling in the Catholic tradition was forbidden.[11]

In 1673, the then apostolic vicar, Johannes van Neercassel, was not satisfied with the way in which the relics were kept at the Collegium. He decided to bring the relics back to the Netherlands and chose the hidden church of St Gertrude's parish in Utrecht as the holding place, which had already taken ownership of the remains of St Willibrord.[12]

The hammer of St Martin

Despite the successful reconstructions of the history of relics outlined above, some relics and their stories can be harder to uncover. This is true even for very distinct relics, such as the hammer of St Martin. The hammer consists of a stone hammerhead from around 1000 BC (**Pl. 6**). This peculiar stone, probably a cult object relating to another pagan religion, somehow became part of the treasury of Utrecht's Dome Church.[13] The placement of the stone within a new Christian context could relate to the canons' desire to Christianize the object. Around 1300 the Dome Church ordered a wooden stalk with a silver mounting to be added with an inscription that reads: 'Idols were knocked down by the axe of St Martin. Do not believe that they, who so easily fall down, are gods.' The story about St Martin destroying idols derives from his *Vita*, written by Sulpicius Severus around AD 420 who details how St Martin built churches and monasteries on the former locations of the idols.

There is minimal information in the archival sources concerning the hammer. The secondary relic is however mentioned in an inventory of 1504. The inventory lists relics in the care of the so-called *questierder*, a travelling 'merchant' who offered laymen the opportunity to venerate the relics he carried with him. This was lucrative for the Dome chapter in two ways. Firstly, the connection between the believers and the chapter became stronger and secondly, the believers could buy indulgences from this *questierder*. In 1504 he was in possession of several relics, one of which was the hammer of St Martin. The inventory provides the *Vita* of St Martin with an exciting twist. St Martin did not smash idols with the hammer, but he fought the devil himself with this instrument![14]

It is here however that we lose sight of the hammer. There are no indications whatsoever about the rescue of this special relic. We do not know when, where or through whom the hammer went into hiding. What we do know however is that at some point it was secluded in the hidden church in Utrecht.

Rescuing relics

The doubts raised concerning the journey of St Martin's hammer prove that reconstructing relic histories is not a simple matter. There are a couple of general reasons for this, the most important being the changed appearance of relics and the loss of the *cedulae* (the small parchment scroll containing critical information about the relic). Often the textile wrappings have been changed – sometimes several times – throughout the centuries. This makes it almost

Plate 6 Hammer of St Martin, *c.* 1000 BC, stalk *c.* 1300, stone, wood and silver, stone, h. 35cm. Museum Catharijneconvent, Utrecht

impossible to connect the description of a relic in a medieval inventory to the actual relic we find today. This kind of research is hindered when the *cedula* is missing.

The successful reconstructions outlined in this study prove that those who rescued relics went to great lengths to preserve the holy remains of the pre-Reformation Catholic church. This was done to guarantee the continued existence of the relics themselves as well as the worship of relics. The relics were crucial for the restoration of the Catholic Church in the Counter-Reformation. Through these relics the Catholic Church found that its identity came from the unbreakable bond with the Roman martyrs who were the founders of their religion. Research on the Utrecht treasure shows that much information can be gained from archival sources. For example, by studying correspondence of the so-called 'relic rescuers' concerning the travails of the relics, it is possible to reconstruct the journeys that holy remains were subjected to. In many cases it is indeed a challenge to unravel the information about relics from the letters and reports in Latin from the 16th and early 17th centuries. However, the results are rewarding as they provide a growing insight into the countless miraculous ways in which relics were saved and preserved.

Notes

1 This article derives from my dissertation (de Kruijf 2011). The footnotes of my dissertation contain a full account of sources and publications used for the research. For further reading on the Old Catholic Church of the Netherlands, see Schoon 2004.
2 Utrecht Archive, HUA OKN 1003-3, f.388-9.
3 De Kruijf 2011, 112.
4 Main altar of St Gertrude's Cathedral, document C-13.
5 Rikhof 1997.
6 Van Ditmarsch 2004, 43.
7 Visser 1933.
8 Utrecht Archive, HUA OKN 1003-19, f.1125.
9 Utrecht Archive, HUA OKN 88-166. Gerrit van den Steen made a list of all the valuables he received.
10 Staal 2000.
11 Van Gruting 1992.
12 Utrecht Archive, HUA OKN OBC-583, f.875r.
13 The medieval cathedral of Utrecht is now known as the Dome Church. The church fell to the Protestants in the late 16th century and has remained a Protestant church ever since. The Roman

Catholics therefore built St Catherine's Cathedral in Utrecht, while the Old Catholics continue to worship in St Gertrude's Cathedral.

14 Utrecht Archive, HUA 216-2505, f.12v.

Bibliography

Archival sources

HUA OKN 88-166: Collected documents of the Old-Catholic Church in the Netherlands, Chapter of Oudmunster: inventory of relics made by Gerrit van der Steen.

HUA 216-2505: Archive of the Dome chapter in Utrecht: inventories of ornaments in the treasury of the Dome church, 1498, 1504, 1530, 1543, 1571.

HUA OKN 1003-3: Archive of the apostolic vicars of the mission in the Netherlands, Sasbout Vosmeer: incoming correspondence, 1583–1614.

HUA OKN 1003-19: Archive of the apostolic vicars of the mission in the Netherlands, Sasbout Vosmeer: outgoing correspondence, 1588–1614.

HUA OKN-OBC-583: Archive of the Oud Bisschoppelijke Clerezie, Johannes van Neercassel: outgoing correspondence, 1663–86.

Secondary sources

De Kruijf, A.C. 2011. *Miraculeus bewaard. Middeleeuwse Utrechtse relieken op reis: de schat van de oud-katholieke Gertrudiskathedraal*, Zutphen.

Rikhof, F. 1997. 'Kathedrale kerk van St. Maarten' in *Bedevaartplaatsen in Nederland* (1997–2004), ed. P.J. Margry and C.M.A. Caspers, Hilversum, 737–47.

Schoon, D.J. 2004. *Van bisschoppelijke Cleresie tot Oud-Katholieke Kerk. Bijdrage tot de geschiedenis van het katholicisme in Nederland in de 19de eeuw*, Nijmegen.

Staal, C. 2000. 'Het bisdom Utrecht: relieken, relikwieën en reliekhouders', in *De weg naar de hemel. Reliekverering in de Middeleeuwen*, ed. H.W. van Os, Amsterdam, 163–98.

Van Ditmarsch, J.N. 2004. *90 jaar kathedrale kerk van Ste. Gertrudis. 6 mei 1914–6 mei 2004. Een terugblik met perspectief*, Utrecht.

Van Gruting, R.R.A. 1992. 'Lotgevallen van relieken van H. Oswald en H. Eusebius uit het bezit van apostolisch-vicaris Sasbout Vosmeer', *Bijdragen en mededelingen van Gelre* 83, 51–83.

Visser, W.J.A. 1933. 'Relieken van de H. Willibrordus, die in 1301 aan de Oudmunster te Utrecht ten geschenke zijn gegeven', *Archief voor de geschiedenis van het aartsbisdom Utrecht* 57, 137–210.

Chapter 24
Change and Continuity in the Display of Relics in England in the Sixteenth and Seventeenth Centuries
The English Catholic Community in a Broader Context

Andrea de Meo Arbore

Following the Act of Supremacy of 1534, an Act of Parliament that declared Henry VIII to be the supreme head of the Church of England, the vilification of the worship of relics became one of the principal goals of royal religious policy. The aim was to gain popular support for the dissolution of the monasteries (which was completed by 1539), where the majority of the most highly regarded relics were preserved and displayed. Through burning relics on pyres and other desacralizing ceremonies that took place from 1536 to 1538, the royal commissioners struck deep at the English people's profound faith in relics.[1] As a result of these acts, a large part of the population gradually accepted the view of relics that had been conveyed through royal propaganda: they were merely 'juggling deceits', set up for the profit of the clergy.[2] The possession of objects identifiable as relics soon became a sign of affiliation to the popish religion and consequently could lead to an accusation of high treason against the monarch, whose title of supreme head of the Church of England had been recognized by parliament in 1531 and confirmed by the Act of Supremacy in 1534.[3]

It is therefore not surprising that in the aftermath of the above events rich or impressive reliquaries were no longer made in England. Firstly, devoting large sums to the making of lavish reliquaries would obviously have been unwise in a country where such items were subject to requisition. Secondly, neither the old relics which survived the post-Reformation destruction nor those of the new martyrs could, in most parts of the country, find a sanctuary, shrine or even a church in which they could be kept and displayed until the second half of the 18th century. Therefore, as Alexandra Walsham explains, 'Despite the constant attempts of the missionary priests to reclaim them into the Church's possession, it is apparent that all too many remained in the hands of those who had rescued them from Protestant destruction'.[4] The combination of lay possession and the danger of requisition not only prevented expensive reliquaries of the type that had previously been displayed in English churches from being made, but it also shaped the appearance and size of the new reliquaries, the majority of which could now be hidden easily in one's pocket in case of a sudden raid by pursuivants (the officials and guards in charge of enforcing the conformity to the Church of England and especially the persecution of the recusants) (**Pl. 1**). The simplicity of the new style of reliquaries should therefore not be considered as an indication of a lesser sense of importance that post-Reformation Catholics gave to relics, but rather instead as a matter of necessity and convenience.

Although many consider reliquaries and relics to be closely connected objects and are aware of the attention that the state and the Church paid to the legitimating power of their collection and display, the survival of so many minor relics in relatively poor reliquaries amongst English Catholics clearly shows that devotion to relics survived. This practice continued even in the absence of churches which could patronise highly decorative reliquaries and at a time when their owners could face criminal charges.

Nevertheless, the devotion to relics of both official and unofficial saints flourished in England during the period

Plate 1 Fragment of St Thomas More's birret (the traditional hat of Catholic priests), metal frame early 17th century, wooden frame late 17th century. Oxford Oratory (courtesy of Father Jerome Bertram)

Plate 2 Reproduction of the visage of Henry Garnet that appeared on a straw-husk by the scaffold at his execution, early 17th century, print. British Museum, London (1856,0614.267)

between the last two decades of the 16th century and 1650. Walsham provides an exhaustive account of relics and associated miracles, covering more than a century of English Catholicism from Henry VIII to the middle of the 17th century: she aims to demonstrate how difficult it is to make a clear and definite division within English Catholicism between the pre-Reformation and post-Reformation period when belief and 'material devotion' escaped the control of an ill-organized and persecuted clergy.[5]

Nevertheless some differences can be detected which help to place the veneration of English relics within a wider history of change and continuity. The question that needs to be asked in order to understand the veneration of relics in post-Reformation England is whether the relic was still the same object of veneration among Catholics both before and after the end of the medieval era. Or were new elements instead introduced in the early modern period which altered the veneration of relics among the English faithful and added further elements to their worship. The example of the English Catholic community is also useful here to outline the more general change in the veneration of relics and attitudes towards religious worship that took place during this period in the majority of Catholic countries. The English Catholic community is not representative of the standard Catholic country at that time, but the conditions which shaped the modern history of that community have affected many Christian countries in the centuries that followed the events examined here. Whereas tradition and

continuity with the past are essential to preserve the unique identity of a persecuted minority, innovation has always been necessary in order to survive the arrival of new and hostile ideologies.

The attitude of post-Reformation English Catholics towards relics certainly had many things in common with medieval traditions, with two aspects deserving particular attention. The first is the mark of the sensational or the wondrous, which underlies the belief in the extraordinary powers of holy remains and the efficacy of touching them. There are many accounts which demonstrate the complete trust of the faithful in the healing powers of any type of relic which had experienced even the slightest of contact with a martyr's body. This applied not only to first class relics which were actual parts of a martyr's corpse, but also to second class relics such as fragments of clothes or even objects like empty medieval reliquaries, which were now seen as relics themselves. One example of this is a linen casket from Glastonbury Abbey which was used to perform healing long after its holy content had been lost.[6] This same wondrous aspect became even more manifest in the stories that soon arose regarding the discovery of martyrs' relics or their miraculous creation. One of the most extraordinary and best known cases concerns a drop of blood shed by the Jesuit priest Father Henry Garnet which fell on a straw husk near the scaffold during his execution in 1606.[7] This piece of straw was discovered a few days after the event to bear the perfect, albeit miniature portrait of Father Garnet which had been miraculously painted in the blood and was collected as a relic (**Pl. 2**). Many people confessed to have seen it, and even the Archbishop of Canterbury Richard Bancroft asked to view this extraordinary relic.[8] It was later brought to the Jesuit house in Liège where it was lost in the aftermath of the French Revolution.

The second aspect of continuation to be considered, which is of a completely different nature to the first, is the awareness of following in the footsteps of martyrs who had suffered on English soil, the most celebrated of whom was St Thomas Becket. The best example of this kind of sentiment and mode of self-representation is Sir Thomas More. In a notable passage from one of his last letters, he wrote that he longed to be executed on St Thomas Becket Eve, as indeed was the case.[9] This passage not only tells us about More's perception of himself as a direct heir of St Thomas Becket, but it was also used by many Catholic writers in the intervening years to draw continuity between the new martyrs and the medieval and more popular English saints.[10]

However at the end of the 16th century, these traditional attitudes towards the veneration of relics were influenced by new elements which introduced a radical change to the way in which relics were conceived and consequently to the devotion which they aroused. Following the persecution of Catholic recusants and the martyrdom of a large number of them, these relics added a new, more vivid value to the traditional aspect of religious and sometimes magical power. The new relics did not relate to distant times and unknown peoples, but they embodied the memory and proof of terrible recent events. They were objects that popular and respected laymen and priests, whose tragic outcomes were deeply fixed in the memory of many, had left behind as tokens of an example to follow. This new element inevitably led to parallels being drawn with other historical contexts. Bypassing the last thousand years, the 16th and 17th centuries became directly linked to the first centuries of Christianity and the era of the early martyrs.

The comparison of contemporary English martyrs with their predecessors in Roman times first appeared in apologetic writings from the end of the 16th century, especially those by Jesuit priests. In the works of authors such as Francisco Suàrez, Thomas Stapleton and Lawrence Anderton,[11] in whose books at least one chapter is always dedicated to relics and martyrs, only ancient authorities are cited to strengthen the assertion that the contemporary figures who suffered for the Catholic faith in England were genuine martyrs and that their relics were therefore a legitimate object of devotion. In fact, explicit references to the most renowned medieval theologians are never found in these writings, which became very popular among the recusants: while Sts Augustine, John Chrysostom, Ambrose and Gregory are frequently quoted, Sts Thomas Aquinas and Bonaventure are barely mentioned.

A reason for this somewhat embarrassing silence was that the teaching of the medieval theologians was often underrated by Protestant writers who placed more authority on the writings of the early Fathers of the Church. By avoiding any explicit reference to medieval sources, the Catholic apologists sought to demonstrate how the present teachings of the Church of Rome were a continuation of those of the authoritative and universally approved Fathers. It was also an attempt to refute prejudiced Protestant accusations: primarily that Catholics continued to worship the remains of saints of uncertain origin, whose lives were largely wrapped in myth and whose cults were deemed as medieval superstitions. Therefore, the historical narrative of continuity within the tradition of medieval Catholic England was overwritten by counter-Reformation scholars and apologists by linking the new martyrs with the ancient pre-medieval ones, whose lives were testified in more prestigious Latin sources.

As a result, the fate of hundreds of people executed during this period in England for their religion assumed a different meaning. Their deaths were no longer seen as a sign of the end of a religious era, but rather as the beginning of a new age of faith and devotion that was fed by the blood of martyrs, in the same way as ancient paganism was forced to yield to Christianity after the killing of the Apostles. The devotion to St Thomas More is once again a good example of this change. If More thought of himself as a successor of St Thomas Becket, 22 years later he was given the title of 'protomartyr' by the Catholic apologist Nicholas Harpsfield. Harpsfield saw strong parallels between More and St Stephen, the protomartyr par excellence. He considered More to be the founder of a new series of martyrs designed to be the seed of the renewal of the Catholic Church in England, in the same way as St Stephen had been the first of the martyrs whose blood had helped to convert the Roman Empire to Christianity.[12] It is interesting to note how Harpsfield made such a significant comparison long before Thomas More had been canonized and his worship fully allowed.

This approach to martyrdom had consequences for the concept of relics, which became something of a sign that martyrs left to the faithful not only to strengthen their faith, but also to encourage them to follow their example. This idea, which was both ancient and modern, had many political consequences. It is significant that it found the strongest support among the Jesuits, who fiercely opposed the Elizabethan regime, and it was not reflected in Stuart religious policy. The perils introduced by this shift in the concept of relics and martyrdom were deeply felt amongst Protestants. By putting aside the old expressions of contempt for relics, Protestant writers were compelled to debate the subject on the same ground as their Catholic counterparts, principally whether the most recent executions were genuine martyrdoms or not.

In 1610 the poet and Church of England minister John Donne, who was from a Catholic family and had attended the execution of a priest in his childhood, published *Pseudo-Martyr*. This work is probably the most famous reply to the Jesuit campaign to promote the veneration of English martyrs, in which Donne strikingly uses the same sources as his Catholic opponents to neutralize their arguments. A year later, the English translation of the Acts of the Apostles in the Authorised Version of the Bible constituted the strongest attack on the cult of relics by omitting the second half of verse 5:15 from the traditional text of the Vulgate which describes how the simple shadow of St Peter caused the sick to be healed. This had traditionally been used as proof of the

ROMA SOTTERRANEA

Plate 3 Detail of the frontispiece of *Roma sotterranea* by Antonio Bosio (Rome, 1632), showing the hypothetical reconstruction of the Roman catacombs and the entombment of Roman martyrs

healing powers of relics, even those which are not part of a saint's body.[13] Nevertheless, the strength of the Catholic argument was so great that, despite their advantageous position, Protestant propagandists felt it necessary to continue their invectives against the cult of martyrs and the veneration of their relics throughout the 17th century.[14]

At the same time an unforeseen event took place in Rome which caused great excitement and produced a significant revival in the worship of relics. In 1578 the ancient catacombs under the Via Salaria were discovered which prompted an extensive exploration of the dungeons in subterranean Rome.[15] These excavations uncovered hundreds of tombs as well as the bones of early Roman Christians with exotic names, accompanied by inscriptions showing the unmistakable signs of martyrdom. The news of the discovery promptly spread throughout the Catholic world, and the newly found ancient relics filled the churches of Italy and travelled widely in Europe. Books were printed about the discoveries in the catacombs, including the beautiful *Roma sotterranea* based on the research carried out by Antonio Bosio, copies of which were highly sought after in London (**Pl. 3**).[16]

The belief that Catholics in England should be seen in the same way as the early Christians in the Roman Empire gradually passed from the Jesuit theologians through to the common faithful. A remarkable example of this can be found in the accounts surrounding the rescue of the corpses of English martyrs in the correspondence of Luisa de Carvajal, a Spanish woman of noble birth who chose to live in London and help the Catholic people, who nurtured the undeclared hope that she would herself die a martyr.[17] In letters of 10 May 1611,[18] 19 October 1612[19] and 31 December 1612,[20] de Carvajal wrote of how her English Catholic companions had managed to rescue the remains of Father John Roberts and Father Maurus Scott, both of whom had been recently executed.

The account given in her correspondence is interesting for a number of reasons. Firstly, when talking about the executed priests, de Carvajal does not hesitate to call them *santos* (saints) and to create relics from their recently deceased bodies, despite the fact that no religious authority had

proclaimed their sanctity. The readiness with which she initiates the production of the relics and sends them to her friends both in England and abroad is indicative of the faith that lay believers placed in the martyrdom of their co-religionists and their certainty of living in an age of martyrs, just as in ancient Rome. Another point of interest is de Carvajal's language and style. Apart from some details, the story told by de Carvajal might easily have taken place amongst the early Christians. Indeed she deliberately uses several words that can be found in the most common Spanish translation of the Gospel account of the entombment of Christ.[21] In this way she constructs an analogy between Christ and the executed priests and between herself and Mary Magdalene, which is conveyed in her letter to the Marquess of Caracena of 10 May 1611 where she states that the linen she used to envelop the relics reminds her of the shroud in which Christ had been wrapped.[22] Finally, one cannot avoid being struck by the attention that she pays to every single material detail surrounding the recovery of the bodies. Despite her almost worship of the bodies of these men who had not yet been declared saints and the fact that she is cutting up their corpses in order to despatch their relics, she does not spare any realistic detail of the proceedings, however gruesome.

It is notable that the worship that surrounded the relics of martyrs collected in this way was different from that shown only a few decades earlier towards relics in churches. These relics had been the destination of pilgrimages and were celebrated mostly for their miraculous powers, but the new relics were now able to add specific new features to these traditional attributes. On the one hand they were the material memory of people whom many of the worshippers had personally met, but on the other hand each relic was the vivid testimony of a martyrdom that was not an isolated episode, but instead part of a critical ongoing moment in history. As a result of these factors – the first linked to personal experience, the second part of a much broader social phenomenon – the use of relics also changed. A number of these relics remained in the hands of devout laymen who, as Sarah Convington explains, preserved the corporal fragments 'for consolatory as well as memorializing purposes'.[23] Other relics were taken abroad by foreign ambassadors or fell into the possession of members of religious orders and as a result they often enriched the display of relics in the English seminaries on the continent, such as those in Rome, Louvain, Seville and Valladolid. The arrival and display of fresh relics obviously had political consequences in the Catholic countries which hosted the English seminaries. The relics became both a public and visible sign of the treatment meted out to Catholics in England and acted as a constant spur to encourage political powers to act in order to achieve religious toleration in England or the re-establishment of the Catholic faith by any possible means.

In conclusion I believe that there was an essential shift in the conception of relics in the 16th and 17th centuries, a change marked by the importance attributed to the historical facts of martyrdom, an accurate description of the event and the stress on the moral example offered by the martyrs. This new position was carefully thought out and used for both pastoral and political purposes, originating amongst educated, often Jesuit, religious circles, but consequently spreading to all the faithful. This change in approach, which concerned relics, religious worship, politics and human emotions, did of course have an effect on reliquaries. If seeing the relic meant also recalling a piece of real history and the disturbing sight of human remains is justified by the moral value of the martyr's sufferings, then it is not surprising that the relic demanded greater visibility and a central place within the composition of a reliquary.

The English reliquaries of martyrs from the early modern era seldom show accurate workmanship and very rarely recall the beauty and lavishness of the earlier containers of relics. The reason for this change is not only a result of functional considerations, as discussed at the start of this chapter, but rather of a new approach to the relic itself which it now became necessary not to hide within a reliquary, but to display openly. It was the relic that mattered, not its glamorous container. Certainly the new documentary value attached to the relic is more vivid when the relic itself is visible and central, and I think this is the reason why numbers of so-called monstrance reliquaries increased across Europe during the 17th and 18th centuries (**Pl. 4**).[24]

The start of this change, which I have studied within the context of the English Catholic community, is perhaps only one episode of a much larger religious and cultural movement that was not exclusive to England. This switch towards a vivid realism in the concept of and in the discourse on relics, as well as in their display, finds parallels in other parts of the continent. This is also reflected in painting and sculpture, such as the works of Carracci[25] and later Caravaggio[25] and their followers in Europe, as well as the wooden painted statues made in Spain,[26] which all strove to produce moving effects in the observer to the extent of generating an 'aesthetic of the pathetic'.[27]

It is impossible to say whether the new kind of reliquaries and these types of artistic production had a common origin beyond their local historical context. However, it may be useful to recall the decree that followed the 25th session of the Council of Trent of 1563 which dealt with the worship of

Plate 4 Bones from the hand of Father John Roberts, a Catholic priest executed in 1611 whose corpse was rescued by Luisa de Carvajal, 17th century brass monstrance reliquary. Downside Abbey, Somerset (courtesy of Dom Benet Watt)

images and relics and listed both under the same title: 'On the invocation, veneration, and Relics of Saints, and on Sacred Images'. In this decree, the worship of images and relics is justified for the same functional reason, namely to recall the supernatural realities through the display of historical facts.[28] This therefore provides a similar explanation to that which I have described in the course of this chapter concerning the changes in the worship of relics amongst English Catholics in the 16th and 17th centuries. The wording of the Tridentine decree should be sufficient to place the aesthetic, historical and theological study of relics and reliquaries alongside that of paintings and other forms of religious art produced during this period, which all strive to highlight the historical and human authenticity of what they represent as well as the accompanying moral exhortation.

Notes

1   See Marshall 2003.
2   Latimer 1844–5, vol. I, 53–4 (sermon of June 1536).
3   The essay by I.D. Thornley (1917) continues to provide a deep and detailed exposition of this subject.
4   Walsham 2003, 797. Walsham later published another essay on a similar subject in which she advances an interpretation of relics within the Protestant context that stresses a gradual shift from iconoclasm to documentary appreciation (Walsham 2010).
5   Walsham 2010.
6   Walsham 2003, 796 from Weston 1955, 111.

7 Foley 1878, 121–33.

8 Bancroft did not manage to see the relic, but had a reproduction made of the husk in red paint with the image of Garnet in an attempt to demonstrate that the pretended miracle was a forgery. His conclusions appeared in Pricket 1607.

9 Rogers 1947, 564: '[T]o morrowe … is S. Thomas evin, and the vtas [octave] of Sainte Peter and therefore to morowe longe I to goe to God, it were a daye very meete and conveniente for me'. See also Lines 2000.

10 For example Stapleton 1588.

11 Suárez 1613; Stapleton 1620; Anderton 1633.

12 In Harpsfield 1932.

13 The controversial words are: '[…] ita ut in plateas eijceret infirmos, et ponerent in lectulis ac grabatis, ut, veniente Petro, saltem umbra illius obumbraret quemquam illorum, et liberarentur ab infirmitatibus suis' (*Acta Apostolorum* 5:15, *Biblia Sacra*, Sisto-Clementina edn, 1592), translated in the Douai-Rheims Bible of 1582 as: 'in so much that they brought forth the sick into the streetes, and laid them on beds and couches, that at the least the shadow of Peter passing by, might overshadow some of them, and they all might be dilivered from their infirmities'. The second half of the verse 'et liberarentur…'. is omitted in the 1611 Authorised Version of the Bible. The last part of the verse had been cited by Augustine in his 39th sermon *De Sanctis*, which was also quoted in Heigham 1623, 104: '[Augustin] sayeth: If the shadow of his body could help then, how much more now, the fulness of his power? Wherein he supposeth two things; The one; that the shadow of his body being here in earth, did both help and heal infirmities. […] The other, that being in heaven, he can still help us by his power.'

14 Examples of the Protestant propaganda against the worship of relics are to be found in pamphlets and polemics, but also in works of religious instruction and within the articles of many Protestant catechisms. The main examples of this kind of works published in the 17th century are: William Perkins, *A Warning Against Idolatry* (1601); John Polyander, *A Disputation against the Adoration of the Reliques of Saints Departed* (1611); Joseph Hall, *No Peace With Rome* (1617); Thomas Cartwright, *A Confutation Of The Rhemists Translation, Glosses And Annotations On The New Testament* (1618); Thomas Jackson, *A Treatise Containing The Original Of Misbelief Concerning The Deity* (1625); Pierre Du Moulin, *The Buckler Of The Faith* (1631); Edward Kellett, *Miscellanies Of Divinity* (1633); George Gillespie, *A Dispute Against The English-Popish Ceremonies Obtruded Upon The Church Of Scotland* (1637); Richard Overton, *New Lambeth fayre* (1642); William Jenkyn, *An Exposition Of The Epistle Of Jude* (1652); Richard Baxter, *The Life Of Faith* (1660); Samuel Annesley, *The Morning Exercises At Cripplegate* (1675); Thomas Manton, *18 Sermons On II Thessalonians* (1679); Anonymous, *Religious reliques, or, the sale at the Savoy; upon the Jesuits Breaking up their School and Chappel* (1688); George Fox, *A Journal Of The Life Of George Fox* (1694).

15 See Bedouelle 2003, 126.

16 One copy of Antonio Bosio's *Roma sotterranea*, was in the possession of the royal family and had been given as a present from Rome by Gregorio Panzani in 1634. See Panzani 1793, 196.

17 Maria Luisa de Carvajal y Mendoza (Jaraicejo 1566 – London 1614), who was from a very noble family in Spain, moved to London in 1605 where she lived in humble conditions and pursued her aim of reconverting England to Catholicism. She died in London and the Spanish authorities arranged for her body to be shipped back to Madrid, where it is still preserved in a velvet coffin in the vestry of the Real Monasterio de la Encarnación. Her life has attracted the attention of scholars in the last two decades with publications in Spanish and English. Warren 2010, 97–147; Pinillos Iglesias 2001; Rhodes 2000. Of particular note is Redworth 2008, which shows a deep understanding of the subject and resists the temptation to portray de Carvajal through literary stereotypes such as gender. The passages from de Carvajal's letters quoted in this essay are taken from: Marañón and Abad 1965. Some of her correspondence is translated in Rees 2002 and the majority of her letters are translated in Redworth 2012.

18 Letter from de Carvajal to Marquess of Caracena, 10 May 1611 (Marañón and Abad 1965, letter 126): '[…] ayer, llegué a merecer, sin merecerlo, el dar la segunda mortaja, o sábana limpia (que me hizo grandemente acordar de la de Cristo), a las reliquias de los dos santos últimos mártires, habiéndolos dado la primera, que, por muy manchada en los adrezos que se pusieron para conservar su carne, era forzoso mudarla en otra. […] mis indignas manos los envolvieron y cosieron en el lienzo, que llaman aquí holanda al que no es grueso. Pesóme no fuese de oro: aunque, en los ojos de la divina piedad, todo lo que se ofrece en su servicio, y de los suyos por él, oro es finísimo.' ('Yesterday I received the undeserved honour of placing a second shroud, a sheet of fresh linen (which reminded me very much of the one of Christ), onto the relics of the last two holy martyrs. I had already given them one, but as it was strongly stained by the ointments applied to conserve their flesh, it was necessary to change it. […] My unworthy hands wrapped and sewed them in a type of linen which here they call "Holland", which is not thick. I regretted it was not gold, although, before his divine mercy, everything that is offered to his service, and by his servants, is finest gold indeed.')

19 Letter from de Carvajal to Marquess of Caracena, 19 October 1612 (Marañón and Abad 1965, letter 151): '[…] cuando los entierran es junto a la horca, en un hoyo hondísimo y muy ancho, que hay mucha cantidad de tierra que quitar, y ponen sobre los Santos los ladrones que ahorcan con ellos. A éstos no los hacen cuartos; y así, bien se ve cuáles son los Santos. Tres días después tuvimos orden cómo robarlos, o mejor decir, tomar nuestro tesoro […] Apercibimos entre nosotras una procesión, cada una con dos candelas en las manos, que fueron doce; y todo el camino de abajo arriba adornado de muchas flores y ramos, llevándolos desde la puerta hasta el altar el mercader y nuestro criado; y con devoción, mezclado gozo y dolor, los pusimos sobre la alfombra, delante el altar, cubiertos con un grande y nuevo tafetán encarnado, con muchas flores odorosas encima; hincadas de rodillas, tuvimos alguna oración allí. […] Este, señora, fue nuestro funeral.' (They bury them near the gallows, in a very deep and broad pit, for which much ground has to be removed, and above the Saints they put the bodies of the common criminals who are executed alongside them. The bodies of the criminals are never dismembered, so that it is easy to tell apart the Saints. After three days we were given instructions on how to steal their bodies, or to be correct, how to seize our treasure [. . .] We gathered in a procession, each of us holding two candles in her hands, twelve in all; and from below all the way above [the oratory] was decorated with an abundance of flowers and branches, while the merchant and one of our servants carried the bodies from the door to the altar. With joy and sorrow, we piously laid them on the carpet before the altar, and covered them with a new crimson taffeta and many fragrant flowers laid onto it. We knelt and prayed. […] Madam, such was our funeral.')

20 Letter from de Carvajal to Don Rodrigo Calderòn, 31 December 1612 (Marañón and Abad 1965, letter 163): '[…] gasto las noches enteras, cansada en aderezarlos con las especias aromáticas, de limpiarlos primero del lodo, coger la sangre que aún brota de algunas de las venas, besando muchas veces sus manos y sus pies, vendando los despedazados miembros con holanda nueva, velando delante dellos y puniéndolos en su sepulcro de plomo, para que puedan conservarse.' (…it took whole nights of hard work, treating them [the corpses] with sweet spices. First I had to clean off the mud from them and collect the blood that was still seeping from some of the veins, kissing often their hands and feet; then we bandaged their dismembered limbs with fresh Holland linen, held a wake over them and finally placed them in their leaden coffins, so that they may be preserved.')

21 Many of her expressions expressively evoke the words used in the editions *Sagradas Escrituras* (1569) and *Reina Valera* (1602), two popular vernacular translations of the Bible which were certainly familiar to de Carvajal and her correspondents. The words *sabana limpia, lienzo, sepulcro* and *especias aromaticas* are especially common in the four Gospels in the description of the entombment of Christ, and the last three terms can be found in John 19:40–1. Other expressions such as 'los ladrones' used to describe the other criminals executed on the same day as the priests and 'tres días después' expressed to indicate the timing of the rescue of the bodies, distinctly recall the *dos ladrones* who were crucified with Christ and *el día tercero* after the crucifixion when the resurrection happened (cf. Matthew 27:38, Mark 15:27 and Matthew 27:64).

22 Letter from de Carvajal to Marquess of Caracena, 10 May 1611 (Marañón and Abad 1965, letter 126): 'dar la segunda mortaja, o sábana limpia (que me hizo grandemente acordar de la de Cristo), a las reliquias de los dos santos últimos mártires'.

23 Convington 2009, 273.

24 To stress the importance of the documentary factor, it is also necessary to recall the increased control of the authenticity of relics through periodic examinations of the collections of relics which became increasingly promoted by bishops during the 18th and 19th centuries.

25 See Jones 1997, 133–62; Boschloo 1974; Spezzaferro 2009.

26 See De Ceballos 2010, 45–58.

27 The definition of 'mentalité pathétique' applied to the artistic expressions of the Baroque art, first coined by Mandrou (1960), has been recently retrieved by Burke 2009.

28 Waterworth 1848, 235–6: 'great profit is derived from all sacred images, […] because the miracles which God has performed by means of the saints, and their salutary examples, are set before the eyes of the faithful; that so they may give God thanks for those things', and later it states: 'Moreover, in the invocation of saints, the veneration of relics, and the sacred use of images, every superstition shall be removed […] in such wise that figures shall not be painted or adorned with a beauty exciting to lust; nor the celebration of the saints, and the visitation of relics be by any perverted into revellings and drunkenness; as if festivals are celebrated to the honour of the saints by luxury and wantonness.'

Bibliography

Anderton, L. 1633. *The Progeny Of Catholics And Protestants*, Rouen.

Bedouelle, G. 2003. *La riforma del cattolicesimo (1480–1620)*, Milan.

Boschloo, A.W. 1974. *Annibale Carracci in Bologna: Visible Reality in Art after the Council of Trent*, The Hague.

Bosio, A. 1632. *Roma sotterranea*, Rome.

Burke, P. 2009. 'The crisis in the arts of the seventeenth century: a crisis of representation?', *Journal of Interdisciplinary History*, XL, 2 239–61.

Convington, S. 2009. 'Consolations on Golgotha', *Journal of Ecclesiastical History* 60, no. 2, 270–93.

De Ceballos, A.R.G. 2010. 'The art of devotion: seventeenth-century Spanish painting and sculpture in its religious context', in *The Sacred made Real: Spanish Painting and Sculpture 1600–1700*, ed. Xavier Bray, London, 45–58.

Foley, H. 1878. *Records of the English Province of the Society of Jesus*, vol. IV, London.

Harpsfield, N. 1932. *The Life and Death of Sir. Thomas Moore, Knight, Sometymes Lord High Chancellor of England* [1557], ed. R.W. Chambers, W. Rastell and E. Vaughan, London.

Heigham, J. 1623. *The Gag of The Reformed Gospel*, Douai.

Jones, P.M. 1997. *Federico Borromeo e l'Ambrosiana: arte e Riforma cattolica nel XVII secolo a Milano*, Milan.

Latimer, H. 1844–5. *Sermons*, ed. G. E. Corrie, 2 vols, London.

Lines, C. 2000. '"Secret violence": Becket, More, and the scripting of martyrdom', in *Religion and Literature* 32, no. 2, 11–28.

Mandrou, R. 1960. 'Le baroque européen: mentalité pathétique et revolution sociale', in *Annales ESC*, V, 898–914.

Marañón, J.G. and Abad, C.M. (eds) 1965. *Epistolario y Poesías de Doña Luisa de Carvajal y Mendoza*, Madrid.

Marshall, P. 2003. 'Forgery and miracles in the reign of Henry VIII', *Past & Present* 178, 39–73.

Panzani, G. 1793. *The Memoirs of Gregorio Panzani*, London.

Pinillos Iglesias, M. 2001. *Hilando oro: vida de Luisa de Carvajal*, Madrid.

Pricket, R. 1607. *The Jesuit Miracles, or New Popish Wonders*, London.

Redworth, G. 2008. *The She-apostle: The Extraordinary Life and Death of Luisa de Carvajal*, Oxford.

Redworth, G. 2012. *The Letters of Luisa de Carvajal y Mendoza*, London.

Rees, M.A. 2002. *The Writings of Doña Luisa de Carvajal y Mendoza, Catholic Missionary to James I's London*, New York.

Rhodes, E. 2000. *This Tight Embrace*, Milwaukee.

Rogers, E. (ed.) 1947. *The Correspondence of Sir Thomas More*, Princeton.

Spezzaferro, L. (ed.) 2009. *Caravaggio e l'Europa: l'artista, la storia, la tecnica e la sua eredità: atti del Convegno internazionale di studi*, Milan.

Stapleton, T. 1588. *Tres Thomae*, Douai.

Stapleton, T. 1620. *Propugnaculum Fidei Primitivae Anglorum*, Paris.

Suárez, F. 1613. *Defensio Fidei Catholicae, Et Apostolicae Adversus Anglicanae Sectae Errores*, Coimbra.

Thornley, I.D. 1917. 'The treason legislation of Henry VIII (1531–1534)', *Transactions of the Royal Historical Society*, 3rd series, vol. 11, 87–123.

Walsham, A. 2003. 'Miracles and the Counter-Reformation mission to England', *The Historical Journal* 46, no. 4. 779–815.

Walsham, A. 2010. 'Skeletons in the cupboard: relics after the English Reformation', in *Relics and Remains*, ed. A. Walsham, Supplement 5 of *Past and Present*, Oxford, 121–43.

Warren, N.B. 2010. *The Embodied Word: Female Spiritualities, Contested Orthodoxies, and English Religious Cultures, 1350–1700*, London.

Waterworth, J. (ed.) 1848. *The Canons and Decrees of the Sacred and Oecumenical Council of Trent*, trans. J. Waterworth, London.

Weston, W. 1955. *Autobiography of an Elizabethan*, ed. P. Caraman, London.

Chapter 25
Bodies, Artefacts and Images
A Cross-cultural Theory of Relics

Steven Hooper

Prologue

This essay begins, where the *Treasures of Heaven* exhibition ended, at the British Museum. In the autumn of 2000 I spent an hour contemplating one exhibit, the remarkable image from Rurutu Island in the Pacific that is covered with 30 smaller images and has a close-fitting panel concealing a carefully excavated chamber at the back (**Pl. 1**). Although perhaps the most famous of all Polynesian sculptures, usually referred to as an image of the god A'a, little is known about its original use prior to it being given to Christian missionaries by newly converted islanders in 1821. I was pondering how the sculpture had been made and why the detachable panel had been carved so precisely to fit the curvature of the head. Also, why had the image been given this deeply hollowed form, which would have involved difficult and time-consuming work with the stone-bladed tools available at this time? Having lived with canoe-builders in eastern Fiji, I knew that Polynesian carpenters would not do technically demanding work without reason. It then occurred to me that the spherical cavity in the head was large enough to admit a human skull and the cylindrical cavity in the body long enough for limb bones. It became clear that the sculpture was a reliquary, a highly accomplished work of art that could be analysed both as a god image and a repository for the relics of a deified ancestor.[1]

This assessment prompted questions about the connections between body parts, containers and images in Polynesia as well as a search for a theory of relics that might illuminate the Polynesian example. In what ways might the A'a image be equivalent to image reliquaries of Christian saints, such as St Foy? Surprisingly, a general theory of relics appeared to be lacking. In most published works the identity of a relic was assumed rather than defined; definitions were implicit rather than explicit. As a result, this essay attempts to provide a cross-cultural definition and theory of relics that includes existing partial definitions and encompasses widespread behaviour that expresses profound human concerns about life, power and causation. Through these means it is hoped that a range of behaviours previously thought to be unconnected can be linked and explained: from the activities of Neolithic people moving bones about the landscape, to the practices of Christians or Buddhists or Polynesians, to the adulation of celebrities such as Lord Nelson or Michael Jackson, to the way we treasure heirlooms or to the value attributed to images, memorabilia and much of what is called 'art'. It is proposed that relic-related behaviour is a cultural practice with very ancient roots and is a fundamental mechanism by which humans have engaged with sources of power to derive benefit from them. A synopsis of the theory will be followed by evidence in the form of a series of short case studies. A brief review of relic-related literature is then followed by a fuller elaboration of the proposed theoretical framework.

A theory of relics

A definition of relics is proposed that distinguishes three types of material manifestation of 'special personages'(gods, ancestors, kings, queens, saints, heroes, celebrities). The three types are: A – body relics, B – contact relics and C – image relics. The inclusion of supposedly 'secular' heroes

Plate 1 Reliquary image of the god A'a, probably 18th century, Rurutu, Austral Islands, wood, h. 117cm. British Museum, London (Oc,LMS 119)

and celebrities in the category 'special personage' and the extension of the definition of relics to include images are significant features of the theory. The aim is to see beyond conventional culture-specific classificatory schemes in order to provide a coherent explanation of the common features of apparently disparate material. All three types of relic are attributed with the life-giving and life-enhancing powers of the original special personage; they embody in different forms the exceptional, thaumaturgic and talented qualities of the prototype and provide a focus for human engagement with such sources of power.

Relic-related behaviour

In 2009, during a tour of Britain, large crowds assembled to venerate the arm and leg relics of St Thérèse of Lisieux contained in an elaborate chasse-like reliquary within a perspex case (**Pl. 2**). On arrival at Portsmouth Cathedral, the *Guardian* reported: 'Many could not resist touching the glass, getting as close as they possibly could to the holiness they believed lay just millimetres away. Others pressed beads, religious figurines, even cuddly toys to the protective case and hoped that the goodness would somehow rub off. The ill prayed to be healed, and relatives of the dying pleaded for a miracle.'[2] St Thérèse died in 1897 and a basilica containing her relics at Lisieux is visited annually by more than two million pilgrims – second only to Lourdes in pilgrimage popularity in France. A major index of the value accorded to relics is the number of people willing to make journeys to see them or make pilgrimages to places whose specialness is determined by their presence, such as Santiago de Compostela in Spain or the Temple of the Tooth in Kandy, Sri Lanka. Such journeys in order to be

close to, interact with and derive benefit (often medical) from relics involve sacrifices of time, energy and resources, including money.

Pilgrimages can also be made to artefacts. At the Marian shrine at Tinos in Greece, built on the site of an earlier Byzantine church and a Dionysian temple, Orthodox Christians, some of whom have crawled up a kilometre-long carpet from the port, queue to bow, prostrate themselves and kiss the jewel-encrusted cover of an icon of the Virgin. The icon is said to have miraculous powers and to have been discovered at that spot in 1823 after a vision by a local nun,

Plate 2 Reliquary for the bones of St Thérèse of Lisieux at the Metropolitan Cathedral of Christ the King, Liverpool, September 2009, during the UK tour of the relics (image courtesy of the Catholic Church, England and Wales)

Plate 3 Wisps of Lord Nelson's and Lady Hamilton's hair, with their provenance document, sold as lot 381 at Holloway's auctioneers, Banbury, England, on 22 February 2011 (courtesy Holloway's, Banbury)

St Pelagia. Along the route to the shrine are numerous stalls selling replica icons and all kinds of memorabilia that have value in a domestic sphere when taken home.[3]

During a visit to the Topkapi Museum in Istanbul in 2011, lines of pilgrims/tourists filed reverentially past the 'Sacred Trusts' – body parts and artefacts – viewable in glazed cabinets behind special barriers. The hair, tooth and footprints of the Prophet, bones of St John the Baptist and Moses's staff were displayed alongside old parts of the Ka'ba and other items from Mecca. In a sumptuous anteroom could be glimpsed an elaborate reliquary-like case containing the Holy Mantle – the Prophet Mohammed's personal robe – one of the greatest treasures of the Topkapi that is periodically brought out from its case for more intimate viewing and which is featured prominently in a lavish publication available at the museum.[4]

Some body relics are commercially available, as was widely the case in medieval Christian history. On 22 February 2011, at Holloway's auctioneers in Banbury, England, a lock of Admiral Lord Horatio Nelson's hair was offered for sale as lot 381. Martyr-victor of the battle of Trafalgar in October 1805 that delivered England from the threat of Napoleonic invasion, Nelson was an English national hero of colossal proportions who received the kind of extreme adulatory attention that can perhaps best be compared to recent behaviour towards Diana, Princess of Wales, in life and in premature death. Vast crowds assembled to cheer Nelson in London during shore leave in August 1805, and huge numbers mourned him during a lengthy funeral procession by river and road to his final resting place in an elaborate tomb-reliquary in the crypt of St Paul's Cathedral. The lock of hair at auction in 2011, according to a manuscript provenance document, had belonged to Lady Hamilton and was accompanied by one of her own – thus providing the additional frisson of their scandalous romantic liaison (**Pl. 3**). With a pre-sale estimate of £3,000–5,000, the two rather insubstantial wisps, folded

within their validating document (strongly reminiscent of labelled Christian relics), sold for £62,400. In addition to pilgrimage, competitive bidding at auction is also an index of cultural value.

Besides body parts, artefactual relics associated with Nelson are also regularly offered for sale. At the bicentennial auction at Sotheby's in London of Trafalgar memorabilia (5 October 2005), a large number of 'Nelson' lots sold well above their pre-sale estimates. Two will be noted here. Lot 184 was 'The Victory Watch', an inscribed pocket watch that was probably carried by Nelson when he died aboard HMS *Victory*. A watch of this type without provenance would have been worth about £10,000–20,000. Sotheby's, knowing a thing or two about relics and celebrity, decided to give it an estimate of £200,000–300,000, but even their optimism paled in the face of a bidder who eventually paid £400,000.

The question arises as to how to account for this enormous difference in value between an ordinary item and one owned by a celebrity – a 'body relic' or 'contact relic' closely associated with a hero's death? A related question emerges in relation to lot 77 in the Trafalgar sale, a portrait of Nelson dating to around 1800 by Lemuel Abbott, a respectable portraitist of the late 18th century. It was one of a series based on a sitting in 1797 (**Pl. 4**). The portrait was given a pre-sale estimate of £80,000–120,000 and it sold for £299,000. Meanwhile, a comparable portrait by Abbott was also in the sale (lot 146), very similar in size, framing and even quantities of oil paint. It was an equivalent artefact to the Nelson portrait in every way, except it was not of Nelson, but was of another now obscure admiral, Sir Robert Bruce-Kingsmill, painted around 1795 (**Pl. 5**). This portrait carried an estimate of £5,000–7,000 and sold for £8,400. The reason for this difference in price between the two pictures, and thus in value according to a major global mechanism of value assessment (an auction), is at once obvious yet problematic. Of course, the Nelson portrait would be worth more because it is of Nelson. But why? Why should a Nelson portrait be worth over 35 times more than an equivalent portrait by the same artist of another admiral? To someone unfamiliar with European history, the only observable differences between the two artefacts are the facial features and minor costume details. This conundrum encapsulates an analytical problem with images, statues and icons, and their relationship to the original body, which this paper attempts to resolve.

Two further cases will be discussed that bear on the issue of premature death and martyrdom, and how auctions are arenas for the establishment of value in the global cash economy. At an Edinburgh auction on 23 March 2003, an early 19th-century walking stick appeared for sale with a silver mount inscribed 'Made of the spear which killed Captain Cook, R.N'. Although an unprovenanced walking stick of this type might have been worth £500, an estimate of £5,000–8,000 was given because of the link to the famous navigator. However, there was no conclusive proof connecting the stick/spear to Cook's death at the hands of Hawaiians in 1779, nor was any claimed by Lyon and Turnbull, the auctioneers. In fact, there is no evidence that it was a spear that killed Cook; the most reliable sources mention a dagger and stones. Nevertheless, at the auction,

Plate 4 Lemuel Francis Abbott (1760–1802), portrait of Admiral Horatio, First Viscount Nelson (1758–1805), c. 1800, oil on canvas, 73.5 x 61cm (image courtesy of Sotheby's)

Plate 5 Lemuel Francis Abbott (1760–1802), portrait of Admiral Sir Robert Bruce-Kingsmill, Bt. (c. 1730–1805), c. 1795, oil on canvas, 71.8 x 57.2cm (image courtesy of Sotheby's)

bidders from all over the world were busy on the telephones and the stick sold for £153,000. Again, how might we account for this extraordinary price difference between an 'ordinary' walking stick and one that might, if disbelief was suspended, have been made from the spear that spilled the celebrated captain's blood?[5]

In 2009 in Los Angeles, the 'moonwalk' glove worn by the recently deceased Michael Jackson was offered at auction with a pre-sale estimate of $40,000–60,000. The following report was released by *Associated Press* (27/11/2009):

> The shimmering white glove Michael Jackson wore when he premiered his trademark moonwalk dance in 1983 was auctioned … on Saturday. Winning bidder Hoffman Ma of Hong Kong will pay $420,000, including taxes and fees, for the rhinestone-studded, modified golf glove.… As the price of the glove soared, fans roared and squealed, echoing the kind of frenzy that accompanied the pop star when he toured the world. 'That's what death brings upon celebrity,' said Brendan Doyle, a college student … 'Jackson's death was such a tragedy at such a young age that it pushed up prices.' The pop icon [*n.b.*] died June 25, aged 50.… Auctioneer Darren Julien said prices for Michael Jackson memorabilia now outstrip those for items belonging to Elvis or Marilyn Monroe.

To bring home the point, also available at that time for purchase online were replica rhinestone-studded 'Michael Jackson Tribute' gloves, priced at $7.50.[6]

Therefore, what do these vignettes, and numerous other case studies, ancient and modern, relating to the high cultural value attributed to Holy Blood, the crown of thorns, the Buddha's tooth, ancestors' bones, early copies of the Qur'an, Jane Austen manuscripts, Gandhi's spectacles and

Marilyn Monroe's dresses have in common?[7] What are the factors that connect them, given they all involve items referred to as relics? In addition, what connects them to images of gods, kings, saints, heroes and celebrities worldwide, including Egyptian, Christian, Buddhist and Hindu statues, Orthodox Christian icons and Andy Warhol portraits of Elvis Presley? Is it analytically useful to classify some as religious relics and others as secular relics? Also, what is the relationship between relics and memorabilia? These and other questions will be addressed by developing a theoretical framework that accommodates apparently disparate material of this kind and also accounts for relic-related behaviour across cultures and throughout human history. However, before outlining this comparative exercise, some terminological and definitional issues need to be resolved.

'Religious', 'secular' and other terminology problems

In order to clear the way for a cross-cultural perspective, some terminological iconoclasm is required since certain key terms that have become commonplace in relic studies merit scrutiny. Culturally specific assumptions, categories and vocabulary deriving from Christian, Islamic, Buddhist, Polynesian or any other tradition need to be set aside or used with care so that widespread underlying patterns of behaviour can be recognized and identified.

To start with basics, etymologically the term relic is related to Greek and Latin words meaning remains or things left behind. At one level of analysis it is a general term applied to things of all kinds, human or otherwise, that remain from the past. The substantive and metaphorical uses of the English term relic, or equivalents in other languages, are often hard to disentangle, although there seems to be agreement that relics are things which have human body properties and associations, or have been connected with human activity through manufacture or use. The body part of a Christian saint or an ordinary person can be called a relic, as are artefacts such as the spear that pierced Christ's side or Nelson's watch. 'Natural' things that are simply old, such as geological specimens or fossils, tend not to be classified as relics, unless the fossil was owned by a famous person, such as Darwin, when it would become a contact relic of Darwin by virtue of being associated with him through ownership and touch, and its cultural and commercial value altered accordingly.

Any study of relics must take account of religion, but familiar European classificatory categories, and especially the oppositional juxtaposition of religious and secular, need to be challenged. In most cultures the religious/secular distinction is neither demonstrable nor illuminating, distorting discussion of behaviour into artificially circumscribed categories that can prove a hindrance to profound understanding. The analytical distinction between religious and secular is deeply ingrained in Western academic writing, yet it is a distinction which for most cultures around the world, including Western ones, is at best problematic. To define domains such as food gathering, house-building, making journeys or buying things as secular does disservice to people's relationships with gods, spirits or ancestors and the pervasive influence of those entities on supposedly mundane 'secular' activities. Relic-related behaviour is most productively viewed as having a religious character, even if it is not explicitly part of the practice of a particular religion. In addition, with respect to Western systems of classification that have often been transferred to the analysis of other cultures' arrangements, Arthur Hocart's perceptive dictum is a salutary corrective: 'How can we make any progress in the understanding of cultures, ancient or modern, if we persist in dividing what the people join, and in joining what they keep apart?'.[8] So, some classificatory scepticism is appropriate, especially in relation to the notion of 'secular', as it frees us to think comparatively about a range of human behaviour. It also permits us to see connections in human behaviour that allow more nuanced understandings of aetiology, religion, medicine and 'celebrity/hero culture' worldwide and over many millennia.

A second heresy needs to be committed in the service of developing the theory, and this is to ignore all culturally specific theological or philosophical expositions about 'belief' (doctrine, dogma, creed) as they are obstructive in terms of a cross-cultural theory. Valuable as written or verbal versions of beliefs are for specific studies of Christianity, Buddhism, Islam and the like, or for comparative religious studies, they can prevent us from observing similarities in practice. Accordingly, an essential process in developing the theory will be to focus on what people do and have done in relation to those persons or things attributed with special powers and qualities, rather than what people say or write about them. The focus will be on practice, not expressed belief. It is argued that throughout human history, practice – what people do – has constituted

religion for the great majority of people, not verbal or written expositions by an elite minority. The scholar of Buddhism, Gregory Schopen, lends support to this approach when he advocates studies 'on the ground'. He recommends that we should be 'preoccupied *not* with what small, literate, almost exclusively male and certainly atypical professionalized subgroups wrote, but rather, with what religious people of all segments of a community actually did and how they lived'.[9] There remain fundamental similarities in practice, if not in doctrine, in all religions: people assemble periodically at special places, often associated with the dead, to sing/dance/process, to recite formulae and to make offerings to sources of power. These sources of power – gods, ancestors and spirits – are attributed with sometimes capricious life-enhancing and life-destroying powers that are nevertheless considered amenable to human influence under prescribed circumstances (ritual). At its core, religious behaviour is about the establishment and maintenance of mutually beneficial exchange relationships between humans and sources of power. Sacrifices of time, skill, energy and resources, including money, animals, plants and even human life, are made to higher powers to solicit divine blessings that bring about abundance, prosperity, health and success – in effect providing the means for the production of new sacrifices to continue the cycle.

Let us take one case study as an example of the usefulness of focusing on practice not dogma and of rejecting the religious/secular distinction in order to see connections in supposedly disparate behaviour. The remains of a saint such as St Thérèse taken on tour – temporarily translated so they can be venerated by devotees who congregate and queue for the purpose – elicits behaviour similar to that associated with large blockbuster exhibitions, such as the 2011–12 Leonardo exhibition at the National Gallery in London or the famous Tutankhamun exhibition at the British Museum in 1972. We may sense intuitively that there are strong similarities between a pilgrimage to Mecca or Lourdes and a journey to Graceland or to a blockbuster exhibition because they involve equivalent behaviours that collapse the unhelpful distinction between pilgrimage to a religious/sacred site and a visit to a secular/profane exhibition. Seen at the level of practice, or behaviour, both activities involve sacrifices of time and resources in order to engage with something that has the power to be life-enhancing physically, spiritually, emotionally, intellectually or socially. The *Treasures of Heaven* exhibition at the British Museum in 2011 is a key example in this regard because of its subject matter and the ambiguity reportedly expressed by many visitors about whether it was a religious or secular experience. Kissing of display cases necessitated extra cleaning.[10] The common observation that museums are the new temples is more than a metaphor – it is true at the level of practice.

Defining/theorizing relics

A survey of recent literature shows burgeoning activity in relic studies, moving away from hagiography to develop increasingly sophisticated analyses and theoretical frameworks for discussing relics in specific cultural and historical contexts, notably Late Antique and medieval

Christianity. This has led to much brilliant scholarship and new insights, apparent in and stimulated by the work of Peter Brown, Patrick Geary and others, and manifested in recent publications such as *Treasures of Heaven*,[11] *Relics and Remains*[12] and *Relics in Comparative Perspective*.[13] The last two publications also exemplify a developing trend in studies of relics in non-Christian traditions including Buddhism and Islam.[14]

However, despite this intellectual energy in relic studies, the theoretical framework proposed here is a definitional exercise that seems not to have been undertaken hitherto. For example, the volume *Relics and Remains* extends the range of relic scholarship by presenting a series of conference papers dealing with Egyptian, Greek, Islamic, Christian and other case studies. Each study is anchored in thorough scholarship, yet underlying many of the essays (and many other publications) appears to be an uncertainty about what is and what is not a relic, and about how to explain why disparate yet patterned behaviours involving bones, images and the like seem to be connected. Most of the papers probe at the relationship between body parts, artefacts, statues, gods, heroes and ordinary mortals, but the full analytical potential of some of the case studies remains unexploited because of the absence of a theoretical framework to structure discussion.

In her introduction, Alexandra Walsham gives perhaps the most recent definitional overview of the term relic, although she considers it 'inappropriate to insist upon a single or precise definition', and acknowledges 'the slippery, elastic, and expansive nature of this concept and category, and the nebulous boundaries that separate it from other classes of entity'.[15] She refers to the two familiar types of corporeal and non-corporeal (or contact) relics, but considers that a relic 'is ontologically different from a representation or an image: it is not a mere symbol or indicator of divine presence, it is an actual physical embodiment of it'.[16] It is with this statement that a fundamental aspect of relics is missed, and one essential to a definitional completeness that can encompass 'other classes of entity'. The notion that images are 'mere' symbols or only indicate divine presence, rather than embody it, seems to be at odds with religious practice in most parts of the world, including Christianized ones. However, she notes the anomalous position of icons and concedes her uncertainty regarding this classification when she writes that 'it is unhelpful to situate relics and replicas, sacred objects and imitative artefacts, in sharp opposition. The interface between them is both unstable and frequently breached'.[17] It is at this interface that we are likely to find insights by connecting rather than separating, an issue also hinted at by Derek Krueger in his opening essay in the *Treasures of Heaven* catalogue. There he notes the 'complex relationship between image and relic' and he refers to the important connection between bodies and images in his discussion of a mosaic of St Demetrios, where he states that 'St Demetrios and his miracle-working power were present and available *here* in the icon'.[18]

In *Relics and Remains*, Robert Morkot wrestles with the apparent absence of relics in ancient Egypt, but his problem seems to reside in a narrow definition of relics as body parts,

which leads him to state that, in Egyptian interactions with the divine world, 'whilst the vehicles used (mainly statues) are not what we would consider to be relics, they did serve some of the same functions'.[19] The restrictive definition of relics as body parts inhibits him from expressing what he intuitively senses from his own extensive knowledge – that images can be relics, in the sense that behaviour in relation to images and to body parts is equivalent. He admits that 'the Egyptian dead were revered, and their tombs became places of pilgrimage for many reasons',[20] yet the absence of much evidence for body-part distribution, aside from the myth of Osiris's murder, dismemberment and the dispersal of his body parts to various cult centres, leads Morkot to conclude that relics were not an important feature of ancient Egyptian religious and cultural practice. If his definition of relics was more encompassing to include images, it could be argued that relic-related behaviour was in fact fundamental to religious practice in Egypt, as elsewhere.

Therefore it is clear that there appears to be no agreed academic definition of relics, and the limiting nature of some definitional assumptions, both about relics and religious/ secular distinctions, troubles scholars who acknowledge the importance of images, memorabilia and celebrity, but struggle to fit them into a coherent scheme. There also does not appear to be a formal Christian definition of relics. Bernie Fife-Shaw of the National Catholic Library, St Michael's Abbey, Farnborough, explained there was only one 'borrowed from practice'.[21] No official definition appears in the authoritative *Catholic Encyclopedia*.[22] With respect to other religions, there are not, as far as I am aware, official definitions of relics in Islam, Buddhism, Judaism or Hinduism.

Christian doctrine concerning relics has been ambivalent, betraying elite theological anxiety about associations with magic, superstition and paganism. However, since at least the 4th century, intense relic-related behaviour has characterized the practice of Christianity by ordinary people and in many cases continues to do so. Among the most valued relics are those associated with the body of Christ and his Passion – pieces of the True Cross, thorns from his crown, the spear that pierced his side and other items such as shrouds (all associated with his blood, similar to 'the spear that killed Captain Cook'). Actual body relics of Christ are rare, though the ingenuity of devotees has provided us with Holy Blood, notably that which impregnated the soil around the base of the Cross, and several prepuces purportedly taken from Christ during circumcision. Also highly valued in Christianity have been the bodily remains of saints, notably martyrs, and of Mary, principally her milk. Items closely associated with saints – for example clothing – have also been regarded as powerful relics, as have other items including *brandea*, pieces of cloth that have come into contact with saints' bodies or relics of the Passion.

Overall, across many traditions, we have a picture of the widespread high valuation of, and veneration for, the body parts of gods and other eminent personages as well as artefacts associated with them. There is also a widespread valuation of, and veneration for, images, although in some traditions this is suppressed and displaced into non-figural artefacts that embody divinity such as books like the Bible and the Qur'an. In addition, we have definitional uncertainty about relics and the deployment of theory, however sophisticated, only in culturally specific studies. The task here is to propose a general cross-cultural theory of relics that connects rather than separates equivalent patterns of human behaviour, while also satisfying, or engaging in debate, relic specialists of different traditions.

A cross-cultural theory: bodies, artefacts and images

In presenting a new theoretical framework, existing terminology is adapted to create a tripartite scheme. Expressions such as 'body/corporeal relic' and 'contact/ touch/secondary relic' have wide currency in relic studies, but added to them here is a third category, image relics, which encompasses images and artworks. Some authors, including Alexander Nagel, have discussed 'relic-images',[23] but not in the context of a formal definitional framework. In the interests of cross-cultural analysis, the largely Western distinction between religious and secular is discarded. The three types of relic proposed are:

Type A
Body relics/corporeal relics, or relics by substance: body remains, whole or fragmentary, of a special personage (Christ's Holy Blood; saints' bones; the Prophet's hair; the Buddha's tooth; Polynesian chiefly bones; Nelson's hair).

Type B
Contact relics/touch relics, or relics by association: artefacts that have come into direct contact with, or close proximity to, the live body or body relics of a special personage (pieces of the True Cross; a saint's tunic; Luther's bed; the Prophet's Holy Mantle; Polynesian chiefly cloaks; reliquaries; Michael Jackson's glove; Nelson's watch; a painting by Leonardo or Picasso).

Type C
Image relics/substitute relics, or relics by equivalence: images or objects that are equivalent to, and/or substitutes for, the body of a special personage (an icon of the Virgin; Leonardo's *Last Supper*; a statue of a saint; a Qur'an; a Bible; Buddhist, Hindu or Polynesian statues; Fijian whale ivory valuables; Nelson's portrait).

In this scheme the special personage in the particular cultural context will be attributed with significant powers and qualities, and will by definition have high status. This context may not be explicitly religious, but the behaviour patterns towards the special personage will have a religious character, involving veneration, adulation, respect and special journeys, leading to altered medical, psychological and emotional states. In recent history the range of special personages has become broader. In addition to gods, saints, kings, queens, ancestors and heroes, specialist practitioners such as artists, musicians, actors and sports stars, whose skills transcend those of 'normal' human beings, have developed a global reach. They become modern-day heroes and the focus of celebrity cults. Over time the status of special personages may wax and wane. Some, such as Christ, the Prophet and the Buddha, maintain or increase popularity, others drift into obscurity as the number of people who sustain their cults diminishes.

With respect to relics, their value is linked to the status of the special personage. For example, relics associated with Christ, the Virgin or a saint will be highly valued in a Christian context, but will be less so or not at all in a non-Christian one. In the context of contemporary global popular culture, relics associated with Elvis Presley have high value, as evidenced by visitor numbers to Graceland and prices for his memorabilia on the market. In a more limited way, relics associated with my grandmother will have value within my family, but not beyond (unless she happened to be a celebrity). Accordingly the value of, and competition for control of, body parts, artefacts and images associated with these kinds of personage will differ. People will not bid large sums at auction for the hair of my grandmother, or for her clothing or her portrait, nor will they make pilgrimages to my house where I might keep such things, but they will do and have done these things for body parts, artefacts and images associated with a Christian saint, the Buddha, the Prophet Mohammed, Nelson, Gandhi, Picasso and Elvis Presley. Graceland, Elvis Presley's house, attracts huge numbers of visitors/pilgrims. Elvis was originally buried in 1977 at Forest Hills Cemetery in Memphis, but, in a telling parallel to medieval Christian practice, his body was translated to the Meditation Garden at Graceland after attempts were made to steal his coffin.

What is the quality that distinguishes a special personage? In many cultures it is characterized as vitality, an active life force, a miraculous power that in gods and ancestors can be life-giving and life-destroying, and that in heroes and artists with god-given talent can be life-enhancing. Saints, prophets and other religious personages, though long dead, are attributed with an enduring power that derives from gods and can affect human life. Artists and celebrities, though not explicitly religious figures, can also be attributed with divine qualities. Mozart and Leonardo are regarded as vehicles for divine intervention in the world, and in popular culture we have screen goddesses, sports stars, pop icons and the like – a vocabulary that gives a cosmological/religious dimension to their status. It is through engagement with these life-giving and life-enhancing special personages or via their material manifestations (defined here as relics) that humans can derive benefit. The main mechanism for engagement is sacrifice, which is the initiating process in what is intended as a productive exchange relationship. Sacrifice involves worship, veneration, adulation, journeys and resource expenditure, nowadays cash, offered in return for blessings that bring health, abundance, prosperity and an enhanced emotional condition.

The quality that suffuses the bodies of special personages and their associated artefacts and images is generally rendered linguistically as power or force. In the Pacific it is *mana* (and cognate terms), an efficacious power deriving from gods that can inhere in humans such as chiefs and healers, and in objects such as images of wood and ivory.[24] Among the Yoruba of Nigeria and diasporic communities in the Americas it is *ase*, translated widely as life-force.[25] In early Christianity this quality was rendered as *virtus* in Latin, *dunamis* in Greek and virtue in English. In his examination of early texts and the cult of relics, Charles Thomas highlighted the healing aspects of the term, noting St Luke's account of how Jesus knew he had healed someone in the midst of an excited throng.[26] Jesus affirmed, '*Somebody* hath touched me; for I perceive that virtue has gone out of me' (Luke 8:43–50). On another occasion a great gathering had come to be healed: 'And the whole multitude sought to touch him; for virtue went out of him, and healed them all' (Luke 6:17–19). Thomas describes *virtus* as 'miraculous power, a miracle in itself, and virtue inherent in God, as well as healing virtue residing by God's will in individual persons'. *Virtus* is also attributed to saints, where in one case it is described as 'a mystic curative influence resident in, and flowing from, the enshrined remains of St Ninian'.

So, the powerful qualities attributed to special personages are immanent in their bodies, and relics derive their value and importance from their connection to the core body. How does this work? With respect to body relics (Type A), it is well established in Christian and Buddhist studies, for example, that body parts are considered to retain the life-giving vitality of the original body and that this is not diminished by fragmentation. They are, in their very substance, the original body, with its associated powers and qualities.[27] With respect to contact relics (Type B), what establishes their value is the link, through touch, to the original core body or to its Type A body relics. By the putative operation of contagious or sympathetic magic, or of 'holy contagion', items that have been touched, used or created by the special personage, or that have touched their remains, have transferred to them the specialness of the core body. Items associated with a martyr's blood, such as pieces of the True Cross or 'the spear that killed Captain Cook', come into this category, as do Nelson's watch and Michael Jackson's 'moonwalk' glove. Other items such as original Mozart scores, Jane Austen manuscripts or Picasso paintings, touched and created by genius, are also highly valued. Digital reproductions of these items, however good, will not have the same value, either in monetary terms or pilgrimage to an exhibition, because the original, touched, matters.[28] Analysing artworks as contact relics helps us understand more clearly the logic of the art market and its anxieties over issues of authenticity. Contact relics also relate to living artists and celebrities; tennis wristbands impregnated with Rafael Nadal's sweat, thrown into the crowd at the end of a heroic triumph, will be fought for, remain unwashed and be treasured by devotees as valuable memorabilia – veritable *brandea* of the modern age.

But what of image relics (Type C)? How do images of gods, saints, heroes or ancestors fit in when they may never have been touched by, or come into close proximity to, the core body? It is here that the crucial issue of representation comes into play, and the nature of 'the power of images'.[29] We need to explain why the Nelson portrait by Abbott attracted a £290,000 premium over his portrait of a little-known admiral, and why a Hindu image, an Orthodox icon or a saint's statue in Mexico can become the focus of intense devotion. Part of the answer is that, in many cultures, images are considered *to be* the personage represented and a material embodiment of them that is

equivalent to a corporeal or contact relic. To many Catholics, Orthodox Christians, Hindus, New Zealand Maori and numerous other groups this is a reality that informs their cultural practices; it causes veneration and pilgrimages to be close to or even kiss the object of devotion, as in the case of icons. Alfred Gell's theoretical work on agency is important here in relation to what might be called a 'principle of equivalence'. He argues persuasively that images, artworks or objects can be substitutes for, and equivalent to, persons (who may be gods, saints, heroes, artists or ancestors – 'special personages'), and that these artefacts can exercise person-like agency in human affairs.[30] In this way Nelson's portrait, or an image of the Virgin, becomes part of what Gell calls their 'distributed personhood',[31] which, like their Type A and B relics, can continue to have effects in the world. A portrait is also part of the distributed personhood and a contact relic of the artist who painted it, although in the case of Abbott, because he is not regarded as significant in the context of British art, this adds little to the value of the Nelson portrait. When both subject and artist are special personages, the value of the work as both image relic and contact relic will be high: an Andy Warhol portrait of Elvis Presley fetched $37 million at Sotheby's in New York on 9 May 2012.

Images can be activated by special procedures during their production, notably consecration. For example, Hindu and Buddhist images can be empowered by painting the eyes, allowing participation in *darshan*, mutual 'seeing' that facilitates human benefit transfer.[32] Such rituals can be repeated to re-activate images when required. Hirini Mead, New Zealand Maori curator of the *Te Maori* exhibition in the USA in 1984, for which opening consecration rituals were performed, considered that for living relatives 'the taonga [treasure/artwork] is more than a representation of their ancestor; the figure is their ancestor, and woe betide anyone who acts indifferently to their tipuna (ancestor)'.[33] For Maori, the act of artistic creation can transfer the essence of the original special personage into the image, which can then serve as a vehicle for that personage to have agency in human affairs. Image relics need not be anthropomorphic or zoomorphic. The violent furore in March 2012 over the US Army's burning of copies of the Qur'an in Afghanistan demonstrates that the book, as an artefactual embodiment of the word of God transmitted through his Messenger, is by the logic of this theory a Type C relic. It is equivalent to and consubstantial with the personages Mohammed and Allah, making its destruction equivalent to homicide and deicide – hence the outrage and retaliatory killing.

Collapsing the person/object distinction and crediting certain objects with animate person-like qualities allows us to understand human behaviour more clearly, especially religious behaviour. Religion is likely to have had its origins in early aetiological concerns with natural events and sickness, and religious practice developed as a means of influencing such things for human benefit by engaging in exchange relationships with gods, the sources of power who were considered to cause them. Blessings and beneficially altered personal conditions are what humans seek from sources of power, and a principal means of engaging with and deriving benefit from them is via relics of the three types enumerated here. Over time, major shifts take place in the value of particular types of relic, and in some Western cultural contexts the enduring importance of relics is masked by a shift away from medieval Christian practices to post-Reformation ones focused on royalty, heroes, artists and celebrities. Classifying art and celebrity memorabilia as relics allows us to understand recent behaviour from a *longue durée* perspective. Because artists and celebrities now have an elevated status that was formerly restricted to gods, kings, saints and heroes, their nature as exceptional, talented and well-known persons is now registered through pre-existing modes of engaging with special personages – adulation, veneration, special journeys, enhanced emotional states and competition for their relics.

It is hoped that this theoretical framework will assist scholars to see some of their materials in a fresh light, and help resolve analytical problems concerning the physical manifestations of human engagement with sources of power. A cross-cultural approach to relics, with a focus on practice and relic-related behaviour, may help us see connections that previous classificatory schemes have obscured.

Acknowledgements

This essay has its origins in an inaugural professorial lecture at the University of East Anglia in 2009. I am grateful to John Mitchell, Sandy Heslop, Margit Thofner, George Lau, John Mack, Karen Jacobs, Aristoteles Barcelos Neto, Matthew Sillence and other colleagues at UEA for feedback, and also to Lloyd de Beer and an anonymous peer reviewer for helpful comments. I also wish to thank James Robinson and Anna Harnden warmly for the invitation to attend the stimulating *Matter of Faith* conference at the British Museum in October 2011, and for considering this paper for publication.

Notes

1 Although very frequently published as a great work of art, this sculpture had not previously been identified as a reliquary. The reliquary hypothesis was proposed at the William Fagg Memorial Lecture at the British Museum in March 2001 and in the book *Pacific Encounters* (Hooper 2006, 194–5). A full study of the image and its history was published in the *Journal of the Polynesian Society* (Hooper 2007). Alongside its great aesthetic and cultural value, its insurance value when loaned to exhibitions is also extremely high.

2 http://www.guardian.co.uk/world/2009/sep/16/st-therese-relics-uk. Relics of St Thérèse have toured the world; in Ireland in 2001 an estimated three million people went to see them, or at least to see the reliquary and be close to its contents (http://www.guardian.co.uk/uk/2001/jul/02/catholicism.religion).

3 The Tinos shrine was visited by the author in August 2009. The icon is purported to be the work of St Luke. See Dubisch 1995 for an extended discussion of the shrine.

4 Aydin 2004, 52–65. See Meri 2010 for discussion of the Topkapi and other important Islamic relics.

5 The significance of spears and holy blood will not be lost on Christian relic specialists. The 2003 Captain Cook 'spear' auction and the Christie's 1972 auction of 'the club that killed Captain Cook' are discussed in an article in *Anthropology Today* (Hooper 2003).

6 The price of Michael Jackson's modified golf glove must be the highest ever paid for a golf glove. Even those worn by deceased golfing 'icons' such as Severiano Ballesteros (died 2011, aged 54) would be unlikely to reach such heights.

7 The last three have fetched high prices recently at auction. Jane Austen's 1804 manuscript draft of *The Watsons* was sold at Sotheby's

in London on 14 July 2011 for £993,250. Gandhi relics, including his spectacles, sold at Antiquorum in New York on 4 March 2009 for $2,096,000, and Marilyn Monroe's 'subway' dress sold at Profiles in History in Los Angeles on 18 June 2011 for $5,200,000.

8 Hocart 1952, 23. On this subject and on the origins of 'government' in ritual/religion see Hocart 1970.

9 Schopen 1997, 114 (emphasis in original).

10 Reissland-Burghart 2011, 30.

11 Bagnoli *et al.* 2010.

12 Walsham 2010a.

13 Trainor 2010.

14 No justice can be done here to the extensive literature on relics, but key publications that have stimulated recent scholarship are by Brown (1981) and Geary (1986, 1990). More recently, Meri (2002, 2010), Schopen (1997), Trainor (1997) and Strong (2004) have made significant contributions to the study of Islamic and Buddhist relics, emphasizing their major, if largely ignored, role in the history of those religions.

15 Walsham 2010b, 11.

16 Ibid., 12.

17 Ibid., 13.

18 Krueger 2010, 12, 15 (emphasis in original).

19 Morkot 2010, 37.

20 Ibid., 40.

21 Pers. comm., 23 March 2012.

22 Herbermann 1913.

23 Nagel 2010, 214.

24 Shore 1989, 139ff.; Hooper 1996, 257–60.

25 Abiodun 1994; Sansi 2007.

26 Thomas 1973, 2–4.

27 Evidence for the widespread attribution in Christianity of active divine power to Holy Blood or saints' bones and for the presence (*praesentia*) of the original holy personage in body relics can be found in Bagnoli *et al.* 2010, and throughout this volume. For Buddhism, Schopen argues that 'relics are characterized by – full of – exactly the same spiritual forces and faculties that characterize, and, in fact, constitute and animate the living Buddha' (1997: 154). Similar observations could be made for body parts of 'the very special dead' (Brown 1981, 69–85) in many cultures, including that which created the A'a reliquary with which this essay began.

28 Within anthropology, the concept of contagious magic was developed by James Frazer in *The Golden Bough* (1990; 12 volume 3rd edition originally published 1906–15) as an aspect of sympathetic magic which privileges contact. John Skorupski proposed the notion of 'contagious transfer', in which the quality of one object can be transferred to another, but not necessarily by contact (1976, 176). Both definitions contribute to the meaning suggested here, which is that contact, or close proximity, facilitates the transfer of qualities from one object or person to another person or object. An informative review of theories concerning the relational power of saints and relics in the context of a study of the Jain case is provided by Flügel (2010), who uses key anthropological sources, such as Tambiah 1984.

29 There is an enormous literature that is culture- or tradition-specific concerning images, but some notable contributions to broader understandings include Belting 1994, Freedberg 1989, Gell 1998, Latour and Weibel 2002, McClanan and Johnson 2005 and Boldrick and Clay 2007.

30 Gell 1998, 5–7.

31 Ibid., 96ff.

32 See Gell 1998, 116–21 and Schopen 1997, 116–17, 137–8.

33 Mead 1997, 184.

Bibliography

Abiodun, R. 1994. 'Ase', *African Arts* 27, 68–103.

Aydin, H. 2004. *The Sacred Trusts, Topkapi Palace Museum*, Istanbul.

Bagnoli, M., Klein, H.A., Mann, C.G. and Robinson, J. (eds) 2010. *Treasures of Heaven: Saints, Relics and Devotion in Medieval Europe*, Baltimore and London.

Belting, H. 1994. *Likeness and Presence: A History of the Image before the Era of Art*, Chicago.

Boldrick, S. and Clay, R. (eds) 2007. *Iconoclasm: Contested Objects, Contested Terms*, Aldershot.

Brown, P. 1981. *The Cult of the Saints: Its Rise and Function in Latin Christianity*, Chicago.

Dubisch, J. 1995. *In a Different Place: Pilgrimage, Gender, and Politics at a Greek Island Shrine*, Princeton.

Flügel, P. 2010. 'The Jaina cult of relic stupas', in *Relics in Comparative Perspective*, special issue of *Numen* 57 (3–4), ed. K. Trainor, 389–504.

Frazer, J.G. 1990. *The Golden Bough* [abridged edition], London.

Freedberg, D. 1989. *The Power of Images: Studies in the History and Theory of Response*, Chicago.

Geary, P.J. 1986. 'Sacred commodities: the circulation of medieval relics', in *The Social life of Things: Commodities in Cultural Perspective*, ed. A. Appadurai, Cambridge, 169–91.

Geary, P.J. 1990. *Furta Sacra: Thefts of Relics in the Central Middle Ages*, (rev. edn, 1st edn 1978), Princeton.

Gell, A. 1998. *Art and Agency: An Anthropological Theory*, Oxford.

Herbermann, C.G. (ed.) 1913. *The Catholic Encyclopedia: An International Work of Reference on the Constitution, Doctrine, Discipline and History of the Catholic Church*, 15 vols, New York.

Hocart, A.M. 1952. *The Life-giving Myth and other Essays*, London.

Hocart, A.M. 1970. *Kings and Councillors: An Essay in the Comparative Anatomy of Human Society*, Chicago (rev. edn, 1st edn 1936), Cairo.

Holsbeke, M. (ed.) 1996. *The Object as Mediator: On the Transcendental Meaning of Art in Traditional Cultures*, Antwerp.

Hooper, S. 1996. 'Who are the chiefs? Chiefship in Lau, Eastern Fiji', in *Leadership and Change in the Western Pacific: Essays Presented to Sir Raymond Firth on the Occasion of his 90th birthday*, ed. R. Feinberg and K. A. Watson-Gegeo, London School of Economics Monographs in Social Anthropology 66, London, 239–71.

Hooper, S. 2003. 'Making a killing? Of sticks and stones and James Cook's 'bones', *Anthropology Today* 19(3), 6–8.

Hooper, S. 2006. *Pacific Encounters: Art and Divinity in Polynesia, 1760–1860*, London.

Hooper, S. 2007. 'Embodying divinity: the life of A'a', *Journal of the Polynesian Society* 116(2), 131–79.

Knight, A. 2010. 'The several legs of Santa Anna: a saga of secular relics', in Walsham 2010a, 227–55.

Krueger, D. 2010. 'The religion of relics in Late Antiquity and Byzantium', in Bagnoli *et al.* 2010, 5–17.

Latour, B. and Weibel, P. (eds) 2002. *Iconoclash*, Karlsruhe.

McClanan, A. and Johnson, J. (eds) 2005. *Negating the Image: Case Studies in Iconoclasm*, Aldershot.

Mead, H. 1997. *Landmarks, Bridges and Visions: Aspects of Maori Culture*, Wellington.

Meri, J. W. 2002. *The Cult of Saints among Muslims and Jews in Medieval Syria*, Oxford.

Meri, J.W. 2010. 'Relics of piety and power in Medieval Islam', in Walsham 2010a, 97–120.

Morkot, R. 2010. 'Divine of Body: the remains of Egyptian kings – preservation, reverence, and memory in a world without relics', in Walsham 2010a, 37–55.

Nagel, A. 2010. 'The afterlife of the reliquary', in Bagnoli *et al.* 2010, 211–22.

Reissland-Burghart, T. 2011. 'Museum worship?', *Anthropology Today* 27(4), 30.

Sansi, R. 2007. *Fetishes and Monuments: Afro-Brazilian Art and Culture in the Twentieth Century*, Oxford.

Schopen, G. 1997. *Bones, Stones, and Buddhist Monks: Collected Papers on the Archaeology, Epigraphy, and Texts of Monastic Buddhism in India*, Honolulu.

Shore, B. 1989. '*Mana* and *Tapu*', in *Developments in Polynesian Ethnology*, ed. A. Howard and R. Borofsky, Honolulu, 137–73.

Skorupski, J. 1976. *Symbol and Theory: A Philosophical Study of Theories of Religion in Social Anthropology*, Cambridge.

Strong, J. 2004. *Relics of the Buddha*, Princeton.

Tambiah, S. 1984. *The Buddhist Saints of the Forest and the Cult of Amulets*, Cambridge.

Thomas, C. 1973. *Bede, Archaeology, and the Cult of Relics*, Jarrow [The Jarrow Lecture, 1973].

Trainor, K. 1997. *Relics, Ritual and Representation in Buddhism: Rematerializing the Sri Lankan Theravāda Tradition*, Cambridge.

Trainor, K. (ed.) 2010. *Relics in Comparative Perspective*, special issue of *Numen* 57(3–4).

Walsham, A. (ed.) 2010a. *Relics and Remains* (*Past and Present* supplement N.S. vol. 5), Oxford.

Walsham, A. 2010b. 'Introduction', in Walsham 2010a, 9–36.

Contributors

Elisabeth Antoine-König is senior curator in the Department of Decorative Arts at the Louvre, with responsibility for the Gothic collections (since 2005) and organized the exhibition *Le Trésor de l'abbaye de Saint-Maurice d'Agaune* in the Louvre in 2014.

Martina Bagnoli is the Andrew W. Mellon Curator in Charge of Medieval Art and Manuscripts at the Walters Art Museum. She co-curated the exhibition *Treasures of Heaven. Saints, Relics and Devotion in Medieval Europe*.

Sarah Blick is Professor of Art History at Kenyon College, edits *Peregrinations: Journal of Medieval Art & Architecture* and publishes on medieval English pilgrimage art and Gothic parish church baptismal font covers.

Barbara Drake Boehm is the Paul and Jill Ruddock Curator in the Department of Medieval Art and The Cloisters at The Metropolitan Museum of Art. A specialist in medieval goldsmiths' work and the cult of relics, she was a contributing author and advisor to *Treasures of Heaven*.

Lloyd de Beer is a curator with responsibility for the late medieval collection at the British Museum. His research is primarily concerned with English art and architecture of the Middle Ages. He is currently working on the alabaster sculptures of medieval England.

Anique de Kruijf specializes in late medieval and early modern devotional art. She is a religious heritage specialist at Museum Catharijneconvent and works as an independent researcher and lecturer.

Andrea de Meo Arbore is an architectural historian who has studied at Scuola Normale Superiore di Pisa, The Warburg Institute, The Paul Mellon Centre for Studies in British Art and UCL. He teaches at Università Europea in Rome.

Lucy Donkin is a Lecturer in History and History of Art at the University of Bristol. Her research focuses on medieval perceptions of place, especially the creation, use and decoration of holy ground.

Terry Drayman-Weisser is Director of Conservation & Technical Research at the Walters Art Museum. Her speciality is objects conservation, focusing on ancient through early 20th-century metalwork, enamels and ivory.

Dee Dyas is a Senior Research Fellow and the Director of the Centre for the Study of Christianity and Culture and of the Centre for Pilgrimage Studies at the University of York.

Glenn Gates is the Conservation Scientist at the Walters Art Museum in Baltimore, Maryland; his research focuses on analytical development and nanotechnology applied to cultural heritage studies.

Stefania Gerevini is Assistant Director of the British School at Rome. Her current research interests include the uses of light and transparency in medieval art and the appropriation and meaning of Byzantine visual language in late medieval Italy.

Kathryn Gerry holds a PhD in art history. Her research interests include medieval manuscripts and portable arts associated with the cult of saints. She is currently Assistant Professor of Art History at the Memphis College of Art, Memphis Tennessee.

Madeleine Gray is Professor of Ecclesiastical History at the University of South Wales. She has written extensively on the visual culture of medieval religion in Wales.

Anna Harnden was Project Curator for *Treasures of Heaven* and *Matter of Faith* conference. She now curates and lectures on a freelance basis and is Programme Manager for VocalEyes, a charity that increases access to the visual arts and heritage sites for the blind and partially sighted.

Kristin Hoefener is a musicologist and conductor specializing in the history and performance of medieval music. In her research at the Musikhistorisches Institut in Würzburg she primarily focuses on medieval liturgical offices and their relationship to saints' cults.

Steven Hooper is Director of the Sainsbury Research Unit for the Arts of Africa, Oceania and the Americas, and Professor of Visual Arts, at the University of East Anglia.

Erik Inglis teaches medieval art history at Oberlin College. He has published a monograph on Jean Fouquet, and is currently researching the medieval art historical imagination.

Susan La Niece, FSA, is the senior metallurgist at the British Museum and has published on subjects including metalworking in medieval Europe and the Middle East, niello, gilding, silvering and decorative patination.

Wolfgang Loseries is a researcher and the project coordinator of the project 'Die Kirchen von Siena' (The churches of Siena) at the Kunsthistorisches Institut in Florenz-Max-Planck-Institut, Florence, and member of the Accademia Senese degli Intronati in Siena.

Scott B. Montgomery is Associate Professor of Art History at the University of Denver. His research focuses on the visual culture of saints' cults and his publications include *Saint Ursula and the Eleven Thousand Virgins of Cologne.*

Vibeke Olson is an Associate Professor of Art History at the University of North Carolina Wilmington. Her research interests include viewer response and the role of bodily fluids in medieval devotion and art.

Shelley Reisman Paine is Exhibitions Conservator at The Field Museum, Chicago, IL. She was the Conservator of Objects at the Cleveland Museum of Art when the portable altar of Countess Gertrude was evaluated.

David M. Perry is Associate Professor of History at Dominican University, in River Forest, IL. He is the author of *Sacred Plunder: Venice and the Aftermath of the Fourth Crusade* (Penn State University Press, 2015).

Samantha Riches is a cultural historian based at Lancaster University. She has a special interest in gender history and the late medieval cults of pseudo-historical saints, especially St George.

James Robinson is Keeper of Art and Design at National Museums Scotland, formerly senior curator of the late medieval collection at the British Museum and co-curator of the exhibition *Treasures of Heaven: Saints, Relics and Devotion in Medieval Europe.*

David B. Saja is Curator of Mineralogy at the Cleveland Museum of Natural History.

Janet E. Snyder is Professor of Art History at West Virginia University. Her research concerns the use of stone and the representation of textiles and clothing in northern European medieval architectural sculpture.

Linda B. Spurlock is Assistant Professor of Anthropology at Kent State University, Kent, OH.

Maickel van Bellegem trained as a goldsmith and metals conservator in the Netherlands. Working for the British Museum since 2005, he has worked on the medieval galleries and the *Treasures of Heaven* exhibition.

Jeremy Warren is the Collections and Academic Director of the Wallace Collection. His specialist interests lie in Medieval and Renaissance sculpture and works of art and has recently published a three-volume catalogue of Medieval and Renaissance sculpture in the Ashmolean Museum.

Leslie Webster was Keeper of the Department of Prehistory and Europe at the British Museum and curator of the Insular early medieval collection. She has written and lectured extensively on Anglo-Saxon art and archaeology.

Index